Lecture Notes in Computer Science   9884

Commenced Publication in 1973
Founding and Former Series Editors:
Gerhard Goos, Juris Hartmanis, and Jan van Leeuwen

Editorial Board

More information about this series at http://www.springer.com/series/7407

Martin Fränzle · Nicolas Markey (Eds.)

Formal Modeling and Analysis of Timed Systems

14th International Conference, FORMATS 2016
Quebec, QC, Canada, August 24–26, 2016
Proceedings

 Springer

Editors
Martin Fränzle
Carl von Ossietzky Universität
Oldenburg
Germany

Nicolas Markey
LSV, ENS de Cachan
Cachan Cedex
France

ISSN 0302-9743   ISSN 1611-3349 (electronic)
Lecture Notes in Computer Science
ISBN 978-3-319-44877-0   ISBN 978-3-319-44878-7   (eBook)
DOI 10.1007/978-3-319-44878-7

Library of Congress Control Number: 2016948265

LNCS Sublibrary: SL1 – Theoretical Computer Science and General Issues

Printed on acid-free paper

This Springer imprint is published by Springer Nature
The registered company is Springer International Publishing AG Switzerland

Preface

This volume of the *Lecture Notes in Computer Science* contains the papers presented at FORMATS 2016, the 14th edition of the International Conference on Formal Modeling and Analysis of Timed Systems, held during August 24–26, 2016, in Quebec City, Canada.

Control and analysis of the timing of computations are crucial to many domains of system engineering, be it, e.g., for ensuring a timely response to stimuli originating in an uncooperative environment or for synchronizing components in VLSI. Reflecting this broad scope, timing aspects of systems from a variety of domains have been treated independently by different communities in computer science and control. Researchers interested in semantics, verification, and performance analysis study models such as timed automata and timed Petri nets, the digital design community focuses on propagation and switching delays, while designers of embedded controllers have to take account of the time taken by controllers to compute their responses after sampling the environment, as well as of the dynamics of the controlled process during this span.

Timing-related questions in these separate disciplines have their particularities. However, there is growing awareness that there are basic problems that are common to all of them. In particular, all these subdisciplines treat systems whose behavior depends upon combinations of logical and temporal constraints; namely, constraints on the temporal distances between occurrences of events. Often, these constraints cannot be separated, as intrinsic dynamics of processes couples them, necessitating models, methods, and tools facilitating their combined analysis.

Reflecting this fact, the aim of FORMATS is to promote the study of fundamental and practical aspects of timed systems, and to bring together researchers from different disciplines that share interests in modeling and analysis of timed systems and, as a generalization, hybrid systems. Typical topics include (but are not limited to):

- Foundations and Semantics: Theoretical foundations of timed systems and languages; comparison between different models (such as timed automata, timed Petri nets, hybrid automata, timed process algebra, max-plus algebra, probabilistic models)
- Methods and Tools: Techniques, algorithms, data structures, and software tools for analyzing or synthesizing timed or hybrid systems and for resolving temporal constraints (e.g., scheduling, worst-case execution time analysis, optimization, model checking, testing, constraint solving)
- Applications: Adaptation and specialization of timing technology in application domains in which timing plays an important role (real-time software, embedded control, hardware circuits, and problems of scheduling in manufacturing and telecommunication, etc.)

FORMATS 2016 continued the tradition of the events previously held in Madrid (2015), Florence (2014), Buenos Aires (2013), London (2012), Aalborg (2011), Klosterneuburg (2010), Budapest (2009), St. Malo (2008), Salzburg (2007), Paris (2006), Uppsala (2005),

Grenoble (2004), and Marseille (2003). It was co-located with the 27th International Conference on Concurrency Theory (CONCUR 2016) and the 13th International Conference on Quantitative Evaluation of Systems (QEST 2016), sharing invited speakers and social events among these conferences, and with the workshops EXPRESS/SOS and TRENDS.

This year FORMATS received 32 full submissions by authors coming from 26 different countries. Each submission had full reviews from three Program Committee (PC) members and their sub-reviewers, plus additional comments from further PC members during an intense discussion phase. The committee finally selected 14 submissions for publication and presentation at the conference, which amounts to a 44 % acceptance rate. In addition, the conference included invited talks by:

- Scott A. Smolka, State University of New York, Stony Brook: "V-Formation as Optimal Control" (joint with Concur and QEST; abstract presented in the proceedings of CONCUR)
- Ufuk Topcu, University of Texas at Austin: "Adaptable yet Provably Correct Autonomous Systems" (joint with QEST, which also includes the abstract in its proceedings)
- Oleg Sokolsky, University of Pennsylvania: "Platform-Specific Code Generation from Platform-Independent Timed Models"

We sincerely thank the invited speakers for accepting our invitation and for providing abstracts of their talks for inclusion in the different proceedings volumes. We are grateful to the 27 PC members and their 33 associated reviewers for their competent and timely reviews of submissions, which were instrumental in securing the scientific standards of FORMATS. The EasyChair conference management system again provided reliable support in the submission phase, during the selection process, and while preparing this volume. We would also like to thank the Steering Committee of FORMATS for giving us the opportunity to put together this exciting event and for their support throughout this process, and Josée Desharnais of the University of Laval, Canada, for the competent and reliable local organization.

Last but not least, we are deeply grateful to all the authors for entrusting us with their papers. Thanks to their contributions we were able to put together the inspiring program reflected in these proceedings.

July 2016

Martin Fränzle
Nicolas Markey

Organization

Program Committee

S. Akshay	IIT Bombay, India
Hanifa Boucheneb	École Polytechnique de Montréal, Canada
Béatrice Bérard	LIP6, Université Pierre et Marie Curie, France
Laura Carnevali	University of Florence, Italy
Franck Cassez	Macquarie University, Australia
Martin Fränzle	University of Oldenburg, Germany
Gilles Geeraerts	Université libre de Bruxelles, Belgium
Michael R. Hansen	Technical University of Denmark
Boudewijn Haverkort	University of Twente, The Netherlands
Franjo Ivancic	Google, USA
Oded Maler	VERIMAG, CNRS, France
Nicolas Markey	LSV, CNRS, ENS Cachan, France
Chris Myers	University of Utah, USA
Jens Oehlerking	Robert Bosch GmbH, Germany
David Parker	University of Birmingham, UK
Karin Quaas	University of Leipzig, Germany
Stefan Ratschan	Czech Academy of Sciences, Czech Republic
Cesar Sanchez	IMDEA Software Institute, Spain
Sriram Sankaranarayanan	University of Colorado, Boulder, USA
Jeremy Sproston	University of Turin, Italy
Jiří Srba	Aalborg University, Denmark
Lothar Thiele	ETH Zurich, Switzerland
Enrico Vicario	University of Florence, Italy
Mahesh Viswanathan	University of Illinois, Urbana-Champaign, USA
James Worrell	University of Oxford, UK
Sergio Yovine	CONICET-UBA, Argentina
Huibiao Zhu	East China Normal University, China

Additional Reviewers

Basset, Nicolas
Bauer, Matthew S.
Berthomieu, Bernard
Bollig, Benedikt
Brenguier, Romain
Chen, Xin
Dang, Thao

Dubikhin, Vladimir
Frehse, Goran
Genest, Blaise
Gray, Travis
Ho, Hsi-Ming
Jensen, Peter Gjøl
Laroussinie, François

Mathur, Umang S.
Mikučionis, Marius
Muniz, Marco
Paolieri, Marco
Phawade, Ramchandra
Poplavko, Peter
Poulsen, Danny Bøgsted
Roohi, Nima
Ruijters, Enno
S., Krishna

Santinelli, Luca
Su, Wen
Sznajder, Nathalie
Ulus, Dogan
Van-Anh, Nguyen
Watanabe, Leandro
Wunderlich, Sascha
Xie, Wanling
Zhang, Zhen

Platform-Specific Code Generation
from Platform-Independent Timed Models
(Invited Keynote)

Oleg Sokolsky

Department of Computer and Information Science, University of Pennsylvania
sokolsky@cis.upenn.edu

Model-based implementation has emerged as an effective approach to systematically develop embedded software for real-time systems. Functional and timing behavior of the software is modeled using modeling languages with formal semantics. We then use formal verification techniques to demonstrate conformance of the model to the timing requirements for the system. Code generation then automatically generates source code from the verified model. The goal of this process is to guarantee that the final implemented system, running on an embedded platform, also conforms to the timing requirements. Several code generation frameworks have emerged, but they rely on restrictive assumptions regarding code execution by the underlying platform or require manual effort to integrate platform-independent code onto the platform. Both may undermine formal guarantees obtained in the course of model-based development.

In this talk, we consider the well-known four-variable model of system execution introduced by Parnas. The four-variable model makes a clear distinction between the external boundary of the system and internal boundary of the software. Timing requirements are typically verified on the external boundary, while generated code operates at the internal boundary of the system. This distinction can lead to a semantic gap between the verified model and generate code. We explore several complementary approaches to account for the distinction between the two boundaries. One approach composes the platform-independent model with a platform execution model for verification, but applies code generation to the platform-independent model only. Another approach uses integer linear programming to calculate a transformation of timing constants in the platform-independent model that keeps effects of platform delays on the occurrence of observable events in the generated code as small as possible.

This talk presents results of a collaboration with my colleagues BaekGyu Kim (currently at Toyota ITC), Insup Lee, Linh T.X. Phan, and Lu Feng. Material covered in this talk relies on ideas published in [1, 2].

References

1. Kim, B., Feng, L., Phan, L., Sokolsky, O., Lee, I.: Platform-specific timing verification framework in model-based implementation. In: Design, Automation and Test in Europe Conference and Exhibition (DATE 2015), pp. 235–240 (2015)
2. Kim, B., Feng, L., Sokolsky, O., Lee, I.: Platform-specific code generation from platform-independent timed models. In: IEEE Real-Time Systems Symposium (RTSS 2015), pp. 75–86 (2015)

Contents

Workload Analysis

Modeling Timed Phenomena

Consistent Timed Semantics for Nested Petri Nets with Restricted Urgency

Leonid W. Dworzanski[✉]

National Research University Higher School of Economics,
Myasnitskaya ul. 20, 101000 Moscow, Russia
leo@mathtech.ru

Abstract. The nested Petri nets are a nets-within-nets formalism convenient for modelling systems that consist of distributed mobile agents with individual behaviour. The formalism is supported by developed verification methods based on structural analysis and model checking techniques. Time constraints are crucial for many safety critical and everyday IoT systems. Recently, the non Turing-complete time semantics for Time Petri nets based on restricted urgency was suggested; and, it was shown that some behavioural analysis problems are decidable under the semantics. In the paper, the semantics is extended to the nested Petri nets formalism and it was demonstrated that some behavioural analysis problems are still decidable. The semantics is illustrated by an example of a health monitoring system.

Keywords: Nested petri nets · Time petri nets · Well structured transition systems · Time semantics

1 Introduction

The ubiquitous propagation of mobile computational devices into the human environment stimulated the rapid spread of distributed systems with mobile agents-components. Not only software components become more distributed and autonomous (web services, mobile agents, cloud applications, ubiquitous computing), but computational devices become more powerful and more autonomous due to intensive development of computing, data storing, and energy accumulating technologies. From safety critical to everyday "internet-of-things" systems — wireless sensor networks, system for coordinating search and rescue operations, corporate and social networks of personal computational devices, automated urban metro subway systems [1] — consist of mobile software and hardware agents moving in informational or physical spaces. The correctness of such systems is becoming more and more crucial to safety and quality of life of individuals. To model and rigorously check the safety of these systems, formal methods techniques should be utilized.

Petri nets evolution resembles the evolution of software systems. From flat unstructured nets, Petri nets have evolved into high-level nets with hierarchical

M. Fränzle and N. Markey (Eds.): FORMATS 2016, LNCS 9884, pp. 3–18, 2016.
DOI: 10.1007/978-3-319-44878-7_1

structure and tokens attributed with complex data and/or individual behaviour. "Nets-within-nets" is a modern approach based on the object-oriented paradigm that introduces individual behaviour to tokens by assigning marked Petri nets to them [25]. The application of the approach for modelling active objects, mobility and dynamics in distributed systems is extensively studied [14,17,24]. Nested Petri nets (NP-nets) [18] are an extension of high-level Petri nets according to the nets-within-nets approach. NP-nets formalism combines value semantics with dynamical hierarchical structure.

An NP-net consists of a high-level system net that coordinates a number of net tokens. Each token has its own behaviour determined by its internal marked Petri net. The levels in an NP-net are synchronized via synchronized transitions (simultaneous firing of transitions in adjacent levels of the net). Because of a loosely-coupled multilevel structure, NP-nets can be used for effective modelling of adaptive distributed systems [13], systems of mobile robots [20], sensor networks of mobile agents [6], innovative space systems architectures [7].

The analysis methods for NP-nets are under active development. In the work [9] the approach to checking properties of NP-nets by translating them into coloured Petri nets was developed. The practical value of the translation is determined by the comprehensive tool support for analysis of coloured Petri nets. In [26] a verification method based on translating recursive NP-nets into PROMELA language and applying SPIN model checker is provided. The compositional approach to inferring liveness and boundedness of NP-nets from liveness and boundedness of NP-nets separate components was introduced in [10] and received software support in [11]. Structural place invariants method for NP-nets was suggested in [8].

For many real world software/hardware systems, time related aspects like performance, time-outs, delays, and latency are crucial for correct functioning. While NP-nets can express many behavioural aspects of distributed systems, the formalism does not capture time constraints. In [6] a time semantics for NP-nets was suggested. But the rigorous study of suggested semantics and the problem of composing synchronization with time semantics was postponed for further research.

The paper introduces Timed NP-nets formalism that incorporates the recently suggested restricted urgency timed semantics into Nested Petri nets formalism and demonstrates that decidability of coverability is preserved under the new time semantics for NP-nets. The approach is illustrated with the model of a health monitoring system.

In the Sect. 2 the model of a health monitoring system is described. The Sect. 3 consists of preliminaries and NP-nets definition. The Sect. 4 introduces Timed Arc NP-nets with restricted urgency (TANPU-nets). The Sect. 5 contains proof of the decidability of coverability of TANPU-nets.

2   Motivating Example

Health monitoring systems allow detection and prevention of diseases on very early stages. The medical microrobots technology widens horizons of such systems and makes them minimally or completely noninvasive. Microrobots systems consist of distributed intercommunicating agents, thus require correct orchestration and choreography as well as any other distributed systems. The lack of correct synchronization or behavioural flaws can easily lead to the loss of expensive equipment and complications of treatment. In this section, we model a health monitoring system with nested Petri nets formalism.

The modelled system is a medical system that monitor the state of a gullet, a stomach, a heart and an intestine. It consists of the devices of three types — a heart sensor, stomach bots, and transport bots. A heart sensor (h-sensor) measures the heart activity for abnormalities. Its behaviour is modeled with the element net E_1 depicted in the Fig. 2. In case of any abnormalities, it communicates with a passing transport bot. A stomach bot (s-bot) is mounted in the stomach and can conduct chemical monitoring or perform a surgical operation depending on the equipped actuator (the element net E_2 in the Fig. 3). A transport bot (t-bot) flows regularly through the human body to communicate with deployed bots, and supply them with necessary equipment and resources (E_3 in the Fig. 2). The system net represents the coordinated behaviour of the agents and the material flow of the system (SN in the Fig. 1). For brevity, by $N{:}pl$ ($N{:}\mathbf{tr}$) we will denote the place pl (the transition $\mathbf{tr}$) of the net N.

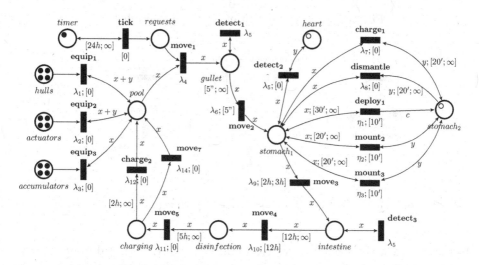

Fig. 1. The health monitoring system: the system net SN

In the initial state, transport bots residue in the external pool ($SN{:}pool$). A t-bot starts its operating cycle when the timer ($SN{:}timer$) generates ($SN{:}\mathbf{tick}$) a request each 24 h. When a request is generated ($SN{:}\mathbf{requests}$), a t-bot is put ($\{SN,E_3\}{:}\mathbf{move}_1$) into the gullet ($SN{:}gullet$). While moving through the gullet, the t-bot may detect an anomaly ($\{SN,E_3\}{:}\mathbf{detect}_1$) and store the data in ($E_3{:}warning$) for further processing. The diagnosis process is not considered here. Passing down the gullet usually takes from 5 to 10 s ($\{SN,E_3\}{:}\mathbf{move}_2$).

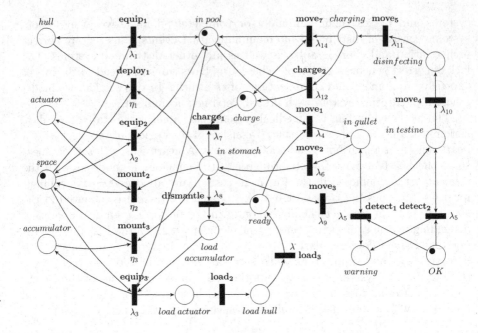

Fig. 2. The element net E_3 of a transport microbot

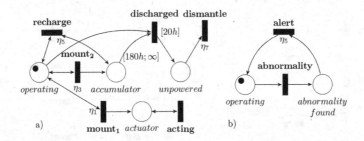

Fig. 3. The element nets: (a) E_2 of a stomach microbot; (b) E_1 of a heart sensor.

In the stomach, the t-bot can receive an alert signal ($\{SN,E_3\}$:**detect**$_2$) from the h-sensor (E_1:*alert*). The alert signal has the highest urgency and shall be processed as soon as possible. The t-bot can charge ($\{SN,E_3\}$:**charge**$_1$) the s-bot (E_2:**recharge**) deployed in the stomach. The charging process takes 20–30 min and consumes the internal charge (E_3:*charge*) of the t-bot. Then the t-bot moves to the intestine ($\{SN,E_3\}$:**move**$_3$). It usually takes from 2 to 3 h. In the intestine again the t-bot can detect ($\{SN,E_3\}$:**detect**$_2$) issues that require attention. The t-bot flows through the intestine (SN:**move**$_4$) for 12 to 24 h. After that the t-bot spends 5 h in the disinfection plant (SN:*disinfection*,E_1:*disinfecting*) and moves ($\{SN,E_3\}$:**move**$_5$) to the charging plant (SN:*charging*,E_3:*charging*). If the internal charge (E_3:*charge*) was expended, then the t-bot spends 2 h in the charging plant and afterward moves to the pool ($\{SN,E_3\}$:**charge$_2$**). If charging is not needed, the t-bot moves immediately to the pool ($\{SN,E_3\}$:**move$_7$**). In the pool (SN:*pool*), the t-bot readings can be analysed to check if medical attention is required (E_3:*warning*) or not (E_3:*OK*).

If an s-bot is fully discharged, then the t-bot must remove it from the stomach and assembly a new s-bot inside the stomach. The practice of assembling microbots on site was considered less invasive; in fact, it allows to transport microbots to otherwise unreachable parts of the human body without surgical interference. If the t-bot while in the stomach finds an uncharged s-bot, it dismantles ($\{SN,E_2,E_3\}$:**dismantle**) the s-bot and changes the state of the internal trigger (from E_3:*ready* to E_3:*load accumulator*) to receive parts from the pool (SN:*pool*) needed for a new s-bot assembly. If the trigger is in the state E_3:*load accumulator*, then the t-bot will be equiped (SN:**equip$_3$**) with an accumulator (SN:*accumulators*,E_3:*accumulator*). Other two t-bots will be equiped ($\{SN,E_3\}$:**equip$_1$**) with a hull (SN:*hulls*,E_3:*hull*) and ($\{SN,E_3\}$:**equip$_2$**) with an actuator (SN:*actuators*,E_3:*actuator*). When a t-bot with a hull is in the stomach, it will deploy (SN:**deploy$_1$**) the hull. When a t-bot with an actuator is in the stomach, it will mount ($\{SN,E_3,E_2\}$:**mount$_2$**) the actuator (E_3:*actuator*) to the hull. Then a t-bot with an accumulator will mount ($\{SN,E_3,E_2\}$:**mount$_3$**) the accumulator (E_3:*accumulator*) to the s-bot.

3   Preliminaries

By $\mathbb{N}$ and $\mathbb{Q}_{\geq 0}$ we denote the sets of non-negative natural and non-negative rational numbers correspondingly. The set of intervals over $\mathbb{Q}_{\geq 0} \cup \{\infty\}$ is denoted by $\mathcal{I}(\mathbb{Q}_{\geq 0})$. For a set S, a *bag (multiset)* m over S is a mapping $m : S \to \mathbb{N}$. The set of all bags over S is denoted by $\mathbb{N}^S$. We use $+$ and $-$ for the sum and the difference of two bags, $\|m\|$ for the number of all elements in m taking into account the multiplicity, and $=, <, >, \leq, \geq$ for comparisons of bags, which are defined in the standard way. We overload the set notation writing $\emptyset$ for the empty bag and $\in$ for the element inclusion.

Petri nets is a well-known formalism for concurrent systems modelling. In this section, we give the definition of coloured Petri nets (CP-nets) parameterized with a value universe U. We slightly adapted the classical definition of CP-nets [15] by adding transition labels. A coloured function for places is defined using the notion of types, and a coloured function for arcs is defined using expressions over the simple additive language $Expr$. Each place is mapped to a type, which is a subset of U. We assume a language $Expr$ for arcs expressions over a set Var of variables and a set Con of constants with some fixed interpretation $\mathcal{I}$, such that for any type-consistent evaluation $\nu : Var \to U$ the value $\mathcal{I}(e, \nu) \in \mathbb{N}^U$ of an expression $e \in Expr$ is defined. We also assume a set Lab of labels for transitions such that $\tau \notin Lab$. The label τ is the "silent" label, while labels from Lab mark externally observable firings. The τ labels are usually omitted on transitions.

Definition 1 (Coloured Petri net). *A coloured net over the universe U is a 6-tuple $(P, T, F, \upsilon, \gamma, \Lambda)$, where*

– P and T are disjoint finite sets of places, respectively transitions;
– $F \subseteq (P \times T) \cup (T \times P)$ is a set of arcs;
– $\upsilon : P \to 2^U$ is a place typing function, mapping P to the subsets of U;
– $\gamma : F \to Expr$ is an arc labelling function;
– $\Lambda : T \to Lab \cup \{\tau\}$ is a transition labelling function.

For an element $x \in P \cup T$ an arc (y, x) is called an *input arc*, and an arc (x, y) an *output arc*; a *preset* ${}^{\bullet}x$ and a *postset* $x^{\bullet}$ are subsets of $P \cup T$ such that ${}^{\bullet}x = \{y | (y, x) \in F\}$ and $x^{\bullet} = \{y | (x, y) \in F\}$. Given a CP-net $N = (P, T, F, \upsilon, \gamma, \Lambda)$ over the universe U, a *marking* in N is a function $m : P \to \mathbb{N}^U$, such that $m(p)$ has $\upsilon(p)$ as a support set. A pair $\langle N, m \rangle$ of a CP-net and a marking is called a marked net.

Let $N = (P, T, F, \upsilon, \gamma, \Lambda)$ be a CP-net. A transition $t \in T$ is *enabled* in a marking m iff $\exists \nu \forall p \in P : (p, t) \in F \Rightarrow m(p) \geq \mathcal{I}(\gamma(p, t), \nu)$. Here $\nu : Var \to U$ is a variable evaluation, called also a *binding*. An enabled transition t may *fire* yielding a new marking $m'(p) = m(p) - \mathcal{I}(\gamma(p, t), \nu) + \mathcal{I}(\gamma(t, p), \nu)$ for each $p \in P$ (denoted $m \xrightarrow{t} m'$). The set of all markings reachable from a marking m (via a sequence of firings) is denoted by $\mathcal{R}(m)$. As usual, a marked coloured net defines a transition system which represents the observable behaviour of the net.

Nested Petri nets (*NP-nets*) are coloured Petri nets over a special universe [18]. This universe consists of elements of some finite set S (called atomic tokens) and marked Petri nets (called net tokens). We consider here only two-level NP-nets, where net tokens are classical place-transition nets.

Let S be a finite set of atomic objects. For a CP-net N by $\mathcal{M}(N, S)$ we denote the set of all marked nets, obtained from N by adding markings over the universe S. Let then $N_1, \ldots, N_k$ be CP-nets over the universe S. Define a universe $\mathcal{U}(N_1, \ldots, N_k) = S \cup \mathcal{M}(N_1, S) \cup \cdots \cup \mathcal{M}(N_k, S)$ with types $S, \mathcal{M}(N_1, S), \ldots, \mathcal{M}(N_k, S)$. We denote $\Omega(N_1, \ldots, N_k) = \{S, \mathcal{M}(N_1, S), \ldots, \mathcal{M}(N_k, S)\}$. By abuse of notation, we say that a place p with a type $\mathcal{M}(N, S)$ is typed by N.

Definition 2 (Nested Petri net). *Let Lab be a set of transition labels and let $N_1, \ldots, N_k$ be CP-nets over the universe S, where all transitions are labelled with labels from $Lab \cup \{\tau\}$.*

An NP-net is a tuple $NP = \langle N_1, \ldots, N_k, SN \rangle$, where $N_1, \ldots, N_k$ are called element nets, and SN is called a system net. A system net $SN = \langle P_{SN}, T_{SN}, F_{SN}, \upsilon, \gamma, \Lambda \rangle$ is a CP-net over the universe $\mathcal{U} = \mathcal{U}(N_1, \ldots, N_k)$, where places are typed by elements of $\Omega = \Omega(N_1, \ldots, N_k)$, transition labels are from $Lab \cup \{\tau\}$, and an arc expression language Expr is defined as follows.

Let Con be a set of constants interpreted over $\mathcal{U}$ and Var – a set of variables, typed with Ω-types. Then an expression in Expr is a multiset of elements over $Con \cup Var$ of the same type with two additional restrictions for each transition $t \in T_{SN}$:

1. *constants or multiple instances of the same variable are not allowed in input arc expressions of t;*
2. *each variable in an output arc expression for t occurs in one of the input arc expressions of t.*

Note that removing the first restriction on system net arc expressions makes NP-nets Turing-powerful [18], since without this restriction there would be a possibility to check, whether inner markings of two tokens in a current marking are equal, and hence to make a zero-test. The second restriction excludes infinite branching in a transition system, representing a behavior of an NP-net.

The interpretation of constants from Con is extended to the interpretation $\mathcal{I}$ of expressions under a given binding of variables in the standard way.

We call a marked element net a net token, and an element from S an atomic token. A marking in an NP-net is defined as a marking in its system net. So, a marking $m : P_{SN} \to \mathbb{N}^{\mathcal{U}}$ in an NP-net maps each place in its system net to a multiset of atomic tokens or net tokens of appropriate type.

A behaviour of an NP-net is composed of three kinds of steps (firings). An *element-autonomous step* is the firing of a transition t, labelled with τ, in one of the net tokens of the current marking according to the usual firing rule for coloured Petri nets. Formally, let m be a marking in an NP-net NP, $\alpha = (N, \mu) \in m(p)$ — a net token residing in the place $p \in P_{SN}$ in m. Let also t be enabled in α and $\mu \xrightarrow{t} \mu'$ in α. Then the element-autonomous step $s = \{t[\alpha]\}$ is enabled in m and the result of s-firing is the new marking m', such that for all $p' \in P_{SN} \setminus p$: $m'(p') = m(p')$, and $m'(p) = m(p) - \alpha + (N, \mu')$. Note, that such a step changes only the inner marking in one of the net tokens.

A *system-autonomous step* is the firing of a transition $t \in T_{SN}$, labelled with τ, in the system net according to the firing rule for coloured Petri nets, as if net tokens were just coloured tokens without an inner marking. Formally, the system-autonomous step $s = \{t\}$ is *enabled* in a marking m iff there exists a binding $\nu : Var \to \mathcal{U}$, such that $\forall p \in P_{SN} : (p, t) \in F_{SN} \Rightarrow m(p) \geq \mathcal{I}(\gamma(p, t), \nu)$. The result of s-firing is the new marking $m'(p) = m(p) - \mathcal{I}(\gamma(p, t), \nu) + \mathcal{I}(\gamma(t, p), \nu)$ for each $p \in P_{SN}$ (denoted $m \xrightarrow{s} m'$). An autonomous step in a system net can move, copy, generate, or remove tokens involved in the step, but does not change their inner markings.

A *(vertical) synchronization step* is the simultaneous firing of a transition $t \in T_{SN}$, labelled with some $\lambda \in Lab$, in the system net together with firings of transitions $t_1, \ldots, t_q$ $(q \geq 1)$ also labelled with λ, in all net tokens involved in (i.e. consumed by) this system net transition firing.

Formally, let m be a marking in an NP-net NP, a transition $t \in T_{SN}$ be labelled with λ and enabled in m via binding ν as a system-autonomous step. We say that a net token α is involved in t-firing via binding ν iff $\alpha \in \mathcal{I}(\gamma(p, t), \nu)$ for some $p \in {}^\bullet t$. Let then $\alpha_1 = (N_{i1}, \mu_1), \ldots, \alpha_q = (N_{iq}, \mu_q)$ be all net tokens involved in the firing of t via binding ν, and for each $1 \leq j \leq q$ there is a transition t_j, labelled with λ in N_{ij}, such that t_j is enabled in μ_j, and $\mu_j \xrightarrow{t_j} \mu'_j$ in N_{ij}. Then the synchronization step $s = \{t, t_1[\alpha_1], \ldots, t_q[\alpha_q]\}$ is enabled in m for NP, and the result of s-firing is the new marking m' defined as follows. For each $p \in P_{SN}$: $m'(p) = m(p) - \mathcal{I}(\gamma(p, t), \nu) + \mathcal{I}(\gamma(t, p), \nu')$, where for a variable x: $\nu(x) = (N, \mu)$ implies $\nu'(x) = (N, \mu')$.

Figure 4 gives an example of a synchronization step. The left part of the picture shows a marked fragment of a system net. A transition t has two input

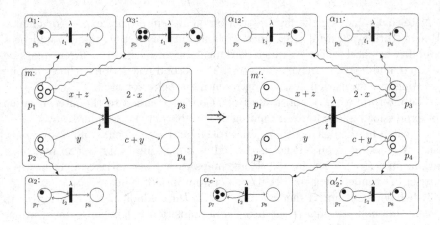

Fig. 4. An example of a synchronization step

places p_1 and p_2, and two output places p_3 and p_4. In the current marking, the place p_1 contains three net tokens; two of them, α_1 and α_3, are explicitly depicted. The place p_2 contains two net tokens, the structure and the marking of one of them are shown in the picture. Only the synchronization step is allowed here, since all transitions are labelled with the synchronization label λ. A possible binding of variables x, y, z in the input arc expressions is $x = \alpha_1, y = \alpha_2$ and $z = \alpha_3$. Then the transitions t in the system net, $t_1[\alpha_1]$, $t_1[\alpha_3]$, and $t_2[\alpha_2]$ fire simultaneously. The resulting marking m' is shown on the right side of the picture. According to the output arc expressions after t-firing two copies of α_1 appear in p_3, the net token α_3 disappears, α_2 with a new marking is transported into the place p_4, and a new net token α_c appears in p_4 being a value of the net constant c.

A transition labelled with $\lambda \in Lab$ in a system net consumes net tokens with enabled transitions labelled with λ. To exclude obviously dead transitions we add to our definition of NP-nets the following syntactical restriction: for each system net transition t labelled with $\lambda \neq \tau$, and for each $p \in {}^\bullet t$, p is typed by an element net with at least one transition labelled with λ.

Thus a step is a set of transitions (a one-element set in the case of an autonomous step). We write $m \xrightarrow{s} m'$ for a step s converting the marking m into the marking m'. By $Steps(NP)$ we denote the set of all (potential) steps in NP.

A run in an NP-net NP is a sequence $\rho = m_0 \xrightarrow{s_1} m_1 \xrightarrow{s_2} \ldots$, where $m_0, m_1, \ldots$ are markings, m_0 is an initial marking, and $s_1, s_2, \ldots$ are steps in NP. For a sequence of steps $\sigma = s_1, \ldots s_n$ we write $m \xrightarrow{\sigma} m'$, and say that m' is reachable from m, if $m = m_0 \xrightarrow{s_1} m_1 \ldots \xrightarrow{s_n} m_n = m'$. By $\mathcal{R}(NP, m)$ we denote the set of all markings reachable from m in NP, and by abuse of notations we write $\mathcal{R}(NP)$ for the set of all markings reachable in NP from its initial marking.

Note that net tokens of the same type (i.e., with the same net structure) are not distinguished in a system net autonomous firing. This follows from the first input arc expressions restriction for NP-nets, which eliminates comparing inner markings of net tokens. Moreover, since all tokens in a system net place are of the same type, enabledness of an autonomous transition in a system net depends only on the numbers of tokens in its input places, and a system net considered as a separate component is actually similar to a p/t-net.

For further details on NP-nets see [18,19]. Note, however, that here we consider a typed variant of NP-nets, where a type is instantiated to each place.

4   Timed-Arc Nested Petri Nets with Restricted Urgency

The real-time constraints are important for many aspects of physical, technical, and information systems. Time constraints have different purposes: to reproduce the speed of modelled processes — biological, chemical, computational, etc.; to impose timing requirements on system actions in order to ensure correct behaviour; to introduce time triggers such as clock generators, watchdog timers, stopwatches, absolute timers. Therefore, many discrete event dynamic formalisms adopted the notion of time [3,21,22].

While nested Petri nets can express many behavioural aspects of multi-agent distributed systems, the formalism does not have means to express time constraints. In [6], a time semantics for nested Petri nets was suggested. But the semantics was not formally grounded, and the problem of composing synchronization with time semantics was suggested for further research. Inaccurate introduction of time semantics may easily lead to intrinsic timing inconsistencies. In [21], a state of a system when the passage of time is blocked due to operational semantics is called a time-deadlock and considered as the timing inconsistency of a specification. Such timing inconsistencies of NP-nets are illustrated in the Fig. 5. If in the Fig. 5(a) transition t_1 of the net token α_1 is enabled at the initial moment of time and its timer is started, then after 1 time unit passed, t_1 must fire. But due to the absence of a token in p_2, the system net transition t is disabled; and, t_1 cannot fire according to the rule of synchronization step execution. A similar inconsistency with the system net transition t can occur in the Fig. 5(b). Such inconsistencies are result of contradictions between time and synchronization constraints.

There are several possible approaches to address the issues with timing inconsistencies. The compositional approach is to introduce structural or behavioural restrictions on the separate components of an NP-net that guarantee the absence of inconsistencies in the composition of the components, i.e. in the whole system. This may require resource consuming checking of behavioural properties and will be the subject of further research. Another approach is syntactical — to define time semantics such that inconsistencies are excluded syntactically. We adopt the latter approach. Informally, only system net synchronization transitions have urgency restrictions, while net tokens transitions with synchronization labels do not. The clock of a system net transition t starts when there is a possible binding of t due to firing rules of NP-nets. As the result, timers start only when corresponding transition is actually ready to fire. Thus, time-deadlocks are excluded by the definition of semantics. The formal definition of the suggested semantics is given in the end of the section.

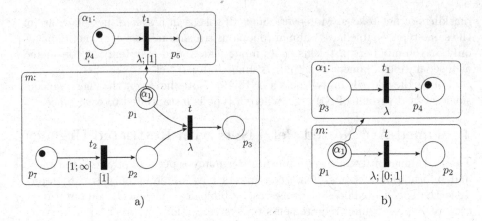

Fig. 5. Two NP-nets with time inconsistencies

There is a lot of ways to introduce time constraints in Petri nets [4,5,22]. One of important notions of time semantics is "urgency" [21], i.e. an enabled transition can be forced to fire by time constraints. While urgency enables to express time-outs and clock signals, the unpleasant effect of adding urgency notion is that it usually makes the Petri net formalism Turing-complete. The cause is that urgency can be utilized to prioritize transitions. With prioritized transitions, we can do zero-testing of a Petri net place as shown in the Fig. 6. The timers of t_1 and t_2 start simultaneously, when a token appears at the *if* place. If the place *capacity* contains tokens, then the transition t_1 will fire when the timer of t_1 is equal to 1; otherwise, t_2 will fire when the timer of t_2 is 2. We can model unbounded counters by combining zero-testing with unbounded places. Consequently, three-counter Minsky machines can be immediately constructed with a time Petri net [16]. The widely known time extensions of Petri nets — Time Petri nets [22] and Timed (Duration) Petri nets [23] — are Turing-complete as they admit urgency and allow to model counters.

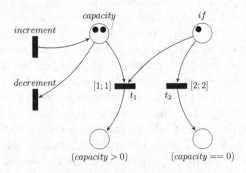

Fig. 6. A time Petri net models a counter.

To address the issue, a time semantics with restricted urgency was recently suggested in [2]. The suggested approach is based on timed-arc Petri net semantics and allows urgent transitions to consume tokens only from the bounded places of a Petri net. As a result, only counters with limited capacity can be modelled, Minsky machines cannot be modelled, and some classes of such Petri nets regain decidability of behavioural properties such as coverability. The proof idea is that as the Petri net fragment with urgency has only finite number of states, it is therefore possible to unfold it to a timed automata, and then convert to a time equivalent timed arc Petri nets without urgency. Then we may combine the resulting timed arc Petri net without urgency with the unbounded residue of the initial Petri net to get a final timed arc Petri net that is time equivalent to the initial net. The absense of urgency in the final net results in monotonicity, which makes it a well-structured transition system and yields decidability of coverability. For further details see [2].

We extend the suggested semantics to NP-nets to obtain NP-nets with timing constraints that still have decidable coverability and related properties. NP-nets are strictly larger than classical Petri nets as they may simulate Petri nets with reset arcs [18]. Consequently, reachability and other related problems are undecidable for NP-nets. In [18] it was proven that coverability and termination problems are decidable for NP-nets using well known theory of well-structured transition systems [12]. It was demonstrated that it is possible to define well-quasi ordering on NP-net markings using injective mapping on nested sets. And as the ordering is transitive compatible with the NP-net transition system, coverability and termination properties are decidable [12]. We omit futher details here.

Now we adapt the definition of Timed-Arc Petri nets with urgency from [2] for NP-nets.

Definition 3 (Timed Arc Nested Petri net with Urgency). *A Timed Arc Nested Petri net with Urgency (TANPU-net) is a tuple* $TNP = \langle N_1, \ldots, N_k, SN, \mathfrak{T} \rangle$, *where*

- $S(TNP) = \langle N_1, \ldots, N_k, SN \rangle$ *is an NP-net called the skeleton of TNP;*
- $\gamma^t : P_{SN} \times T_{SN} \cup P_{E_1} \times T_{E_1} \cup \cdots \cup P_{E_k} \times T_{E_k} \rightarrow \mathcal{I}(\mathbb{Q}_{\geq 0})$ *is a set of token-age constraints on arcs;*
- $U : T_{SN} \cup T_{E_1} \cup \cdots \cup T_{E_k} \rightarrow \mathbb{Q}_{\geq 0}$ *is a set of urgency constraints on transitions.*

The γ^t *and* U *functions have the following restrictions:*

1. *if an element net transition* t *is labelled with a synchronization label* $(\Lambda(t) \neq \tau)$, *then it has* $[0; \infty]$ *timing interval and* U *is undefined at* t;
2. *if a transition* t *has unbounded places in its preset* ${}^\bullet t$, *then* U *is undefined on* t;

Boundedness of places can be determined by different means. Here we imply that a place p is bounded iff it is bounded in the skeleton of TNP. The marking $m = \langle m_s, m_t, m_u \rangle$ of a TANPU-net TNP consists of a marking m_s of the NP-net $S(TNP)$, a time marking $m_t : Tok^*(m_s) \rightarrow \mathbb{Q}_{\geq 0}$ that assigns clocks to tokens, and an urgency marking $m_U : T^*(m_s) \rightarrow \mathbb{Q}_{\geq 0}$ that assigns clocks to transitions, where $T^*(m_s)$ comprises all transitions and $Tok^*(m_s)$ comprises all tokens of the marked NP-net $\langle S(TNP), m_s \rangle$. The urgency constraint $U(t)$ means that t must fire if t has been enabled for $U(t)$ units of time. The token-age constraint $\gamma^t(p,t)$ means that t may fire only if there is an atomic or net token α in p with $m_t(\alpha) \in \gamma^t(p,t)$. The urgency U of a transition is depicted as a number near the transition. The time constraints γ^t of an arc are depicted as an interval near the arc.

The operational semantics of TANPU-nets is defined by incorporating time constraints into the firing rules of NP-nets. A step $s = \{t_1, \ldots, t_k\}$ is enabled in the marking $m = \langle m_s, m_t, m_u \rangle$, if s is enabled in $\langle S(TNP), m_s \rangle$ and for each t_i time constraints are satisfied, i.e. each token α from a place p involved in the firing of t_i satisfies $m_t(\alpha) \in \gamma^t(p, t_i)$. The step s can be an element-autonomous, a system-autonomous, or a synchronization step.

A *time elapsing* step corresponds to elapsing δ time units in each clock of the marking m. We assume that all arcs and transitions clocks run at the same pace. We denote by $m + \delta$ the marking with all clocks increased by δ, i.e. for each token $\alpha \in m_s : (m_t + \delta)(\alpha) = m_t(\alpha) + \delta$ and for each transition $t : (m_u + \delta)(t) = m_u(t) + \delta$. Under urgency restrictions, time elapsing step δ is allowed if there are no $\delta' \in [0, \delta)$ such that the $m + \delta'$ marking has urgent transitions.

5   Consistency and "well-structuredness" of TANPU-nets

Time-deadlocks results from contradictions between synchronization and time (urgent) restrictions of synchronized transitions.

Proposition 1. *TANPU-nets are time-deadlock free.*

By the restriction 1 of the Definition 3 of TANPU-nets, net tokens transitions synchronization does not have urgency restrictions; consequently, such contradictions are excluded syntactically. The obvious drawback of such syntactical exclusion is that we are not able to express local time constraints on synchronization actions of system components. But such local constraints can be modelled indirectly, by introducing watchdog τ transitions with urgent constraints.

To show decidability of coverability for TANPU-nets without urgent transitions we use the notion of well-structured transition systems [12]. A well-structured transition system is a transition system/structure induced by system behaviour that is compatible with well-quasi ordering.

Definition 4. *A well-quasi ordering (wqo) is a quasi ordering $\leq$ such that for any infinite sequence $x_1, x_2 \ldots$ in a set X there exist indices $i < j$ such that $x_i \leq x_j$.*

Definition 5. *A well-structured transition system (wsts) is a transition system $\langle S, \rightarrow, \leq \rangle$ with the wqo ordering $\leq \subset S \times S$ compatible with S, i.e. if $s_1 \leq s_2$ and $s_1 \rightarrow s_1'$, then there exist s_2' such that $s_2 \rightarrow s_2'$ and $s_1' \leq s_2'$.*

Markings of NP-nets can be represented as rooted trees. It is possible to define wqo ordering on rooted trees based on injective mapping between set of nodes of rooted trees.

Definition 6. *Let NPN be an NP-net. For $m_1, m_2 \in \mathcal{M}(NPN) : m_1 \preceq m_2$ iff for all $p \in P_{SN}$ there exists an injective function $j_p : m_1(p) \to m_2(p)$ such that $\forall \alpha = \langle E_i, \mu \rangle \in m_1(p)$: either $j_p(\alpha) = \alpha$ or $j_p(\alpha) = \langle E_i, \mu' \rangle$ and $\mu \leq \mu'$.*

By showing the compatibility of the j ordering with the transition system induced by an NP-net, it was shown that NP-nets are well-structured transition systems, and decidability of coverability follows directly.

Theorem 1. *TANPU-nets without urgent transitions are well-structured transition systems.*

Proof sketch. The proof is conducted by common "freeze" argument. Let *NPN* be a TANPU-net without urgent restrictions. If we have two markings $m_1, m_2 \in \mathcal{M}(NPN)$ such that $m_1 \preceq m_2$, then m_2 contains some extra atomic and net tokens comparing to m_1: $\Delta = m_2 - m_1$. Let $m_1 \xrightarrow{s} m_1'$. As there are no urgent transitions in *NPN*, we may forget about all extra tokens Δ, i.e. do not take into account their presence and still execute step s in m_2: $m_2 \xrightarrow{s} m_2'$ such that $m_2' = m_1' + \Delta$ and $m_1' \preceq m_2'$. Thus, the wqo ordering j is compatible with TANPU-nets; and, TANPU-nets are well-structured transition systems. Decidability of coverability for TANPU-nets follows from this.

Now, we allow restricted urgency only in net tokens.

Theorem 2. *Coverability is decidable for TANPU-nets with restricted urgent transitions only in element nets.*

Proof sketch. This can be proved by reduction the problem to the coverability problem for TANPU-net without urgent transition. Let *NPN* be a TANPU-net with restricted urgent transitions only in element nets. Element nets in two-level NP-nets are classical place-transition nets. So we may directly apply translation from [2] to obtain time equivalent timed-arc Petri nets without urgent transitions from element nets with restricted urgency. When we apply the translation to all element tokens with restricted urgency, we obtain TANPU-net *NPN'* without urgent transitions that is time equivalent to *NPN*. Due to the Theorem 1 we may check the coverability for *NPN'*. As *NPN'* is time equivalent to *NPN*, they have the same reachability set, even if their transition systems can be very different.

Theorem 3. *Coverability is decidable for TANPU-nets with restricted urgent transitions.*

Proof sketch. Let *NPN* be a TANPU-net with restricted urgent transitions. Proving coverability of *NPN* with urgent transitions in the system net is complex, as the translation from [2] does not preserve the complex structure of the system net. To remove urgency and preserve the structure of the system net we suggest the following technique. We consider the system net as a flat timed arc Petri net.

Then we apply the translation from [2] to obtain time equivalent timed arc Petri net (TAPN) without urgent transition. Then we remove time constraints from the transitions in the system net of *NPN* and fuse them with the corresponding transitions of the obtained TAPN with the same names. As the result we obtain the TANPU-net which preserve the structure of initial *NPN* net and has extra TAPN without urgent transitions that guarantee time equivalence of *NPN* and result net. As in the previous proof, the initial *NPN* and final nets may have quite different transition system, but their reachability sets will be equal. This concludes the proof.

Coverability problem allows to check many important behavioural properties of distributed systems. As reachability problem is undecidable even for untimed NP-nets, the problem is certainly undecidable for TANPU-nets. However, when the net tokens of an NP-net are bounded, NP-net is as expressive as classical P/T-net. So it is interesting to check if under some restrictions reachability problem is decidable for TANPU-nets.

6   Conclusion

In this paper we have defined a consistent time operational semantics for Nested Petri nets based on the recently suggested semantics of Timed Arc Petri nets with restricted urgency. The suggested semantics enables to perform simulation and rigorous analysis of TANPU-nets models. The coverability problem of TANPU-nets is decidable. The work is the first step of combining Nested Petri nets with timing constraints. The use of the formalism for modelling was demonstrated by the example of a health monitoring system.

The timed-arc semantics with restricted urgency for two-level NP-nets can be extended to multi-level NP-nets. It is possible to conduct such extension, as synchronization transitions are structurally local, i.e. they synchronize only transitions of two adjacent levels. Then time constraints should be allowed only on the level, which is closer to the system net.

The further research directions are: to adapt algorithms for constructing state classes and reachable essential integer states graphs of TANPU-nets; to study other time semantics that preserve decidability of behavioural properties; to develop compositional methods of composing separate timed components while avoiding time inconsistencies.

Acknowledgments. This work is supported by Russian Foundation for Basic Research, project No. 16-37-00482 mol_a.

The authors would like to thank three anonymous referees for the very helpful and insightful comments.

References

1. A Fleet of Self-Driving Trucks Just Completed a 1,000-Mile Trip Across Europe, 7 April 2016. http://www.popularmechanics.com
2. Akshay, S., Genest, B., Hélouët, L.: Timed-arc petri nets with (restricted) urgency. In: Proceedings of Application and Theory of Petri Nets and Concurrency - 37th International Conference, PETRI NETS, Torun, Poland, 19–24 June 2016. Springer, Berlin Heidelberg (2016)
3. Baeten, J.C.M., Middelburg, C.A.: Process Algebra with Timing. Springer, Heidelberg (2013)
4. Bérard, B., Cassez, F., Haddad, S., Lime, D., Roux, O.H.: Comparison of different semantics for time petri nets. In: Peled, D.A., Tsay, Y.-K. (eds.) ATVA 2005. LNCS, vol. 3707, pp. 293–307. Springer, Heidelberg (2005)
5. Brown, C., Gurr, D.: Timing petri nets categorically. In: Kuich, W. (ed.) ICALP 1992. LNCS, vol. 623, pp. 571–582. Springer, Heidelberg (1992)
6. Chang, L., et al.: Applying a nested petri net modeling paradigm to coordination of sensor networks with mobile agents. In: Proceedings of PNDS 2008, Xian, China, pp. 132–45 (2008)
7. Cristini, F., Tessier, C.: Nets-within-nets to model innovative space system architectures. In: Haddad, S., Pomello, L. (eds.) PETRI NETS 2012. LNCS, vol. 7347, pp. 348–367. Springer, Heidelberg (2012)
8. Dworzanski, L.W., Lomazova, I.A.: Structural place invariants for analyzing the behavioral properties of nested petri nets. In: Kordon, F., Moldt, D. (eds.) PETRI NETS 2016. LNCS, vol. 9698, pp. 325–344. Springer, Heidelberg (2016). doi:10.1007/978-3-319-39086-4_19
9. Dworzański, L.W., Lomazova, I.A.: CPN tools-assisted simulation and verification of nested petri nets. Autom. Control Comput. Sci. **47**(7), 393–402 (2013)
10. Dworzański, L.W., Lomazova, I.A.: On compositionality of boundedness and liveness for nested petri nets. Fundamenta Informaticae **120**(3–4), 275–293 (2012)
11. Dworzanski, L., Frumin, D.: NPNtool: modelling and analysis toolset for nested petri nets. In: Proceedings of SYRCoSE 2013, pp. 9–14 (2013)
12. Finkel, A., Schnoebelen, P.: Well-structured transition systems everywhere!. Theor. Comput. Sci. **256**(1–2), 63–92 (2001)
13. van Hee, K.M., et al.: Checking properties of adaptive workflow nets. Fundamenta Informaticae **79**(3–4), 347–362 (2007)
14. Hoffmann, K., Ehrig, H., Mossakowski, T.: High-level nets with nets and rules as tokens. In: Ciardo, G., Darondeau, P. (eds.) ICATPN 2005. LNCS, vol. 3536, pp. 268–288. Springer, Heidelberg (2005)
15. Jensen, K., Kristensen, L.M.: Coloured Petri Nets - Modelling and Validation of Concurrent Systems. Springer, Heidelberg (2009)
16. Jones, N.D., Landweber, L.H., Lien, Y.E.: Complexity of some problems in petri nets. Theor. Comput. Sci. **4**(3), 277–299 (1977)
17. Köhler, M., Farwer, B.: Object nets for mobility. In: Kleijn, J., Yakovlev, A. (eds.) ICATPN 2007. LNCS, vol. 4546, pp. 244–262. Springer, Heidelberg (2007)
18. Lomazova, I.A.: Nested petri nets - a formalism for specification and verification of multi-agent distributed systems. Fundamenta Informaticae **43**(1), 195–214 (2000)
19. Lomazova, I.A.: Nested petri nets: multi-level and recursive systems. Fundamenta Informaticae **47**(3–4), 283–293 (2001)
20. Lopez-Mellado, E., Almeyda-Canepa, H.: A three-level net formalism for the modelling of multiple mobile robot systems. In: IEEE International Conference on Systems, Man and Cybernetics, vol. 3, pp. 2733–2738, October 2003

21. Nicollin, X., Sifakis, J.: An overview and synthesis on timed process algebras. In: de Bakker, J.W., Huizing, C., de Roever, W.P., Rozenberg, G. (eds.) REX 1991. LNCS, vol. 600, pp. 526–548. Springer, Heidelberg (1991)
22. Popova-Zeugmann, L.: Time and Petri Nets. Springer, Heidelberg (2013)
23. Ramchandani, C.: Analysis of asynchronous concurrent systems by timed petri nets. Technical report, Cambridge (1974)
24. Valk, R.: Object petri nets. In: Desel, J., Reisig, W., Rozenberg, G. (eds.) Lectures on Concurrency and Petri Nets. LNCS, vol. 3098, pp. 819–848. Springer, Heidelberg (2004)
25. Valk, R.: Petri nets as token objects: an introduction to elementary object nets. In: Desel, J., Silva, M. (eds.) ICATPN 1998. LNCS, vol. 1420, pp. 1–25. Springer, Heidelberg (1998)
26. Venero, M.L.F., da Silva, F.S.C.: Model checking multi-level and recursive nets. Softw. Syst. Model. 15, 1–28 (2016)

On the Expressiveness of Parametric Timed Automata

Étienne André[1,2]($\boxtimes$), Didier Lime[2], and Olivier H. Roux[2]

[1] Université Paris 13, Sorbonne Paris Cité, LIPN CNRS,
UMR 7030, 93430 Villetaneuse, France
`Etienne.Andre@univ-paris13.fr`
[2] École Centrale de Nantes, IRCCyN, CNRS, UMR 6597, Nantes, France

Abstract. Parametric timed automata (PTAs) are a powerful formalism to reason about, model and verify real-time systems in which some constraints are unknown, or subject to uncertainty. In the literature, PTAs come in several variants: in particular the domain of parameters can be integers or rationals, and can be bounded or not. Also clocks can either be compared only to a single parameter, or to more complex linear expressions. Yet we do not know how these variants compare in terms of expressiveness, and even the notion of expressiveness for parametric timed models does not exist in the literature. Furthermore, since most interesting problems are undecidable for PTAs, subclasses, such as L/U-PTAs, have been proposed for which some of those problems are decidable. It is not clear however what can actually be modeled with those restricted formalisms and their expressiveness is thus a crucial issue. We therefore propose two definitions for the expressiveness of parametric timed models: the first in terms of all the untimed words that can be generated for all possible valuations of the parameters, the second with the additional information of which parameter valuations allow which word, thus more suitable for synthesis issues. We then use these two definitions to propose a first comparison of the aforementioned PTA variants.

Keywords: Parametric timed automata · L/U-PTAs · Hidden parameters

1 Introduction

Designing real-time systems is a challenging issue and formal models and reasoning are key elements in attaining this objective. In this context, timed automata (TAs) [1] are a powerful and popular modeling formalism. They extend finite automata with timing constraints, in which clocks are compared to integer constants that model timing features of the system. In the early design phases

This work is partially supported by the ANR national research program "PACS" (ANR-14-CE28-0002).

M. Fränzle and N. Markey (Eds.): FORMATS 2016, LNCS 9884, pp. 19–34, 2016.
DOI: 10.1007/978-3-319-44878-7_2

these features may not be known with precision and therefore parametric timed automata (PTAs) [2] allow these constants to be replaced by unknown parameters, the correct values of which will be synthesized as part of the verification process. Unfortunately, most interesting problems are undecidable for PTAs, including the basic question of the existence of values for the parameters such that a given location is reachable [2] (sometimes called EF-emptiness problem).

Since the seminal definition, many variants of PTAs have been defined in the literature, both as an effort to further increase the convenience of modeling by allowing complex linear expressions on parameters in the timing constraints (such as in [11,12]), or in order to better assess the frontier of decidability for PTAs. In the latter objective, parameters have been considered to be integers [2,5,6,8,9,12,13] or rationals [2,5,10–13], possibly bounded a priori [12], or even restricted to be used as either always upper bounds or always lower bounds, giving so-called L/U-PTAs [8,11].

In order to be able to compare these definitions, one must first agree on a notion of expressiveness for timed parametric models, since none exists in the literature. This is the main objective of this work.

Contribution. We propose the following two definitions of expressiveness: (1) as the union over all parameter valuations of the accepting untimed words ("untimed language"); (2) as the pairs of untimed words with the parameter valuations that allow them ("constrained untimed language").

We first prove that considering rational parameter valuations or unbounded integer parameter valuations in PTAs and L/U-PTAs is actually equivalent with respect to the untimed language.

We also prove that, whereas the untimed language recognized by a PTA with a single clock and arbitrarily many parameters is regular, adding a single non-parametric clock (i. e., a clock compared at least once to a parameter), even with a single parameter, gives a language that is at least context-sensitive, hence beyond the class of regular languages.

We then compare the expressiveness, w.r.t. untimed language and constrained untimed language, of several known subclasses of PTAs with integer parameters, in particular L/U-PTAs, and PTAs with bounded parameters. It turns out that, when considering the expressiveness as the untimed language, most subclasses of PTAs with integer parameters (including PTAs with bounded parameters, and L/U-PTAs) are in fact not more expressive than TAs. However, classical PTAs remain strictly more expressive than TAs. We also show that adding fully parametric constraints (i. e., comparison of parametric linear terms with 0, without any clock) does not increase the expressiveness of PTAs seen as the untimed language.

We also propose and focus on a new class of PTAs in which some parameters are hidden, i. e., do not occur in the constrained untimed language. While adding hidden parameters does not increase the expressiveness w.r.t. the untimed language (since in that case all parameters can be considered as hidden), when considering the expressiveness as the constrained untimed language, we show that hidden parameters strictly extend the expressiveness of PTAs.

And interestingly, for this second definition of expressiveness, L/U-PTAs with bounded parameters turn out to be incomparable with classical L/U-PTAs.

Outline. We introduce the basic notions in Sect. 2. We propose our two definitions of expressiveness in Sect. 3. We then show that rational-valued parameters are not more expressive than integer-valued parameters for the untimed language (Sect. 4). Focusing on integer-valued parameters, we then classify PTAs, their subclasses, and their extensions with hidden parameters w.r.t. the untimed language (Sect. 5) and the constrained untimed language (Sect. 6). We conclude and outline perspectives in Sect. 7.

2 Preliminaries

2.1 Clocks, Parameters and Constraints

Let $\mathbb{N}$, $\mathbb{Z}$, and $\mathbb{R}_+$ denote the sets of non-negative integers, integers, and non-negative real numbers respectively. Let $\mathcal{I}(\mathbb{N})$ denote the set of closed intervals on $\mathbb{N}$, i. e., the set of intervals $[a, b]$ where $a, b \in \mathbb{N}$ and $a \leq b$.

Throughout this paper, we assume a set $X = \{x_1, \ldots, x_H\}$ of *clocks*, i. e., real-valued variables that evolve at the same rate. A clock valuation is a function $\mu : X \to \mathbb{R}_+$. We write $\mathbf{0}$ for the clock valuation that assigns 0 to all clocks. Given $d \in \mathbb{R}_+$, $\mu + d$ denotes the valuation such that $(\mu + d)(x) = \mu(x) + d$, for all $x \in X$. Given $R \subseteq X$, we define the *reset* of a valuation μ, denoted by $[\mu]_R$, as follows: $[\mu]_R(x) = 0$ if $x \in R$, and $[\mu]_R(x) = \mu(x)$ otherwise.

We assume a set $P = \{p_1, \ldots, p_M\}$ of *parameters*, i. e., unknown integer-valued constants (except in Sect. 4 where parameters can also be rational-valued). A parameter *valuation* v is a function $v : P \to \mathbb{N}$.

In the following, we assume $\prec \in \{<, \leq\}$ and $\sim \in \{<, \leq, \geq, >\}$. Throughout this paper, *lt* denotes a linear term over $X \cup P$ of the form $\sum_{1 \leq i \leq H} \alpha_i x_i + \sum_{1 \leq j \leq M} \beta_j p_j + d$, with $\alpha_i, \beta_j, d \in \mathbb{Z}$. Similarly, *plt* denotes a parametric linear term over P, that is a linear term without clocks ($\alpha_i = 0$ for all i). A *constraint* C (i. e., a convex polyhedron) over $X \cup P$ is a conjunction of inequalities of the form $lt \sim 0$. Given a parameter valuation v, $v(C)$ denotes the constraint over X obtained by replacing each parameter p in C with $v(p)$. Likewise, given a clock valuation μ, $\mu(v(C))$ denotes the Boolean value obtained by replacing each clock x in $v(C)$ with $\mu(x)$.

A *guard* g is a constraint over $X \cup P$ defined by inequalities of the form $x \sim plt$.

2.2 Parametric Timed Automata with Hidden Parameters

Parametric timed automata (PTAs) extend timed automata with parameters within guards and invariants in place of integer constants [2].

We actually first define an extension of PTAs (namely hPTAs) that will allow us to compare models with a different number of parameters, by considering that some of them are hidden. We will define PTAs as a restriction of hPTAs.

Definition 1 (PTA with hidden parameters). *A parametric timed automa-ton with hidden parameters (hereafter hPTA)* A *is a tuple* $(\Sigma, L, l_0, F, X, P, I, E)$, *where: (i)* Σ *is a finite set of actions, (ii)* L *is a finite set of locations, (iii)* $l_0 \in L$ *is the initial location, (iv)* $F \subseteq L$ *is a set of accepting locations, (v)* X *is a finite set of clocks, (vi)* $P = P_{\overline{v}} \uplus P_v$ *is a finite set of parameters partitioned into hid-den parameters* $P_{\overline{v}}$ *and visible parameters* P_v, *(vii)* I *is the invariant, assigning to every* $l \in L$ *a guard* $I(l)$, *(viii)* E *is a finite set of edges* $e = (l, g, a, R, l')$ *where* $l, l' \in L$ *are the source and target locations,* $a \in \Sigma \cup \{\epsilon\}$ *(ϵ being the silent action),* $R \subseteq X$ *is a set of clocks to be reset, and* g *is a guard.*

We define a *PTA* as an hPTA in which $P = P_v$.

Observe that we allow ϵ-transitions (or silent transitions), i.e., transitions not labeled with any action.

Given an hPTA A and a parameter valuation v, we denote by $v(A)$ the non-parametric timed automaton where all occurrences of a parameter p_i have been replaced by $v(p_i)$.

Definition 2 (Concrete semantics of a TA). *Given an hPTA* A $= (\Sigma, L, l_0, F, X, P, I, E)$, *and a parameter valuation* v, *the concrete semantics of* $v(A)$ *is given by the timed transition system* $(S, s_0, \rightarrow)$, *with* $S = \{(l, \mu) \in L \times \mathbb{R}_+^H \mid \mu(v(I(l)))$ *is true*$\}$, $s_0 = (l_0, \mathbf{0})$, *and* $\rightarrow$ *consists of the discrete and (continuous) delay transition relations:*

- *discrete transitions:* $(l, \mu) \xrightarrow{e} (l', \mu')$, *if* $(l, \mu), (l', \mu') \in S$, *there exists* $e = (l, g, a, R, l') \in E$, $\mu' = [\mu]_R$, *and* $\mu(v(g))$ *is true.*
- *delay transitions:* $(l, \mu) \xrightarrow{d} (l, \mu + d)$, *with* $d \in \mathbb{R}_+$, *if* $\forall d' \in [0, d], (l, \mu + d') \in S$.

A *(concrete) run* is a sequence $\rho = s_1 \alpha_1 s_2 \alpha_2 \cdots s_n \alpha_n \cdots$ such that $\forall i, (s_i, \alpha_i, s_{i+1}) \in \rightarrow$. We consider as usual that concrete runs strictly alternate delays d_i and discrete transitions e_i and we thus write concrete runs in the form $\rho = s_1 \xrightarrow{(d_1, e_1)} s_2 \xrightarrow{(d_2, e_2)} \cdots$. We refer to a state of a run starting from the initial state of a TA A as a *concrete state* (or just as a *state*) of A. Note that when a run is finite, it must end with a state. The *duration* of a concrete run is the sum of all the delays d_i appearing in this run.

An *untimed* run of $v(A)$ is a sequence $l_1 e_1 l_2 e_2 \cdots l_n \cdots$ such that for all i there exist a clock valuation μ_i and $d_i \geq 0$ such that $(l_1, \mu_1) \xrightarrow{(d_1, e_1)} (l_2, \mu_2) \xrightarrow{(d_2, e_2)} \cdots (l_n, \mu_n) \xrightarrow{(d_n, e_n)} \cdots$ is a run of $v(A)$. Given a run ρ, we denote by $\mathsf{Untime}(\rho)$ its corresponding untimed run.

The *trace* of an untimed run $l_1 e_1 l_2 e_2 \cdots l_n \cdots$ is the sequence $e_1 e_2 \cdots e_n \cdots$.

The *(untimed) trace* of a concrete run ρ is the trace of $\mathsf{Untime}(\rho)$.

A run ρ is *accepted* by $v(A)$ if it is finite and the location of its last state belongs to F. An untimed run is accepted by $v(A)$ if it is finite and its last location belongs to F.

The *(untimed) language* of $v(A)$ is the set of the traces of runs accepted by $v(A)$.

2.3 Subclasses of Parametric Timed Automata

L/U-PTAs have been introduced as a subclass of PTAs for which the EF-emptiness problem (i.e., the existence of values for the parameters such that a given location is reachable) is decidable [11]:

Definition 3 (hL/U-PTA). *An hL/U-PTA is an hPTA where the set of parameters is partitioned into a set of lower-bound parameters P^- and a set of upper-bound parameters P^+. A parameter p belongs to P^+ (resp. P^-), if it appears in constraints $x \leq plt$ or $x < plt$ always with a non-negative (resp. non-positive) coefficient, and in constraints $x \geq plt$ or $x > plt$ always with a non-positive (resp. non-negative) coefficient.*

Just as for PTAs, we define an *L/U-PTA* as an hL/U-PTA in which $P = P_v$.

Decidability comes from the fact that in L/U-PTAs increasing the value of an upper bound parameter or decreasing that of a lower bound parameter always only increase the possible behavior:

Lemma 1 (monotonicity of hL/U-PTAs [11]). Let A be an hL/U-PTA and v be a parameter valuation. Let v' be a valuation such that for each upper-bound parameter p^+, $v'(p^+) \geq v(p^+)$ and for each lower-bound parameter p^-, $v'(p^-) \leq v(p^-)$. Then any run of $v(A)$ is a run of $v'(A)$.

Given an hL/U-PTA, we denote by $v_{0/\infty}$ the special parameter valuation (mentioned in, e.g., [11]) assigning 0 to all lower-bound parameters and ∞ to all upper-bound parameters.[1]

Let us now define a bounded PTA as a PTA where the domain of each parameter is bounded, i.e., ranges between two integer-valued constants.

Definition 4 (bounded hPTA). *A bounded hPTA is $A_{|bounds}$, where A is an hPTA, and bounds : $P \to \mathcal{I}(\mathbb{N})$ assigns to each parameter p an interval $[\min, \max]$, with $\min, \max \in \mathbb{N}$.*

3 Defining the Expressiveness of PTAs

In the following, we denote by $\mathcal{V}(P)$, $\mathcal{V}(P_v)$, and $\mathcal{V}(P_{\overline{v}})$ the sets of valuations of respectively all the parameters, the visible parameters, and the hidden parameters of an hPTA.

Definition 5 (untimed language of an hPTA). *Given an hPTA A, the untimed language of A, denoted by UL(A) is the union over all parameter valuations v of the sets of untimed words accepted by $v(A)$, i.e.,*

$$\bigcup_{v \in \mathcal{V}(P)} \left\{ w \mid w \text{ is an untimed word accepted by } v(A) \right\}$$

---

[1] Technically, $v_{0/\infty}$ is not a parameter valuation, as the definition of valuation does not allow ∞. However, we will use it only to valuate an L/U-PTA (or an hL/U-PTA) with it; observe that valuating an L/U-PTA with $v_{0/\infty}$ still gives a valid TA.

TA is a subclass of PTA, hence, given a TA A, we also denote UL(A) its untimed language.

We propose below another definition of language for hPTAs, in which we consider not only the accepting untimed words, but also the parameter valuations associated with these words; this definition is more suited to compare the possibilities offered by parameter synthesis. Note that we only expose the *visible* parameter valuations.

Definition 6 (constrained untimed language of an hPTA). *Given an hPTA* A, *the* constrained untimed language *of* A, *denoted by* CUL(A) *is*

$$\bigcup_{v \in \mathcal{V}(P_v)} \Big\{ (w, v) \mid \exists v' \in \mathcal{V}(P_{\overline{v}}) \text{ s.t. } w \text{ is an untimed word accepted by } v(v'(\mathsf{A})) \Big\}$$

Note that since P_v and $P_{\overline{v}}$ are disjoint, we can write indifferently $v(v'(\mathsf{A}))$ and $v'(v(\mathsf{A}))$.

We use the word "constrained" because another way to represent the constrained language of an hPTA is in the form of a set of elements (w, K), where w is an untimed word, and K is a parametric constraint such that for all v in K, then w is an untimed word accepted by $v(v'(\mathsf{A}))$ for some $v' \in \mathcal{V}(P_{\overline{v}})$.

Example 1. Let us consider the hPTA A of Fig. 1a, where $P_v = \{p_1\}$ and $P_{\overline{v}} = \{p_2\}$.

- Its untimed language is UL(A) = $\{a\} \cup \{ba^n \mid n \in \mathbb{N}\}$ that we note with the rational expression UL(A) = $a + ba^*$.
- Its constrained untimed language is CUL(A) = $\Big\{ (a, p_1 = i) \mid 0 \le i \le 1 \Big\} \cup \Big\{ (ba^n, p_1 = i) \mid i \in \mathbb{N}, n \in \mathbb{N} \Big\}$ that we can also note CUL(A) = $\Big\{ (a, p_1 \le 1), (ba^*, p_1 \ge 0) \Big\}$, with $p_1 \in \mathbb{N}$. Note that both the parameter p_2 and the fact that p_2 must be at least 1 to go to l_2 are hidden.

Definition 7 (regular constrained language). *The* constrained untimed language *of an hPTA* A *is* regular *if for all visible parameter valuations* $v \in \mathcal{V}(P_v)$, *the language* $\{w \mid (w, v) \in \mathsf{CUL}(\mathsf{A})\}$ *is regular.*

Remark 1. Since valuating a PTA with any rational parameter valuation gives a TA, the constrained untimed language of any PTA is regular in the sense of Definition 7.

Note that the idea of combining the untimed language with the parameter valuations leading to it is close to the idea of the behavioral cartography of parametric timed automata [4], that consists in computing parameter constraints together with a "trace set", i.e., the untimed language (that also includes in [4] the locations).

In the following, a *class* refers to an element in the set of TAs, bounded L/U-PTAs, L/U-PTAs, bounded PTAs and PTAs, and their counterparts with hidden parameters. An *instance* of a class is a model of that class.

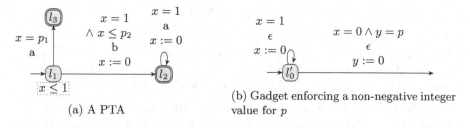

(a) A PTA

(b) Gadget enforcing a non-negative integer value for p

Fig. 1. An example of PTA, and a PTA gadget

A first class is strictly more expressive than a second one w.r.t. the untimed language if (i) for any instance of the second one, their exists an instance of the first one that has the same untimed language, and (ii) there exists an instance of the first one for which no instance of the second one has the same untimed language. Two classes are equally expressive w.r.t. the untimed language if for any instance of either class, their exists an instance of the other class that has the same untimed language. The comparison of the expressiveness w.r.t. the constrained untimed language can be defined similarly, with the additional requirement that the two instances must contain the same visible parameters (possibly after some renaming).

4   An Equivalence Between Integer and Rational Parameters

In the literature, some works focus on integer parameters [6,8,9], some others on rational parameters [10,11], and also some propose constructions working in both settings [2,5,12,13].

In this section, we prove that considering rational parameter valuations or unbounded integer parameter valuations in PTAs and L/U-PTAs is actually equivalent with respect to untimed languages.[2]

First, remark that any PTA with rational parameter valuations can be constrained to accept only non-negative integer parameter valuations. We just need to insert a copy of the gadget in Fig. 1b for each parameter p before the initial location. We connect them to each other in sequence, in any order, and x and y can be clocks from the original PTA. In that gadget x is zero only when y is a non-negative integer and therefore p must be a non-negative integer to permit the exit from l'_0. Clearly, when considering only non-negative integer parameter valuations, both PTAs have the same untimed language.

With the above construction, we can filter out non-integer valuations. We can actually go a bit further and establish the following result:

---

[2] Comparing constrained languages would make no sense since obviously the parameter valuations cannot match in general in the rational and integer settings.

Lemma 2. *For each PTA* A, *there exists a PTA* A' *such that:*

1. *for all rational parameter valuations v of* A *there exists an integer parameter valuation v' of* A' *such that $v(A)$ and $v'(A')$ have the same untimed language.*
2. *for all integer parameter valuations v' of* A' *there exists a rational parameter valuation v of* A *such that $v(A)$ and $v'(A')$ have the same untimed language.*

Proof. The idea of the proof is to scale all the expressions to which clocks are constrained so that they are integers. However, since we do not know in advance by how much we have to scale, we use an additional parameter to account for this scaling factor.

Let A be a PTA. Let p be a fresh parameter and let A'' be the PTA obtained from A by replacing every inhomogeneous (i. e., constant) term c in the linear expressions of guards and invariants by $c * p$. For instance, the constraint $x \leq 3p_1 + 2p_2 + 7$ becomes $x \leq 3p_1 + 2p_2 + 7p$.

We now build A' as follows: we add a new location (which will be the initial location of A'), from which two transitions, labeled ϵ and resetting all clocks, exit. The first one has guard $x \neq 0 \land x = p$ and goes to the initial location of A''. The second has guard $x = 0 \land x = p$ and goes to the initial location of an exact copy of A. By construction the first one can be taken only if $p \neq 0$ and the second one only if $p = 0$.

1. Let v be a rational parameter valuation of A. Let m be the least common multiple (LCM) of the denominators of the values assigned to parameters by v. Let v' be defined as: $\forall p_i \neq p, v'(p_i) = m * v(p_i)$ and $v'(p) = m$. Then, by construction, v' is an integer valuation of A', $v'(p) \neq 0$ and $v'(A'')$ is a TA that is scaled by m from the TA $v(A)$. Then by [1, Lemma 4.1], $v(A)$ and $v'(A'')$ have the same untimed runs up to renaming. And finally, $v(A)$ and $v'(A')$ have the same untimed language.
2. The opposite direction works similarly: let v' be an integer parameter valuation of A'. If $v'(p) = 0$, then in A'' we can only go to the copy of A. We can therefore choose $v(p_i) = v'(p_i)$ and obtain the same untimed language. If $v'(p) \neq 0$, we define v by $v(p_i) = \frac{v'(p_i)}{v'(p)}$. Then v is a rational parameter valuation of A and $v(A)$ is a scaled down version of $v'(A'')$, which therefore has the same untimed runs. And again, $v(A)$ and $v'(A')$ have the same untimed language.   □

First remark that, in order to show the equivalence between integer- and rational-valued parameters, we provided a construction that added one additional parameter, and possibly some parametric clocks. This is consistent with the fact that PTAs with integer parameters typically have decidability results for slightly more parametric clocks and parameters than with rational parameters. For instance, the existence of a rational parameter valuation such that a given location is reachable is undecidable for PTAs with 1 parametric clock (a clock compared to parameters) and 3 normal clocks [13], while the existence of an *integer* parameter valuation is decidable in that setting [6].

Second, in the construction, we need the integer parameters to be unbounded because the LCM can be arbitrarily big.

Finally, this result is not directly applicable to L/U-PTAs as we cannot ensure that the parameterized scaling factor would be the same for upper bound inhomogeneous terms as for lower bound ones. However, for L/U-PTAs, we can derive the same result from the monotonicity property:

Lemma 3. *For an L/U-PTA A, the set of untimed runs produced with only integer parameter valuations or with all rational parameter valuations is the same.*

Proof. Clearly the set of untimed runs produced by considering only integer parameter valuations is included in the one obtained by considering all rational parameter valuations.

In the other direction: let v be a rational parameter valuation of A and let v' be the integer parameter valuation obtained from v by rounding up the values for upper bound parameters, and rounding down for lower bound parameters. Then, by Lemma 1, $v'(A)$ contains all the untimed runs of $v(A)$.   □

Here also we need integer parameters to be unbounded because the rational parameter valuations can themselves be arbitrarily big and we get accordingly big integers when rounding up.

We can now conclude the following:

Proposition 1. *PTAs (resp. L/U-PTAs) with rational parameters and PTAs (resp. L/U-PTAs) with unbounded integer parameters are equivalent with respect to the untimed language.*

When the parameters are bounded, we will see in Proposition 2 that the integer setting leads to regular languages. So, when bounded, PTAs with rational parameters are obviously strictly more expressive than their integer parameter counterpart. For L/U-PTAs, using again the monotonicity property, we trivially see that the valuation setting all upper-bound parameters to the maximal value allowed by the bounded domain, and lower-bound parameters to the minimal value gives all the untimed runs that are possible with other valuations. That "extremal" valuation is an integer valuation by definition. So, even when bounded, L/U-PTAs are still equally expressive in the rational and integer settings.

5   Expressiveness as the Untimed Language

5.1   PTAs in the Hierarchy of Chomsky

Let us show that (without surprise) Turing-recognizable languages (type-0 in Chomsky's hierarchy) can be recognized by PTAs (with enough clocks and parameters).

Lemma 4. *Turing-recognizable languages are also recognizable by PTAs.*

Proof. Consider a Turing-machine: it can be simulated by a 2-counter machine (with labelled instructions), which can in turn be simulated by a PTA. The transitions of the encoding PTA can be easily labeled accordingly (using also ϵ transitions). Assume that a word is accepted by the machine when it halts (i. e., it reaches l_{halt}). If the machine does not halt, l_{halt} is reachable for no parameter valuation, hence the language of the machine is empty and that of the encoding PTA also. If the machine halts, l_{halt} is reachable for parameter valuations correctly encoding the machine (i. e., depending on the proof, large enough or small enough to correctly encode the maximum value of the two counters). Hence, by taking the union over all parameter valuations of all untimed words accepted by the encoding PTA, one obtains exactly the language recognized by the machine. $\square$

Lemma 4 only holds with enough clocks and parameters, typically 3 parametric clocks and 1 integer-valued or rational-valued parameter [6], or 1 parametric clock, 3 non-parametric clocks and 1 rational-valued parameter [13].

For lower numbers, either decidability of the EF-emptiness problem is ensured (in which case the language cannot be type-0), or this problem remains open.

Let us point out a direct consequence of a result of [5] on PTAs with a single (necessarily parametric) clock.

Lemma 5. *The untimed language recognized by a PTA with a single clock and arbitrarily many parameters is regular.*

Proof. In [5, Theorem 20], we proved that the parametric zone graph (an extension of the zone graph for PTAs, following e. g., [12]) of a PTA with a single (necessarily parametric) clock and arbitrarily many parameters is finite. This gives that the language recognized by a PTA with a single clock is regular. $\square$

We now show that adding to the setting of Lemma 5 a single non-parametric clock, even with a single parameter, may give a language that is at least context-sensitive, hence beyond the class of regular languages.

Theorem 1. *PTAs with 1 parametric clock, 1 non-parametric clock and 1 parameter can recognize languages that are context-sensitive.*

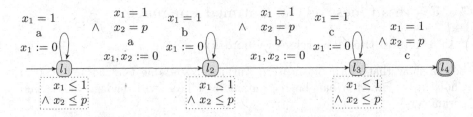

Fig. 2. A PTA with untimed language $a^n b^n c^n$

Proof. Consider the PTA A in Fig. 2. Consider an integer parameter valuation v such that $v(p) = i$, with $i \in \mathbb{N}$. The idea is that we use the parameter to first count the number of as, and then ensure that we perform an identical number of bs and cs; such counting feature is not possible in TAs (at least not for any value of i as is the case here). Clearly, due to the invariant $x_1 \leq 1$ in l_1, one must take the self-loop on l_1 every 1 time unit; then, one can take the transition to l_2 only after i such loops. The same reasoning applies to locations l_2 and l_3. Hence, the language accepted by the TA $v(A)$ is $a^{i+1}b^{i+1}c^{i+1}$.

Hence the union over all parameter valuations of the words accepted by A is $\{a^n b^n c^n \mid n \geq 1\}$. This language is known to be in the class of context-sensitive languages (type-1 in Chomsky's hierarchy), hence beyond the class of regular languages (type-3). □

This result is interesting for several reasons. First, it shows that adding a single clock, even non-parametric, to a PTA with a single clock immediately increases its expressiveness. Second, it falls into the interesting class of PTAs with 2 clocks, for which many problems remain open: the PTA exhibited in the proof of Theorem 1 (1 parametric clock and 1 non-parametric) falls into the class of 1 parametric clock, arbitrarily many non-parametric clocks and arbitrarily many integer-valued parameters, for which the EF-emptiness is known to be decidable [6]. When replacing the integer-valued with a rational-valued parameter (which does not fundamentally change our example), it also falls into the class of 1 parametric clock, 1 non-parametric clock and 1 rational-valued parameter, for which the EF-emptiness is known to be open [3]. In both cases, it gives a lower bound on the class of languages recognized by such a PTA.

5.2   Comparison of Expressiveness

In this section, we compare the expressiveness of PTAs w.r.t. their untimed language UL.

First, we show in the following lemma that the untimed language of an L/U-PTA is equal to that of the same L/U-PTA valuated with $v_{0/\infty}$.

Lemma 6. *Let A be an L/U-PTA. Then:* $\mathsf{UL}(A) = \mathsf{UL}(v_{0/\infty}(A))$.

Proof. ⊆ Let us first show that any accepting run of A for some parameter valuation is also an accepting run of $v_{0/\infty}(A)$, in the spirit of [11]. Let v be a parameter valuation. Let ρ be an accepting run of $v(A)$. Observe that, by definition, the guards and invariants of $v_{0/\infty}(A)$ are more relaxed than that of $v(A)$. Hence, any transition of ρ is also enabled in $v_{0/\infty}(A)$. Hence, ρ is also an accepting run of $v_{0/\infty}(A)$.
⊇ Conversely, let us show that, for any accepting run of $v_{0/\infty}(A)$, there exists a parameter valuation v such that this run is also an accepting run of $v(A)$. It suffices to show that, for a given run, there exists one parameter valuation accepting this run, as we define UL as the union over all parameter valuations. Let $\rho : s_0 \xrightarrow{(e_0, d_0)} s_1 \xrightarrow{(e_1, d_1)} \cdots \xrightarrow{(e_{m-1}, d_{m-1})} s_m$ be an accepting run of $v_{0/\infty}(A)$.

Let d be the duration of this run. Let $k = \lceil d \rceil + 1$. Let $v_{0/k}$ be the parameter valuation assigning 0 to all lower-bound parameters, and k to all upper-bound parameters. Now, observe that $v_{0/\infty}(\mathsf{A})$ and $v_{0/k}(\mathsf{A})$ are identical TAs, with the exception that some guards and invariants in $v_{0/k}(\mathsf{A})$ may include additional constraints of the form $x \leq i \times k$ or $x < i \times k$ (for some clock x and some $i > 0, i \in \mathbb{N}$). Since the duration of ρ is strictly less than k, then no clock will reach value k and therefore this run cannot be impacted by these additional constraints; hence, ρ is an accepting run of $v_{0/k}(\mathsf{A})$ too. □

Proposition 2. *TAs, L/U-PTAs and bounded PTAs are equally expressive w.r.t. the union of untimed languages.*

Proof. **L/U-PTAs = TAs** Direct from Lemma 6, and the fact that any TA is an L/U-PTA with no parameter.

bounded PTAs = TAs The untimed language of a PTA is the union of the untimed language of the TAs over all possible parameter valuations. As we consider integer-valued parameters, there is a finite number of valuations in a bounded PTA. Since the language recognized by a TA is a regular language, and the class of regular languages is closed under finite union, then bounded PTAs also recognize regular languages, and are therefore equally expressive with TAs. □

Proposition 3. *L/U-PTAs and hL/U-PTAs are equally expressive w.r.t. the union of untimed languages.*

Proof. Consider an L/U-PTA A. Let A_h be the hL/U-PTA that is identical to A and contains no hidden parameters (i.e., $P_v = P$ and $P_{\overline{v}} = \emptyset$). Then $\mathsf{UL}(\mathsf{A}_h) = \mathsf{UL}(\mathsf{A})$.

Conversely, consider an hL/U-PTA A_h with visible parameters P_v and hidden parameters $P_{\overline{v}}$. Let A be the L/U-PTA such that $P = P_v \cup P_{\overline{v}}$. Then $\mathsf{UL}(\mathsf{A}) = \mathsf{UL}(\mathsf{A}_h)$. □

Proposition 4. *PTAs are strictly more expressive than TAs w.r.t. the union of untimed languages.*

Proof. Since the untimed words recognized by TA form a regular language [1], then the PTA exhibited in Theorem 1 recognizes a language not recognized by any TA. Conversely, any TA is a PTA (with no parameter) which gives that the expressiveness of PTAs is strictly larger than that of TAs. □

In the following, we show that neither hidden parameters nor fully parametric linear constraints increase the expressive power of PTAs w.r.t. the union of untimed languages.

Proposition 5. *PTAs and hPTAs are equally expressive w.r.t. the union of untimed languages.*

Proof. Following the same reasoning as in Proposition 3. □

Impact of the Syntax of the Guards. Recall that our guards and invariants are of the form $x \sim plt$, with plt a parametric linear term. Several alternative definitions exist in the literature. In addition to the PTAs defined in Definition 1, we consider here two other definitions, one that can be seen as the most restrictive (and used in e.g., [2]), and one that is very permissive, with even constraints involving no clocks. We denote by a *simple guard* a constraint over $X \cup P$ defined by inequalities of the form $x \sim z$, where z is either a parameter or a constant in $\mathbb{Z}$. We define an *AHV93-PTA* as a PTA the guards and invariants of which are all conjunctions of simple guards. We define a PTA with fully parametric constraints (*fpc-PTA*) as a PTA the guards and invariants of which are conjunctions of inequalities either of the form $x \sim plt$ ("guards"), or $plt \sim 0$ ("fully parametric guards"). Let us show that all three definitions are equivalently expressive w.r.t. the untimed language.

Proposition 6. *PTAs and AVH93-PTAs are equally expressive w.r.t. the union of untimed languages.*

This result extends in a straightforward manner to fpc-PTAs.

Proposition 7. *PTAs and fpc-PTAs are equally expressive w.r.t. the union of untimed languages.*

6   Expressiveness as the Constrained Untimed Language

In this section, we compare the expressiveness of PTAs w.r.t. their visible constrained untimed language.

Proposition 8. *Bounded PTAs are strictly less expressive than PTAs w.r.t. the constrained untimed language.*

Proof. Bounded PTAs can easily be simulated using a non-bounded PTA, by bounding the parameters using one clock and appropriate extra locations and transitions prior to the original initial location of the PTA. For example, if x is reset when entering l_1', the gadget in Fig. 3a ensures that $p \in [\min, \max]$. All such gadgets (one per parameter) must be added in a sequential manner, resetting x prior to each gadget, and resetting all clocks when entering the original initial location after the last gadget.

Now, it is easy to find a PTA that has a larger constrained untimed language than any bounded PTA. This is the case of any PTA for which a word is accepting for parameter valuations arbitrarily large (e.g., Fig. 3b).   □

We now show that, interestingly, this result does not extend to L/U-PTAs, i.e., bounded L/U-PTAs are not strictly less expressive than but incomparable with L/U-PTAs.

Proposition 9. *Bounded L/U-PTAs are incomparable with L/U-PTAs w.r.t. the constrained untimed language.*

(a) Bounding a PTA   (b) PTA accepting a for any valuation

Fig. 3. A PTA gadget and a PTA

Proof. – Let us show that the constrained untimed language of a given bounded L/U-PTA cannot be obtained for any L/U-PTA. Consider a bounded U-PTA with a single parameter p^+ with bounds such that $p^+ \in [0,1]$, and accepting a for any valuation of $p^+ \in [0,1]$. From Lemma 1, if this run is accepted in an L/U-PTA A′, then this run is also accepted for any valuation v' such that $v'(p^+) \geq 0$, including for instance $v'(p^+) > 1$. Hence accepting a only for valuations of $p^+ \in [0,1]$ cannot be obtained in an L/U-PTA, and therefore no L/U-PTA yields this constrained untimed language.
  – This converse is immediate: assume an L/U-PTA with a single parameter p^+, accepting a for any valuation of $p^+ \in [0, \infty)$. From the definition of bounded (L/U-)PTAs, all parameters must be bounded, and therefore there exists no bounded L/U-PTA that can accept a run for $p^+ \in [0, \infty)$. Hence no bounded L/U-PTA yields this constrained untimed language.   □

We now show that hidden parameters do not extend the expressiveness of L/U-PTAs.

Proposition 10. *hL/U-PTAs are equally expressive with L/U-PTAs w.r.t. the constrained untimed language.*

Hidden parameters however strictly extend the expressiveness of PTAs.

Lemma 7. *There exists an hPTA A such that* CUL(A) *is not regular.*

Proof. Assume a PTA with no parameter. Its constrained untimed language is a set of pairs (w, v), where v is a degenerate parameter valuation (i.e., a valuation $v : \emptyset \to \mathbb{N}$ as this PTA contains no parameter). The projection of this set of pairs onto the words (i.e., $\{w \mid (w, v) \in$ CUL(A)$\}$) yields a regular language, as a PTA without parameters is a TA, the class of language recognized by which is that of regular languages. Now consider an hPTA where all parameters are hidden. This time, from Theorem 1 the projection of its constrained untimed language onto the words yields a language that goes beyond the class of regular languages. Hence there exists an hPTA for which the constrained untimed language is not regular.   □

Remark 2. The idea used in the proof of Lemma 7 uses a PTA with no (visible) parameter. But such a result can be generalized to a PTA with an arbitrary number of visible parameters: assume such a PTA, and assume one of its parameter valuations v. We can extend this PTA into a PTA A′ with a single hidden parameter such that, for the valuation v (of the visible parameters), the PTA will produce $a^n b^n c^n$ using the construction in Theorem 1. Hence, the constrained untimed language of A' is not regular.

Proposition 11. *hPTAs are strictly more expressive than PTAs w.r.t. the constrained untimed language.*

Proof. From Remark 1 and Lemma 7. □

Let us finally show that PTAs and fpc-PTAs (involving additionally $plt \sim 0$) are not more expressive than AHV93-PTAs with hidden parameters.

Proposition 12. *PTAs and fpc-PTAs are not more expressive than AHV93-PTAs with hidden parameters w.r.t. the constrained untimed language.*

Proof. In Propositions 6 and 7, we used a construction to show the equivalent expressiveness of the untimed language of PTAs, fpc-PTAs and AHV93-PTAs. This construction transforms a PTA or an fpc-PTA into an AHV93-PTAs. Since we use extra parameters in this construction, it suffices to hide these extra parameters, and we therefore obtain an AHV93-PTA with the same CUL as the original (fpc-)PTA. □

7 Conclusion and Perspectives

In this paper, we proposed a first attempt at defining the expressiveness of parametric timed automata, also introducing the notion of hidden parameters to compare models with different numbers of parameters. When considering the union over all parameter valuations of the untimed language, it turns out that all subclasses of PTAs with integer parameters are not more expressive than TAs. However, PTAs are strictly more expressive than TAs (from 1 parametric clock and 1 non-parametric clock); extending PTAs with hidden parameters or fully parametric constraints does not increase their expressiveness. In addition, integer-valued or rational-valued parameters turn out to be equivalent.

When considering the set of accepting untimed words together with their associated parameter valuations, then subclasses of PTAs with integer parameters have a varying expressiveness. An interesting result is that bounded L/U-PTAs turn out to be incomparable with L/U-PTAs. In addition, hidden parameters strictly extend the expressiveness of PTAs.

Future Works. We compared so far general formalisms; it now remains to be studied what consequences on decidability the forms of guards and invariants together with a fixed number of clocks and parameters may have: a ultimate goal would be to unify the wealth of (un)decidability results from the literature with all different syntactic contexts.

We showed that rational-valued parameters are not more expressive than integer-valued parameters; our construction makes use of an extra parameter. It remains to be shown whether this construction is optimal or not.

Finally, forbidding ϵ-transitions may also change our comparison of formalisms, as such silent transitions have an impact on the expressiveness of TAs (see [7]).

References

1. Alur, R., Dill, D.L.: A theory of timed automata. Theor. Comput. Sci. **126**(2), 183–235 (1994)
2. Alur, R., Henzinger, T.A., Vardi, M.Y.: Parametric real-time reasoning. In: STOC, pp. 592–601. ACM (1993)
3. André, É.: What's decidable about parametric timed automata? In: Artho, C., et al. (eds.) FTSCS 2015. CCIS, vol. 596, pp. 52–68. Springer, Heidelberg (2016). doi:10.1007/978-3-319-29510-7_3
4. André, É., Fribourg, L.: Behavioral cartography of timed automata. In: Kučera, A., Potapov, I. (eds.) RP 2010. LNCS, vol. 6227, pp. 76–90. Springer, Heidelberg (2010)
5. André, É., Markey, N.: Language preservation problems in parametric timed automata. In: Sankaranarayanan, S., Vicario, E. (eds.) FORMATS 2015. LNCS, vol. 9268, pp. 27–43. Springer, Heidelberg (2015)
6. Beneš, N., Bezděk, P., Larsen, K.G., Srba, J.: Language emptiness of continuous-time parametric timed automata. In: Halldórsson, M.M., Iwama, K., Kobayashi, N., Speckmann, B. (eds.) ICALP 2015. LNCS, vol. 9135, pp. 69–81. Springer, Heidelberg (2015)
7. Bérard, B., Petit, A., Diekert, V., Gastin, P.: Characterization of the expressive power of silent transitions in timed automata. Fundamenta Informaticae **36**(2–3), 145–182 (1998)
8. Bozzelli, L., La Torre, S.: Decision problems for lower/upper bound parametric timed automata. Formal Meth. Syst. Des. **35**(2), 121–151 (2009)
9. Bundala, D., Ouaknine, J.: Advances in parametric real-time reasoning. In: Csuhaj-Varjú, E., Dietzfelbinger, M., Ésik, Z. (eds.) MFCS 2014, Part I. LNCS, vol. 8634, pp. 123–134. Springer, Heidelberg (2014)
10. Doyen, L.: Robust parametric reachability for timed automata. Inf. Process. Lett. **102**(5), 208–213 (2007)
11. Hune, T., Romijn, J., Stoelinga, M., Vaandrager, F.W.: Linear parametric model checking of timed automata. J. Logic Algebraic Program. **52–53**, 183–220 (2002)
12. Jovanović, A., Lime, D., Roux, O.H.: Integer parameter synthesis for timed automata. Trans. Softw. Eng. **41**(5), 445–461 (2015)
13. Miller, J.S.: Decidability and complexity results for timed automata and semi-linear hybrid automata. In: Lynch, N.A., Krogh, B.H. (eds.) HSCC 2000. LNCS, vol. 1790, pp. 296–309. Springer, Heidelberg (2000)

Modelling Attack-defense Trees Using Timed Automata

Olga Gadyatskaya[1], René Rydhof Hansen[2], Kim Guldstrand Larsen[2],
Axel Legay[3], Mads Çhr. Olesen[2], and Danny Bøgsted Poulsen[2]($\boxtimes$)

[1] SnT, University of Luxembourg, Luxembourg City, Luxembourg
[2] Department of Computer Science, Aalborg University, Aalborg, Denmark
dannybpoulsen@hotmail.com
[3] Inria Rennes – Bretagne Atlantique, Rennes, France

Abstract. Performing a thorough security risk assessment of an organisation has always been challenging, but with the increased reliance on outsourced and off-site third-party services, i.e., "cloud services", combined with internal (legacy) IT-infrastructure and -services, it has become a very difficult and time-consuming task. One of the traditional tools available to ease the burden of performing a security risk assessment and structure security analyses in general is *attack trees* [19, 23, 24], a tree-based formalism inspired by *fault trees*, a well-known formalism used in safety engineering.

In this paper we study an extension of traditional attack trees, called *attack-defense trees*, in which not only the attacker's actions are modelled, but also the defensive actions taken by the attacked party [15]. In this work we use the attack-defense tree as a goal an attacker wants to achieve, and separate the behaviour of the attacker and defender from the attack-defense-tree. We give a fully stochastic timed semantics for the behaviour of the attacker by introducing *attacker profiles* that choose actions probabilistically and execute these according to a probability density. Lastly, the stochastic semantics provides success probabilities for individual actions. Furthermore, we show how to introduce costs of attacker actions. Finally, we show how to automatically encode it all with a *network of timed automata*, an encoding that enables us to apply state-of-the-art model checking tools and techniques to perform fully automated quantitative and qualitative analyses of the modelled system.

1 Introduction

In the past few years, we have witnessed a rapid increase in the number and severity of security breaches, ranging from theft of personal information about millions of US government employees[1] to sophisticated targeted malware attacks on security vendors[2]. This problem is exacerbated by the fact that it has become

---

Research leading to these results was partially supported by the European Union Seventh Framework Programme under grant agreement no. 318003 (TREsPASS).

[1] https://www.opm.gov/cybersecurity/cybersecurity-incidents/.
[2] http://usa.kaspersky.com/about-us/press-center/press-releases/
duqu-back-kaspersky-lab-reveals-cyberattack-its-corporate-netwo.

© Springer International Publishing Switzerland 2016
M. Fränzle and N. Markey (Eds.): FORMATS 2016, LNCS 9884, pp. 35–50, 2016.
DOI: 10.1007/978-3-319-44878-7_3

difficult to perform an adequate *risk assessment* of an organisation's security stance, with many organisations relying on a complex mix of off-site third party IT-services, e.g., "cloud services" and internally supported IT services. One of the tools available to help structure risk assessments and security analyses is *attack trees*, recommended, e.g., by NATO Research and Technology Organisation (RTO) [20] and OWASP [22]. Attack trees [19,23,24] is a tree based formalism inspired by *fault trees*, a well-known formalism used in safety engineering. The formalism was initially introduced by [24] and given a formal definition by Mauw and Oostdijk [19]. Kordy et al. [16] provide a survey on attack trees and related formalisms. While basic quantitative analysis, i.e., a bottom-up computation for a single parameter (e.g., cost, probability or time of an attack), can be performed directly on attack trees [4], several proposals exist to extend the basic attack tree formalism in order to support better analysis. For example, Buldas et al. [6], Jürgenson and Willemson [14] introduced multi-parameter attack trees with interdependent variables; Dalton et al. [7] have proposed analysing attack trees as Generalized Stochastic Petri Nets; Arnold et al. [2] applied interactive Input/Output Markov Chains to enhance temporal and stochastic dependencies analysis in attack trees. Kumar et al. [17] have considered priced timed automata for analysis of attack trees. This work defines a translation for each leaf node and each gate in an attack tree into a priced timed automaton. The approach allows to translate the full attack tree into an automaton that can be analysed using the UPPAAL CORA model checker. The research community interest in attack trees has been recently reinvigorated by new techniques to automatically generate attack trees and attack-defense trees from socio-technical organizational models [11,13], paving the way towards automating risk assessment.

Attack-defense trees are a notable extension of attack trees that include, besides attacker's actions, also defender's actions and model their interplay [3,15]. This extended formalism allows capturing more detailed scenarios, and incorporating the defender's perspective into an analysis. For example, burglar-resistance classes for physical security mechanisms, such as doors and windows, define how much time an attacker equipped with certain tools needs to spend on the intrusion [25]. Explicit consideration of defenses in the analysis allows the domain experts to get a better picture of the scenario [4,15]. Recently, Hermanns et al. [12] have created the attack-defense-diagrams formalism extending attacke-defense trees with trigger and reset gates, which allow expressing temporal behaviours. The work [21] likewise introduces a sequential gate to attack-defense trees and considers a two-player stochastic game interpretation of this.

Our paper introduces a framework for analysing complex temporal scenarios of interactions of attackers and defenders, beyond the expressiveness of classic attack-defense trees. For doing this we develop a modelling framework for expressing the temporal behaviour of the attacker with the formalism *networks of timed automata*. Unlike the work of [17] the attack-defense-tree is not encoded as a timed automata-instead it is encoded as a boolean formula, which the attacker wishes to become true. This encoding allows us to apply state-of-the-art model checking tools and techniques to perform fully automated analyses of the modelled system, both qualitative (boolean) analysis and quantitative (probabilistic) analysis. The modelling framework is accompanied by an automatic translation script. The script reads an attack-defense-tree and outputs a UPPAAL [18] timed automata model which can subsequently be queried several questions: among these questions are "what is the probability that an attack succeeds within τ" and "what is the expected cost of the attacker within τ time units" for a specific behaviour of the attacker. Using UPPAAL-STRATEGO [10], a recent extension of UPPAAL, we are furthermore capable of finding an attacker that minimises the expected cost of an attack.

2   Attack Defense Trees

We will now define an attack-defense tree (Definition 1), along with the standard boolean semantics for such a tree. Thereafter a temporal semantics with time, cost and stochasticity is introduced. This temporal semantics is the first contribution of this paper.

Definition 1 (AD-tree). *An AD-tree over the attacker actions A_a and defender actions A_d is generated by the syntax*

$$t ::= p \mid t \wedge t \mid t \vee t \mid \sim t$$

where $p \in A_a \cup A_d$. We denote by $\mathcal{L}(A_a, A_d)$ all AD-trees over A_a and A_d.

Let $t \in \mathcal{L}(A_a, A_d)$, let $A \subseteq A_a$ be the set of selected attacker actins and let $D \subseteq A_d$ be the set of selected defender actions; then we inductively define $[\![t]\!]A, D$ as

- $[\![p]\!]D, A = \mathtt{tt}$ if $p \in A \cup D$, $\mathtt{ff}$·otherwise
- $[\![t_1 \wedge t_2]\!]D, A = ([\![t_1]\!]D, A) \wedge ([\![t_2]\!]D, A)$
- $[\![t_1 \vee t_2]\!]D, A = ([\![t_1]\!]D, A) \vee ([\![t_2]\!]D, A)$
- $[\![\sim t]\!]D, A = \neg([\![t]\!]D, A)$

As an example of an attack-defense-tree consider Fig. 1. This tree explains how an attacker may succefully remove an RFID-tag from a warehouse. Among the possible ways is infiltrating management and order a replacement tag. The example is lifted from [3].

To make attack-defense-trees well-formed, we follow Aslanyan and Nielson [3] and impose a type system on top of the abstract syntax of Definition 1 – in this system there are two types d and a corresponding to defender and attacker. The type system is captured in Fig. 2. The negation operator $\sim$ acts like the switch operator of Aslanyan and Nielson [3] and changes the type of the subtree. Unlike Aslanyan and Nielson [3], we do not have a normal negation operator: the reason is we only want an attacker (or defender for that matter) to do positive things i.e. the attacker should only do something beneficial for him. In the remainder we only consider well-formed trees according to this type-system and we restrict our attention to trees t where $t \vdash a$. The major interest of attack-defense trees is whether there exists a set of defense measures such that an attack can never occur.

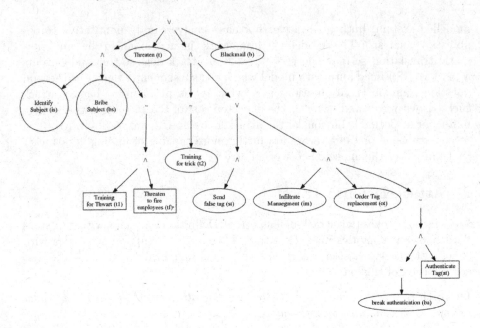

Fig. 1. An example of an attack-defense-tree. Square items correspond to defender's actions and circles to the attacker.

Question 1. For an attack-defense tree $t \in \mathcal{L}(\mathsf{A}_a, \mathsf{A}_d)$, does there exist $D \subseteq \mathsf{A}_d$, such that for all $A \subseteq \mathsf{A}_a$, $[\![t]\!]D, A = \mathtt{ff}$?

This encapsulates our view that defense measures are selected ahead of time and fixed, while the attacker selects a set of attack measures. Our view is in accordance with the classical definition of attack-defense trees by [15]. Let λ be a symbol not in A_a, which indicates that an attacker chooses to do no actions. We denote by A_a^λ the set $\mathsf{A}_a \cup \{\lambda\}$.

Definition 2. *Let* $t \in \mathcal{L}(\mathsf{A}_a, \mathsf{A}_d)$ *be an AD-tree. The Attack-Defense-Graph over* t *is the tuple* $\mathcal{G}^t = (\mathcal{V}, v^0, \to, \to_\neg, \dashrightarrow, F)$ *where*

- $\mathcal{V} = 2^{\mathsf{A}_d} \times 2^{\mathsf{A}_a}$ *is a set of vertices containing currently true attacker and defender actions,*
- $v^0 = (\emptyset, \emptyset)$ *is the initial vertex,*
- $\to \subseteq (\mathcal{V} \times \mathsf{A}_a^\lambda \times \mathcal{V})$ *is a set of edges where* $((D, A), a, (D', A')) \in \to$ *if and only if* $D = D'$, $A' = A \cup (\{a\} \cap \mathsf{A}_a)$ *and* $a \notin A$,
- $\to_\neg \subseteq (\mathcal{V} \times \mathsf{A}_a \times \mathcal{V})$ *is a set of edges where* $((D, A), a, (D, A)) \in \to_\neg$ *if and only if* $a \notin A$
- $\dashrightarrow = \{(v^0, D, S) \mid D \in 2^{\mathsf{A}_d} \wedge S = (D, \emptyset)\}$ *is the "select defense" edges and*
- $F = \{(D, A) \in \mathcal{V} \mid [\![t]\!]D, A = \mathtt{tt}\}$ *is a set of final vertices.*

An attack-defense graph is essentially laying out all the possible steps an attacker may take to achieve a successful attack. Notice the edges in $\to_\neg$ correspond to

$$\frac{}{\mathsf{A}_d, \mathsf{A}_a \vdash p : a}, p \in \mathsf{A}_a \qquad \frac{}{\mathsf{A}_d, \mathsf{A}_a \vdash p : d}, p \in \mathsf{A}_d \qquad \frac{\mathsf{A}_d, \mathsf{A}_a \vdash t_1 : r \qquad \mathsf{A}_d, \mathsf{A}_a \vdash t_2 : r}{\mathsf{A}_d, \mathsf{A}_a \vdash t_1 \wedge t_2 : r}$$

$$\frac{\mathsf{A}_d, \mathsf{A}_a \vdash t_1 : r \qquad \mathsf{A}_d, \mathsf{A}_a \vdash t_2 : r}{\mathsf{A}_d, \mathsf{A}_a \vdash t_1 \vee t_2 : r} \qquad \frac{\mathsf{A}_d, \mathsf{A}_a \vdash t_1 : r}{\mathsf{A}_d, \mathsf{A}_a \vdash \sim t_1 : r^{-1}}, r^{-1} = \begin{cases} a & \text{if } r = d \\ d & \text{if } r = a \end{cases}$$

Fig. 2. Type system to make attack-defense trees well-formed

trying to execute an atomic attack and failing. We allow this loop back as in this way we are able to model an attacker who selects what action to perform and an environment deciding whether that action succeeds.

For an attack-defense graph (ADG) $\mathcal{G}^t = (\mathcal{V}, v^0, \rightarrow, \rightarrow_\neg, \dashrightarrow, F)$ we write $v \overset{D}{\dashrightarrow} v'$ whenever $(v, D, v') \in \dashrightarrow$ and similarly we write $v \overset{a}{\rightarrow} v'$ ($v \overset{\neg a}{\rightarrow} v'$) if $(v, a, v') \in \rightarrow$ ($(v, a, v') \in \rightarrow_\neg$). An *attack-defense scenario* (ADS) for $\mathcal{G}^t$ is a sequence $\omega = v_0 D v_1 \alpha_1 v_2 \alpha_2 \ldots \alpha_{n_1} s_n \ldots$, where $v_0 = v^0$, for all i, $\alpha_i \in \{a, \neg a \mid a \in \mathsf{A}_a\} \cup \{\lambda\}$, $v_0 \overset{D}{\dashrightarrow} v_1$ and for all $j > 0$, $v_j \overset{\alpha_j}{\rightarrow} v_{j+1}$. We call ω a *successful ADS* if there exists j such that $v_j \in F$, denoted $\omega \vDash t$, and we call it a *failed ADS* if for all j, $v_j \notin F$, denoted $\omega \nvDash t$. We denote by $\Omega(t)$ all ADSs over t and furthermore let $\Omega^D(t) = \{\pi = v^0 \overset{D}{\dashrightarrow} v_0 \overset{a_1}{\rightarrow} \cdots \mid \pi \in \Omega(t)\}$ be all the ADSs initiated by the defender selecting defense measure D.

Lemma 1. *Let $t \in \mathcal{L}(\mathsf{A}_a, \mathsf{A}_d)$ be an attack-defense-tree and let $D \subseteq \mathsf{A}_d$. If for all $\omega \in \Omega^D(t)$, $\omega \nvDash t$ then for all $A \subseteq \mathsf{A}_a$ $[\![t]\!]D, A = \mathtt{ff}$.*

Lemma 2. *Let $t \in \mathcal{L}(\mathsf{A}_a, \mathsf{A}_d)$ be an attack-defense-tree and let $D \subseteq \mathsf{A}_d$. If there exists $\omega \in \Omega^D(t)$, $\omega \vDash t$ then there exists $A \subseteq \mathsf{A}_a$ such that $[\![t]\!]D, A = \mathtt{tt}$.*

In reality we wish to analyse the possible attacks after the defender has selected some defense measures. For this we remove the choice of defense measures from the ADG to get an attack graph (AG). Let $\mathcal{G}^t = (\mathcal{V}, v^0, \rightarrow, \rightarrow_\neg, \dashrightarrow, F)$ be the ADG for $t \in \mathcal{L}(\mathsf{A}_a, \mathsf{A}_d)$; then the AG responding to $D \subseteq \mathsf{A}_d$ is the graph $(\mathcal{V}, v^\mathcal{A}, \rightarrow, \rightarrow_\neg, F)$ where $v^0 \overset{D}{\dashrightarrow} v^\mathcal{A}$. We denote this AG by $\mathcal{G}^t_D$. Due to Lemmas 1 and 2 then Question 1 is answerable by a pure reachability check on $\mathcal{G}^t_D$ for all $D \subseteq 2^{\mathsf{A}_d}$.

2.1   Adding Timed Behaviour

Intuitively speaking, an attacker observes the state of an ADG and choose an action. The attacker is memoryless and does, for instance, not remember how many times a specific attack has been attempted. The execution time of an action p_a is given by interval $[L_{p_a}, U_{p_a}]$, and thus an abstract timed attacker (Definition 3) is essentially a timed transition system.

Definition 3 (Abstract Timed Attacker). *Let* $t \in \mathcal{L}(\mathsf{A}_a, \mathsf{A}_d)$. *An abstract timed attacker over the ADG* $\mathcal{G}^t = (\mathcal{V}, v^0, \to, \to_\neg, \dashrightarrow, F)$ *is a tuple* (S, M, Ac) *where*

- S *is a set of states,*
- $M : \mathcal{V} \to \mathsf{S}$ *maps vertices to attacker states, and*
- $Ac : \mathsf{S} \to 2^{\mathsf{A}_a^\lambda \times \mathbb{R}_{\geq 0}}$ *gives the possible actions and delays for an attacker, with the requirements that*
  - *if* $\mathsf{s} = M(v)$ *and* $(p_a, r) \in Ac(\mathsf{s})$ *then* $v \xrightarrow{p_a} v'$ *for some* v',
  - *if* $(p_a, t) \in Ac(\mathsf{s})$ *then* $L_{p_a} \leq t \leq U_{p_a}$ *and* $\{(p_a, t') | L_{p_a} \leq t' \leq U_{p_a}\} \subseteq Ac(\mathsf{s})$,
  - *if* $(\lambda, t) \in Ac(\mathsf{s})$ *then* $Ac(\mathsf{s}) = \{(\lambda, t') \mid t' \in \mathbb{R}_{\geq 0}\}$,
  - *if* $\mathsf{s} = M(v)$, $v = D, A$, *then* $(\lambda, 0) \in Ac(\mathsf{s})$ *if and only if* $v \in F$ *or* $A = \mathsf{A}_a$ *and*
  - *for all* $\mathsf{s} \in \mathsf{s}$, $Ac(\mathsf{s}) \neq \emptyset$

Let $\mathcal{G}^t = (\mathcal{V}, v^0, \to_a, \to_\neg, \dashrightarrow, F)$ be an ADG and let $\mathcal{A} = (\mathsf{S}, M, Ac)$ be an abstract timed attacker for $\mathcal{G}^t$. For $D \subseteq \mathsf{A}_d$, we denote by $\mathcal{G}^t_D | \mathcal{A}$ the transition system with state space $\mathcal{V} \times \mathsf{S}$, initial state $(v^{\mathcal{A}}, M(v^{\mathcal{A}}))$ and transition relation defined by the rules

- $(v, \mathsf{s}) \xrightarrow{p_a, t} (v', M(v'))$ if $(p_a, t) \in Ac(\mathsf{s})$ and $v \xrightarrow{p_a} v'$
- $(v, \mathsf{s}) \xrightarrow{\neg p_a, t} (v', M(v'))$ if $(p_a, t) \in Ac(\mathsf{s})$ and $v \xrightarrow{\neg p_a} v'$
- $(v, \mathsf{s}) \xrightarrow{\lambda, t} (v', M(v'))$ if $(\lambda, t) \in Ac(\mathsf{s})$ and $v \xrightarrow{\lambda} v'$.

A timed attack over $\mathcal{G}^t_D | \mathcal{A}$, $t \in \mathcal{L}(\mathsf{A}_a, \mathsf{A}_d)$ is a sequence $v_0 d_0 \alpha_0, v_1 d_1 \alpha_1 \ldots$, where $v_0 = v^{\mathcal{A}}$, for all i, $d_i \in \mathbb{R}_{\geq 0}$, $\alpha_i \in \{p_a, \neg p_a \mid p_a \in \mathsf{A}_a\} \cup \{\lambda\}$ and there exists a sequence of states and transitions $(v_0, M(v_0)) \xrightarrow{\alpha_0, d_0} (v_1, \mathsf{s}^1) \ldots$. We denote by $\Omega^\tau(\mathcal{G}^t_D | \mathcal{A})$ all timed attacks of $\mathcal{G}^t_D | \mathcal{A}$. Let $\omega = v_0 d_0 \alpha_0, v_1 d_1 \alpha_1 \ldots$ be a timed attack, then we write $\omega \vDash^\tau t$ if there exists i, s.t. $[\![t]\!]v = \mathbf{tt}$ and $\sum_{i=0}^{i-1} d_i \leq \tau$.

Having introduced time, a defender may consider to not guarantee that an attack can never occur, but to make it very difficult time-wise i.e. that any succeeding attack will require more than τ time units - captured by Question 2. Obviously, an attacker wishes to find an attack in response to $D \subseteq \mathsf{A}_d$ that succeeds before τ time units i.e. to answer Question 3.

Question 2. For an attack-defense tree $t \in \mathcal{L}(\mathsf{A}_a, \mathsf{A}_d)$, abstract timed attacker $\mathcal{A}$ and time limit τ, does there exist a $D \subseteq \mathsf{A}_d$, such that for all $\omega \in \Omega^\tau(\mathcal{G}^t_D | \mathcal{A})$, $\omega \not\vDash^\tau t$?

Question 3. For an attack-defense tree $t \in \mathcal{L}(\mathsf{A}_a, \mathsf{A}_d)$, abstract timed attacker $\mathcal{A}$, time limit τ and $D \subseteq \mathsf{A}_d$ does there exist $\omega \in \Omega^\tau(\mathcal{G}^t_D | \mathcal{A})$, such that $\omega \vDash^\tau t$?

2.2 Adding Stochasticity

A stochastic attacker is a tuple $\mathcal{A}^{\mathcal{S}} = (\mathcal{A}, \gamma, \{\delta_{p_a} | p_a \in \mathsf{A}_a^\lambda\})$, where $\mathcal{A}$ is an attacker defining allowed behaviour by the stochastic attacker, $\gamma : \mathsf{S} \to \mathsf{A}_a^\lambda \to \mathbb{R}_{\geq 0}$ assigns a probability mass to attacker's actions and for all $p_a \in \mathsf{A}_a^\lambda, \delta_{p_a} : \mathsf{S} \to \mathbb{R}_{\geq 0} \to \mathbb{R}_{\geq 0}$ assigns a density to the execution time of p_a. A few requirements are in order here:

1. $\sum_{a \in \mathsf{A}_a^\lambda} \gamma(\mathsf{s})(a) = 1$,
2. $\int_{\mathbb{R}_{\geq 0}} \delta_a(\mathsf{s})(t) \, dt = 1$ for all $a \in \mathsf{A}_a^\lambda$,
3. $\gamma(\mathsf{s})(a) \cdot \delta_a(\mathsf{s})(t) \neq 0$ implies $(a, t) \in Ac(\mathsf{s})$.

Requirement 1 states that $\gamma(\mathsf{s})$ must be a probability mass function, 2 requires that $\delta_a(\mathsf{s})$ is a probability density, and finally the most interesting rule 3 requires that whenever a probability density is assigned to a pair (a, t) then the attacker must in fact be able to do those according to the timed semantics. Finally, to make a complete stochastic semantics we need to resolve the non-determinism of selecting an outcome of performing an action p_a. We assume there is a static probability of an action succeeding, and thus we assume a probability mass function $\gamma_{Succ} : \mathsf{A}_a \to \{p_a, \neg p_a\} \to]0, 1[$ that assigns success and failure probabilities to actions with the requirement that any action must have a non-zero probability of succeeding.

Forming the core of a σ-algebra over timed attacks of $\mathcal{G}_D^t | \mathcal{A}^{\mathcal{S}}$, consider the finite sequence $\pi = v_0 I_0 \alpha_0 v_1 I_1 \alpha_1 \ldots v_n$, where for all i; $\alpha_i \in \{p_a, \neg p_a \mid p_a \in \mathsf{A}_a\}$, I_i is an interval with rational end-points and $v_i \in \mathcal{V}$. The set of runs (cylinder) of this sequence is

$$\mathcal{C}_{\mathcal{G}_D^t | \mathcal{A}^{\mathcal{S}}}(\pi) = \{v_0 d_0 \alpha_0, v_1 d_1 \alpha_1 \ldots v_n d_n \alpha_n \cdots \in \Omega^\tau(\mathcal{G}_D^t | \mathcal{A}) \mid \forall i < d_i \in I_i\}.$$

The probability of these timed attacks runs from (v, s) are recursively defined by

$$F_{(v,\mathsf{s})}(\pi) = (v_0 = v) \cdot \gamma(\mathsf{s})(c(\alpha)) \cdot \int_{\mathbb{R}_{\geq 0}} \delta_{c(\alpha)}(\mathsf{s})(t) \, dt \cdot \gamma_{Succ}(\alpha) F_{[(v,\mathsf{s})]^{\alpha,t}}(\pi^1),$$

where $\pi^1 = v_1 d_1 \alpha_1 \ldots v_n d_n \alpha_n$, $c(p_a) = c(\neg p_a) = p_a$ and $(v, \mathsf{s}) \xrightarrow{\alpha,t} [(v, \mathsf{s})]^{\alpha,t}$ and base case $F_{(v,\mathsf{s})}(\epsilon) = 1$.

Remark 1. The stochastic semantics above is given for arbitrary time distributions. For the remainder we will however restrict our attention to stochastic attacker using only uniform distributions.

Let $\mathcal{G}_D^t = (\mathcal{V}, v^{\mathcal{A}}, \to_a, \to_\neg, F)$ be an AG and let $\mathcal{A}^{\mathcal{S}} = ((S, M, Ac), \gamma, \{, \delta_{p_a} | p_a \in \mathsf{A}_a^\lambda\})$ then we let $F_{\mathcal{G}_D^t | \mathcal{A}^{\mathcal{S}}}(\pi) = F_{(v^{\mathcal{A}}, M(v^{\mathcal{A}}))}(\pi)$. With the above in place, the probability of a succesful attack within a time-bound τ is

$$\mathbb{P}_{\mathcal{G}_D^t | \mathcal{A}^{\mathcal{S}}}(\Diamond_{\leq \tau} t) = \int_{\omega \in \Omega^\tau(\mathcal{G}_D^t | \mathcal{A}^{\mathcal{S}})} \left(\begin{cases} 0 & \text{if } \omega \not\models^\tau t \\ 1 & \text{if } \omega \models^\tau t \end{cases} \right) dF_{\mathcal{G}_D^t | \mathcal{A}^{\mathcal{S}}}.$$

Question 4. Given an attack-defense tree $t \in \mathcal{L}(\mathsf{A}_a, \mathsf{A}_d)$, stochastic attacker $\mathcal{A}^\mathcal{S}$ and time limit τ; find $D^* = \arg\min_{D \in 2^{\mathsf{A}_d}} \left(\mathbb{P}_{\mathcal{G}_D^t | \mathcal{A}^\mathcal{S}}(\lozenge_\tau t) \right)$

Notice that Question 4 has the time bound requirement for how quickly an attacker must succeed in an attack. If this time bound was not present and we thus gave an attacker unlimited time, then if a successful attack exists (no matter how unlikely) it would eventually succeed. This is evidenced by the plot in Fig. 3 with the time limit on the x-axis and the probabilities of an attack on the y-axis. The dashed line in the figure is the lower bound of the 99 % confidence level and the solid line is the upper bound.

2.3   Adding Cost

Considering that an attacker is not only constrained by time, but also by his available resources e.g. money, we want to reflect the concept of a resource in our modelling. For this purpose we consider that an attacker only has one resource and that each action has an associated cost per attempted execution. We capture this cost by a function $\mathsf{C} : \mathsf{A}_a^\lambda \to \mathbb{R}_{\geq 0}$ that assigns the cost to actions with the requirement that $\mathsf{C}(\lambda) = 0$.

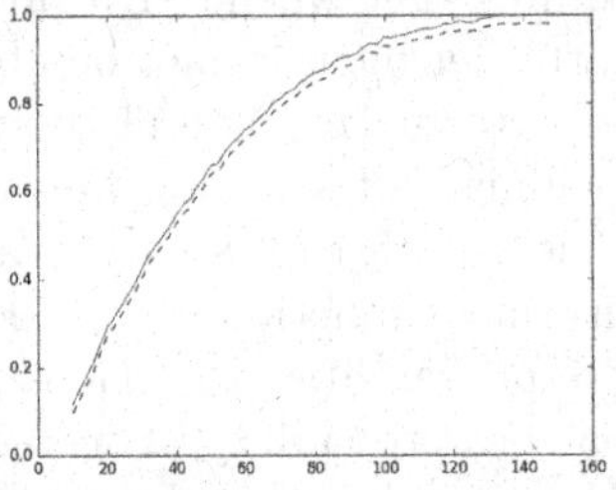

Fig. 3. Plot of probabilities of a successful attack for a uniform attacker.

Let $\omega = v_0 d_0 \alpha_0 \ldots$ be a timed attack; then we define the cost of ω up till step j as $\mathsf{C}(\omega, j) = \sum_{i=0}^{j-1} \mathsf{C}(c(\alpha_i))$, where $c(\lambda) = \lambda$ and $c(p_a) = c(\neg p_a) = p_a$, i.e., we just sum up the individual costs along the attack before the jth step. Now we can define the expected cost of a stochastic attacker, $\mathcal{A}^\mathcal{S}$, responding to a set of defense measures D with a time limit τ

$$\mathbb{E}_{\mathcal{G}_D^t | \mathcal{A}^\mathcal{S}}(C : \lozenge_{\leq \tau} t) = \int_{\omega \in \Omega^\tau(\mathcal{G}_D^t | \mathcal{A}^\mathcal{S})} \left(\begin{cases} \mathsf{C}(\pi, j) & \text{if } \omega \not\vDash^\tau t \land j = \max\{i \mid \sum_{k=0}^i d_k \leq \tau\} \\ \mathsf{C}(\pi, j) & \text{if } \omega \vDash^\tau t \land j = \min\{i \mid [\![t]\!] v_i = \mathtt{tt}\} \end{cases} \right) dF_{\mathcal{G}_D^t | \mathcal{A}^\mathcal{S}}.$$

Question 5. Given an attack-defense tree $t \in \mathcal{L}(\mathsf{A}_a, \mathsf{A}_d)$, stochastic attacker $\mathcal{A}^\mathcal{S}$, time limit τ and $D \subset \mathsf{A}_d$, find $\mathbb{E}_{\mathcal{G}_D^t | \mathcal{A}^\mathcal{S}}(C : \lozenge_{\leq \tau} t)$.

Consider that we fix the distribution over execution times and the success probabilities of execution attacks, but let γ range freely among all possible probability mass functions. Thus, we have a range of possible stochastic attackers, parameterised by γ, i.e. a range of attackers $\mathcal{A}^\mathcal{S}_1, \mathcal{A}^\mathcal{S}_2 \ldots$, where $\mathcal{A}^\mathcal{S}_i = (\mathcal{A}, \gamma_i, \{\delta_{p_a} | p_a \in \mathsf{A}_a^\lambda\})$. Then we are interested in finding the attacker that minimises the cost.

Question 6. Given an attack-defense tree $t \in \mathcal{L}(\mathsf{A}_a, \mathsf{A}_d)$ time limit τ, $D \subset \mathsf{A}_d$ and a collection of attackers $\mathcal{A}^\mathcal{S}_1, \mathcal{A}^\mathcal{S}_2 \ldots$ parameterised by γ; find a stochastic attacker, $\mathcal{A}^\mathcal{S}$, minimising $\mathbb{E}_{\mathcal{G}_D^t | \mathcal{A}^\mathcal{S}}(C : \lozenge_{\leq \tau} t)$.

3   Timed Automata

In this paper we use the expressive *network of timed automata* (TA) formalism [1] extensively. An efficient model checking technique exists for this formalism, and the tool UPPAAL [5,18] uses an extended version as its modelling language. As an example consider the three automata in Fig. 4, modelling two persons and a door.

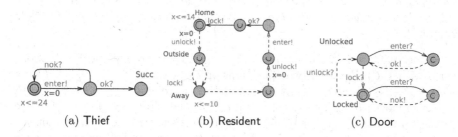

(a) Thief   (b) Resident   (c) Door

Fig. 4. Model of a Thief, a Resident and a Door.

One of the persons is a Resident of a house and the other is a Thief who wants to enter the house while the Resident is not home. The Resident is initially at Home with the door locked for 14 h - indicated by the expression $x <= 14$. The expression $x <= 14$ is an invariant expression and is something that should always be true whenever the automata is in the given location. From Home the resident may *unlock*! the door and go Outside, from where he can either *Lock*! the door or just leave the location to go Away. The "U" in Outside means this location is *urgent* and thus no time may pass while any automata is in such a location. The Door is initially Locked – from here someone may request to *enter*?, after which the Door responds with *ok*!: the "C" in the location means *committed* and is similar to urgent locations, but in addition to stopping time, it also ensures that only components in committed locations may move next. The door may be *lock*?ed - from which it responds to an *enter*? with a *nok*!. The Thief chooses some time, between 0 and 24 to attempt *enter*!ing – if he succeeds and gets an *ok*? from the Door he is happy and enters Succ. In case he is unlucky he receives an *nok*? and tries again later. Although simple, the above example contains the key elements of timed automata. To summarise, a timed automaton consists of locations and edges between locations. On locations one can write invariant expressions based on the values of clocks, like $x <= 14$. A clock is a real-valued counter that increases as time progresses. While moving along an edge, a TA may synchronise with another over a set of channels: in UPPAAL the convention is that *a*! means "send on a", and *a*? means "receive on a". Not shown in the example is that edges can be "guarded" by expressions over clocks.

Let c be a clock then we call an element $c \leq n$ ($c \geq n$) an upper (lower) bound and denote by $\mathcal{B}^{\leq}(\mathcal{C})$ ($\mathcal{B}^{\geq}(\mathcal{C})$) the set of all finite conjunctions of lower (upper) bounds. For a finite set of channels Σ we denote by $\Sigma_o = \{a! | a \in \Sigma\}$ and $\Sigma_i = \{a? | a \in \Sigma\}$ the output and input actions over Σ respectively.

Definition 4 (Timed Automaton). *A timed automaton (TA) is a 6-tuple* $\mathcal{A} = (L, \mathcal{C}, \ell_0, \mathsf{A}, \rightarrow, I)$, *where (1) L is a finite set of locations, (2) $\ell_0 \in L$ is the initial location, (3) $\mathcal{C}$ is a finite set of clocks, (4) Σ is a finite set of channels, (5) $\rightarrow \subseteq L \times \mathcal{G}(\mathcal{C}) \times 2^{\mathcal{C}} \times L$ is the (non-deterministic) transition relation. We write $\ell \xrightarrow{g,a,R} \ell'$ for a transition, where ℓ is the source and ℓ' the target location, $g \in \mathcal{B}^{\leq}(\mathcal{C})$ is a guard, $a \in \Sigma_o \cup \Sigma_i$ is a label, and $R \subseteq \mathcal{C}$ is the set of clocks to reset, and (6) $I: L \rightarrow \mathcal{B}^{\geq}(\mathcal{C})$ is an invariant function, mapping locations to a set of invariant constraints.*

A clock valuation is a function $v : \mathcal{C} \rightarrow \mathbb{R}_{\geq 0}$. We denote all clock valuations over $\mathcal{C}$ with $\mathcal{V}(\mathcal{C})$. We need two operations on clock valuations: $v' = v + d$ for a *delay* of $d \in \mathbb{R}_{\geq 0}$ time units, s.t. $\forall c \in \mathcal{C}: v'(c) = v(c) + d$, and *reset* $v' = v[R]$ of a set of clocks $R \subseteq \mathcal{C}$, s.t. $v'(c) = 0$ if $c \in R$, and $v'(c) = v(c)$ otherwise. We write $v \vDash g$ to mean that the clock valuation v satisfies the clock constraint g.

The semantics of a TA $(L, \mathcal{C}, \ell_0, \mathsf{A}, \rightarrow, I)$ is a timed transition system with states $L \times \mathcal{V}(\mathcal{C})$ and initial state (ℓ_0, v_0), where v_0 assigns zero to all clocks. From a state (ℓ, v) the TA may transit via a discrete transition $(\ell, v) \xrightarrow{a} (\ell', v')$ if there exists an edge $\ell \xrightarrow{g,a,r} \ell'$, $v \vDash g$ and $v' = v[r]$. Time-wise the TA can perform a delay $d \in \mathbb{R}_{\geq 0}$ via a time transition $(\ell, v) \xrightarrow{d} (\ell, v + d)$ if $v + d \vDash I(\ell)$.

Several TAs $\mathcal{A}_1, \mathcal{A}_2, \ldots, \mathcal{A}_n$, $\mathcal{A}_i = (L_i, \mathcal{C}_i, \ell_0^i, \Sigma, \rightarrow_i, I_i)$ may be joined into a network of timed automata. The state space of such a composition is the product of the individual TAs state spaces. From a state $(s_1, s_2, \ldots, s_n)$ the network can do a

- discrete output transition $(s_1, s_2, \ldots, s_n) \xrightarrow{a!} (s_1', s_2', \ldots, s_n')$, if there exists an i, such that $s_i \xrightarrow{a!} s_i'$ and for all $j \neq i$ $s_j \xrightarrow{a?} s_j'$
- or it can can delay d time units, $(s_1, s_2, \ldots, s_n) \xrightarrow{d} (s_1', s_2', \ldots, s_n')$, if for all i $s_i \xrightarrow{d} s_i'$.

Notice we are using broadcast synchronisation for accommodating the use of UPPAAL SMC. Furthermore, we will assume that components are input-enabled and action-deterministic thus for any action there is at most one successor and for any input action there is at least one.

Stochastic Semantics. The stochastic semantics of networks of timed automata was laid out by David et al. [8]. In a state, each timed automaton is given a delay density and a probability mass function for selecting output actions. The semantics is now race based: components select a delay, t, according to their delay distribution, and the one with the smallest delay is selected the winner. After the entire network performs the delay, the winner selects an output according to its probability mass function. The remaining network respond to this output by performing the corresponding input. Afterwards a new race commences. In UPPAAL SMC bounded delays (i.e. the current location has an invariant) are selected from a uniform distribution ranging from the minimal delay before some guard is satisfied and the maximal delay, where the invariant is still satisfied. For unbounded delays the delay is selected from an exponential distribution.

In the preceding example, the probability that the Thief enters the house without the Resident being home within 12 time units is:

$$\int_0^{12} \frac{1}{14} \cdot \left(\int_t^{24} \frac{1}{24} \, dt' \right) \cdot \frac{1}{2} \cdot \int_0^{12-t} \frac{1}{24-t} \, d\tau \, dt \approx 0.13$$

Game Semantics. In recent works [9,10] the simple stochastic timed automata model has been given a game semantics. In this semantics the edges of timed automaton $\mathcal{A} = (L, \mathcal{C}, \ell_0, \mathsf{A}, \rightarrow, I)$ are partitioned into a controllable set of edges, $\rightarrow_C$, and uncontrollable set of edges $\rightarrow_U$. The uncontrollable edges are controlled by stochastic environment behaving according to the stochastic semantics above, while the controllable set of edges is controlled by an actor that tries to "drive" the system into a given goal state. In Fig. 4 the dashed edges correspond to uncontrollable edges and the controllable edges are the solid edges.

A tool like UPPAAL-STRATEGO can, by using reinforcement learning, find deterministic strategies for minimising the expected time (or cost) of reaching a goal - taking the stochastic environment into account.

4   Timed Automata Encoding

The timed automata encoding of the attack-defense tree semantics given in the previous sections consists of three automata; one encoding the attacker, one encoding the defender and one encoding the environment selecting an outcome for the execution of attacker actions (γ_{Succ}). Furthermore, the encoding has one boolean variable b_p_a per atomic proposition, p, in the attack-defense tree. The state of these boolean variables directly corresponds to the states of the ADG.

4.1   Environmental Modelling

Let A_a be the set of attacker actions in the attack-defense-tree, then for each $p_a \in \mathsf{A}_a$ we create a channel c_p_a that is used by the attacker to indicate that he wishes to execute p_a. The environment responds to this by deciding an outcome in accordance with γ_{Succ}. Figure 5 depicts the modelling of the environment for an attack-defense tree, where there is only one attacker action (p_a); here $1 - p$ is the probability that p_a succeeds.

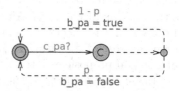

Fig. 5. Environmental modelling. In the figure $p = 1\text{-}\gamma_{Succ}(p_a)(p_a)$.

4.2   Defender Modelling

Let A_d be the set of defender actions available
to the defender. For each $D \in 2^{A_d}$ the defender
has an edge, where he sets all boolean variables,
$p_d \in D$, to true. In Fig. 6 an example modelling
of this is shown with two defender actions. As
the edges of this defender are uncontrollable, the
defender would select a set of defense measures
by a uniform choice among all the edges. For
analysing possible attack scenarios in response
to a specific set of defense measures D we would
delete edges of the defender until only the edge
corresponding to D remains.

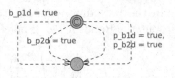

Fig. 6. Modelling the environment with two defender actions,
p_d^1 and p_d^2.

4.3   Attacker Modelling

In the formal development of an attacker we just defined general requirements
that any attacker should respect. Firstly, we present a non-deterministic attacker
that is as general as possible, which can be used for learning; afterwards we
create one specific attacker profile, where the non-determinism is resolved by a
probability mass function.

Non-deterministic Attacker. Assume we have
$A_a = \{p_a\}$ as our set of attacker actions
and let each of the attacker propositions
have a lower execution bound (L_pa) and
an upper execution bound (U_pa) – an execution time that is not controllable by the
attacker and thus will be selected according
to a uniform distribution by the environment.
Figure 7 depicts an attacker with only one

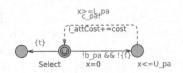

Fig. 7. Non-deterministic attacker
modelling

action: from the initial state, the attacker can decide to perform p_a, if it is
not already true and the tree is not already true ($!\{t\}$); after which it enters a
location, where the environment decides how long the execution takes according
to the uniform distribution. After this waiting time the environment is informed
of the attempt to execute p_a and decides on the outcome. Also, during this transition the cost of executing p_a is added to the variable $i\_attCost$. For the case
with several propositions, the cycle in Fig. 7 is added for each proposition.

In case the tree is true, the attacker only has one option, namely, to enter the
location, where he cannot do anything.

Uniform Attacker. The uniform attacker is essentially the non-deterministic
attacker, where the non-determinism of selecting an action is resolved by a uniform choice among all possible actions.

5   Tool Support

The translation into timed automata described in the preceding section has been implemented as a python script. This script takes the attack-defense tree, the description of the cost of atomic attacker actions, the execution time and their probability of succeeding. Having translated into timed automata, we can now take advantage of the UPPAAL [5] model checking engine to answer some of the questions raised in the previous sections. For instance, Question 3 is answerable by a simple timed reachability check by UPPAAL. In the following we focus on answering Questions 5 and 6. We consider the attack-defense tree in Fig. 1. The success probability and cost of the

	L	U	C	F
is	0	20	80	0.80
bs	0	20	100	0.70
t	0	20	700	0.70
b	0	20	700	0.70
st	0	20	50	0.50
ba	0	20	85	0.60
im	0	20	70	0.50
ot	0	20	0	0.60

Fig. 8. Experimental setup.

various attacker actions are summarised in Fig. 8. The L column is the lower bound of the execution time, U is the upper bound, C is the cost of the actions and F is the success probability.

5.1   Expected Cost

We first show how to answer Question 5 by finding expected cost of the uniform attacker within 300 time units. The cost of the attacker is estimated by the UPPAALsmc with the query

$$E[<= 300; 1000](\max : \text{i\_attCost}).$$

Table 1. Expected cost for the uniform attacker and for synthesised strategies.

Defenses	$\{t1,tf/at,t2\}$	$\{tf,at/t2\}$	$\{t1,at/t2\}$	$\{at/t2\}$	$\{t1,tf/t2\}$	$\{tf/t2\}$	$\{t1/t2\}$	$\{t2\}$	$\{t1,tf/at\}$	$\{tf/at\}$	$\{t1/at\}$	$\{at\}$	$\{t1/tf\}$	$\{tf\}$	$\{t1\}$	$\emptyset$
Uniform	1030.51 ±33.20	873.15 ±28.68	880.81 ±29.0	891.17 ±29.7	1027.29 ±33.3	881.74 ±37.7	881.68 ±28.7	894.91 ±37.1	867.83 ±32.7	747.09 ±26.82	742.3 ±25.4	738.0 ±8.9	773.0	659.19 ±27.9	659.4 ±27.1	675.6 ±27.64
UPPAAL-STRATEGO	855.86 ±31.6	292.76 ±13.2	256.11 ±6.4	256.25 ±6.6	976.12 ±31.4	242.62 ±5.8	246.02 ±5.9	287.14 ±7.5	498.58 ±32.3	240.22 ±8.62	183.32 ±7.9	197.310 ±8.9	304.14 ±31.1	219.13 ±17.43	173.95 ±8.74	115.03 ±7.10

The estimates for various defense measures are given in Table 1 in the "Uniform" row. From the results we can see that the highest cost (unsurprisingly) is obtained when all possible defender's actions are selected, and the smallest when none of them are selected. Also the results indicate that by performing $t2, t1, tf$ the expected cost is equivalent to performing all of the defense measures. This is because this set jointly blocks large parts of the attack-defense tree, leaving only the expensive "threaten" and "blackmail" for an attacker to succeed.

5.2   Finding Good Attacker Profile

Next we answer Question 6 i.e. we focus on a stochastic attacker, who minimises his costs in response to various defense measures. For doing this, we apply the non-deterministic attacker of our encoding and use the UPPAAL-STRATEGO to minimise the cost variable. The queries for the UPPAAL-STRATEGO are

$$\texttt{strategy s} = \texttt{minE(bi\_attCost)}[<= 300] :<> \texttt{t}$$
$$\texttt{E}[<= 300; 1000](\texttt{max} : \texttt{bi\_attCost}) \texttt{ under s},$$

where t is the attack-defense tree translated into the UPPAAL syntax.

The result of executing these queries for different defenders are reported in Table 1 in the UPPAAL-STRATEGO row. As can be seen, the synthesized attacker generally obtains a reduced expected cost. The reason is that he can avoid attempting attacks he knows are blocked due to the defender's measures. Another reason is that this attacker actively attempts to minimise his costs; meaning he will not take the expensive "threaten" or "bribe" if it can be avoided.

6   Conclusion

In this paper we have shown how to separate the modelling of attacker's and defender's behaviours from the attack-defense tree. In this way we allow modelling complex temporal behaviours without compromising the intuitively simple description of various ways of achieving an attack expressed in the attack-defense tree. This stands in opposition with, for example, the work [12] that adds temporal behaviours by introducing sequential gates, trigger gates and reset gates, which may clutter the description of possible attacks. Experiments reported in the paper have shown the different analyses that can be performed on our encoding using the UPPAAL SMC and UPPAAL-STRATEGO: among these are finding an attacker who minimises his costs, and estimating the probability of an attack for a specific attacker.

In the future we wish to extend the current framework by describing the actual behaviour of the attacker in a more thorough way. This may include incorporating parts of the work by Hermanns et al. [12], but we will maintain them in a separate modelling language.

References

1. Alur, R., Dill, D.: Automata for modeling real-time systems. In: Paterson, M.S. (ed.) Automata, Languages and Programming. LNCS, vol. 443, pp. 322–335. Springer, Heidelberg (1990). ISBN: 3-540-52826-1
2. Arnold, F., Guck, D., Kumar, R., Stoelinga, M.: Sequential and parallel attack tree modelling. In: Koornneef, F., van Gulijk, C. (eds.) Computer Safety, Reliability, and Security. LNCS, vol. 9338, pp. 291–299. Springer International Publishing, Switzerland (2015)

3. Aslanyan, Z., Nielson, F.: Pareto efficient solutions of attack-defence trees. In: Focardi, R., Myers, A. (eds.) POST 2015. LNCS, vol. 9036, pp. 95–114. Springer, Heidelberg (2015). doi:10.1007/978-3-662-46666-7_6

4. Bagnato, A., Kordy, B., Meland, P.H., Schweitzer, P.: Attribute decoration of attack-defense trees. Int. J. Secure Softw. Eng. (IJSSE) **3**(2), 1 (2012)

5. Behrmann, G., David, A., Larsen, K.G.: A tutorial on UPPAAL. In: Bernardo, M., Corradini, F. (eds.) SFM-RT 2004. LNCS, vol. 3185, pp. 200–236. Springer, Heidelberg (2004). doi:10.1007/978-3-540-30080-9_7

6. Buldas, A., Laud, P., Priisalu, J., Saarepera, M., Willemson, J.: Rational choice of security measures via multi-parameter attack trees. In: López, J. (ed.) CRITIS 2006. LNCS, vol. 4347, pp. 235–248. Springer, Heidelberg (2006)

7. Dalton, G.C., Mills, R.F., Colombi, J.M., Raines, R.A., et al.: Analyzing attack trees using generalized stochastic petri nets. In: 2006 IEEE Information Assurance Workshop, pp. 116–123. IEEE (2006)

8. David, A., Larsen, K.G., Legay, A., Mikučionis, M., Poulsen, D.B., van Vliet, J., Wang, Z.: Statistical model checking for networks of priced timed automata. In: Fahrenberg, U., Tripakis, S. (eds.) FORMATS 2011. LNCS, vol. 6919, pp. 80–96. Springer, Heidelberg (2011)

9. David, A., Jensen, P.G., Larsen, K.G., Legay, A., Lime, D., Sørensen, M.G., Taankvist, J.H.: On time with minimal expected cost!. In: Cassez, F., Raskin, J.-F. (eds.) ATVA 2014. LNCS, vol. 8837, pp. 129–145. Springer, Heidelberg (2014). doi:10. 1007/978-3-319-11936-6_10. ISBN: 978-3-319-11935-9

10. David, A., Jensen, P.G., Larsen, K.G., Mikucionis, M., Taankvist, J.H.: Uppaal stratego. In: Baier, C., Tinelli, C. (eds.) Tools and Algorithms for the Construction and Analysis of Systems. LNCS, vol. 9035, pp. 206–211. Springer, Heidelberg (2015). doi:10.1007/978-3-662-46681-0_16. ISBN: 978-3-662-46680-3

11. Gadyatskaya, O.: How to generate security cameras: towards defence generation for socio-technical systems. In: Mauw, S., et al. (eds.) GraMSec 2015. LNCS, vol. 9390, pp. 50–65. Springer, Heidelberg (2016). doi:10.1007/978-3-319-29968-6_4

12. Hermanns, H., Krämer, J., Krcál, J., Stoelinga, M.: The value of attack-defence diagrams. In: Piessens, F., et al. (eds.) POST 2016. LNCS, vol. 9635, pp. 163–185. Springer, Heidelberg (2016). doi:10.1007/978-3-662-49635-0_9

13. Ivanova, M.G., Probst, C.W., Hansen, R.R., Kammüller, F.: Transforming graphical system models to graphical attack models. In: Mauw, S., et al. (eds.) GraMSec 2015. LNCS, vol. 9390, pp. 82–96. Springer, Heidelberg (2016). doi:10.1007/978-3-319-29968-6_6

14. Jürgenson, A., Willemson, J.: Computing exact outcomes of multi-parameter attack trees. In: Meersman, R., Tari, Z. (eds.) OTM 2008, Part II. LNCS, vol. 5332, pp. 1036–1051. Springer, Heidelberg (2008)

15. Kordy, B., Mauw, S., Radomirović, S., Schweitzer, P.: Attack-defense trees. J. Logic Comput. **24**(1), 55–87 (2014)

16. Kordy, B., Piètre-Cambacédès, L., Schweitzer, P.: DAG-based attack and defense modeling: don't miss the forest for the attack trees. Comput. Sci. Rev. **13–14**, 1–38 (2014). doi:10.1016/j.cosrev.2014.07.001

17. Kumar, R., Ruijters, E., Stoelinga, M.: Quantitative attack tree analysis via priced timed automata. In: Sankaranarayanan, S., Vicario, E. (eds.) FORMATS 2015. LNCS, vol. 9268, pp. 156–171. Springer, Heidelberg (2015)

18. Larsen, K.G., Pettersson, P., Yi, W.: UPPAAL in a nutshell. STTT **1**(1–2), 134–152 (1997). doi:10.1007/s100090050010

19. Mauw, S., Oostdijk, M.: Foundations of attack trees. In: Won, D.H., Kim, S. (eds.) ICISC 2005. LNCS, vol. 3935, pp. 186–198. Springer, Heidelberg (2006)

20. NATO Research and Technology Organisation (RTO). Improving Common Security Risk Analysis. Technical report AC/323(ISP-049)TP/193, North Atlantic Treaty Organisation, University of California, Berkeley (2008)
21. Nielson, F., Aslanyan, Z., Parker, D.: Quantitative verification and synthesis of attack-defense scenarios. In: CSF 2016 (2016, to appear)
22. OWASP. CISO AppSec Guide: Criteria for managing application security risks (2013)
23. Salter, C., Saydjari, O.S., Schneier, B., Wallner, J.: Toward a secure system engineering methodology. In: Proceedings of the 1998 New Security Paradigms Workshop (NSPW 1998), pp. 2–10, Charlottesville, Virginia, US, September 1998
24. Schneier, B.: Attack trees: modeling security threats. Dr. Dobb's J. (1999)
25. SITEC. Burglar resistance. https://www.sitec.de/en/information-and-advice/burglar-resistance/

Stochasticity and Hybrid Control

Input/Output Stochastic Automata
Compositionality and Determinism

Pedro R. D'Argenio[1], Matias David Lee[2], and Raúl E. Monti[1(✉)]

[1] CONICET, Universidad Nacional de Córdoba, Córdoba, Argentina
{dargenio,rmonti}@famaf.unc.edu.ar
[2] LIP, Université de Lyon, CNRS, ENS de Lyon, Inria, UCBL, Lyon, France

Abstract. Stochastic automata provide a way to symbolically model systems in which the occurrence time of events may respond to any continuous random variable. We introduce here an input/output variant of stochastic automata that, once the model is closed —i.e., all synchronizations are resolved—, the resulting automaton does not contain non-deterministic choices. This is important since fully probabilistic models are amenable to simulation in the general case and to much more efficient analysis if restricted to Markov models. We present here a theoretical introduction to input/output stochastic automata (IOSA) for which we (i) provide a concrete semantics in terms of non-deterministic labeled Markov processes (NLMP), (ii) prove that bisimulation is a congruence for parallel composition both in NLMP and IOSA, (iii) show that parallel composition commutes in the symbolic and concrete level, and (iv) provide a proof that a closed IOSA is indeed deterministic.

1 Introduction

The difficulty of the modeling and analysis of a system grows rapidly with the size and complexity of the system itself. In this sense the advantages of compositional approaches to modeling complex systems are unquestionable: they facilitate systematic design and the interchange of components, enable compositional analysis and help for the compact representation of state spaces and other ways of attacking the state explosion problem. Compositional modeling allows the designer to focus on the modeling of the rather discernible operational behaviour of the components and the evident synchronization among them (compare to the difficulty of figuring out the whole behaviour in a monolithic model).

If these models are aimed at performance and dependability analysis, there is a need to consider general distributions. Although (negative) exponential distributions yield analytically tractable models (namely, continuous time Markov chains), and are useful for many applications, they are not realistic for modeling many phenomena. Phenomena such as timeouts in communication protocols, hard deadlines in real-time systems, human response times or the variability of the delay of sound and video frames (so-called jitter) in modern multi-media

Supported by ANPCyT PICT-2012-1823 and SeCyT-UNC 05/BP12 and 05/B497.

M. Fränzle and N. Markey (Eds.): FORMATS 2016, LNCS 9884, pp. 53–68, 2016.
DOI: 10.1007/978-3-319-44878-7_4

communication systems are typically described by non-memoryless distributions such as uniform, log-normal, or Weibull distributions.

To attack the compositional modeling of this type of systems stochastic process algebras with general continuous distributions have been devised (see e.g. [4] and references therein), and notably the modeling language MODEST [3]. The problem with all these languages is that they introduce non-determinism. In general, it is not possible to analyze generally distributed stochastic processes, let alone if they are also non-deterministic. However, deterministic stochastic processes can be simulated using discrete event simulation. Simulation is instead not feasible in general if the models are non-deterministic. (Though there are approaches to simulate Markov decission processes either by recognizing spurious non-determinism [2,16] or by sampling schedulers [9], it is not clear how these techniques scale to continuous settings.)

Starting from the notion of stochastic automata [7,8], we restrict this framework to obtain input/output stochastic automata (IOSA). While stochastic automata were constructed to naturally accept the non-determinism interacting with continuous probabilities, we designed IOSA so that parallel composition works naturally and, moreover, the system becomes fully probabilistic (i.e., it does not contain non-determinism) as soon as the system is closed (i.e. all interactions are resolved). Thus, we split actions into input and output and let them behave in a reactive and generative manner respectively (see [15] for the concepts of reactive and generative transitions), following ideas proposed in [22]. Since outputs behave generatively, we let their occurrence time be controlled by a random variable (encoded in a *clock*). As inputs are reactive, they are passive and hence their occurrence time can only depend on their interaction with outputs. Thus, IOSA combines in a single model the two interpretations of stochastic automata (either as open or as closed systems [7,8].)

The paper presents a theoretical introduction to IOSA. For this, we present the model in Sect. 3 and give its concrete semantics in terms of non-deterministic labeled Markov processes (NLMP) [10,21]. Next (Sect. 4) we define the parallel composition on IOSA and show that the model is closed under composition. We also define parallel composition on NLMPs and show that, when it is well defined, bisimulation is a congruence for parallel composition on NLMPs. Moreover, we prove that parallel composition commutes in the symbolic (IOSA) and concrete (NLMP) level through isomorphism and as a corollary have that bisimulation is a congruence for parallel composition on IOSAs. In Sect. 5, we define precisely what we mean by a deterministic IOSA, show several properties of the underlying NLMP, and prove that a closed IOSA (i.e., a IOSA without input actions) is indeed deterministic. In addition, we provide the essential background on measure theory in Sect. 2, and conclude the paper in Sect. 6.

2   Preliminaries on Measure Theory

In this section, we recall some fundamental notions of measure theory that will be useful throughout the paper.

Given a set S and a collection Σ of subsets of S, we call Σ a σ-*algebra* iff $S \in \Sigma$ and Σ is closed under complement and denumerable union. By $\sigma(\mathcal{G})$ we denote the σ-*algebra generated by* the family $\mathcal{G} \subseteq 2^S$, i.e., the minimal σ-algebra containing $\mathcal{G}$. Each element of $\mathcal{G}$ is called a *generator* and $\mathcal{G}$ is called the *generator set*. We call the pair (S, Σ) a *measurable space*. A *measurable set* is a set $Q \in \Sigma$. Let (L, Λ) and (S, Σ) be measurable spaces. A *measurable rectangle* is a set $A \times B$ with $A \in \Lambda$ and $B \in \Sigma$. The *product σ-algebra* on $L \times S$ is the smallest σ-algebra containing all measurable rectangles, and is denoted by $\Lambda \otimes \Sigma$. The *coproduct σ-algebra* $\Lambda \oplus \Sigma$ of L and S is defined in the disjoint union $L \uplus S$ and it is generated by the set $\Lambda \cup \Sigma$.

A function $\mu : \Sigma \to [0, 1]$ is a *probability measure* if (i) it is σ-additive, i.e. $\mu(\bigcup_{i \in \mathbb{N}} Q_i) = \sum_{i \in \mathbb{N}} \mu(Q_i)$ for all countable family of pairwise disjoint measurable sets $\{Q_i \mid i \in \mathbb{N}\} \subseteq \Sigma$, and (ii) $\mu(S) = 1$. By δ_a we denote the Dirac probability measure concentrated in $\{a\}$. Given measures μ and μ' on (L, Λ) and (S, Σ) respectively, the product measure $\mu \times \mu'$ on the product space $(L \times S, \Lambda \otimes \Sigma)$ is defined as the unique measure such that $(\mu \times \mu')(A \times B) = \mu(A) \cdot \mu'(B)$ for all $A \in \Lambda$ and $B \in \Sigma$. Any measure μ on (L, Λ) can be naturally extended into a measure $\hat{\mu}$ in the coproduct space $(L \uplus S, \Lambda \oplus \Sigma)$ by taking $\hat{\mu}(A) = \mu(A \backslash S)$, and similarly for measures on (S, Σ). Let $\Delta(S)$ denote the set of all probability measures over the measurable space (S, Σ). We let $\mu, \mu', \mu_1, \ldots$ range over $\Delta(S)$. Let (S_1, Σ_1) and (S_2, Σ_2) be two measurable spaces. A function $f : S_1 \to S_2$ is said to be *measurable* if for all $Q_2 \in \Sigma_2$, $f^{-1}(Q_2) \in \Sigma_1$, i.e., its inverse image maps measurable sets to measurable sets. In this case we denote $f : (S_1, \Sigma_1) \to (S_2, \Sigma_2)$.

A σ-algebra is *Borel* if it is generated by the set of all open sets in a topology. Particularly, the Borel σ-algebra on the real line is $\mathcal{B}(\mathbb{R}) = \sigma(\{(a, b) \mid a, b \in \mathbb{R} \text{ and } a < b\})$. Similarly, $\mathcal{B}([0, 1])$ is the Borel σ-algebra on the interval $[0, 1]$ generated by the open sets in the interval $[0, 1]$.

There is a standard construction by Giry [14] to endow $\Delta(S)$ with a σ-algebra as follows: $\Delta(\Sigma)$ is defined as the σ-algebra generated by the sets of probability measures $\Delta^{\geq p}(Q) \doteq \{\mu \mid \mu(Q) \geq p\}$, with $Q \in \Sigma$ and $p \in [0, 1]$. We let ξ range over $\Delta(\Sigma)$.

To give structure to non-determinism on NLMP, we will use hit σ-algebras [10] on $\Delta(\Sigma)$. Thus, the hit σ-algebra $H(\Delta(\Sigma))$ is defined to be the minimal σ-algebra containing all sets $H(\xi) \doteq \{\zeta \in \Delta(\Sigma) \mid \zeta \cap \xi \neq \varnothing\}$ with $\xi \in \Delta(\Sigma)$.

3   Input/Output Stochastic Automata (IOSA)

Stochastic automata [7,8] use clock variables to control and observe the passage of time. Since in our context the time at which events occur is random, clocks are in fact random variables. When a clock is set, it takes a random value whose probability depends on the distribution function of the clock. As time evolves, clocks count down synchronously, i.e., all do so at the same rate. When a clock reaches the value zero, "the clock expires" and this may enable some events. Starting from the notion of stochastic automata, we restrict this framework to obtain IOSA. We split actions into inputs and outputs and let them behave in a reactive and generative manner respectively (see [15] for the concepts of reactive and generative transitions), somehow following ideas proposed in [22]. We could also think that inputs are externally controlled actions and outputs are locally controlled actions. Precisely because of this, the occurrence time of output actions is controlled by a random variable, while inputs are passive and hence their occurrence time can only depend on their interaction with outputs. A set of restrictions which we will explain later ensures that, almost surely, no two outputs actions are enabled at the same time.

Definition 1. *An input/output stochastic automaton (IOSA for short) is a structure $(\mathcal{S}, \mathcal{A}, \mathcal{C}, \rightarrow, \mathcal{C}_0, s_0)$, where $\mathcal{S}$ is a (denumerable) set of states, $\mathcal{A}$ is a (denumerable) set of labels partitioned into disjoint sets of input labels $\mathcal{A}^I$, and output labels $\mathcal{A}^O$, $\mathcal{C}$ is a (finite) set of clocks such that each $x \in \mathcal{C}$ has associated a continuous probability measure μ_x on $\mathbb{R}$ (hence $\mu_x(d) = 0$ for any $d \in \mathbb{R}$) also satisfying that $\mu_x(\mathbb{R}_{>0}) = 1$, $\rightarrow \subseteq \mathcal{S} \times \mathcal{C} \times \mathcal{A} \times \mathcal{C} \times \mathcal{S}$ is a transition function, $\mathcal{C}_0$ is the set of clocks that are initialized in the initial state, and $s_0 \in \mathcal{S}$ is the initial state. In addition a IOSA should satisfy the following constraints:*

(a) *If $s \xrightarrow{C,a,C'} s'$ and $a \in \mathcal{A}^I$, then $C = \varnothing$.*

(b) *If $s \xrightarrow{C,a,C'} s'$ and $a \in \mathcal{A}^O$, then C is a singleton set.*

(c) *If $s \xrightarrow{\{x\},a_1,C_1} s_1$ and $s \xrightarrow{\{x\},a_2,C_2} s_2$ then $a_1 = a_2$, $C_1 = C_2$ and $s_1 = s_2$.*

(d) *If $s \xrightarrow{\{x\},a,C} s'$ then, for every transition $t \xrightarrow{C_1,b,C_2} s$, either $x \in C_2$, or $x \notin C_1$ and there exists a transition $t \xrightarrow{\{x\},c,C_3} t'$.*

(e) *If $s_0 \xrightarrow{\{x\},a,C} s$ then $x \in \mathcal{C}_0$.*

(f) *For every $a \in \mathcal{A}^I$ and state s, there exists a transition $s \xrightarrow{\varnothing,a,C} s'$.*

(g) *For every $a \in \mathcal{A}^I$, if $s \xrightarrow{\varnothing,a,C_1} s_1$ and $s \xrightarrow{\varnothing,a,C_2} s_2$, $C_1 = C_2$ and $s_1 = s_2$.*

The occurrence of an action is controlled by the expiration of clocks. Thus, whenever $s \xrightarrow{\{x\},a,C} s'$ and the system is in state s, output action a will occur once the value of clock x reaches 0. At this point, the system moves to state s' setting the values of every clocks $y \in C$ to a value sampled according to the distribution μ_y. For input transitions $s \xrightarrow{\varnothing,a,C} s'$, the behaviour is similar, only that its occurrence can potentially occur at any time which will become definite once the action interacts with an output.

Restriction (a) states that every input is reactive and hence their occurrence is controlled by the environment. Hence no internal clock controls its occurrence. Restriction (b) states that each output is generative (or locally controlled) so it has associated a clock which determines its occurrence time. We also limit the set to exactly one clock, to have a clean definition. Restriction (c) forbids that a single clock enables two different transitions, otherwise two output actions would become enable simultaneously. Besides, notice that if clocks are used when they have already expired they would immediately enable the respective output transition, which may lead to a simultaneous enabling if the system arrives to a states with two expired clocks enabling two different transitions. Restrictions (d) and (e) ensure that a clock would never be used when it has already expired. Particularly (d) states that an enabling clock x at state s should either be set on arrival ($x \in C_2$) or it has not been used immediately before ($x \notin C_1$) but should be also enabling on the immediately preceding state. Since clocks are set by sampling from a continuous random variable, the probability that the values of two different clocks are equal is 0. This last fact, together with restrictions (c), (d) and (e), guarantees that almost never two different output transitions are enabled at the same time. Restrictions (f) and (g) are usual restrictions on I/O-like automata: (f) ensures that outputs are not blocked in a composition, and (g) that determinism is preserved after composition.

The semantics of IOSA is defined in terms of NLMP [10,21]. An NLMP is a generalization of probabilistic transition systems with continuous domain. More particularly, it extends LMP [11] with *internal* non-determinism.

Definition 2. *A non-deterministic labeled Markov process (NLMP for short) is a structure $(\boldsymbol{S}, \Sigma, \{T_a \mid a \in \mathcal{L}\})$ where Σ is a σ-algebra on the set of states $\boldsymbol{S}$, and for each label $a \in \mathcal{L}$ we have $T_a : \boldsymbol{S} \to \Delta(\Sigma)$ is measurable from Σ to the hit σ-algebra $H(\Delta(\Sigma))$.*

The formal semantics of a IOSA is defined by an NLMP with two classes of transitions: one that encodes the discrete steps and contains all the probabilistic information introduced by the sampling of clocks, and other describing the time steps, that only records the passage of time synchronously decreasing the value of all clocks. In order to simplify the definition, we assume that the set of clocks has a particular order and their current values follow the same order in a vector.

Definition 3. *Given a IOSA $\mathcal{I} = (\mathcal{S}, \mathcal{A}, \mathcal{C}, \to, \mathcal{C}_0, s_0)$ with $\mathcal{C} = \{x_1, \ldots, x_N\}$, its semantics is defined by the NLMP $\mathcal{P}(\mathcal{I}) = (\boldsymbol{S}, \mathscr{B}(\boldsymbol{S}), \{T_a \mid a \in \mathcal{L}\})$ where*

- $\boldsymbol{S} = (\mathcal{S} \cup \{\mathsf{init}\}) \times \mathbb{R}^N$, $\mathcal{L} = \mathcal{A} \cup \mathbb{R}_{>0} \cup \{\mathsf{init}\}$, with $\mathsf{init} \notin \mathcal{S} \cup \mathcal{A} \cup \mathbb{R}_{>0}$
- $T_{\mathsf{init}}(\mathsf{init}, \vec{v}) = \{\delta_{s_0} \times \prod_{i=1}^{N} \mu_{x_i}\}$,
- $T_a(s, \vec{v}) = \{\mu_{\vec{v}, C', s'} \mid s \xrightarrow{C, a, C'} s', \bigwedge_{x_i \in C} \vec{v}(i) \leq 0\}$, for all $a \in \mathcal{A}$, where $\mu_{\vec{v}, C', s'} = \delta_{s'} \times \prod_{i=1}^{N} \overline{\mu}_{x_i}$ with $\overline{\mu}_{x_i} = \mu_{x_i}$ if $x_i \in C'$ and $\overline{\mu}_{x_i} = \delta_{\vec{v}(i)}$ otherwise, and
- $T_d(s, \vec{v}) = \{\delta_{(s, \vec{v})}^{-d} \mid 0 < d \leq \min\{\vec{v}(i) \mid \exists a \in \mathcal{A}^O, C' \subseteq \mathcal{C}, s' \in S : s \xrightarrow{\{x_i\}, a, C'} s'\}\}$ for all $d \in \mathbb{R}_{\geq 0}$, where $\delta_{(s, \vec{v})}^{-d} = \delta_s \times \prod_{i=1}^{N} \delta_{\vec{v}(i) - d}$.

The state space is the product space of the states of the IOSA with all possible clock valuations. A distinguished initial state init is added to encode the random initialization of all clocks (it would be sufficient to initialize clocks in C_0 but we decided for this simplification). Such encoding is done by transition T_{init}. The state space is structured in the usual Borel σ-algebra. The discrete step is encoded by T_a, with $a \in \mathcal{A}$. Notice that, at state $(s, \vec{v})$, the transition $s \xrightarrow{C, a, C'} s'$ will only take place if $\bigwedge_{x_i \in C} \vec{v}(i) \leq 0$, that is, if the current values of all clocks in C are not positive. For the particular case of the input actions this will always be true. The next actual state would be determined randomly as follows: the symbolic state will be s' (this corresponds to $\delta_{s'}$ in $\mu_{\vec{v},C',s'} = \delta_{s'} \times \prod_{i=1}^{N} \overline{\mu}_{x_i}$), any clock not in C' preserves the current value (hence $\overline{\mu}_{x_i} = \delta_{\vec{v}(i)}$ if $x_i \notin C'$), and any clock in C' is set randomly according to its respective associated distribution (hence $\overline{\mu}_{x_i} = \mu_{x_i}$ if $x_i \in C'$). The time step is encoded by $\mathcal{T}_d(s,\vec{v})$ with $d \in \mathbb{R}_{\geq 0}$. It can only take place at d units of time if there is no output transition enabled at the current state within the next d time units (this is verified by condition $0 < d \leq \min\{\vec{v}(i) \mid \exists a \in \mathcal{A}^O, C' \subseteq \mathcal{C}, s' \in S : s \xrightarrow{\{x_i\},a,C'} s'\}$). In this case, the system remains in the same symbolic state (this corresponds to δ_s in $\delta_{(s,\vec{v})}^{-d} = \delta_s \times \prod_{i=1}^{N} \delta_{\vec{v}(i)-d}$), and all clock values are decreased by d units of times (represented by $\delta_{\vec{v}(i)-d}$ in the same formula).

We still need to show that $\mathcal{P}(\mathcal{I})$ is indeed an NLMP. For this we have to prove that $\mathcal{T}_a$ maps into measurable sets in $\Delta(\mathscr{B}(\mathbf{S}))$ (Lemma 4), and that $\mathcal{T}_a$ is a measurable function for every $a \in \mathcal{L}$ (Lemma 5).

Lemma 4. $\mathcal{T}_a(s,\vec{v}) \in \Delta(\mathscr{B}(\mathbf{S}))$ *for all* $a \in \mathcal{L}$ *and* $(s,\vec{v}) \in \mathbf{S}$.

Proof. The proof makes use of Lemma 3.1 in [10], from which we know that for all $\mu \in \Delta(\mathbf{S})$, $\{\mu\} \in \Delta(\mathscr{B}(\mathbf{S}))$ (since $\mathscr{B}(\mathbf{S})$ is generated by a discrete π-system).

Notice that for any $\vec{v} \in \mathbb{R}^N$, $\mathcal{T}_{\text{init}}(\text{init},\vec{v})$ is a singleton set and hence measurable. Similarly, notice that for every $d \in \mathbb{R}$, $s \in \mathcal{S}$, and $\vec{v} \in \mathbb{R}^N$, $\mathcal{T}_d(s,\vec{v})$ is either a singleton set or the empty set, and hence measurable. Finally, since there is only a denumerable number of transitions in a IOSA, for every $a \in \mathcal{A}$, $s \in \mathcal{S}$, and $\vec{v} \in \mathbb{R}^N$, $\mathcal{T}_a(s,\vec{v})$ is a denumerable union of singleton sets, and hence also measurable. □

Lemma 5. *For all* $a \in \mathcal{L}$, T_a *is measurable from* $\mathscr{B}(\mathbf{S})$ *to* $H(\Delta(\mathscr{B}(\mathbf{S})))$.

Proof. We need to show that for every $a \in \mathcal{L}$ and every $\xi \in \Delta(\mathscr{B}(\mathbf{S}))$, $\mathcal{T}_a^{-1}(H(\xi)) = \{(s,\vec{v}) \mid \mathcal{T}_a(s,\vec{v}) \cap \xi \neq \varnothing\}$ is measurable.

We divide the proof in three cases depending on the nature of the label on the transition function. First, notice that $\mathcal{T}_{\text{init}}^{-1}(H(\xi)) = \{\text{init}\} \times \mathbb{R}^N$ if $\delta_{s_0} \times \prod_{i=1}^{N} \mu_{x_i} \in \xi$ and $\mathcal{T}_{\text{init}}^{-1}(H(\xi)) = \varnothing$ otherwise, and both sets are measurable.

We analyze now the case of $a \in \mathcal{A}$, for which we can calculate

$$\mathcal{T}_a^{-1}(H(\xi)) = \{(s,\vec{v}) \mid \{\mu_{\vec{v},C',s'} \mid s \xrightarrow{C,a,C'} s', \bigwedge_{x_i \in C} \vec{v}(i) \leq 0\} \cap \xi \neq \varnothing\}$$

$$= \bigcup_{s \xrightarrow{C,a,C'} s'} \{(s,\vec{v}) \mid \bigwedge_{x_i \in C} \vec{v}(i) \leq 0\} \cap \{(s,\vec{v}) \mid \mu_{\vec{v},C',s'} \in \xi\}$$

Since the union is denumerable, it is sufficient to prove that the two intersecting sets are measurable. First, notice that $\{(s,\vec{v}) \mid \bigwedge_{x_i \in C} \vec{v}(i) \leq 0\} = \{s\} \times \prod_{i=1}^{N} V_i$ where $V_i = (-\infty, 0]$ if $x_i \in C$ and $V_i = \mathbb{R}$ otherwise. Hence, it is measurable.

For the second case, define $f_{C',s'} : \mathbb{R} \to \Delta(\mathbf{S})$ by $f_{C',s'}(\vec{v}) = \mu_{\vec{v},C',s'}$. Then $\{(s,\vec{v}) \mid \mu_{\vec{v},C',s'} \in \xi\} = \{(s,\vec{v}) \mid f_{C',s'}(\vec{v}) \in \xi\} = \{s\} \times f_{C',s'}^{-1}(\xi)$. So, it only remains to prove that $f_{C',s'}$ is a measurable function. Using [20, Lemma 3.6], we only have to prove that $f_{C',s'}^{-1}(\Delta^{\geq q}(A \times \prod_{i=1}^{N} V_i))$ with $A \subseteq \mathbf{S}$ and $V_i \in \mathscr{B}(\mathbb{R})$, $1 \leq i \leq N$, is measurable, for which we can calculate

$$f_{C',s'}^{-1}(\Delta^{\geq q}(A \times \textstyle\prod_{i=1}^{N} V_i)) = \{\vec{v} \mid \mu_{\vec{v},C',s'}(A \times \textstyle\prod_{i=1}^{N} V_i) \geq q\}$$
$$= \{\vec{v} \mid s' \in A, (\textstyle\prod_{x_i \in C'} \mu_{x_i})(\textstyle\prod_{x_i \in C'} V_i) \geq q, \forall x_i \notin C' : \vec{v}(i) \in V_i\}$$

Then, if $s' \in A$ and $(\prod_{x_i \in C'})(\prod_{x_i \in C'} V_i) \geq q$, $f_{C',s'}^{-1}(\Delta^{\geq q}(A \times \prod_{i=1}^{N} V_i)) = \prod_{i=1}^{N} \overline{V_i}$ with $\overline{V_i} = \mathbb{R}$ if $x_i \in C'$, $\overline{V_i} = V_i$ if $x_i \notin C'$, or $f_{C',s'}^{-1}(\Delta^{\geq q}(A \times \prod_{i=1}^{N} V_i)) = \varnothing$ otherwise, and in both cases the sets are measurable.

For the case of $d \in \mathbb{R}$, notice that

$$\mathcal{T}_d^{-1}(H(\xi)) = \{(s,\vec{v}) \mid \delta_{(s,\vec{v})}^{-d} \in \xi\} \cap$$

$$\{(s,\vec{v}) \mid 0 < d \leq \min\{\vec{v}(i) \mid \exists a \in \mathcal{A}^O, C' \subseteq \mathcal{C}, s' \in S : s \xrightarrow{\{x_i\},a,C'} s'\}$$

The second set is equal to $\mathbf{S} \times \prod_{i=1}^{N} V_i$ where $V_i = [d, \infty)$ if $s \xrightarrow{\{x_i\},a,C'} s'$, and $V_i = \mathbb{R}$ otherwise. Hence it is measurable. For the first set, define $f_d : \mathbf{S} \to \Delta(\mathbf{S})$ by $f_d(s,\vec{v}) = \delta_{(s,\vec{v})}^{-d}$. Then $\{(s,\vec{v}) \mid \delta_{(s,\vec{v})}^{-d} \in \xi\} = f_d^{-1}(\xi)$ and hence it suffices to show that f_d is measurable. So, we have to prove that $f_d^{-1}(\Delta^{\geq q}(Q))$ is measurable for any $Q \in \mathscr{B}(\mathbf{S})$. But $f_d^{-1}(\Delta^{\geq q}(Q)) = \{(s,\vec{v}) \mid \delta_{(s,\vec{v})}^{-d}(Q) \geq q\} = \{(s,\vec{v}) \mid (s, \vec{v} - d) \in Q \wedge q = 1\}$. That is $f_d^{-1}(\Delta^{\geq q}(Q)) = \{(s,\vec{v}) \mid (s, \vec{v} - d) \in Q\}$ if $q = 1$ or $f_d^{-1}(\Delta^{\geq q}(Q)) = \varnothing$ otherwise, and in both cases the sets are measurable. $\square$

4 Composition and Bisimulation as a Congruence

In this section we define parallel composition of IOSAs and show that IOSAs are closed for parallel composition. We also show that bisimulation is a congruence for the parallel composition and we achieve it through defining parallel composition on NLMPs.

Since we intend outputs to be autonomous (or locally controlled), we do not allow synchronization between outputs. Besides, we need to avoid name clashes on the clock, so that the intended behaviour of each component is preserved and moreover, to ensure that the resulting composed automata is indeed a IOSA. Thus we require to compose only *compatible* IOSAs.

Definition 6. *Two IOSAs $\mathcal{I}_1$ and $\mathcal{I}_2$ are said to be compatible if they do not share output actions nor clocks, i.e. $\mathcal{A}_1^O \cap \mathcal{A}_2^O = \varnothing$ and $\mathcal{C}_1 \cap \mathcal{C}_2 = \varnothing$.*

Definition 7. *Given two compatible IOSAs $\mathcal{I}_1$ and $\mathcal{I}_2$, the parallel composition $\mathcal{I}_1 \| \mathcal{I}_2$ is a new IOSA $(\mathcal{S}_1 \times \mathcal{S}_2, \mathcal{A}, \mathcal{C}, \to, \mathcal{C}_0, s_0^1 \| s_0^2)$ where (i) $\mathcal{A}^O = \mathcal{A}_1^O \cup \mathcal{A}_2^O$ (ii) $\mathcal{A}^I = (\mathcal{A}_1^I \cup \mathcal{A}_2^I) \setminus \mathcal{A}^O$ (iii) $\mathcal{C} = \mathcal{C}_1 \cup \mathcal{C}_2$ (iv) $\mathcal{C}_0 = \mathcal{C}_0^1 \cup \mathcal{C}_0^2$ and $\to$ is the smallest relation defined by rules in Table 1 where we write $s \| t$ instead of (s,t).*

The previous definition is only structural. We need to show that the seven restrictions that define IOSAs also hold.

Table 1. Parallel composition on IOSAs

$$\frac{s_1 \xrightarrow{C,a,C'}_1 s_1'}{s_1\|s_2 \xrightarrow{C,a,C'} s_1'\|s_2} \quad a \in \mathcal{A}_1\backslash\mathcal{A}_2 \quad (1) \qquad \frac{s_2 \xrightarrow{C,a,C'}_2 s_2'}{s_1\|s_2 \xrightarrow{C,a,C'} s_1\|s_2'} \quad a \in \mathcal{A}_2\backslash\mathcal{A}_1 \quad (2)$$

$$\frac{s_1 \xrightarrow{C_1,a,C_1'}_1 s_1', \quad s_2 \xrightarrow{C_2,a,C_2'}_2 s_2'}{s_1\|s_2 \xrightarrow{C_1\cup C_2,a,C_1'\cup C_2'} s_1'\|s_2'} \quad (3)$$

Theorem 8. *Let $\mathcal{I}_1$ and $\mathcal{I}_2$ be two compatible IOSAs. Then $\mathcal{I}_1\|\mathcal{I}_2$ is indeed a IOSA.*

Proof. The proof of restrictions (a), (b), (f), (e), and (g) follow by straightforward inspection on the rules, considering that $\mathcal{I}_1$ and $\mathcal{I}_2$ also satisfy the respective restriction, and doing some case analysis. Since $\mathcal{I}_1$ and $\mathcal{I}_2$ are compatible, restriction (c) also follows by inspecting the rules taking into account, in addition, that $\mathcal{I}_1$ and $\mathcal{I}_2$ satisfy restriction (g).

So, we only focus on (d). Suppose $s_1\|s_2 \xrightarrow{\{x\},a,C} s_1'\|s_2'$. We analyze the case in which $a \in \mathcal{A}_1$ and $x \in C_1$. The other is symmetric. Moreover, we only consider the case in which $a \in \mathcal{A}_1 \cap \mathcal{A}_2$ since the case $a \in \mathcal{A}_1 \setminus \mathcal{A}_2$ follows similarly.

In this case, we have that $s_1 \xrightarrow{\{x\},a,C_1}_1 s_1'$, $s_2 \xrightarrow{\varnothing,a,C_2}_2 s_2'$, and $C = C_1 \cup C_2$. Let $t_1\|t_2 \xrightarrow{C',b,C''} s_1\|s_2$. We distinguish three cases:

(i) Suppose $b \in \mathcal{A}_1 \setminus \mathcal{A}_2$. Then $t_1 \xrightarrow{C',b,C''} s_1$ and $t_2 = s_2$. Because $\mathcal{I}_1$ satisfies (d), then either $x \in C''$, or $x \notin C'$ and there exist $t_1 \xrightarrow{\{x\},c,C_3}_1 t_1'$. Hence $x \in C''$, or $x \notin C'$ and there exist t_2' and C_3' such that $t_1\|t_2 \xrightarrow{\{x\},c,C_3'} t_1'\|t_2'$ (which may occur either by rule (1) or (3) if $c \in \mathcal{A}_1 \cap \mathcal{A}_2$).

(ii) If $b \in \mathcal{A}_2 \setminus \mathcal{A}_1$, then $t_2 \xrightarrow{C',b,C''}_2 s_2$ and $t_1 = s_1$. Notice that $C', C'' \subseteq C_2$ and hence $x \notin C'$ and $x \notin C''$. Moreover, since $\mathcal{I}_2$ is input enabled (restriction (f)), $t_2 \xrightarrow{\varnothing,a,C_3}_2 t_2'$ for some C_3 and t_2'. Then, by rule (3), $s_1\|t_2 \xrightarrow{\{x\},a,C_1\cup C_3} s_1'\|t_2'$ which proves this case.

(iii) If $b \in \mathcal{A}_1 \cap \mathcal{A}_2$, then, by rule (3), $t_1 \xrightarrow{C_1',b,C_1''}_1 s_1$, $t_2 \xrightarrow{C_2',b,C_2''}_2 s_2$, $C' = C_1' \cup C_2'$ and $C'' = C_1'' \cup C_2''$. Because $\mathcal{I}_1$ satisfies (d), then either $x \in C_1''$, or $x \notin C_1'$ and there exist $t_1 \xrightarrow{\{x\},c,C_3}_1 t_1'$. If $x \in C_1''$, then $x \in C''$ partially proving this case. If instead $x \notin C_1'$ and there exist $t_1 \xrightarrow{\{x\},c,C_3}_1 t_1'$, then $x \notin C''$ (since $x \notin C_2''$ by compatibility), and there exist t_2' and C_3' such that $t_1\|t_2 \xrightarrow{\{x\},c,C_3'} t_1'\|t_2'$ (which may occur either by rule (1) or (3) if $c \in \mathcal{A}_1 \cap \mathcal{A}_2$), finally proving this case. □

To prove that bisimulation is a congruence on IOSAs, we first define a parallel composition on NLMPs, prove congruence in this setting, and then show that the semantics of the parallel composition of two IOSAs is isomorphic to the parallel composition of the semantics of each IOSA. From this, it follows that bisimulation is also a congruence for the parallel composition of IOSAs. An important consideration is that NLMPs are not closed for parallel composition [13] in general. So we will need to require that the parallel composition of NLMPs is also an NLMP as a hypothesis of the congruence theorem on NLMP.

Definition 9. *Let $\mathcal{P}_i = (S_i, \Sigma_i, \{T_a^i \mid a \in \mathcal{L}_i\})$, $i \in \{1, 2\}$, be two NLMPs. We define the parallel composition by $\mathcal{P}_1 \| \mathcal{P}_2 = (S_1 \times S_2, \Sigma_1 \otimes \Sigma_2, \{T_a \mid a \in \mathcal{L}_1 \cup \mathcal{L}_2\})$ where, writing $s_1 \| s_2$ instead of (s_1, s_2),*

(i) $T_a(s_1 \| s_2) = \{\mu_1 \times \delta_{s_2} \mid \mu_1 \in T_a^1(s_1)\}$, if $a \in \mathcal{L}_1 \setminus \mathcal{L}_2$,
(ii) $T_a(s_1 \| s_2) = \{\delta_{s_1} \times \mu_2 \mid \mu_2 \in T_a^2(s_2)\}$, if $a \in \mathcal{L}_2 \setminus \mathcal{L}_1$, and
(iii) $T_a(s_1 \| s_2) = \{\mu_1 \times \mu_2 \mid \mu_1 \in T_a^1(s_1), \mu_2 \in T_a^2(s_2)\}$, if $a \in \mathcal{L}_1 \cap \mathcal{L}_2$.

Probabilistic bisimulation was introduced by Larsen and Skou [18] in a discrete setting and adapted to a continuous setting like NLMP in [10,11]. The idea behind the bisimulation equivalence is that from two equivalent states, an a-transition should lead with equal probability to any measurable aggregate of equivalence classes (properly speaking, to any measurable set that results from an arbitrary union of equivalence classes).

Given a relation $R \subseteq S \times S$, a set $Q \subseteq S$ is R-*closed* if $R(Q) \subseteq Q$. If R is symmetric, Q is R-closed iff for all $s, t \in S$ such that $s \, R \, t$, $s \in Q \Leftrightarrow t \in Q$. Using this definition, a symmetric relation R can be lifted to an equivalence relation in $\Delta(S)$ as follows: $\mu \, R \, \mu'$ iff for every R-closed $Q \in \Sigma$, $\mu(Q) = \mu'(Q)$.

Definition 10. *A relation $R \subseteq S \times S$ is a* bisimulation *on the NLMP $\mathcal{P} = (S, \Sigma, \{T_a \mid a \in \mathcal{L}\})$ if it is symmetric and for all $a \in \mathcal{L}$, $s \, R \, t$ implies that for all $\mu \in T_a(s)$, there is $\mu' \in T_a(t)$ s.t. $\mu \, R \, \mu'$. We say that $s, t \in S$ are* bisimilar, *denoted by $s \sim t$, if there is a bisimulation R such that $s \, R \, t$.*

We know that $\sim$ is an equivalence relation [10]. The next theorem states that $\sim$ is a congruence for parallel composition whenever the resulting composition is indeed an NLMP.

Theorem 11. *Let $\mathcal{P}_i = (S_i, \Sigma_i, \{T_a^i \mid a \in \mathcal{L}_i\})$ $i \in \{1, 2\}$, be two NLMPs. If $\mathcal{P}_1 \| \mathcal{P}_2$ is an NLMP, then for all $s_1, s_1' \in S_1$ and $s_2 \in S_2$, if $s_1 \sim s_1'$, then $s_1 \| s_2 \sim s_1' \| s_2$ and $s_2 \| s_1 \sim s_2 \| s_1'$.*

Proof. We only prove that $s_1 \| s_2 \sim s_1' \| s_2$. The other case is symmetric. Let $R \subseteq S_1 \times S_1$ be a bisimulation relation. Define $R' \subseteq (S_1 \times S_2) \times (S_1 \times S_2)$ by $R' = \{(s_1 \| s_2, s_1' \| s_2) \mid (s_1, s_1') \in R, s_2 \in S_2\}$. We prove that R' is a bisimulation by doing case analysis on the definition of the transition relation in the parallel composition.

Suppose in general that $s_1 \| s_2 \, R' \, s_1' \| s_2$, and consider the case in which $T_a(s_1 \| s_2)$ results from (i) in Definition 9. Let $\mu_1 \times \delta_{s_2} \in T_a(s_1 \| s_2)$ with $\mu_1 \in T_a^1(s_1)$. Since $s_1 \, R \, s_1'$, there exists $\mu_1' \in T_a^1(s_1')$ such that $\mu_1 \, R \, \mu_1'$. Let $Q \in$

$\Sigma_1 \otimes \Sigma_2$ be R'-closed and define $Q|_{s_2} = \{s_1 \mid s_1||s_2 \in Q\}$. $Q|_{s_2}$ is measurable in Σ_1 [1], and can be easily proven to be R-closed. Now we can calculate:

$$(\mu_1 \times \delta_{s_2})(Q) = (\mu_1 \times \delta_{s_2})(Q|_{s_2} \times \{s_2\}) = \mu_1(Q|_{s_2})$$

$$\stackrel{(*)}{=} \mu_1'(Q|_{s_2}) = (\mu_1' \times \delta_{s_2})(Q|_{s_2} \times \{s_2\}) = (\mu_1' \times \delta_{s_2})(Q)$$

where equality $(*)$ follows from $\mu_1 \ R \ \mu_1'$, and hence $(\mu_1 \times \delta_{s_2}) \ R' \ (\mu_1' \times \delta_{s_2})$.

Case (ii) in Definition 9 follows with a similar analysis, so we focus on case (iii). Let $\mu_1 \times \mu_2 \in T_a(s_1||s_2)$ with $\mu_1 \in T_a^1(s_1)$. Since $s_1 \ R \ s_1'$, there exists $\mu_1' \in T_a^1(s_1')$ such that $\mu_1 \ R \ \mu_1'$. Let $Q \in \Sigma_1 \otimes \Sigma_2$ be R'-closed. Using Fubini's theorem [1], we calculate:

$$(\mu_1 \times \mu_2)(Q) = \int_{\mathbf{S}_2}\int_{\mathbf{S}_1} 1_Q(x,y) \, d\mu_1(x) \, d\mu_2(y) = \int_{\mathbf{S}_2}\int_{\mathbf{S}_1} 1_{Q|_y}(x) \, d\mu_1(x) \, d\mu_2(y)$$

$$= \int_{\mathbf{S}_2} \mu_1(Q|_y) \, d\mu_2(y) \stackrel{(*)}{=} \int_{\mathbf{S}_2} \mu_1'(Q|_y) \, d\mu_2(y) = (\mu_1' \times \mu_2)(Q)$$

where 1_Q is the usual characteristic function, and $(*)$ follows from $\mu_1 \ R \ \mu_1'$. Therefore $(\mu_1 \times \mu_2) \ R' \ (\mu_1' \times \mu_2)$. $\qquad\square$

Next, we prove that the semantic interpretation of IOSAs and parallel composition commutes, that is, that the NLMP resulting from interpreting a parallel composition of two IOSAs is isomorphic to the parallel composition of the two NLMPs interpreting each of the IOSAs.

Theorem 12. *Given two IOSAs $\mathcal{I}_1$ and $\mathcal{I}_2$, there is an isomorphism between (the reachable parts of) $\mathcal{P}(\mathcal{I}_1||\mathcal{I}_2)$ and $\mathcal{P}(\mathcal{I}_1)||\mathcal{P}(\mathcal{I}_2)$.*

Proof. Let N and M be the number of clocks in $\mathcal{I}_1$ and $\mathcal{I}_2$, respectively. Let $\mathbf{S} = ((\mathcal{S}_1 \times \mathcal{S}_2) \cup \{\text{init}\}) \times \mathbb{R}^{N+M}$ and $\mathbf{S}' = ((\mathcal{S}_1 \times \mathbb{R}^N) \times (\mathcal{S}_2 \times \mathbb{R}^M)) \cup ((\{\text{init}\} \times \mathbb{R}^N) \times (\{\text{init}\} \times \mathbb{R}^M))$ be the states of $\mathcal{P}(\mathcal{I}_1||\mathcal{I}_2)$ and $\mathcal{P}(\mathcal{I}_1)||\mathcal{P}(\mathcal{I}_2)$, respectively[1]. The isomorphism is given by function $f : \mathbf{S} \to \mathbf{S}'$ defined by $f(\text{init}, \vec{v}_1\vec{v}_2) = (\text{init}, \vec{v}_1)||(\text{init}, \vec{v}_2)$, and $f((s_1||s_2), \vec{v}_1\vec{v}_2) = (s_1, \vec{v}_1)||(s_2, \vec{v}_2)$ for all $s_1 \in \mathcal{S}_1$, $s_2 \in \mathcal{S}_2$, and vectors $\vec{v}_1$ and $\vec{v}_2$ which represent valuations on the sets of clocks $\mathcal{C}_1$ and $\mathcal{C}_2$ respectively. f is clearly bijective, and it can be proved straightforwardly that both f and f^{-1} are measurable (i.e. f is *bimeasurable*). From this, it follows that the measurable spaces $(\mathbf{S}, \mathscr{B}(\mathbf{S}))$ and $(\mathbf{S}', \mathscr{B}(\mathbf{S}'))$ are isomorphic.

Following [12], f induces a map $\Delta f : \Delta(\mathbf{S}) \to \Delta(\mathbf{S}')$ defined by $\Delta f(\mu) = \mu \circ f^{-1}$. It is not difficult to prove that Δf is bijective and bimeasurable. Hence, $(\Delta(\mathbf{S}), \Delta(\mathscr{B}(\mathbf{S})))$ and $(\Delta(\mathbf{S}'), \Delta(\mathscr{B}(\mathbf{S}')))$ are isomorphic.

---

[1] Strictly speaking, $\mathcal{P}(\mathcal{I}_1)||\mathcal{P}(\mathcal{I}_2)$ should also contain states of the form $(s, \vec{v}_1)||(\text{init}, \vec{v}_2)$ and $(\text{init}, \vec{v}_1)||(s, \vec{v}_2)$ with $s \neq \text{init}$. Nonetheless, these states are not reachable. Thus, we do not consider them since otherwise the result would not be strictly an isomorphism and it would only add irrelevant technical problems to the proof.

We can lift f a second time to obtain an isomorphism on hit σ-algebras. Define[2] $Hf : \Delta(\mathscr{B}(\mathbf{S}')) \rightarrow \Delta(\mathscr{B}(\mathbf{S}))$ by $Hf = (\Delta f)^{-1}$. Again Hf can be proven to be bijective and bimeasurable and hence, $(\Delta(\mathscr{B}(\mathbf{S})), H(\Delta(\mathscr{B}(\mathbf{S}))))$ and $(\Delta(\mathscr{B}(\mathbf{S}')), H(\Delta(\mathscr{B}(\mathbf{S}'))))$ are isomorphic.

Now, it is not difficult to see that for all $a \in \mathcal{L}$, $\mathcal{T}_a(r) = Hf(\mathcal{T}_a'(f(r)))$ for all $r \in \mathbf{S}$ where $\mathcal{T}_a$ and $\mathcal{T}_a'$ are the transition functions on $\mathcal{P}(\mathcal{I}_1 \| \mathcal{I}_2)$ and $\mathcal{P}(\mathcal{I}_1) \| \mathcal{P}(\mathcal{I}_2)$, respectively. This proves that both NLMPs are isomorphic.   □

Given two NLMPs $\mathcal{P}_1$ and $\mathcal{P}_2$ with the same set of labels, the definition of bisimulation can be extended to states in the different NLMPs by constructing the NLMP induced by the coproduct σ-algebra. The NLMP $\mathcal{P}_1 \oplus \mathcal{P}_2$ is defined by the structure $(\mathbf{S}_1 \uplus \mathbf{S}_2, \Sigma_1 \oplus \Sigma_2, \{\mathcal{T}_a \mid a \in \mathcal{L}\})$ where, for all $s \in \mathbf{S}_1 \uplus \mathbf{S}_2$ and $a \in \mathcal{L}$, $\mathcal{T}_a(s) = \mathcal{T}_a^1(s)$ if $s \in \mathbf{S}_1$ and $\mathcal{T}_a(s) = \mathcal{T}_a^2(s)$ if $s \in \mathbf{S}_2$. Thus, if s_1 and s_2 are states of $\mathcal{P}_1$ and $\mathcal{P}_2$ respectively, $s_1 \sim s_2$ whenever they are bisimilar in $\mathcal{P}_1 \oplus \mathcal{P}_2$.

By [12, Proposition 3.6], the next corollary follows immediately from Theorem 12.

Corollary 13. *For any $\vec{v}_1$ and $\vec{v}_2$ representing valuations of clocks in $\mathcal{I}_1$ and $\mathcal{I}_2$, resp., $(\text{init}, \vec{v}_1 \vec{v}_2) \sim (\text{init}, \vec{v}_1) \| (\text{init}, \vec{v}_2)$ and $((s_1 \| s_2), \vec{v}_1 \vec{v}_2) \sim (s_1, \vec{v}_1) \| (s_2, \vec{v}_2)$.*

We say that two IOSAs $\mathcal{I}_1$ and $\mathcal{I}_2$ are bisimilar, notation $\mathcal{I}_1 \sim \mathcal{I}_2$ whenever $(\text{init}, \vec{v}_1) \sim (\text{init}, \vec{v}_2)$ for any vectors $\vec{v}_1$ and $\vec{v}_2$ representing the valuations of clocks in $\mathcal{I}_1$ and $\mathcal{I}_2$, respectively.

Then, the fact that bisimulation equivalence is a congruence on IOSAs follows from Theorem 11 and Corollary 13 and it is stated in the following theorem.

Theorem 14. *Let $\mathcal{I}_1$ and $\mathcal{I}_2$ be two IOSAs such that $\mathcal{I}_1 \sim \mathcal{I}_2$. Then, for any IOSA $\mathcal{I}_3$, $\mathcal{I}_1 \| \mathcal{I}_3 \sim \mathcal{I}_2 \| \mathcal{I}_3$ and $\mathcal{I}_3 \| \mathcal{I}_1 \sim \mathcal{I}_3 \| \mathcal{I}_2$.*

5   Closed IOSAs are Deterministic

A *closed* IOSA is a IOSA in which all synchronizations have been resolved through parallel composition. Therefore, it has no input actions (i.e. $\mathcal{A}^I = \varnothing$).

In this section we show that a closed IOSA is deterministic in the sense that it is amenable for discrete event simulation or, in case all its clocks are exponentially distributed random variables, also amenable for analysis as a continuous time Markov chain. We will say that a IOSA is deterministic if almost surely at most one discrete transition is enabled at every time point. To avoid referring explicitly to time, we say instead that a IOSA is deterministic if it almost never reaches a state in which two different discrete transitions are enabled.

---

[2] Note that the domain and image of Hf appear apparently inverted. This is necessary in [12] since they only deal with morphisms, and we are following their definitions. In our case, we could have also defined a direct map from $\Delta(\mathscr{B}(\mathbf{S}))$ to $\Delta(\mathscr{B}(\mathbf{S}'))$ since Δf is bimeasurable, namely $H(f^{-1}) = (\Delta(f^{-1}))^{-1}$.

Definition 15. *A IOSA $\mathcal{I}$ is* deterministic *whenever in* $\mathcal{P}(\mathcal{I}) = (\boldsymbol{S}, \mathscr{B}(\boldsymbol{S}), \{\mathcal{T}_a \mid a \in \mathcal{L}\})$, *a state* $(s, \vec{v}) \in \boldsymbol{S}$ *such that* $\bigcup_{a \in \mathcal{A} \cup \{\text{init}\}} \mathcal{T}_a(s, \vec{v})$ *contains at least two different probability measures, is almost never reached from any* $(\text{init}, \vec{v}') \in \boldsymbol{S}$.

By "almost never" we mean that the measure of the set of all paths leading to a state $(s, \vec{v}) \in \boldsymbol{S}$ such that $\bigcup_{a \in \mathcal{A} \cup \{\text{init}\}} \mathcal{T}_a(s, \vec{v})$ contains at least two elements is 0. A strictly formal definition of this requires a series of definitions related to schedulers and measures on paths in NLMPs which is not crucial for the developing of the result. (For a formal definition of scheduler and probability measures on paths in NLMPs see [21, Chap. 7].)

The previous definition only makes sense if $\mathcal{P}(\mathcal{I})$ satisfies *time additivity*, *time determinism*, and *maximal progress* [23]. Particularly, by maximal progress we understand that time cannot progress if an output transition is enabled.

Theorem 16. *For a IOSA $\mathcal{I}$, its semantics* $\mathcal{P}(\mathcal{I}) = (\boldsymbol{S}, \mathscr{B}(\boldsymbol{S}), \{\mathcal{T}_a \mid a \in \mathcal{L}\})$ *satisfies, for all* $(s, \vec{v}) \in \boldsymbol{S}$, $a \in \mathcal{A}^O$ *and* $d, d' \in \mathbb{R}_{>0}$,

maximal progress: $\mathcal{T}_a(s, \vec{v}) \neq \varnothing \Rightarrow \mathcal{T}_d(s, \vec{v}) = \varnothing$
time determinism: $\mu, \mu' \in \mathcal{T}_d(s, \vec{v}) \Rightarrow \mu = \mu'$, *and*
time additivity: $\delta_{(s,\vec{v})}^{-d} \in \mathcal{T}_d(s, \vec{v}) \wedge \delta_{(s,\vec{v}-d)}^{-d'} \in \mathcal{T}_{d'}(s, \vec{v} - d) \Leftrightarrow \delta_{(s,\vec{v})}^{-(d+d')} \in \mathcal{T}_{d+d'}(s, \vec{v})$.

Proof. Notice that if $\mathcal{T}_a(s, \vec{v}) \neq \varnothing$, with $a \in \mathcal{A}^O$, then there exists a transition $s \xrightarrow{\{x_j\}, a, C'} s'$ such that $\vec{v}(j) \leq 0$. Suppose by contradiction that $\mathcal{T}_d(s, \vec{v}) \neq \varnothing$, then $0 < d \leq \min\{\vec{v}(i) \mid \exists a \in \mathcal{A}^O, C' \subseteq \mathcal{C}, s' \in S : s \xrightarrow{\{x_i\}, a, C'} s'\} \leq \vec{v}(j) \leq 0$, which is a contradiction.

Time determinism is immediate by Definition 3 since either $\mathcal{T}_d(s, \vec{v}) = \{\delta_{(s,\vec{v})}^{-d}\}$ or $\mathcal{T}_d(s, \vec{v}) = \varnothing$.

For time additivity, let $\hat{d} = \min\{\vec{v}(i) \mid \exists a \in \mathcal{A}^O, C \subseteq \mathcal{C}, s' \in \mathcal{S} : s \xrightarrow{\{x_i\}, a, C} s'\}$. Suppose $\delta_{(s,\vec{v})}^{-d} \in \mathcal{T}_d(s, \vec{v})$ and $\delta_{(s,\vec{v}-d)}^{-d'} \in \mathcal{T}_{d'}(s, \vec{v} - d)$. By Definition 3, $0 < d \leq \hat{d}$ and $0 < d' \leq \hat{d} - d$, i.e. $0 < d + d' \leq \hat{d}$. Thus $\delta_{(s,\vec{v})}^{-(d+d')} \in \mathcal{T}_{d+d'}(s, \vec{v})$. Suppose now that $\delta_{(s,\vec{v})}^{-(d+d')} \in \mathcal{T}_{d+d'}(s, \vec{v})$. Then $0 < d + d' \leq \hat{d}$ and thus $0 < d \leq \hat{d}$ and $0 < d' \leq \hat{d} - d$, which implies that $\delta_{(s,\vec{v})}^{-d} \in \mathcal{T}_d(s, \vec{v})$ and $\delta_{(s,\vec{v}-d)}^{-d'} \in \mathcal{T}_{d'}(s, \vec{v} - d)$. $\square$

The following is the main theorem of this section.

Theorem 17. *Every closed IOSA is deterministic.*

The rest of the section is devoted to proving this theorem. From now on, we work with the closed IOSA $\mathcal{I} = (\mathcal{S}, \mathcal{C}, \mathcal{A}, \rightarrow, s_0, \mathcal{C}_0)$, with $|\mathcal{C}| = N$, and its semantics $\mathcal{P}(\mathcal{I}) = (\boldsymbol{S}, \mathscr{B}(\boldsymbol{S}), \{\mathcal{T}_a \mid a \in \mathcal{L}\})$. We recall that IOSAs only admit sampling clock values from continuous random variables, which is essential for the validity of Theorem 17.

For every state $s \in \mathcal{S}$, let $active(s) = \{x \mid s \xrightarrow{\{x\}, a, C} s'\}$ be the set of active clocks at state s. By Definition 1(d) it follows that $active(s') \subseteq (active(s) \backslash \{x\}) \cup C$ whenever $s \xrightarrow{\{x\}, a, C} s'$.

The idea of the proof of Theorem 17 is to show that the property that all active clocks have non-negative values and they are different from each other is almost surely an invariant of $\mathcal{I}$, and that at most one transition is enabled in every state satisfying such invariant. Formally, the invariant is the set

$$\mathsf{Inv} = \{(s, \vec{v}) \mid s \in \mathcal{S}, \vec{v}(i) \neq \vec{v}(j), \text{ and } \vec{v}(i) \geq 0$$
$$\text{for all } x_i, x_j \in active(s) \text{ with } i \neq j\} \cup (\{\mathsf{init}\} \times \mathbb{R}^N) \quad (4)$$

therefore, its complement set is

$$\mathsf{Inv}^c = \{(s, \vec{w}) \mid s \in \mathcal{S}, \vec{w}(i) = \vec{w}(j) \text{ for some } x_i, x_j \in active(s) \text{ with } i \neq j\}$$
$$\cup \{(s, \vec{w}) \mid s \in \mathcal{S}, \vec{w}(i) < 0 \text{ for some } x_i \in active(s)\} \quad (5)$$

The next lemma states that Inv^c is almost never reached in one step from a state satisfying the invariant.

Lemma 18. *For all $(s, \vec{v}) \in \mathsf{Inv}$, $a \in \mathcal{L}$, and $\mu \in \mathcal{T}_a(s, \vec{v})$, $\mu(\mathsf{Inv}^c) = 0$.*

Proof. We proceed analyzing by cases, according a is init, in $\mathcal{A}$, or in $\mathbb{R}_{>0}$.

For $a = \mathsf{init}$, we only consider states of the form $(\mathsf{init}, \vec{v})$ since $\mathcal{T}_{\mathsf{init}}(s, \vec{v}) \neq \varnothing$ iff $s = \mathsf{init}$. So, let $\mu \in \mathcal{T}_{\mathsf{init}}(\mathsf{init}, \vec{v})$. Then $\mu = \delta_{s_0} \times \prod_{i=1}^N \mu_{x_i}$. Since each μ_{x_i} is a continuous probability measure (hence the likelihood that two clocks are set to the same value is 0) and $\mu_{x_i}(\mathbb{R}_{>0}) = 1$, then $\mu(\mathsf{Inv}^c) = 0$.

For $a \in \mathcal{A}$, take $\mu \in \mathcal{T}_a(s, \vec{v})$ with $(s, \vec{v}) \in \mathsf{Inv}$. Notice that $s \in \mathcal{S}$. By Definition 3 and because $\mathcal{I}$ is closed, there exists $s \xrightarrow{\{x\}, a, C} s'$ with $\vec{v}(i) \leq 0$ and $\mu = \mu_{\vec{v}, C, s'} = \delta_{s'} \times \prod_{i \in I} \mu_{x_i} \times \prod_{j \in J} \delta_{\vec{v}(j)}$ where $I = \{i \mid x_i \in C\}$ and $J = \{j \mid x_j \notin C\}$.

For each $x_i, x_j \in active(s')$ define $\mathsf{Inv}_{ij}^c = \{(s'', \vec{w}) \mid s'' \in \mathcal{S}, \vec{w}(i) = \vec{w}(j)\}$ whenever $i \neq j$, and $\mathsf{Inv}_i^c = \{(s'', \vec{w}) \mid s'' \in \mathcal{S}, \vec{w}(i) < 0\}$. Notice that $\mathsf{Inv}^c = \bigcup \mathsf{Inv}_{ij}^c \cup \bigcup \mathsf{Inv}_i^c$ and, since the unions are finite, $\mu(\mathsf{Inv}^c) = 0$ iff $\mu(\mathsf{Inv}_{ij}^c) = 0$ and $\mu(\mathsf{Inv}_i^c) = 0$, for every i, j. In the following, we show this last statement.

Let $x_i \in active(s')$. Then $x_i \in (active(s) \backslash \{x\}) \cup C$. If $x_i \in C$, then $\mu(\mathsf{Inv}_i^c) = 0$ because $\mu_i(\mathbb{R}_{\geq 0}) = 1$. If instead $x_i \in active(s) \backslash \{x\}$, then $\mu(\mathsf{Inv}_i^c) = 0$ because $\delta_{\vec{v}(i)}(\mathbb{R}_{\geq 0}) = 1$, since $(s, \vec{v}) \in \mathsf{Inv}$ and hence $\vec{v}(i) \geq 0$.

Let $x_i, x_j \in active(s')$ with $i \neq j$. Then $x_i, x_j \in (active(s) \backslash \{x\}) \cup C$. If $x_i \in C$ then μ_i is a continuous probability measure and hence $\mu(\mathsf{Inv}_{ij}^c) = 0$. Similarly if $x_j \in C$. If instead $x_i, x_j \in active(s) \backslash \{x\}$, then $\delta_{\vec{v}(i)} \neq \delta_{\vec{v}(j)}$ because $(s, \vec{v}) \in \mathsf{Inv}$ and hence $\vec{v}(i) \neq \vec{v}(j)$. Therefore $\mu(\mathsf{Inv}_{ij}^c) = 0$. This proves that $\mu(\mathsf{Inv}^c) = 0$ for this case.

Finally, take $d \in \mathbb{R}_{>0}$ and suppose that $\mathcal{T}_d(s, \vec{v}) = \{\delta_{(s, \vec{v})}^{-d}\}$ with $(s, \vec{v}) \in \mathsf{Inv}$. Notice that $s \in \mathcal{S}$. By Definition 3, $0 < d \leq \min\{\vec{v}(k) \mid s \xrightarrow{\{x_k\}, a, C'} s', a \in \mathcal{A}^O\}$ and $\delta_{(s, \vec{v})}^{-d} = \delta_s \times \prod_{i=1}^N \delta_{\vec{v}(i)-d}$. We take sets Inv_{ij}^c and Inv_i^c as before and follow a similar reasoning. For $x_i \in active(s)$, $\vec{v}(i)-d \geq \min\{\vec{v}(k) \mid s \xrightarrow{\{x_k\}, a, C'} s', a \in \mathcal{A}^O\} - d \geq 0$ and hence $\delta_{\vec{v}(i)-d}(\mathbb{R}_{\geq 0}) = 1$. Therefore $\mu(\mathsf{Inv}_i^c) = 0$. For $x_i, x_j \in active(s)$ with $i \neq j$, $\delta_{\vec{v}(i)-d} \neq \delta_{\vec{v}(j)-d}$ because

$(s, \vec{v}) \in$ Inv and hence $\vec{v}(i) \neq \vec{v}(j)$. So $\mu(\mathsf{Inv}_{ij}^c) = 0$. This proves that $\mu(\mathsf{Inv}^c) = 0$ for this case, and hence the lemma. $\qquad\square$

From Lemma 18 we have the following corollary.

Corollary 19. *The set* Inv^c *is almost never reachable in* $\mathcal{P}(\mathcal{I})$.

The proof of the corollary requires, again, the definitions related to schedulers and measures on paths in NLMPs. We omit it here since the proof eventually boils down to directly applying Lemma 18 and seeing that the measure of all paths leading to a state in Inv^c is 0 for all possible schedulers.

The next lemma states that any state in the invariant Inv has at most one discrete transition enabled.

Lemma 20. *For all* $(s, \vec{v}) \in$ Inv, *the set* $enabled(s, \vec{v}) = \bigcup_{a \in \mathcal{A} \cup \{\mathrm{init}\}} \mathcal{T}_a(s, \vec{v})$ *is either a singleton set or the empty set.*

Proof. By Definition 3, $enabled(\mathrm{init}, \vec{v}) = \mathcal{T}_{\mathrm{init}}(s, \vec{v}) = \{\delta_{s_0} \times \prod_{i=1}^{N} \mu_{x_i}\}$, which proves this case. So, let $(s, \vec{v}) \in$ Inv with $s \in \mathcal{S}$ and suppose that $enabled(s, \vec{v}) \neq \varnothing$. By Definition 3, there is at least one transition $s \xrightarrow{\{x_i\}, a, C} s'$ such that $\vec{v}(i) \leq 0$. Because, $(s, \vec{v}) \in$ Inv and $x_i \in active(s)$, then $\vec{v}(i) = 0$ and for all $x_j \in active(s)$ with $i \neq j$, $\vec{v}(j) > 0$. Condition (c) in Definition 1 ensures that there is no other transition $s \xrightarrow{\{x_i\}, b, C'} s''$ and, as a consequence, $enabled(s, \vec{v})$ is a singleton set. $\qquad\square$

Finally, the proof of Theorem 17 is a direct consequence of Corollary 19 and Lemma 20.

Proof (of Theorem 17). Let $\mathsf{En}_{\geq 2} = \{(s, \vec{v}) \in \mathbf{S} \mid |enabled(s, \vec{v})| \geq 2\}$. By Corollary 19, $\mathsf{En}_{\geq 2} \subseteq \mathsf{Inv}^c$. Therefore, by Lemma 20, $\mathsf{En}_{\geq 2}$ is almost never reachable. $\qquad\square$

6   Conclusion

We introduced IOSA, a stochastic and compositional modeling formalism which turns to be deterministic when all synchronizations are resolved, i.e., the IOSA models a closed system. It supports arbitrary continuous probability distributions to model the stochastic timed behavior of a system. These characteristics make it highly suitable for modeling and simulating systems with more realistic results than Markov models such as CTMCs. Moreover, in case the model uses only exponential distributions, the closed IOSA is amenable to analysis as a CTMC.

As we have already mentioned, our work is related to [22]. This work presents an input/output variant of probabilistic automata where outputs are locally controlled, and hence their occurrence time is governed by exponential distributions, while inputs are externally controlled. Thus it also has the generative/reactive view. In these settings, a closed system forms a CTMC. Our mathematical treatment and theirs is nonetheless very different since the memoryless nature of the exponential distribution can be encoded directly rather than through clocks. Also related to our work, it is the work on weak determinism by Crouzen [6, Chap. 8]. Rather than ensuring by construction that the model is deterministic, this work provides a technique based on Milner's [19, Chap. 11] that, by doing some static analysis, determines if a model, given as a composite I/O-IMC (an input/output variant of IMCs [17]), is weak bisimilar to a deterministic I/O-IMC. The technique may report false negatives.

Currently, we are using IOSA as input language for a discrete event simulation tool —a successor of Bluemoon [5]—that is being developed in our group, and plan to use it as an intermediate language to compile from graphical modeling languages.

Acknowledgments. We thank Pedro Sánchez Terraf for the help provided in measure theory, and Carlos E. Budde for early discussions on IOSAs.

References

1. Ash, R., Doléans-Dade, C.: Probability and Measure Theory. Academic Press, Cambridge (2000)
2. Bogdoll, J., Ferrer Fioriti, L.M., Hartmanns, A., Hermanns, H.: Partial order methods for statistical model checking and simulation. In: Bruni, R., Dingel, J. (eds.) FORTE 2011 and FMOODS 2011. LNCS, vol. 6722, pp. 59–74. Springer, Heidelberg (2011)
3. Bohnenkamp, H.C., D'Argenio, P.R., Hermanns, H., Katoen, J.: MODEST: a compositional modeling formalism for hard and softly timed systems. IEEE Trans. Softw. Eng. **32**(10), 812–830 (2006)
4. Bravetti, M., D'Argenio, P.R.: Tutte le algebre insieme: concepts, discussions and relations of stochastic process algebras with general distributions. In: Baier, C., Haverkort, B.R., Hermanns, H., Katoen, J.-P., Siegle, M. (eds.) Validation of Stochastic Systems. LNCS, vol. 2925, pp. 44–88. Springer, Heidelberg (2004)
5. Budde, C.E., D'Argenio, P.R., Hermanns, H.: Rare event simulation with fully automated importance splitting. In: Beltrán, M., Knottenbelt, W.J., Bradley, J.T. (eds.) Computer Performance Engineering. LNCS, vol. 9272, pp. 275–290. Springer International Publishing, Switzerland (2015)
6. Crouzen, P.: Modularity and Determinism in Compositional Markov Models. Ph.D. thesis, Universität des Saarlandes, Saarbrücken (2014)
7. D'Argenio, P.R.: Algebras and Automata for Timed and Stochastic Systems. Ph.D. thesis, University of Twente, Enschede (1999)
8. D'Argenio, P.R., Katoen, J.P.: A theory of stochastic systems part I: stochastic automata. Inf. Comput. **203**(1), 1–38 (2005)
9. D'Argenio, P.R., Legay, A., Sedwards, S., Traonouez, L.: Smart sampling for lightweight verification of Markov decision processes. STTT **17**(4), 469–484 (2015)
10. D'Argenio, P.R., Sánchez Terraf, P., Wolovick, N.: Bisimulations for nondeterministic labelled Markov processes. Math. Struct. Comput. Sci. **22**(1), 43–68 (2012)

11. Desharnais, J., Edalat, A., Panangaden, P.: Bisimulation for labelled Markov processes. Inf. Comput. **179**(2), 163–193 (2002)
12. Doberkat, E.E., Sánchez Terraf, P.: Stochastic non-determinism and effectivity functions. J. Logic Comput. (2015, to appear). doi:10.1093/logcom/exv049
13. Gburek, D., Baier, C., Klüppelholz, S.: Composition of stochastic transition systems based on spans and couplings. In: ICALP 2016. LIPICS (2016, to appear)
14. Giry, M.: A categorical approach to probability theory. In: Banaschewski, B. (ed.) Categorical Aspects of Topology and Analysis. Lecture Notes in Mathematics, vol. 915, pp. 68–85. Springer, Heidelberg (1982)
15. van Glabbeek, R.J., Smolka, S.A., Steffen, B.: Reactive, generative and stratified models of probabilistic processes. Inf. Comput. **121**(1), 59–80 (1995)
16. Hartmanns, A., Timmer, M.: Sound statistical model checking for MDP using partial order and confluence reduction. STTT **17**(4), 429–456 (2015)
17. Hermanns, H.: Interactive Markov Chains: and the Quest for Quantified Quality. Springer, Heidelberg (2002)
18. Larsen, K.G., Skou, A.: Bisimulation through probabilistic testing. Inf. Comput. **94**(1), 1–28 (1991)
19. Milner, R.: Communication and Concurrency. Prentice-Hall Inc., Upper Saddle River (1989)
20. Viglizzo, I.: Coalgebras on Measurable Spaces. Ph.D. thesis, Indiana University, Argentina (2005)
21. Wolovick, N.: Continuous Probability and Nondeterminism in Labeled Transition Systems. Ph.D. thesis, Universidad Nacional de Córdoba, Argentina (2012)
22. Wu, S., Smolka, S.A., Stark, E.W.: Composition and behaviors of probabilistic I/O automata. Theor. Comput. Sci. **176**(1–2), 1–38 (1997)
23. Yi, W.: Real-time behaviour of asynchronous agents. In: Baeten, J.C.M., Klop, J.W. (eds.) CONCUR '90 Theories of Concurrency: Unification and Extension. LNCS, vol. 458, pp. 502–520. Springer, Heidelberg (1990)

On Optimal Control of Stochastic Linear Hybrid Systems

Susmit Jha[✉] and Vasumathi Raman

United Technology Research Center, Berkeley, USA
{jhask,ramanv}@utrc.utc.com

Abstract. Cyber-physical systems are often hybrid consisting of both discrete and continuous subsystems. The continuous dynamics in cyber-physical systems could be noisy and the environment in which these stochastic hybrid systems operate can also be uncertain. We focus on multimodal hybrid systems in which the switching from one mode to another is determined by a schedule and the optimal finite horizon control problem is to discover the switching schedule as well as the control inputs to be applied in each mode such that some cost metric is minimized over the given horizon. We consider discrete-time control in this paper. We present a two step approach to solve this problem with respect to convex cost objectives and probabilistic safety properties. Our approach uses a combination of sample average approximation and convex programming. We demonstrate the effectiveness of our approach on case studies from temperature-control in buildings and motion planning.

1 Introduction

Hybrid systems can be used to model cyber-physical systems with both discrete and continuous components. Determining a low-cost strategy to control a hybrid system to complete an objective while satisfying a set of safety constraints is a common design challenge in cyber-physical systems. Further, the system dynamics are often noisy in practice due to inherent uncertainty in physical plant as well as modeling approximations. This can cause the system to violate any qualitative Boolean constraints under extreme situations which happen with very low probability. For example, an autonomous airborne vehicle might have noisy dynamics due to air drag in strong winds. Hence, only a probabilistic safety guarantee of not colliding with obstacles is possible. Furthermore, the safety constraints themselves could have uncertainty. For example, the obstacle map perceived by an autonomous vehicle could be noisy due to sensor inaccuracies or due to the presence of other mobile agents whose position is only approximately known. Several other applications such as efficient energy management of buildings and robot-assisted surgery share these characteristics due to uncertainties in process dynamics, sensor data and environment state. These uncertainties, in addition to the mixed continuous and discrete nature of multimodal hybrid systems, make the task of determining an optimal control strategy for the system extremely challenging.

© Springer International Publishing Switzerland 2016
M. Fränzle and N. Markey (Eds.): FORMATS 2016, LNCS 9884, pp. 69–84, 2016.
DOI: 10.1007/978-3-319-44878-7_5

In this paper, we address this challenge and present a novel approach to the synthesis of low-cost control for stochastic linear hybrid systems. We focus on hybrid systems with linear dynamics and a fixed time horizon. The synthesized controller is a discrete-time controller. Our approach uses chance constrained programming [37] to find a low-cost control strategy while satisfying probabilistic safety constraints. Directly solving the chance constrained programs using standard single-shot sampling techniques is impractical for hybrid systems due to the large dimension of the optimization problem. Further, sampling based approaches do not provide any guarantees on satisfaction of constraints, and thus, the generated system might violate probabilistic safety requirements. We split the task of synthesizing optimal control for hybrid systems into two steps. The first step uses constant control approximation and sampling over a small parameter space to determine a low-cost mode sequence and the schedule for switching between different modes in the sequence. The second step synthesizes control inputs in each mode to optimally connect the entry and exit states in each mode. The chance constrained program in the second phase is reduced to a probabilistically conservative but efficiently solvable convex program. This theoretical reduction is key to making our approach practical and scalable. The proposed approach provides a balance between efficiency and optimality (demonstrated through case-studies) while guaranteeing the satisfaction of probabilistic safety properties, and we apply it to a set of case studies from temperature control in buildings and motion planning under uncertainty for autonomous vehicles.

2   Related Work

Automated synthesis of controllers for continuous and hybrid dynamical systems has been widely studied [4,14,44]. Synthesis of continuous controllers and discrete switching logic controllers for noise-free hybrid systems [5,17,19,27,38] is also an active area of research. The control of stochastic systems has been extensively investigated beginning with the work of Pontryagin [33] and Bellman [7]. Its applications include optimal guidance for spacecrafts [3] and flight-simulators [6]. Probabilistic reachability of discrete-time stochastic hybrid systems has also been studied [10,24,34,36]. The focus has been on the safety problem where the goal is to determine a control policy that maximizes the probability of remaining within a safe set during a finite time horizon [2]. This safe control problem is reformulated as a stochastic optimal control problem with multiplicative cost for a controlled Markov chain. Dynamic programming is then used to solve this problem. The solution to value iteration equations obtained using the dynamic programming approach cannot be written out explicitly. In practice, the safety problem is solved using approximation methods. Under appropriate continuity assumptions on the transition probabilities that characterize the stochastic hybrid systems dynamics, [1] proposes a numerical solution obtained by standard gridding scheme that asymptotically converges as the gridding scale approaches zero. The computation burden associated with this approach makes it less scalable and not applicable to realistic situations. This problem is partially alleviated in [22] where neural approximation of the value function is used to mitigate the curse of dimensionality in approximate value iteration algorithm. The goal of these techniques is not optimization of a cost function against probabilistic constraints but instead, the maximization of the probability of staying within a safety condition described by deterministic constraints.

An approximate linear programming solution to the probabilistic invariance problem for stochastic hybrid systems is proposed in [29]. In [12], the authors approximate the constraints in a feedback linearized model of an aircraft so as to make them convex, thereby enabling on-line usage of model predictive control. While we also extract a convex problem, it is based not on approximation of constraints but rather on a practical assumption on the probability bound in safety constraints. In [35], the authors propose a randomized approach to stochastic MPC, for linear systems subject to probabilistic constraints that have to be satisfied for all the disturbance realizations except with probability smaller than a given threshold. At each time step, they solve the finite-horizon chance-constrained optimization problem by first sampling a random finite number of disturbance realizations, and then replacing the probabilistic constraints with hard constraints associated with these extracted realizations only. In this work, we avoid the computationally expensive step of sampling a large number of disturbance realizations or constraints used in these approaches.

The optimization of control for satisfaction of probabilistic constraints can be naturally modeled as chance constrained programs [11,30]. It has been used in various engineering fields that require reasoning about uncertainty such as chemical engineering [25] and artificial intelligence [41]. A detailed survey of existing literature on chance constrained programming and different approaches to solve this problem is given in [37]. Our work relies on solving the chance constrained finite-horizon control problem for the case of uncertainty modeled as Gaussian distribution and continuous dynamics in different modes of hybrid system restricted to being linear. One of the key challenge to this problem arises from evaluating an integral over a multivariate Gaussian. There is no closed form solution to this problem. A table lookup based method to evaluate this integral is possible for univariate Gaussians but the size of the table grows exponentially with the number of variables. Approximate sampling techniques [8,25,26] and conservative bounding methods [9,39] have been proposed to solve this problem. While the number of samples required in sampling techniques grow exponentially with the number of Gaussian variables, the conservative approach also suffers from increased approximation error with an increase in the number of variables.

A conservative ellipsoidal set bounding approach is used to satisfy chance constraints in [39]. This approach finds a deterministic set such that the state is guaranteed to be in the set with a certain probability. An alternative approach based on Boole's inequality is proposed in [9,31]. Bounding approaches tend to be over-conservative such that the true probability of constraint violation is far lower than the specified allowable level. Further, these approaches have been applied only in the context of optimal control of continuous dynamical systems. A two-stage optimization approach is proposed in [32] for continuous dynamical systems. Our work uses a hybrid approach of combining sampling and convex programming to find a low cost control of hybrid systems. The sampling approach allows decomposition of hybrid control problem into a set of continuous control problems by finding the right switching points. The convex programming provides a scalable efficient solution to finding control parameters for the continuous control problem. This ensures that we achieve a good trade-off between optimization and scalability while guaranteeing satisfaction of probabilistic specifications. The use of statistical verification and optimization techniques for synthesis have also been explored in recent literature [43]. Automatic synthesis of controllers from chance-constraint signal temporal logic [18] for dynamical systems have also been proposed in literature.

3   Problem Definition

In this section, we formally define the problem of finding optimal finite time horizon control for discrete-time stochastic hybrid systems where the mode switches are controlled by a schedule. Let us consider a hybrid system consisting of m modes. A finite parametrization of such a system assuming piecewise constant control input sequence yields the following: $x_{k+1} = A_j x_k + B_j u_k + C_j w_k$, where $j = j_1 \ldots j_M$ denotes modes from the set $j_i \in [1, m], x_k \in \mathcal{R}^{n_x}$ is the system state in n_x dimensions, $u_k \in \mathcal{R}^{n_u}$ denotes the n_u control inputs and $w_k \in \mathcal{R}^{n_w}$ denotes n_w dimensional Gaussian noise vector $w_k \sim \mathcal{N}(0, \Sigma_w)$. M is the upper bound on the number of mode switches. Further, the control inputs lie in a convex region $\mathcal{F}_u$, that is,

$$\mathcal{F}_u \triangleq \bigwedge_{i=1}^{N_g} (g_i^T u \leq c_i); \quad \bigwedge_k u_k \in \mathcal{F}_u$$

where $\mathcal{F}_u$ is represented as the intersection of N_g half-planes. The state variables are restricted to be in a convex safe region $\mathcal{F}_x$ with a specified probability lower-bound. This restriction to safe region being convex can be lifted using standard branch and bound techniques [32].

$$\mathcal{F}_x \triangleq \bigwedge_{i=1}^{N_h} (h_i^T x \leq b_i); \quad Pr(\bigwedge_k x_k \in \mathcal{F}_x) \geq 1 - \alpha_x$$

where $h_i^T x \leq b_i$ is i-th linear inequality defining the convex region and the constant α_x determines the probabilistic bound on violating these constraints. The dynamics in each mode of the hybrid systems is described using stochastic differential equations. The time spent in each mode is called the *dwell-time* of that mode. The sum of the dwell times must be equal to the fixed time horizon τ. The dwell-times, $\hat{\tau} = \tau_1 \tau_2 \ldots \tau_M$, can also be restricted to a convex space. The synthesized control needs to be minimized with respect to a convex cost function $f(x, u)$ over the state variables and the control inputs. Since the system is stochastic, the optimization goal is to minimize the expected cost $E[f(x, u)]$.

The corresponding chance constrained optimization problem is as follows:

$$\min_{m_1..m_M, u_1..u_\tau, \tau_1..\tau_M} E_{w,x_0}[f(x_1..x_\tau, u_1..u_{\tau-1})] \text{ subject to}$$

(1) $x_{k+1} = \mathbb{A}_k x_k + \mathbb{B}_k u_k + \mathbb{C}_k w_k$ for $0 \leq k < \tau$ where $\mathbb{A}_k = A_{m_j}, \mathbb{B}_k = B_{m_j}, \mathbb{C}_k = C_{m_j}$

for $\sum_{i=1}^{j-1} \tau_i \leq k < \sum_{i=1}^{j} \tau_i, 1 < j \leq M$, and $\mathbb{A}_k = A_{m_1}, \mathbb{B}_k = B_{m_1}, \mathbb{C}_k = C_{m_1}$, for $0 \leq k < \tau_1$

$w \sim \mathcal{N}(0, \Sigma_w)$, $x_0 \sim \mathcal{N}(x_0^{mean}, \Sigma_{x_0}), m_1 \ldots m_j$ is mode sequence and $\sum_{i}^{M} \tau_i = \tau$

(2) $\bigwedge_{i=1}^{N_g} g_i^T u_k \leq c_i$ and $\bigwedge_{i=1}^{N_l} (l_i^T \hat{\tau} \leq d_i)$ where g_i^T, c_i, d_i are given constants.

(3) $Pr(\bigwedge_{i=1}^{N_h} h_i^T x_k \leq b_i) \geq 1 - \alpha_x$ for all $0 \leq k \leq \tau$ where h_i, b_i are given constants.

The minimization is done with respect to following parameters:

- the sequence of modes $m_1 \ldots m_M$,
- the control parameters $u_1 \ldots u_\tau$,
- the vector of dwell-times in each mode $\hat{\tau} = \langle \tau_1 \ldots \tau_M \rangle$.

The following observations highlight the challenges in solving the stochastic optimization problem described above.

- Firstly, the overall system dynamics is nonlinear due to the discrete switching between different linear systems.
- Second, the probabilistic safety constraint is not convex even when the distribution is assumed to be Gaussian. Standard sampling approach [20,37] to solving such stochastic optimization problem requires sampling in $O(n_x \tau m)$ dimensions to compute the multidimensional integral needed to evaluate $Pr(\wedge_k x_k \in \mathcal{F}_x)$ even for a fixed mode sequence.

Thus, solving such a non-convex stochastic optimization problem with a large set of optimization parameters is not tractable. We address these challenges using mode-sequence discovery technique previously proposed in literature [15,19] and a novel two-level optimization approach presented in Sect. 4. Sample average approximation is used for coarse-level exploration to determine the dwell-times of each mode. The problem of synthesizing optimal control in each mode is reduced to a convex program, which in turn can be solved efficiently.

Illustrative Example Application. We consider temperature control in two interconnected zones where the control objective is to maintain zone temperatures within a comfort range and minimize a quadratic cost function of the control inputs. Let C_k be the aggregate thermal capacitance of the k-th zone, R_1^a and R_2^a represent the thermal resistance of zone walls isolating zone air from outside, T_{oa} be the outside ambient temperature, R be the thermal resistance of the walls separating both zones, T_1 and T_2 be the perceived air temperature of the two zones, and P_1 and P_2 represent the disturbance load of the two zones induced by solar radiation, occupancy, electrical devices etc. The inputs u_1^h and u_2^h represent the two heating agents in both zones. The model of system dynamics is given by the following equations:

$$C_1 \dot{T}_1 = u_1^h + \frac{T_{oa} - T_1}{R_1^a} + \frac{T_2 - T_1}{R} + P_1$$

$$C_2 \dot{T}_2 = u_2^h + \frac{T_{oa} - T_2}{R_2^a} + \frac{T_1 - T_2}{R} + P_2$$

The system operates in four modes: M_1, M_2, M_3, M_4. M_1 is the mode when the zones are occupied and the heater is off, M_2 is the mode when the zones are occupied and the heater is on, M_3 is the mode when the zones are unoccupied and the heater is on, and M_4 is the mode when the zones are unoccupied and the heater is off. We couple the heaters together to reduce the number of modes. The parameters P_1 and P_2 are assumed to be identical and their values are: $P_{\{1,2\}} = P_{const} + P_{occ}$ in M_1, M_2 and $P_{\{1,2\}} = P_{const}$ in M_3, M_4. The control inputs u_h^1 and u_h^2 are non-negative and lie in the $[0.5, 8\,kW]$ range in modes M_2 and M_3, defined by the physical constraints when the heaters are on. The control inputs are 0 in modes M_1 and M_4 when the heaters are off. The parameter values are based on data gathered from Doe library building in UC Berkeley [40]. The outside temperature T_{oa} is set using the weather information at UC Berkeley and the uncertainty in prediction is Gaussian distributed with one standard deviation of $\sigma_{T_{oa}} = 0.71\,°C$. The variable occupancy load P_{occ} is a Gaussian distribution with mean $10\,kW$ and standard deviation $0.63\,kW$. Thus, the uncertainty in this example is due to the deviation of outside temperature from the weather prediction, and the variation in occupancy load. The goal of the controller is to maintain the perceived zone temperature T between 18 and 28 degrees Celsius when the zones are unoccupied and between 21 and 25 degrees Celsius when the zones are occupied. The zones are occupied from 7 AM to 5 PM every day, and the zones are unoccupied for the remaining $14\,h$. The corresponding optimization problem is as follows for the mode sequence M_1, M_2, M_3, M_4:

$$\min_{u, \tau_1, \tau_2, \tau_3, \tau_4} \mathrm{E}_\mathrm{P}[\sum_{k=0}^{\tau-1} u_k^T u_k] \quad \text{subject to}$$

the state $x_k = (T_1, T_2)$ at k-th step is restricted by the dynamics equations presented earlier, $x_0 = [22, 22], \tau_1 + \tau_2 = 10, \tau_3 + \tau_4 = 14, Pr(x_k \in \mathcal{F}^x) \geq 1 - \alpha_x, u_k \in \mathcal{F}^u$ $u = [u_1^h; u_2^h], w = [P_1; P_2; T_{oa}], \mathcal{F}^x = [18, 28]^2$ in M_1, M_2 and $\mathcal{F}^x = [21, 25]^2$ in M_3, M_4, $\mathcal{F}^u = [0.5, 8]^2$ in M_2, M_3 and $[0, 0]^2$ in M_1, M_4 modes

Param	Value	Param	Value	Param	Value	Param	Value
C_1	$1.1e4\ J/^{\circ}C$	C_2	$1.3e4\ J/^{\circ}C$	R_1	$41.67\ ^{\circ}C/W$	R_2	$35.71\ ^{\circ}C/W$
R	$35.00\ ^{\circ}C/W$	Δt	$0.5\ hr$	τ	48	ϵ	10^{-4}
α_x	0.05	τ	48	$\sigma_{T_{oa}}$	0.71	$u_h^1, u_h^2(on)$	$[0.5, 8]\ kW$
P_{const}	$0.1\ kW$	P_{occ}	$\mathcal{N}(10, .6)\ kW$				

4 Synthesis Approach

First, we perform a high level design space exploration of control space by fixing the control input in each mode to be a constant which intuitively represents the average input. The number of optimization parameters reduce from $O(\tau + M)$ to $O(M)$ and since the number of modes in the switching sequence M is usually much smaller than the time horizon τ, we can now use sample average approximation techniques coupled with existing greedy techniques for finding mode sequence to solve the optimization problem in the first step. We use the entry and exit states discovered at the end of the first step to formulate decomposed chance-constrained problems for each mode of the system. We prove that these decomposed problems can be conservatively approximated as convex optimization problems, and thus, solved efficiently. Convexity ensures that any local minimum of the decomposed problems is also a global minimum. We now describe each of these two steps in detail.

4.1 Mode Sequence and Optimal Dwell Times

Mode deletion or insertion from an initial guess of mode sequence has been used in [16,19,21] to synthesize the mode sequence for optimal control of hybrid systems. We use a similar approach here. We adopt addition of modes proposed in [16] because it performed better experimentally that other techniques. Theoretical guarantees of this approach with requisite assumptions on the dynamics can be found in [16]. The approach begins with a mode sequence initialization which can be just the initial mode as a single-mode sequence. New modes are greedily

---

Initialize mode sequence m_0 with an initial guess or the initial state if no guesses are available, and $i = 0$, $done = \texttt{false}$;
while $i <= M$ **and** $done = \texttt{false}$ **do**
  | For each $\texttt{length}(m_i) + 1$ possible insertion position in the sequence m_i, create a new sequence m_{ijk} by adding mode j to the position k ;
  | Pick $m^* = m_{ijk}$ with the lowest cost $\texttt{fixedModeOpt}(m_{ijk})$ for all j, k;
  | **if** $\texttt{fixedModeOpt}(m^*) < \texttt{fixedModeOpt}(m_i)$ **then**
  | | $i = i + 1; m_i = m^*$;
  | **else**
  | | $done = \texttt{true}$;
  | **end**
end
Algorithm 1. Mode Sequence Selection Using Iterative Insertion [16]

added to the sequence if they reduce the cost. This is continued till either we reach the maximum number of modes allowed in the sequence or addition of new modes does not reduce the cost. Let `fixedModeOpt(`m`)` denote the cost obtained for a given fixed mode sequence m, the mode insertion algorithm uses $O(Mm)$ calls to the optimization routine computing `fixedModeOpt` to find the low cost mode sequence as shown below.

In order to compute `fixedModeOpt`, we modify the chance constrained program presented in Sect. 3 by fixing the mode sequence and setting the control inputs in each mode to be a constant. The revised cost metric for schedule switched system:

$$\min_{u_1^\mu..u_M^\mu,\tau_1..\tau_M} E_{w,x_0}[f(x_1..x_\tau, u_1..u_{\tau-1})]$$

where τ_i denotes the dwell-time in the i-the mode of the fixed sequence and u_i denotes the constant control input for that mode. The dimension of the optimization problem has been reduced from $O(\tau + M)$ to $O(M)$. We can now use sample average approximation to solve this optimization problem. This is a standard technique to solve nonlinear stochastic optimization problems. We only sketch the approach here, and details can be found in textbooks on stochastic optimization [20,37]. The overall idea in sample average approximation is to use sampling followed by deterministic optimization. The chance constrained formulation presented earlier can be translated to the standard form:

$$\min_{\vec{x}\in X} f(x) \text{ subject to } Pr\{G(x,\zeta) \leq 0\} \geq 1-\alpha \quad [CCP]$$

where ζ are the random variables representing noise parameters and dwell time for externally controlled hybrid systems, and only noise parameters for schedule controlled systems, f is the optimization function and x includes all the variables being optimized: the control variables for externally controlled hybrid systems, and the control variables and dwell times for the schedule controlled systems. Monte Carlo sampling can be used to generate N samples $\zeta^1,\ldots,\zeta^N$, and let $\hat{q}_N(x)$ denote the proportional of samples with $G(x,\zeta^j) > 0$ in the sample. The sample average approximation of the chance constrained problem has the following form:

$$\min_{x\in X} f(x) \text{ subject to } \hat{q}_N(x) \leq \epsilon \quad\quad [SAA]$$

The above problem is a deterministic optimization problem which can be solved using nonlinear optimization routines in packages such as CPLEX and Gurobi. The following theorem from [23] relates the solution of this deterministic problem to the original stochastic version.

Theorem 1 [23]. *The solution to sample average approximation of the chance constrained problem in Equation SAA approaches the solution of the original problem in Equation CCP with probability 1 as the number of samples (N) approaches infinity, provided the set X is compact, the cost function f is continuous and G(x,·) is measurable.*

Thus, sufficiently sampling the initial states and the noise parameters yields *approximately optimal* control parameters u and dwell times in each mode τ_i. We now describe how the synthesized control parameters and dwell times can be used to obtain the entry and exit states for each mode of the stochastic hybrid system. Since the dynamics is linear, repeated multiplication of the system matrices (described in [39]) can be used to lift the system dynamics to the following form: $x_k = \mathbb{A}_k x_0 + \mathbb{B}_k U_k + \mathbb{C}_k W_k$ where $U_k = [u_0 u_1 \ldots u_{k-1}]^T$ is obtained using the sample average approximation technique described above, $W_k = [w_0 w_1 \ldots w_{k-1}]^T$ is the vector of Gaussian noise, and the initial state x_0 is a Gaussian distribution. Hence, x_k is Gaussian with mean and variance given by: $x_k^\mu = \mathbb{A}_k x_0^\mu + \mathbb{B}_k U_k + \mathbb{C}_k W_k^\mu$, $\Sigma_{x_k} = \mathbb{A}_k \Sigma_{x_0} \mathbb{A}_k^T + \mathbb{C}_k \Sigma_{W_k} \mathbb{C}_k^T$.

The cumulative time T_i is the sum of time spent in modes upto i-th mode in the fixed mode sequence, that is, $T_i = \sum_{j=1}^{i} \tau_j$ for $j \geq 1$ and $T_0 = 0$. The entry-state $\mathbf{in}_i$ and exit-states $\mathbf{out}_i$ for each mode i with dwell time τ_i, are: $\mathbf{in}_i = x_{T_{i-1}}$ and $\mathbf{out}_i = x_{T_i}$. Thus, the entry-state $\mathbf{in}_i$ and exit-state $\mathbf{out}_i$ are also Gaussian distributions. We denote their respective means as $\mathbf{in}_i^\mu, \mathbf{out}_i^\mu$, and the variances as $\Sigma_{\mathbf{in}_i}, \Sigma_{\mathbf{out}_i}$.

4.2 Mode Tuning and Optimal Control Inputs

Given the entry and exit state distributions $\mathbf{in}_i$ and $\mathbf{out}_i$, and the dwell time τ_i for each mode i, the goal of second step is to find control inputs u such that the trajectory in mode i starts from $\mathbf{in}_i$ and exits at $\mathbf{out}_i$ with minimum cost and satisfies the probabilistic safety constraint. We define a new distance between two states $d(x_i, x_j) = (x_i^\mu - x_j^\mu)(x_i^\mu - x_j^\mu)^T + (\Sigma_{x_i} - \Sigma_{x_j})(\Sigma_{x_i} - \Sigma_{x_j})^T$. We revise the original cost metric f by adding the distance of the state reached at the end of trajectory from the specified exit state to the cost. The revised cost metric is $f + Md$ where the constant M is set high enough to force the end state of the trajectory to be the exit state. Both f and d are convex functions over the same domain, and hence the revised cost is also convex. We can now formulate the chance constrained problem for the second step of mode tuning. For each mode, mode tuning is done separately. The chance constrained program for a mode i is as follows:

$$\min_{u_{T_{i-1}} \ldots u_{T_i-1}} E_{w,x_0}[f(x_{T_{i-1}} \ldots x_{T_i}, u_{T_{i-1}} \ldots u_{T_i-1}) + Md(x_{T_i}, \mathbf{out}_i)] \text{ subject to}$$

$$1.\ x_{k+1} = \mathbb{A}_k x_k + \mathbb{B}_k u_k + \mathbb{C}_k w_k \qquad 2.\ \bigwedge_{i=1}^{N_g} g_i^T u_k \leq c_i$$

$$3.\ Pr(\bigwedge_{i=1}^{N_h} h_i^T x_k \leq b_i) \geq 1 - \alpha_x \text{ for all } T_{i-1} \leq k < T_i$$

Next, we show that the above chance constrained problem can be solved using convex programming by a conservative approximation of the probabilistic constraints as long as the violation probability bound $\alpha_x < 0.5$, that is, the probabilistic constraint is required to be satisfied with a probability more than 0.5.

This assumption is very reasonable in many applications where the system is expected to be mostly safe. In practice, the violation probability bounds α_x are often close to zero.

The key challenge in solving the above chance constraint program is due to constraint (3). The probabilistic safety constraint is not convex. But we show how to approximate it as a convex constraint. Firstly, let y_{ik} denote the projection of x_k on the i-th constraint, that is, $y_{ik} = h_i^T x_k$. A, B, C are fixed matrices for dynamics in a given mode. Since x_k is Gaussian distribution, y_{ik} is also a Gaussian distribution with the following mean and variance:

$$y_{ik}^\mu = h_i^T \mathbb{A}_k x_0^\mu + h_i^T \mathbb{B}_k \mathbb{U}_k + h_i^T \mathbb{C}_k \mathbb{W}_k^\mu = h_i^T \sum_{i=0}^{t-1} A^{t-i-1} Bu_i + h_i^T A^t x_0^\mu$$

$$\Sigma_{y_{ik}'} = h_i^T \mathbb{A}_k \Sigma_{x_0} \mathbb{A}_k^T h_i + h_i^T \mathbb{C}_k \Sigma_{W_k} \mathbb{C}_k^T h^i = h_i^T (\sum_{i=0}^{k-1} A^i \Sigma_{x_0} (A^T)^i + A^k \Sigma_{w_k} (A^T)^k) h_i$$

Thus, the probabilistic constraint can be rewritten as:

$$3'. \ Pr(\bigwedge_{i=1}^{N_h} y_{ik} \leq b_i) \geq 1 - \alpha_x \text{ for all } \mathcal{T}_{i-1} \leq k < \mathcal{T}_i$$

We can use Boole's inequality [31] to conservatively bound the above probabilistic constraint. The probability of union of events is at most the sum of the probability of each event, that is, $Pr(\bigvee_{i=1}^{N_h} y_{ik} > b_i) \leq \sum_{i=1}^{N_h} Pr(y_{ik} > b_i)$. Thus,

$$3''. \ Pr(\bigwedge_{i=1}^{N_h} y_{ik} \leq b_i) = 1 - Pr(\bigvee_{i=1}^{N_h} y_{ik} > b_i) \geq 1 - \sum_{i=1}^{N_h} Pr(y_{ik} > b_i) = 1 - \sum_{i=1}^{N_h} (1 - Pr(y_{ik} \leq b_i))$$

The above constraint can be now decomposed into univariate probabilistic constraints.

$$3.1 \ Pr(y_{ik} \leq b_i) \geq 1 - \alpha_x^{ik} \text{ for all } \mathcal{T}_{i-1} \leq k < \mathcal{T}_i, 1 \leq i \leq N_h$$

$$3.2 \ \sum_{i=1}^{N_h} \alpha_x^{ik} \leq \alpha_x \text{ for all } \mathcal{T}_{i-1} \leq k < \mathcal{T}_i$$

We can show that the univariate probabilistic constraints over Gaussian variables in 3.1 is a linear constraint if the violation probability bound is smaller than 0.5.

Lemma 1. $Pr(y_{ik} \leq b_i) \leq 1 - \alpha_x^{ik}$ for a Gaussian variable y_{ik} and $\alpha_x^{ik} < 0.5$ is a linear constraint.

Proof. y_{ik} is a Gaussian random variable. So,

$$Pr(y_{ik} \leq b_i) \leq 1 - \alpha_x^{ik} \text{ iff } y_{ik}^\mu \geq \sqrt{2\Sigma_{y_{ik}}} \text{erf}^{-1}(1 - 2\alpha_x^{ik})$$

when $\alpha_x^{ik} < 0.5$. $\mathtt{erf}^{-1}$ is the inverse of error function $\mathtt{erf}$ for Gaussian distribution: $\mathtt{erf}(x) = 2/\sqrt{\pi} \int_0^x e^{-t^2} dt$. From Eq. 2, $\Sigma_{y_{ik}}$ does not depend on u_k. So, the right-hand side of the inequality can be computed using Maclaurin series or a look-up table beforehand. Let this value be some constant δ_{ik}. From Eq. 1, the left-hand side y_{ik}^μ is linear in the control inputs u_i. So, the probabilistic constraint is equivalent to the following linear constraint: $h_i^T \sum_{i=0}^{t-1} A^{t-i-1} B u_i + h_i^T A^t x_0^\mu \geq \delta_{ik}$ $\square$

Theorem 2. *If $\alpha_x < 0.5$, then the conservative chance-constrained formulation above can be solved as a deterministic convex program.*

Proof. $\sum_{i=1}^{N_h} \alpha_x^{ik} \leq \alpha_x$ and α_x^{ik} are probability bounds and hence, must be non-negative. Consequently, $\alpha_x^{ik} < 0.5$ for all i, k if $\alpha_x < 0.5$. Consequently, all constraints in (3.1) are linear constraints using Lemma 1. We can conservatively choose $\alpha_x^{ik} = \alpha_x/N_k$ and the overall optimization problem becomes a convex optimization problem which can be optimally solved using deterministic optimization techniques. $\square$

In practice correctness constraints are modelled as *likely* probabilistic constraints with probability at least 0.5, and hence $\alpha_{i,j} < 0.5$.

Thus, solving a convex program yields the control inputs for each mode of the hybrid system such that the cost is minimized and the system dynamics starts from the entry state and ends in the exit state found in the first step of our approach. Although our approach uses convex programming in the second step, we can not make guarantees of global optimality for the overall control synthesized by our approach. Nonetheless, the proposed method in this section presents a more systematic alternative to existing sampling based approaches for solving a very challenging problem of designing optimal control for stochastic hybrid systems as illustrated in Sect. 5.

5   Case Studies

In this section, we present results on two other case-studies in addition to the example application presented in Sect. 3. We use quadratic costs in the case-studies and so, we can compare results obtained using the proposed method with the results obtained by using probabilistic particle control [8] for mode selection followed by linear quadratic Gaussian (LQG) control [42] to generate the control inputs for each mode. But in general, the proposed approach (CVX) can be used with any convex cost function while LQG control based approach (LQG) are applicable only when the cost is quadratic. We consider three metrics for comparison: the satisfaction of probabilistic constraints, the cost of synthesized controller and the runtime of synthesis.

5.1   Two Zone Temperature Control

In Fig. 1, we compare the quality of control obtained using our approach and that obtained directly from sampling. The comparison is done using 100 different simulation runs of the system. The proposed approach (CVX) took 476 s to solve this problem while the LQG took 927 s. The controller synthesized by CVX satisfies the probabilistic constraint with a probability of 98.9 % which is greater than required 95 %. On the other hand, the controller synthesize using LQG satisfied the probabilistic constraint with a probability of 92 %. Further, we observe that the proposed approach is able to exploit switching between the heater being on and off when the zones are occupied to produce a more efficient controller with 0.92 times the cost of controlled obtained using sample average approximation.

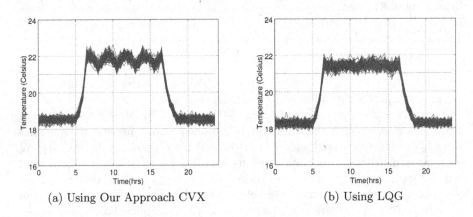

(a) Using Our Approach CVX   (b) Using LQG

Fig. 1. System behavior: Temperature vs Time

5.2   HVAC Control

The HVAC system is used to maintain air quality and temperature in a building. It consists of air handling units (AHUs) and variable air volume (VAV) boxes (see [28] for details). The temperature dynamics for a single zone is:

$$T_{k+1} = \sum_{q=0}^{q=2}(p_{1,q}T^{oa}_{k-q} + p_{2,q}R_{k-q}) + p_3(T^s_k - T_k)\dot{m}_k + \sum_{q=0}^{q=2}(p_{4,q}T_{k-q}) + p_6 + p_{occ}$$

where T_k is the temperature of the zone at time k, $\dot{m}_k$ is the supply air mass flow rate, T^s_k is the supply air temperature, R_k denotes the solar radiation intensity and p_{occ} denotes the noise due to occupancy. All parameters were taken from the model in [28]. The system dynamics can be linearized by introducing deterministic virtual inputs $u^s_k = \dot{m}_k T^s_k$ and $u^z_k = \dot{m}_k T_k$. The goal is to minimize power consumed by the HVAC system while ensuring temperature stays within

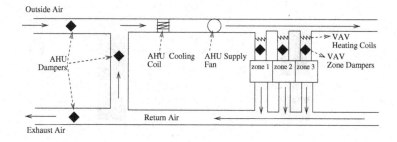

Fig. 2. Schematics of HVAC showing AHU and VAV

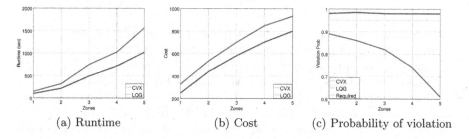

(a) Runtime	(b) Cost	(c) Probability of violation

Fig. 3. Comparison between proposed approach (CVX) and LQG for 1–5 zones

comfortable range. The probabilistic safety property modeling the comfort constraints is the same as Sect. 3. We scale the example from just a single zone to five zones. CVX consistently outperforms LQG in terms of cost and runtime. It is probabilistically more conservative. We compare the runtime, controller cost and probability of violation obtained through 100 simulations in Fig. 3 (Fig. 2).

5.3 Motion Planning

We consider motion planning for an autonomous underwater vehicle moving described in [13] with two modes: *move* and *turn*. The heading in the mode *move* is constant while the propeller maintains a constant speed in the mode *turn*. In practice, the heading and speed control are not perfect and we model the uncertainty using Gaussian distribution. The system dynamics in the two modes: move and turn, are: $\epsilon_{1,2} = \mathcal{N}(0.5, 0.01), \epsilon_3 = \mathcal{N}(0.02, 0.002), 0 \leq v \leq 10$ in the mode *move*; p_k is the control input. $\epsilon_{1,2} = \mathcal{N}(0.2, 0.01), \epsilon_3 = \mathcal{N}(0.01, 0.002)$ $0 \leq \omega \leq 0.5$ in the mode *turn*; q_k is the control input.

$$\begin{pmatrix} x_{k+1} \\ y_{k+1} \\ \alpha_{k+1} \end{pmatrix} = \begin{pmatrix} x_k \\ y_k \\ \alpha_k \end{pmatrix} + \begin{pmatrix} p_k \cos \alpha_k \\ p_k \sin \alpha_k \\ 0 \end{pmatrix} + \begin{pmatrix} \epsilon_1 \cos \alpha_k \\ \epsilon_2 \sin \alpha_k \\ \epsilon_3 \end{pmatrix}, \begin{pmatrix} x_{k+1} \\ y_{k+1} \\ \alpha_{k+1} \end{pmatrix} = \begin{pmatrix} x_k \\ y_k \\ \alpha_k \end{pmatrix} + \begin{pmatrix} 0 \\ 0 \\ q_k \end{pmatrix} + \begin{pmatrix} \epsilon_1 \\ \epsilon_2 \\ \epsilon_3 \end{pmatrix}$$

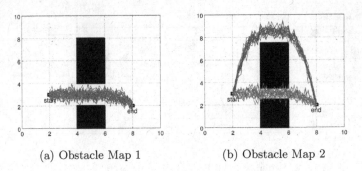

(a) Obstacle Map 1   (b) Obstacle Map 2

Fig. 4. Motion planning

We consider two different obstacle maps shown in Fig. 4. We require that the system state is out of obstacle zone with a probability of 95 %. The trajectory synthesized by our approach is shown in blue and the one synthesized by sample average approximation is shown in red. We simulate the system 200 times to test the robustness of paths. For the first obstacle map, the trajectories synthesized by both approaches are close to each other. LQG is able to synthesize this trajectory in 38 s compared to 98 s taken by our approach. For the second obstacle map, our approach takes 115 s but LQG computes a probabilistically unsafe trajectory even after 182 s.

6   Conclusion

In this paper, we proposed a two-step approach to synthesize low-cost control for stochastic hybrid system such that it satisfies probabilistic safety properties. The first step uses sample average approximation to find switching sequence of modes and the dwell-times. The second step is used to tune the control inputs in each mode using convex programming. The experimental evaluation illustrates the effectiveness of our approach.

References

1. Abate, A., Amin, S., Prandini, M., Lygeros, J., Sastry, S.S.: Computational approaches to reachability analysis of stochastic hybrid systems. In: Bemporad, A., Bicchi, A., Buttazzo, G. (eds.) HSCC 2007. LNCS, vol. 4416, pp. 4–17. Springer, Heidelberg (2007)
2. Abate, A., Prandini, M., Lygeros, J., Sastry, S.: Probabilistic reachability and safety for controlled discrete time stochastic hybrid systems. Automatica **44**(11), 2724–2734 (2008)
3. Acikmese, B., Ploen, S.R.: Convex programming approach to powered descent guidance for Mars landing. J. Guidance Control Dyn. **30**(5), 1353–1366 (2007)
4. Alur, R.: Formal verification of hybrid systems. In: EMSOFT, pp. 273–278. IEEE (2011)

5. Asarin, E., Bournez, O., Dang, T., Maler, O., Pnueli, A.: Effective synthesis of switching controllers for linear systems. Proc. IEEE **88**(7), 1011–1025 (2000)
6. Barr, N.M., Gangsaas, D., Schaeffer, D.R.: Wind models for flight simulator certification of landing and approach guidance and control systems. Technical report, DTIC Document (1974)
7. Bellman, R.E.: Introduction to the Mathematical Theory of Control Processes, vol. 2. IMA (1971)
8. Blackmore, L., Ono, M., Bektassov, A., Williams, B.C.: A probabilistic particle-control approximation of chance-constrained stochastic predictive control. IEEE Trans. Robot. **26**(3), 502–517 (2010)
9. Campi, M.C., Garatti, S., Prandini, M.: The scenario approach for systems and control design. Ann. Rev. Control **33**(2), 149–157 (2009)
10. Cassandras, C.G., Lygeros, J.: Stochastic Hybrid Systems, vol. 24. CRC Press, Boca Raton (2006)
11. Charnes, A., Cooper, W.W., Symonds, G.H.: Cost horizons and certainty equivalents: an approach to stochastic programming of heating oil. Manage. Sci. **4**(3), 235–263 (1958)
12. Deori, L., Garatti, S., Prandini, M.: A model predictive control approach to aircraft motion control. In: American Control Conference, ACC 2015, 1–3 July 2015, Chicago, IL, USA, pp. 2299–2304 (2015)
13. Fang, C., Williams, B.C.: General probabilistic bounds for trajectories using only mean and variance. In: ICRA, pp. 2501–2506 (2014)
14. Frank, P.M.: Advances in Control: Highlights of ECC. Springer Science & Business Media, New York (2012)
15. Gonzalez, H., Vasudevan, R., Kamgarpour, M., Sastry, S., Bajcsy, R., Tomlin, C.: A numerical method for the optimal control of switched systems. In: CDC 2010, pp. 7519–7526 (2010)
16. Gonzalez, H., Vasudevan, R., Kamgarpour, M., Sastry, S.S., Bajcsy, R., Tomlin, C.J.: A descent algorithm for the optimal control of constrained nonlinear switched dynamical systems (2010)
17. Jha, S., Gulwani, S., Seshia, S.A., Tiwari, A.: Synthesizing switching logic for safety and dwell-time requirements. In: ICCPS, pp. 22–31 (2010)
18. Jha, S., Raman, V.: Automated synthesis of safe autonomous vehicle control under perception uncertainty. In: Rayadurgam, S., Tkachuk, O. (eds.) NFM 2016. LNCS, vol. 9690, pp. 117–132. Springer, Heidelberg (2016). doi:10.1007/978-3-319-40648-0_10
19. Jha, S., Seshia, S.A., Tiwari, A.: Synthesis of optimal switching logic for hybrid systems. In: EMSOFT, pp. 107–116 (2011)
20. Kall, P., Wallace, S.: Stochastic Programming. Wiley-Interscience Series in Systems and Optimization. Wiley, New York (1994)
21. Kamgarpour, M., Soler, M., Tomlin, C.J., Olivares, A., Lygeros, J.: Hybrid optimal control for aircraft trajectory design with a variable sequence of modes. In: 18th IFAC World Congress, Italy (2011)
22. Kariotoglou, N., Summers, S., Summers, T., Kamgarpour, M., Lygeros, J.: Approximate dynamic programming for stochastic reachability. In: ECC, pp. 584–589. IEEE (2013)
23. Kleywegt, A.J., Shapiro, A., Homem-de Mello, T.: The sample average approximation method for stochastic discrete optimization. SIAM J. Optim. **12**(2), 479–502 (2002)

24. Koutsoukos, X.D., Riley, D.: Computational methods for reachability analysis of stochastic hybrid systems. In: Hespanha, J.P., Tiwari, A. (eds.) HSCC 2006. LNCS, vol. 3927, pp. 377–391. Springer, Heidelberg (2006)
25. Li, P., Arellano-Garcia, H., Wozny, G.: Chance constrained programming approach to process optimization under uncertainty. Comput. Chem. Eng. 32(1–2), 25–45 (2008)
26. Li, P., Wendt, M., Wozny, G.: A probabilistically constrained model predictive controller. Automatica 38(7), 1171–1176 (2002)
27. Liberzon, D.: Switching in Systems and Control. Springer Science & Business Media, New York (2012)
28. Ma, Y.: Model predictive control for energy efficient buildings. Ph.D. Thesis, Department of Mechanical Engineering, UC Berkeley (2012)
29. Margellos, K., Prandini, M., Lygeros, J.: A compression learning perspective to scenario based optimization. In: CDC 2014, pp. 5997–6002 (2014)
30. Miller, B.L., Wagner, H.M.: Chance constrained programming with joint constraints. Oper. Res. 13(6), 930–945 (1965)
31. Nemirovski, A., Shapiro, A.: Convex approximations of chance constrained programs. SIAM J. Optim. 17(4), 969–996 (2006)
32. Ono, M., Blackmore, L., Williams, B.C.: Chance constrained finite horizon optimal control with nonconvex constraints. In: ACC, pp. 1145–1152. IEEE (2010)
33. Pontryagin, L.: Optimal control processes. Usp. Mat. Nauk 14(3), 3–20 (1959)
34. Prajna, S., Jadbabaie, A., Pappas, G.J.: A framework for worst-case and stochastic safety verification using barrier certificates. IEEE Trans. Autom. Control 52(8), 1415–1428 (2007)
35. Prandini, M., Garatti, S., Lygeros, J.: A randomized approach to stochastic model predictive control. In: CDC 2012, pp. 7315–7320 (2012)
36. Prandini, M., Hu, J.: Stochastic reachability: theory and numerical approximation. Stochast. Hybrid Syst. Autom. Control Eng. Ser. 24, 107–138 (2006)
37. Prékopa, A.: Stochastic Programming, vol. 324. Springer Science & Business Media, New York (2013)
38. Sastry, S.S.: Nonlinear Systems: Analysis, Stability, and Control. Interdisciplinary Applied Mathematics. Springer, New York (1999). Numrotation dans la coll. principale
39. Van Hessem, D., Scherer, C., Bosgra, O.: LMI-based closed-loop economic optimization of stochastic process operation under state and input constraints. In: 2001 Proceedings of the 40th IEEE Conference on Decision and Control, vol. 5, pp. 4228–4233. IEEE (2001)
40. Vichik, S., Borrelli, F.: Identification of thermal model of DOE library. Technical report, ME Department, Univ. California at Berkeley (2012)
41. Vitus, M.P., Tomlin, C.J.: Closed-loop belief space planning for linear, Gaussian systems. In: ICRA, pp. 2152–2159. IEEE (2011)
42. Xue, D., Chen, Y., Atherton, D.P.: Linear feedback control: analysis and design with MATLAB, vol. 14. SIAM (2007)
43. Zhang, Y., Sankaranarayanan, S., Somenzi, F.: Statistically sound verification and optimization for complex systems. In: Cassez, F., Raskin, J.-F. (eds.) ATVA 2014. LNCS, vol. 8837, pp. 411–427. Springer, Heidelberg (2014)
44. Zhu, F., Antsaklis, P.J.: Optimal control of switched hybrid systems: a brief survey. Discrete Event Dyn. Syst. 23(3), 345–364 (2011). ISIS

Scheduling of Controllers' Update-Rates for Residual Bandwidth Utilization

Majid Zamani[1(✉)], Soumyajit Dey[2], Sajid Mohamed[2], Pallab Dasgupta[2], and Manuel Mazo Jr.[3]

[1] Technical University of Munich, Munich, Germany
zamani@tum.de
[2] Indian Institute of Technology, Kharagpur, India
{soumya,sajidm,pallab}@cse.iitkgp.ernet.in
[3] Delft University of Technology, Delft, The Netherlands
m.mazo@tudelft.nl

Abstract. We consider the problem of incorporating control tasks on top of a partially loaded shared computing resource, whose current task execution pattern is characterizable using a window based pattern. We consider that the control task to be scheduled is allowed to switch between multiple controllers, each with different associated sampling rate, in order to adjust its requirement of computational bandwidth as per availability. We provide a novel control theoretic analysis that derives a Timed Automata (TA) based specification of allowable switchings among the different controller options while retaining the asymptotic stability of the closed loop. Our scheduling scheme computes a platform level residual bandwidth pattern from individual task level execution patterns. We then leverage the TA based controller specification and the residual bandwidth pattern in order to synthesize a Linearly Priced Timed Automata for which the minimum cost reachability solution provides realizable multi-rate control schedules. The provided scheduler not only guarantees the asymptotic stability of the control loop but also increases the robustness and control performance of the implementation by maximizing the bandwidth utilization.

1 Introduction

Traditionally, digital implementations of controllers employ constant periodic sampling and control update mechanisms. The engineers designing such implementations tend to over-provision (communication and/or computing) bandwidth to the implemented controllers. Two main reasons justify sampling as fast as possible in a controller implementation: (i) the control engineer is allowed to design a controller with continuous time tools without worrying about the selection of sampling times; and, (ii) the faster the sampling, the quicker a controller

---

This work is partially supported by the German Research Foundation (DFG) through the grant ZA 873/1-1.

M. Fränzle and N. Markey (Eds.): FORMATS 2016, LNCS 9884, pp. 85–101, 2016.
DOI: 10.1007/978-3-319-44878-7_6

can react to external disturbances. However, current trends for the implementation of complex cyber-physical systems are shifting from traditional federated architectures, where each feature runs on a dedicated Electronic Control Unit (ECU), to integrated architectures, where multiple features execute on a shared ECU. These new architectures demand flexibility and efficiency in the use of resources. In a modern automobile, for instance, features may be engaged and disengaged dynamically depending on the state of the system (e.g. the processing of data from the rear parking sensors is not necessary when moving forward). When a feature is not engaged, the residual bandwidth made available by the tasks omitted can be potentially harnessed by the other features running on the same processor. Such plug-and-play nature of control features is recommended by modern automotive standards like AUTOSAR [25], and is also being adopted in cyber-physical system architectures beyond the automotive domain.

We consider architectures in which a simple ECU executes a set of tasks. We assume that tasks are described by arrival patterns expressed in *Real Time Calculus* (RTC), and the scheduling scheme is known for the system. This allows us to find periodic upper bounds on the ECU utilization and compute a recurring pattern of bandwidth availability. We address the problem of scheduling a control task in such a shared ECU under the described assumptions. The goal of the controller scheduler that we design is to maximize the use of the available bandwidth by the newly added control task. We seek to maximize the use of the available bandwidth in order to achieve the highest possible performance in terms of disturbance rejection, as argued earlier. For a small set of tasks with relatively simple periodic specifications, the methodology is lightweight enough to be considered as an online scheduler which can deal with task characterization changing dynamically.

In our solution, we consider control tasks with the ability to select their update (periodic) frequency and we name them "variable-rate" control tasks. This can be achieved by associating to each control task a set of controllers among which one can switch, each requiring a different update frequency. This differs from other aperiodic control alternatives, such as event-triggered [22] (ETC) or self-triggered [2] (STC) control implementations, in that the execution times of our controllers is adjustable by the scheduler, as opposed to being dictated by the plant, as in ETC or STC. Thus in our proposal, once the pattern of ECU availability is known, the scheduler can select a sequence specifying the controller, with its associated update frequency, active at each time interval. The sequence provided shall guarantee the stability of the control task and simultaneously maximize the available resource utilization. The choice of controller sequences, unless exercised judiciously, can result in system instability and suboptimal utilization of ECU bandwidth.

Technically, the variable-rate control systems we consider are switched sampled-data systems. The switching signal determines the closed-loop dynamics through the selection of a controller and an associated sampling time. The stability of switched systems has been studied in depth [4,11] and, as pointed out earlier, it is well known that not every possible switching sequence results in stable closed-loops, even when switching between stable systems (as in our case). Much work has also been devoted in recent years to the computation of adequate sampling intervals to retain the stability of closed-loops under sample-and-hold controller implementations [14,22]. We leverage ideas from both the literature on switched systems and sampled-data systems, to construct a timed automaton dictating when switching to a different controller (also termed mode) is allowed in order to retain stability of the closed-loop. In turn, this automaton implicitly defines a sequence of sampling rates that results in stable operation of the system. In this sense, the type of abstraction provided in the current paper resembles the one proposed in [19] for scheduling event-triggered systems. This automaton can be referenced by the scheduler to affect the switching between the sampling modes without having to compute dwell time constraints at run-time. To this end we leverage tools from linearly priced timed automata [3,18] to synthesize schedulers that maximize the resource utilization. In a related line of work, [5] proposes adaptive assignment of sampling periods to different control loops based on external disturbances while assuming a constant available bandwidth. However, our notion of adaptive switching builds on the premise of time varying bandwidth availability due to other tasks loading the system.

The idea of using multiple sampling rates to schedule control loops has been investigated previously. In [8] sampling schedules are synthesized first, and an iterative procedure is proposed to synthesize a unique controller providing stable operation. However, the algorithm proposed is highly heuristic and there is no guarantee of convergence. A different approach is taken in [17] by constructing automata that provide state-based conditions forcing a change of the controller update frequency. The main shortcoming there is that no proof is given for the stability of the system across transitions. Closer to our proposal are the works [7,24] in which automata are constructed representing mode switches that retain stability of the system. The work reported in [7,24] prescribes recurrent controller scheduling patterns which satisfy exponential stability requirements unlike our approach which derives asymptotically stable switched multi-rate controller schedules that maximally utilize available computational bandwidth. Moreover, unlike [7,24], our approach is directly applicable to non-linear systems. Also very closely related to our work and [7,24], is the work from [9,16], and subsequent publications, developing anytime control algorithms. In that line of work, schedulers are designed that are capable of resolving a trade-off between quality of control (measured as a stochastic notion of stability) and bandwidth utilization, under a stochastic scheduling framework which models channel availability in a probabilistic fashion. Again these developments are restricted to linear time-invariant systems.

2 Notation and Preliminaries

2.1 Notation

The symbols $\mathbb{N}$, $\mathbb{N}_0$, $\mathbb{Q}_0^+$, $\mathbb{R}$, $\mathbb{R}^+$, and $\mathbb{R}_0^+$ denote the set of natural, non-negative integer, nonnegative rational, real, positive, and nonnegative real numbers, respectively. The symbols I_n, 0_n, and $0_{n \times m}$ denote the identity matrix, zero vector, and zero matrix in $\mathbb{R}^{n \times n}$, $\mathbb{R}^n$, and $\mathbb{R}^{n \times m}$, respectively. Given a vector $x \in \mathbb{R}^n$, we denote by $\|x\|$ the Euclidean norm of x. Given a matrix $M = \{m_{ij}\} \in \mathbb{R}^{n \times m}$, we denote by $\|M\|$ the induced two norm of M. A continuous function $\gamma : \mathbb{R}_0^+ \to \mathbb{R}_0^+$, is said to belong to class $\mathcal{K}$ if it is strictly increasing and $\gamma(0) = 0$; γ is said to belong to class $\mathcal{K}_\infty$ if $\gamma \in \mathcal{K}$ and $\gamma(r) \to \infty$ as $r \to \infty$. A continuous function $\beta : \mathbb{R}_0^+ \times \mathbb{R}_0^+ \to \mathbb{R}_0^+$ is said to belong to class $\mathcal{KL}$ if, for each fixed s, the map $\beta(r, s)$ belongs to class $\mathcal{K}$ with respect to r and, for each fixed nonzero r, the map $\beta(r, s)$ is decreasing with respect to s and $\beta(r, s) \to 0$ as $s \to \infty$. Given a measurable function $f : \mathbb{R}_0^+ \to \mathbb{R}^n$, the (essential) supremum of f is denoted by $\|f\|_\infty$. Given a tuple S, we denote by $\sigma := (S)^\omega$ the infinite sequence generated by repeating S infinitely, i.e. $\sigma := SSSSS \ldots$.

2.2 Control Systems

The class of control systems considered in this paper is defined as:

Definition 1. *A control system Σ is a tuple $\Sigma = (\mathbb{R}^n, \mathsf{U}, \mathcal{U}, f)$, where $\mathbb{R}^n$ is the state space, $\mathsf{U} \subseteq \mathbb{R}^m$ is the input set, $\mathcal{U}$ is the set of control inputs from intervals in $\mathbb{R}_0^+$ to U, and f is the vector field. A continuous curve $\xi : \mathbb{R}_0^+ \to \mathbb{R}^n$ is said to be a trajectory of Σ if there exists $\upsilon \in \mathcal{U}$ satisfying $\dot{\xi}(t) = f(\xi(t), \upsilon(t))$ for any $t \in \mathbb{R}_0^+$.*

We write $\xi_{x\upsilon}(t)$ to denote the point reached at time t under the input υ from the initial condition $x = \xi_{x\upsilon}(0)$. Here, we assume some standard regularity assumptions on $\mathcal{U}$ and f guaranteeing existence and uniqueness of the point $\xi_{x\upsilon}(t)$ at any $t \in \mathbb{R}_0^+$ [20]. A control system Σ is said to be forward complete [1] if every trajectory is defined on an interval of the form $[0, \infty[$.

In the remainder of this paper we assume $f(0_n, 0_m) = 0_n$ which implies that 0_n is an equilibrium point for the control system $\Sigma = (\mathbb{R}^n, \{0_m\}, \mathcal{U}, f)$. Here, we recall two stability notions, introduced in [12], as defined next.

Definition 2. *A control system $\Sigma = (\mathbb{R}^n, \{0_m\}, \mathcal{U}, f)$ is globally asymptotically stable (GAS) if it is forward complete and there exists a $\mathcal{KL}$ function β such that for any $t \in \mathbb{R}_0^+$ and any $x \in \mathbb{R}^n$, the following condition is satisfied:*

$$\|\xi_{x\upsilon}(t)\| \leq \beta(\|x\|, t), \tag{2.1}$$

where $\upsilon(t) = 0_m$ for any $t \in \mathbb{R}_0^+$.

Definition 3. *A control system $\Sigma = (\mathbb{R}^n, \mathsf{U}, \mathcal{U}, f)$ is input-to-state stable (ISS) with respect to inputs $\upsilon \in \mathcal{U}$ if it is forward complete and there exist a $\mathcal{KL}$ function β and a $\mathcal{K}_\infty$ function γ such that for any $t \in \mathbb{R}_0^+$, any $x \in \mathbb{R}^n$, and any $\upsilon \in \mathcal{U}$, the following condition is satisfied:*

$$\|\xi_{x\upsilon}(t)\| \leq \beta(\|x\|, t) + \gamma(\|\upsilon\|_\infty). \tag{2.2}$$

It can be readily seen, by observing (2.1) and (2.2), that ISS implies GAS by restricting the set of inputs to $\{0_m\}$. Note that a linear control system $\dot{\xi} = A\xi + Bv$ is GAS or ISS iff A is Hurwitz[1] and the functions β and γ in (2.1) and (2.2) can be computed as:

$$\beta(r,s) = \|e^{As}\|r, \quad \gamma(r) = \|B\| \left(\int_0^\infty \|e^{As}\| \mathrm{d}s \right) r.$$

One can characterize the aforementioned ISS property with respect to some Lyapunov function, as defined next.

Definition 4. *A function $V : \mathbb{R}^n \to \mathbb{R}_0^+$ which is continuous on $\mathbb{R}^n$ and smooth on $\mathbb{R}^n \backslash \{0_n\}$ is said to be an ISS Lyapunov function for the closed-loop system*

$$\dot{\xi} = f(\xi, K(\xi + \varepsilon)), \tag{2.3}$$

where $K : \mathbb{R}^n \to \mathbb{R}^m$, if there exist $\mathcal{K}_\infty$ functions $\underline{\alpha}, \overline{\alpha}, \gamma$, and some constant $\kappa \in \mathbb{R}^+$ such that for all $x, e \in \mathbb{R}^n$ the following inequalities are satisfied:

$$\underline{\alpha}(\|x\|) \leq V(x) \leq \overline{\alpha}(\|x\|), \tag{2.4}$$

$$\frac{\partial V(x)}{\partial x} f(x, K(x+e)) \leq -\kappa V(x) + \gamma(\|e\|). \tag{2.5}$$

The following theorem, borrowed from [21], characterizes the ISS property for the closed-loop system (2.3) in terms of the existence of an ISS Lyapunov function.

Theorem 1. *The closed-loop system (2.3) is ISS with respect to measurement errors ε if and only if there exists an ISS Lyapunov function for (2.3).*

3   Problem Formulation

Consider a control system Σ and assume that there exist p different controllers $K_i : \mathbb{R}^n \to \mathbb{R}^m$, $i \in \mathsf{S} := \{1, \ldots, p\}$, rendering the closed-loop system

$$\dot{\xi} = f(\xi, K_i(\xi + \varepsilon)) \tag{3.1}$$

ISS with respect to measurement errors $\varepsilon : \mathbb{R}_0^+ \to \mathbb{R}^n$, with associated ISS Lyapunov functions V_i and corresponding $\mathcal{K}_\infty$ functions $\underline{\alpha}_i, \overline{\alpha}_i, \gamma_i$ and positive constants $\kappa_i \in \mathbb{R}^+$ as in Definition 4. Now consider a variable-rate control system $\hat{\Sigma} = (\Sigma, P, \mathsf{S}, \mathcal{S})$ representing a sample-and-hold implementation of the closed loop of Σ with different controllers K_i with the associated sampling times h_i, where $P = \{K_1, \ldots, K_p\}$, $\mathsf{S} = \{1, \ldots, p\}$, and

---

[1] A square matrix A is called Hurwitz if the real parts of its eigenvalues are negative.

– $\mathcal{S}$ denotes a subset of the set of all piecewise constant cádlág (i.e. right-continuous and with left limits) functions from $\mathbb{R}_0^+$ to S with a finite number of discontinuities on every bounded interval in $\mathbb{R}_0^+$ (no Zeno behaviour). Each $\pi \in \mathcal{S}$ represents a schedule dictating which controller is active at any time $t \in \mathbb{R}_0^+$. Given any $\pi \in \mathcal{S}$, denoting the switching times as $t_0, t_1, t_2, \ldots$ (occurring at the discontinuity points of π), we denote by $p_i \in$ S the value of the switching signal on the interval $[t_i, t_{i+1}[$. We assume also that the set $\mathcal{S}$ contains only elements for which there exists constants $\tau_{p_i p_{i+1}} \in \mathbb{Q}_0^+$ such that $\tau_{p_i p_{i+1}} \leq t_{i+1} - t_i$, for any $i \in \mathbb{N}_0$, and $\tau_{p_i p_{i+1}} \geq h_{p_i}$ for any $p_i, p_{i+1} \in$ S. Note that the previous assumption on the switching times ensures that the switching signal dwells in mode p_i for at least one associated sampling time h_{p_i} before switching to mode p_{i+1}.

A continuous-time curve $\xi : \mathbb{R}_0^+ \to \mathbb{R}^n$ is said to be a *trajectory* of $\hat{\Sigma}$ if there exists a switching signal $\pi \in \mathcal{S}$ satisfying:

$$\dot{\xi}(t) = f(\xi(t), v(t)) \tag{3.2}$$
$$v(t) = K_{\pi(t)}(\xi(\ell h_{\pi(t)})), \ t \in [\ell h_{\pi(t)}, (\ell+1)h_{\pi(t)}[, \ \forall \ell \in \mathbb{N}_0.$$

We now introduce the main problem which we plan to solve in this paper.

Problem 1. Consider a set T of real-time tasks scheduled on a computing platform and a control task defined as in (3.2). Determine the schedule $\pi \in \mathcal{S}$ of controllers and associated sampling times (K_i, h_i) for the control task so that the utilization of the residue bandwidth left by the real-time tasks is maximal on the average (thus increasing the robustness of the controller implementation to external disturbances) while simultaneously guaranteeing the stability of the control task.

4   Adaptive Scheduling of Variable-Rate Control Tasks

In order to compute a stability aware schedule for the incoming control task on an existing platform, we need: (i) to construct an abstraction of the scheduling constraints that need to be respected to guarantee stability of the control task; (ii) to estimate the available processing bandwidth left by the real-time tasks already present in the platform. We address these challenges in the following.

4.1   Control Task Scheduling Constraints

Consider a control task defined as in (3.2) satisfying the following assumption.

Assumption 2. *Each of the pairs (K_i, h_i), $i \in$ S, of controller and associated sampling times are such that each sampled-data control system (3.2) satisfies*

$$\frac{\partial V_i(\xi(t))}{\partial x} f(\xi(t), v(t)) \leq -\hat{\kappa}_i V_i(\xi(t)), \tag{4.1}$$
$$v(t) = K_i(\xi(\ell h_i)), \ t \in [\ell h_i, (\ell+1)h_i[, \ \forall \ell \in \mathbb{N}_0,$$

for some $\hat{\kappa}_i \in \mathbb{R}^+$, guaranteeing that each mode of the sampled-data closed-loop system is GAS.

Remark 1. There is an abundant literature allowing to design together such pairs of controllers and sampling times satisfying Assumption 2, see e.g. [15] and references therein. Alternatively, one can consider that a continuous time controller is available and compute an adequate sampling time under very mild assumptions on the plant and controller (namely, continuity of the dynamics of plant and controller) such that Assumption 2 holds, see e.g. [14]. Additionally, the large bulk of literature on event-triggered control provides an alternative way of computing sampling times h_i satisfying our requirements through the closely related methods to compute minimum inter-sample times, see e.g. [22]. Note also that the results hereby presented can be directly extended to the case of locally asymptotically stable systems, if one instead assumes (4.1) only holds on a compact set.

We define a timed automaton $\mathcal{T}_{ad} = (L, L_0, C, E, \mathsf{Inv})$, where $L = \mathsf{S}$, $L_0 = L$, $C = \{\zeta\}$, and

- the set E of edges is given by the collection of all tuples (i, g, r, j) such that $i, j \in \mathsf{S}$, $g = \{\zeta \mid \zeta \geq \tau_{ij}\}$ is the transition guard, and the clock reset set r is given by $\{\zeta\}$;
- the (location) invariant for mode i is given by $\mathsf{Inv}(i) := \{\zeta \mid \zeta \geq 0\}$, $\forall i \in \mathsf{S}$,

describing the set, denoted by $\mathcal{S}_{ad}$, of admissible switching policies between different controllers K_i, i.e. $\mathcal{S}_{ad} \subseteq \mathcal{S}$, guaranteeing GAS of the variable-rate closed-loop system. An example of such automaton for the case of $\mathsf{S} = \{1, 2, 3\}$ is depicted in Fig. 1.

In the following, we establish which properties τ_{ij}, $i \in \mathsf{S}$ and $j \in \mathsf{S}\backslash\{i\}$, need to satisfy so that indeed $\mathcal{T}_{ad}$ characterizes a set $\mathcal{S}_{ad} \subseteq \mathcal{S}$ of stabilizing switching sequences.

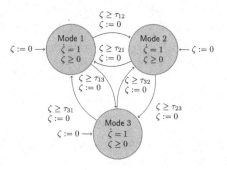

Fig. 1. Timed automaton $\mathcal{T}_{ad}$ for 3 controllers.

Assumption 3. *For any pair of $i, j \in$ S, there exits a constant $\mu_{ij} \geq 1$ such that*

$$\forall x \in \mathbb{R}^n, \quad V_i(x) \leq \mu_{ij} V_j(x). \tag{4.2}$$

Theorem 4. *Consider the variable-rate control system $\hat{\Sigma}$ in (3.2) and let Assumptions 2 and 3 hold. If $\log \frac{\mu_{ij}}{\rho} < \hat{\kappa}_j \tau_{ji}$, for any $i, j \in \mathsf{S}$, $i \neq j$, and some $\rho \in]0, 1[$, then Σ is GAS and $\mathcal{T}_{ad}$ using these τ_{ij} characterizes a set $\mathcal{S}_{ad}$ of stabilizing switching sequences.*

Proof. We show the result for the case of infinite number of switches. A proof for the case of finite switches can be written in a similar way. Let $a \in \mathbb{R}^n$ be any initial condition, $t_0 = 0$, and let $p_i \in \mathsf{S}$ denote the value of the switching signal on the interval $[t_i, t_{i+1}[$, for $i \in \mathbb{N}_0$. For all $i \in \mathbb{N}_0$ and $t \in [t_i, t_{i+1}[$ and using inequality (4.1), one gets

$$\dot{V}_{p_i}(\xi_{av}(t)) \leq -\hat{\kappa}_{p_i} V_{p_i}(\xi_{av}(t)).$$

For all $i \in \mathbb{N}_0$, $t \in [t_i, t_{i+1}]$, and by continuity of V_{p_i}, we have

$$V_{p_i}(\xi_{av}(t)) \leq V_{p_i}(\xi_{av}(t_i)) e^{-\hat{\kappa}_{p_i}(t-t_i)}. \tag{4.3}$$

Particularly, for $t = t_{i+1} \, \forall i \in \mathbb{N}_0$ and using inequality (4.2), one gets

$$V_{p_{i+1}}(\xi_{av}(t_{i+1})) \leq \mu_{p_{i+1}p_i} e^{-\hat{\kappa}_{p_i}(t_{i+1}-t_i)} V_{p_i}(\xi_{av}(t_i)).$$

Then, by induction, we have that for all $i \in \mathbb{N}_0$

$$V_{p_i}(\xi_{av}(t_i)) \leq \mu_{p_i p_{i-1}} e^{-\hat{\kappa}_{p_{i-1}}(t_i-t_{i-1})} \times \tag{4.4}$$
$$\mu_{p_{i-1}p_{i-2}} e^{-\hat{\kappa}_{p_{i-2}}(t_{i-1}-t_{i-2})} \ldots \mu_{p_1 p_0} e^{-\hat{\kappa}_{p_0}(t_1-t_0)} V_{p_0}(a).$$

Combining (4.3) and (4.4), for all $i \in \mathbb{N}_0$ and $t \in [t_i, t_{i+1}]$, one obtains

$$V_{p_i}(\xi_{av}(t)) \leq e^{-\hat{\kappa}_{p_i}(t-t_i)} \mu_{p_i p_{i-1}} e^{-\hat{\kappa}_{p_{i-1}}(t_i-t_{i-1})} \times$$
$$\mu_{p_{i-1}p_{i-2}} e^{-\hat{\kappa}_{p_{i-2}}(t_{i-1}-t_{i-2})} \ldots \mu_{p_1 p_0} e^{-\hat{\kappa}_{p_0}(t_1-t_0)} V_{p_0}(a).$$

Since we consider only switching signals in $\mathcal{S}$, i.e. such that $\exists \tau_{p_i p_{i+1}} \in \mathbb{Q}_0^+$: $\tau_{p_i p_{i+1}} \leq t_{i+1} - t_i$ for any $i \in \mathbb{N}_0$, one can further bound as:

$$V_{p_i}(\xi_{av}(t)) \leq e^{-\hat{\kappa}_{p_i}(t-t_i)} \mu_{p_i p_{i-1}} e^{-\hat{\kappa}_{p_{i-1}}\tau_{p_{i-1}p_i}} \times$$
$$\mu_{p_{i-1}p_{i-2}} e^{-\hat{\kappa}_{p_{i-2}}\tau_{p_{i-2}p_{i-1}}} \ldots \mu_{p_1 p_0} e^{-\hat{\kappa}_{p_0}\tau_{p_0 p_1}} V_{p_0}(a)$$
$$\leq \mu_{p_i p_{i-1}} e^{-\hat{\kappa}_{p_{i-1}}\tau_{p_{i-1}p_i}} \times$$
$$\mu_{p_{i-1}p_{i-2}} e^{-\hat{\kappa}_{p_{i-2}}\tau_{p_{i-2}p_{i-1}}} \ldots \mu_{p_1 p_0} e^{-\hat{\kappa}_{p_0}\tau_{p_0 p_1}} V_{p_0}(a).$$

Finally, since $\log \frac{\mu_{ij}}{\rho} < \hat{\kappa}_j \tau_{ji}$, for any $i, j \in \mathsf{S}$, $i \neq j$, and some $\rho \in]0, 1[$, we obtain:

$$V_{p_i}(\xi_{av}(t)) \leq \rho^i V_{p_0}(a). \tag{4.5}$$

Using inequalities in (2.4) and (4.5), one gets

$$\underline{\alpha}_{p_i}(\|\xi_{av}(t)\|) \leq V_{p_i}(\xi_{av}(t)) \leq \rho^i V_{p_0}(a) \leq \rho^i \overline{\alpha}_{p_0}(\|a\|),$$

which reduces to

$$\|\xi_{av}(t)\| \leq \underline{\alpha}_{p_i}^{-1}(\rho^i \overline{\alpha}_{p_0}(\|a\|)), \tag{4.6}$$

due to $\underline{\alpha}_{p_i} \in \mathcal{K}_\infty$. As t goes to infinity and since the number of switches are infinite (i.e. $i \to \infty$), from (4.6) we conclude that $\|\xi_{av}(t)\|$ converges to zero asymptotically which completes the proof.

4.2   Task Set Characterization

We consider an ECU platform for which the arrival pattern of each task in an existing task set T is known. For a task $\theta_i \in T$, the RTC arrival curves (α_i^l, α_i^u) are functions from $\mathbb{R}^+$ to $\mathbb{N}$ [6,23] such that the number of instances of θ_i arriving in any time window of size t is lower bounded by $\alpha_i^l(n)$ and upper bounded by $\alpha_i^u(n)$. Let us consider the deadline of each instance of θ_i to be e_i time units. The maximum number of task instances of type θ_i that may arrive in a period of size e_i is given by a_i where $a_i := \alpha_i^u(e_i)$. A computational bandwidth which allows sufficient scheduling slots for executing a_i instances of θ_i in every interval of length e_i is sufficient for scheduling θ_i since e_i represents the deadline of each instance of θ_i.

Consider now the worst case execution time (WCET) of θ_i to be w_i CPU cycles. Thus, $a_i w_i$ number of CPU cycles need to be made available for task θ_i in every consecutive real-time interval of size e_i. Let the total available bandwidth offered by the CPU be given as H computation cycles per time unit. Assume that the existing scheduling policy for the platform allocates a $y_i \in [0,1]$ fraction of the total bandwidth to θ_i. We consider an *as late as possible* (ALAP) scheduling of the tasks in the period e_i, meaning that the fraction of bandwidth y allocated to task θ_i is provided in intervals of time of length $\delta_i := \frac{a_i w_i}{H y_i}$ whose end coincides with multiples of e_i. We provide a formal definition of these utilization patterns in the following.

Definition 5. *The* bandwidth utilization pattern *of a task θ_i, with period e_i, bandwidth utilization fraction y_i, and utilization time δ_i, is a function $\sigma_{\theta_i}^{(e_i, y_i, \delta_i)}$: $\mathbb{R}_0^+ \to [0,1]$ satisfying the following properties:*

- $\sigma_{\theta_i}^{(e_i, y_i, \delta_i)}(t + e_i) = \sigma_{\theta_i}^{(e_i, y_i, \delta_i)}(t);$
- $\sigma_{\theta_i}^{(e_i, y_i, \delta_i)}(t) = 0, t \in [0, e_i - \delta_i[;$
- $\sigma_{\theta_i}^{(e_i, y_i, \delta_i)}(t) = y_i, t \in [e_i - \delta_i, e_i[.$

Given the task set $T = \{\theta_1, \ldots, \theta_n\}$ with corresponding deadlines $\{e_1, \ldots, e_n\}$ and fraction of bandwidth allocated $\{y_1, \ldots, y_n\}$, one can compute their respective δ_i's as indicated earlier. Adding up the bandwidth utilization scenarios of each of those tasks a total bandwidth utilization pattern can

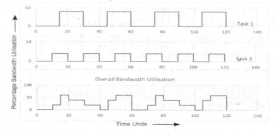

Fig. 2. ALAP Bandwidth budgets

be obtained $\overline{\sigma}_T = \sum_{i=1}^n \sigma_{\theta_i}^{(e_i, y_i, \delta_i)}$. Note that this bandwidth utilization pattern is also a periodic function $\overline{\sigma}_T : \mathbb{R}_0^+ \to [0,1]$ with period $\overline{e} = l.c.m.(e_1, \ldots, e_n)$, where *l.c.m.* stands for least common multiple, but this is not necessarily a bandwidth utilization pattern (the last two conditions of the definition may not hold for $\overline{\sigma}_T$). It may be noted that budgeting processor bandwidths in the way as discussed above is useful for satisfying the bandwidth requirement for any scheduling policy which do not allow deadline violation.

Example 1. Let us consider two tasks θ_1, θ_2 with $e_1 = 30$ and $e_2 = 20$ time units so that $a_1 = \alpha_1^u(30) = 2$ and $a_2 = \alpha_1^u(20) = 10$. Let the WCET of θ_1, θ_2 be 30000 and 2000 CPU cycles, respectively. The CPU offers 10000 computation cycles (H) per time unit and the scheduler offers 40 % and 20 % of overall CPU bandwidth to θ_1 and θ_2, respectively, during execution (i.e. $y_1 = 0.4$, $y_2 = 0.2$). This means θ_1 and θ_2 gets 4000 and 2000 computation cycles per time unit, respectively, while executing. This results in the execution of every instance of θ_1 consuming $30000/4000 = 7.5$ time units. Thus, to satisfy the total worst case demand of θ_1, i.e. 2 instances in periodic intervals of size 30 time units, we require 15 time units of CPU given a bandwidth of 40%. Similarly, we require 10 time units in periodic intervals of size 20 given a bandwidth of 20% for θ_2. Adding up these requirements point-wise, a worst case bandwidth requirement pattern, which recurs every $l.c.m.(30, 20) = 60$ time units, is computed. The resulting bandwidth pattern is illustrated in Fig. 2.

4.3   Scheduler Design

As discussed earlier, given a control system with p different controllers (from a set $P = \{K_1, \ldots, K_p\}$) having sampling rates $\{f_1 < f_2 < \cdots < f_p\}$, $(f_i = h_i^{-1})$, we can construct a TA $\mathcal{T}_{ad}$ having p number of modes, where each mode $1 \le i \le p$ signifies the use of controller K_i. For every possible mode switch from some mode i to some mode j, the automaton provides a timing constraint τ_{ij} signifying what is the minimum duration of using mode i (using K_i) so that a switching can be performed to mode j (start using K_j) guaranteeing that the overall closed loop system is GAS. Let the WCET of controller K_i

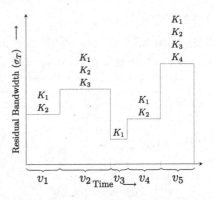

Fig. 3. Admissible controllers

be ω_i^c (in CPU cycles), and thus its computational requirement is $\omega_i^c f_i$ cycles per time unit. Given H available computing cycles per time unit, the fraction of bandwidth required by the controller is $r_i = \frac{\omega_i^c f_i}{H}$, and so one can compute the bandwidth requirements $\{r_1, \ldots, r_p\}$ of all controllers in P.

Given the total bandwidth utilization pattern $\overline{\sigma}_T$ for the task set T, with period $\bar{e}$, denote by $\underline{\sigma}_T := 1 - \overline{\sigma}_T$ the residual bandwidth pattern. Let us consider such a pattern $\underline{\sigma}_T$ and describe it by a string $\underline{s}_T := ((l_1, v_1), \ldots, (l_\nu, v_\nu))^\omega$, with $\sum_{i=1}^{\nu} v_i = \bar{e}$, denoting the infinitely repeating concatenation of time intervals of length v_i and associated fraction of bandwidth available l_i, with $i = 1, \ldots, \nu$. We refer to the i-th tuple in the sequence as the *i-th stage* of the pattern and to the period $\bar{e}$ as the *recurrence length* of the pattern. We also denote by $\underline{s}_T[\bar{e}] := ((l_1, v_1), \ldots, (l_\nu, v_\nu))$. We use the sequence description $\underline{s}_T$ and the availability pattern $\underline{\sigma}_T$ interchangeably in what follows. Consider now the available bandwidth string $\underline{s}_T$, and define $S := \langle S_1, \ldots, S_\nu \rangle$ with $S_i \subseteq 2^P$, $\forall i \in \{1, \ldots, \nu\}$, such that $S_i = \{K_j \,|\, r_j \leq l_i\}$. The list S_i contains the controllers which are schedulable at each of the i-th stages of $\underline{s}_T$ in terms of the available bandwidth (but possibly leading to an unstable closed-loop operation).

Example 2. Given the instance of $\underline{\sigma}_T$ as shown in Fig. 3, a possible list S for the case of 4 controllers, could take the form $S_1 = \{K_1, K_2\}, S_2 = \{K_1, K_2, K_3\}, S_3 = \{K_1\}, S_4 = \{K_1, K_2\}, S_5 = \{K_1, K_2, K_3, K_4\}$, where we have assumed that $r_i < r_j$ if $i < j$.

We specify a switching sequence ς as a string $\varsigma = ((K_{i_1}, t_{i_1}), \ldots, (K_{i_k}, t_{i_k}), \ldots, (K_{i_n}, t_{i_n}))$ indicating that controller K_{i_k} is used inside the k-th time interval $\left[\sum_{j=1}^{k-1} t_{i_j}, \sum_{j=1}^{k} t_{i_j} \right]$, of duration t_{i_k}. We consider only nontrivial sequences in the sense that $K_{i_j} \neq K_{i_{j+1}}$ for all j in a sequence. The *length* of such a sequence is given by $|\varsigma| = \sum_{j=1}^{n} t_{i_j}$. One can therefore construct from such a sequence ς a switching signal $\pi \in \mathcal{S}$ (c.f. Sect. 3) by letting $\pi(t) = i_k$ if $t \in \left[\sum_{j=1}^{k-1} t_{i_j} + \bar{e}s, \sum_{j=1}^{k} t_{i_j} + \bar{e}s \right]$ for some $s \in \mathbb{N}_0$.

Note that the timed automaton $\mathcal{T}_{ad}$ derived in Sect. 4.1, provides us with a set of timing constraints $\{\tau_{ij} \,|\, 1 \leq i \leq p \wedge 1 \leq j \leq p, \ i \neq j\}$ where a constraint τ_{ij} signifies the minimum amount of time controller K_i should execute (i.e. sojourn in mode i of the automaton) before a switch to controller K_j is allowed. Given $\underline{\sigma}_T$, the list S, and $\mathcal{T}_{ad}$, an admissible switching sequence can be defined as follows.

Definition 6. *Given a bandwidth pattern $\underline{\sigma}_T$ described by the string $\underline{s}_T := ((l_1, v_1), \ldots, (l_\nu, v_\nu))^\omega$ with recurrence length $\bar{e}$, the list S of admissible controllers, the timed automaton $\mathcal{T}_{ad}$, a switching sequence $\varsigma = ((K_{i_1}, t_{i_1}), \ldots, (K_{i_k}, t_{i_k}), \ldots, (K_{i_n}, t_{i_n}))$ is considered admissible if:*

- $|\varsigma| = l \times \bar{e}$, *for some $l \in \mathbb{N}$;*
- $\forall k \in \mathbb{N}, 1 \leq k \leq n$, *if $\exists m \in \mathbb{N}, 0 \leq m < l$, and $\exists q \in \mathbb{N}, 1 \leq q \leq \nu$, such that the intervals $\left[\sum_{j=1}^{k-1} t_{i_j}, \sum_{j=1}^{k} t_{i_j} \right]$ and $\left[m \times \bar{e} + \sum_{j=1}^{q-1} v_j, m \times \bar{e} + \sum_{j=1}^{q} v_j \right]$ intersect, i.e., for every k-th time interval in ς if there is a non-null intersection with an interval v_q of $\underline{\sigma}_T$, then $K_{i_k} \in S_q$ and $t_{i_k} \geq \tau_{i_k i_{k+1}}$.*

We define the notion of *bandwidth rejection* by an admissible switching sequence as follows.

Definition 7. *Given a bandwidth pattern $\underline{\sigma}_T$ with recurrence length $\bar{e}$ and the list S of admissible controllers, the bandwidth rejection by an admissible switching sequence $\varsigma = ((K_{i_1}, t_{i_1}), \ldots, (K_{i_k}, t_{i_k}), \ldots, (K_{i_n}, t_{i_n}))$ is given by $rej(\varsigma) = \int_0^{l \times \bar{e}} (\underline{\sigma}_T(t) - r(t)) dt$, where $|\varsigma| = l \times \bar{e}$, for some $l \in \mathbb{N}$, and $r : \mathbb{R}_0^+ \to [0, 1]$ is defined as $r(t) = r_{i_k}$ for $t \in \left[\sum_{j=1}^{k-1} t_{i_j}, \sum_{j=1}^{k} t_{i_j} \right[$.*

In order to formally capture the set of admissible switching sequences, we construct a Linearly Priced Timed Automaton (LPTA) [3,18]. Given the list S, $\underline{\sigma}_T$, and the timing constraints for stable switching as captured by the timed automaton $\mathcal{T}_{ad}$ derived in Sect. 4.1, the LPTA $\mathcal{T} = (L, L_0, C, E, \mathsf{Inv}, \mathcal{P})$ is defined as follows.

- $L = \{m_{i,j} \mid \exists (i,j) \in \{1,\ldots,\nu\} \times \{1,\ldots,p\} \text{ s.t. } K_j \in S_i\}$. A location $m_{i,j}$ denotes a possible choice of controller K_j inside the time interval v_i.
- $L_0 = \{m_{1,k} \in L \mid K_k \in S_1\}$.
- $C = \{c, x, c_g\}$. Clock c is used to keep track of the total time elapsed using the same controller mode across a sequence of intervals. Clock x tracks the time spent on all locations inside the same stage while c_g serves as a global clock.
- E contains three types of edges:
    1. *inter-stage* edges: for $m_{i,j}, m_{i+1,k} \in L$, $(m_{i,j}, \phi, C', m_{i+1,k}) \in E$ if $(K_j \in S_i) \wedge (K_k \in S_{i+1})$.
    2. *intra-stage* edges: for $m_{i,j}, m_{i,k} \in L$, $(m_{i,j}, \phi, C', m_{i,k}) \in E$ if $(K_j \in S_i) \wedge (K_k \in S_i)$.
    3. *final stage* edges: for $m_{\nu,j}, m_{1,j} \in L$, $(m_{\nu,i}, \phi, C', m_{1,j}) \in E$ if $K_i \in S_\nu$, where v_ν is the last interval defining $\underline{\sigma}_T$.
- An inter-stage edge $(m_{i,j}, \phi, C', m_{i+1,k}) \in E$ has a clock reset set $C' = \{c, x\}$ if $j \neq k$ and $C' = \{x\}$ otherwise.
- An inter-stage edge $(m_{i,j}, \phi, C', m_{i+1,k}) \in E$ has a guard $\phi = (c \geq \tau_{jk}) \wedge (x \geq v_i)$ if $j \neq k$ and $\phi = (x \geq v_i)$ otherwise.
- An intra-stage edge $(m_{i,j}, \phi, C', m_{i,k}) \in E$ shall always have $j \neq k$ by construction. For such a transition, $\phi = (c \geq \tau_{jk})$ and $C' = \{c\}$.
- A final-stage edge $(m_{\nu,j}, \phi, C', m_{1,j}) \in E$ has a clock reset set $C' = \{c, x\}$ if $i \neq j$ and $C' = \{x\}$ otherwise.
- A final-stage edge $(m_{\nu,j}, \phi, C', m_{1,j}) \in E$ has a guard $\phi = (c \geq \tau_{ij}) \wedge (x \geq v_i)$ if $i \neq j$ and $\phi = (x \geq v_i)$ otherwise.
- $\mathsf{Inv}(m_{i,j}) = \{x \leq v_i\}$, $\forall m_{i,j} \in L$. These invariants force the automaton to leave $m_{i,j}$ after spending v_i time in the mode. This takes care of the bandwidth availability requirement.
- For a location (mode) $m_{i,j}$, the cost rate function $\mathcal{P}$ is defined as, $\mathcal{P}(m_{i,j}) = (l_i - r_j)$, $\forall m_{i,j} \in L \setminus \{f\}$, and $\mathcal{P}(e) = 0$ $\forall e \in E$. The cost rate at $m_{i,j}$ is the difference between the bandwidth offered inside the interval v_i, and the bandwidth required by controller K_j, i.e. r_j. We do not assign any costs to the edge transitions.

Remark 2. By construction, any run of $\mathcal{T}$ with length being an integer multiple of $\bar{e}$ is an admissible switching sequence.

Based on the notion of on-the-average non-utilized bandwidth, we define a switching sequence as optimal as follows.

Definition 8. *An admissible switching sequence ς^* is considered optimal if for every other admissible switching sequence ς, we have $\frac{rej(\varsigma^*)}{|\varsigma^*|} \leq \frac{rej(\varsigma)}{|\varsigma|}$.*

It may be noted that in general an admissible switching sequence can be of length which is any integer multiple of $\bar{e}$. Hence, it makes sense to consider optimality among admissible switching sequences upto a maximum length.

Definition 9. *An admissible switching sequence* $\varsigma^* = (K^*_{i_1}, t^*_1)(K^*_{i_2}, t^*_2)$ $\cdots (K^*_{i_k}, t^*_k)$ *with* $i_1, \ldots, i_k \in \mathsf{S}$ *is considered optimal in N-unfolding of* $\underline{\sigma}_T$ *if* $|\varsigma^*| \leq N \times \bar{e}$ *and among all admissible switching sequences with length* $\leq N \times \bar{e}$, ς^* *incurs the least (average) bandwidth rejection, i.e. for any other admissible switching sequence* ς *with* $|\varsigma| < N \times \bar{e}$, *we have* $\frac{rej(\varsigma^*)}{|\varsigma^*|} \leq \frac{rej(\varsigma)}{|\varsigma|}$.

Computing Recurrent Schedules. As a scheduling solution, we are interested in switching sequences which follow a recurring pattern just like the bandwidth pattern that recurs every $\bar{e}$ time units.

Definition 10. *Given a bandwidth pattern* $\underline{\sigma}_T$ *and the TA* $\mathcal{T}_{ad}$, *an admissible switching sequence* $\varsigma^* = (K^*_{i_1}, t^*_1)(K^*_{i_2}, t^*_2) \cdots (K^*_{i_k}, t^*_k)$ *with* $i_1, \ldots, i_k \in \mathsf{S}$ *is considered recurrent and optimal in* N *unfolding of* $\underline{\sigma}_T$ *if* ς^* *is optimal in* N *unfolding of* $\underline{\sigma}_T$ *and* $t^*_k \geq \tau_{i_k i_1}$.

The second condition captures the requirement to be satisfied by a finite length pattern to be able to recur, according to the constraints imposed by $\mathcal{T}_{ad}$. We denote such a sequence by ς^*_N.

Observe that the period $\bar{e}$ of the repeating bandwidth pattern can be very large by itself for a potentially large task set (it is the *l.c.m* of all task deadlines). In this work, we restrict our search for recurrent optimal switching sequences to some preset N levels of unfolding of the bandwidth pattern. Let us denote the switching sequence corresponding to the run of $\mathcal{T}$ which leads to minimum cost reachability of a state (location/vertex $= l$, clock valuation $= \mathbf{v}$) by $\varsigma^*(\mathcal{T}, (l, \mathbf{v}))$. Similarly, for some initial vertex $l \in L_0$, let $\varsigma^*_r(\mathcal{T}, (l, \mathbf{V}))$ denote the recurring switching sequence corresponding to the run which starts at l (with all clock valuations being '0') and reaches l with some valuation $\mathbf{v} \in \mathbf{V}$ at minimal cost. In our case, minimal cost implies minimal rejection of available bandwidth. Such minimal cost runs, if exist, can be found by restricting the set of initial vertices of $\mathcal{T}$ to $\{l\}$ and applying minimum cost reachability analysis [3,18] for the vertex l with the valuation set as per the specification of $\mathbf{V}$.

Remark 3. For the LPTA $\mathcal{T}$ constructed from a bandwidth pattern $\underline{\sigma}_T$ of length $\bar{e}$ and TA $\mathcal{T}_{ad}$ using methods outlined earlier, if ς^*_N is the admissible switching sequence recurrent and optimal in N unfolding of $\underline{\sigma}_T$, then

$$\frac{rej(\varsigma^*_N)}{|\varsigma^*_N|} = \min \left\{ \frac{rej(\varsigma)}{|\varsigma|} \,\Big|\, \varsigma = \varsigma^*_r(\mathcal{T}, (l, \{c_g = i \times \bar{e}\})), l \in L_0, i \in \mathbb{N}, 1 \leq i \leq N \right\}.$$

The quantity is non-trivial if there exists at least one switching sequence which recurs with period $\in \{i \times \bar{e} \mid i \in \mathbb{N}, 1 \leq i \leq N\}$. For computing ς^*_N, the set $\{\varsigma = \varsigma^*_r(\mathcal{T}, (l, \{c_g = i \times \bar{e}\})) \mid l \in L_0, i \in \mathbb{N}, 1 \leq i \leq N\}$ is enumerated. This essentially means running $N \times |L_0|$ number of minimum cost reachability analysis over the LPTA where the time taken for each analysis is not uniform and increases with c_g.

5   Simulation Results

We are interested in using the residue ECU bandwidth to schedule a control loop for which multiple controller options with different possible sampling rates are available. We have applied the proposed approach to a Batch Reactor Process Σ [10]. The dynamic of the system Σ is given by $\dot{\xi} = A\xi + Bv$, for matrices A and B of appropriate dimensions. For the system, we construct p stabilizing controllers $\{K_1, \ldots, K_p\}$ using classical results in linear control theory. For any $i \in S$, we find Lyapunov functions $V_i(x) := x^T M_i x$, for any $x \in \mathbb{R}^n$ and some positive definite matrix $M_i \in \mathbb{R}^{n \times n}$, for the closed loop of Σ equipped with the controller K_i. The computed Lyapunov functions V_i satisfy the inequality (4.1) with $\hat{\kappa}_i = i/2$ and the associated sampling periods $\{h_1, \ldots, h_p\}$. The controller update rates are then obtained as $f_i = (1/h_i)$. Using Theorem 4, we can compute τ_{ij} by choosing $\rho = 0.5$. We consider the WCET of controller K_i to be ω_i^c (in CPU cycles) and so one can compute the bandwidth requirements for the controllers, i.e. $\{r_1, \ldots, r_p\}$, as $r_i = \frac{\omega_i^c f_i}{H}$. Given the $\underline{\sigma}_T$ for the current platform load, we can then compute the list S of admissible controllers. Using our modeling method from Sect. 4.3, we create the LPTA specification for this scenario in UPPAAL CORA [13] to obtain the minimum cost schedule. It may be noted that we have implemented the entire methodology in the form of an automated tool-flow.

We revisit the task set $T = \{\theta_1, \theta_2\}$ with the parameters as discussed in Example 1. The different parameters for the example are listed in Table 1. Considering the overall available bandwidth (H) to be 10000 cycles per time unit with one time unit being 0.1 seconds, the residual bandwidth pattern is computed as

Table 1. A sample set of tasks

Task(θ_i)	θ_1	θ_2
Deadline(e_i)	$e_1 = 30$	$e_2 = 20$
$a_i = \alpha^u(e_i)$	2	10
WCET (CPU cycles)	30000	2000
% Bandwidth Allocated	40 %	20 %

$\underline{\sigma}_{T1} = ((l_1, v_1), \ldots)^\omega = ((1, 10), (0.8, 5), (0.4, 5), (0.6, 10), (0.8, 10), (1, 5), (0.6, 5), (0.4, 10))^\omega$. Now consider as control task a Batch Reactor Process whose matrices A and B are given in [10] as

$$A = \begin{bmatrix} 1.50 & 0 & 70 & -5 \\ -0.50 & -4 & 0 & 0.50 \\ 1 & 4 & -6 & 6 \\ 0 & 4 & 1 & -2 \end{bmatrix}, \quad B = \begin{bmatrix} 0 & 0 \\ 5 & 0 \\ 1 & -3 \\ 1 & 0 \end{bmatrix}.$$

We consider a maximum of $p = 14$ controllers. Due to lack of space, we do not provide matrices K_i and M_i. For $i \in S$, the sampling periods are $h_i = 10^{-3} \times \{2.09, 2.33, 2.60, 2.71, 2.91, 3.25, 3.61, 4.17, 4.56, 4.95, 5.38, 5.49, 5.80, 6.04\}$. The values of τ_{ij} are not mentioned in order to save space. Consider the controllers WCETs $\omega_i^c = \{23\}$. The bandwidth requirements for the controllers are computed as $r_i = \{0.96, 0.86, 0.77, 0.74, 0.69, 0.62, 0.59, 0.51, 0.49, 0.45, 0.41, 0.41, 0.40, 0.39\}$. The simulation results are summarized in Table 2 for a single instance (no unfolding) of the bandwidth pattern.

Table 2. Results for batch reactor process with $N = 1$ (no unfolding).

p	Controllers	Switching sequence	Cost
3	K_4, K_{12}, K_{14}	$[(K_{12}, 15), (K_{14}, 7), (K_{12}, 28), (K_{14}, 10)]^\omega$	14.74
4	$K_4,\ K_{12}, K_{13},\ K_{14}$	$[(K_{12}, 15), (K_{14}, 7), (K_{12}, 28),\ (K_{14}, 10)]^\omega$	1457
5	$K_4, K_{11}, \ldots, K_{14}$	$[(K_{12}, 15), (K_{13}, 5), (K_{12}, 10), (K_{14}, 15), (K_{12}, 5), (K_{13}, 10)]^\omega$	1455
6	$K_4, K_{10}, \ldots, K_{14}$	$[(K_{12}, 15), (K_{11}, 5), (K_{12}, 30),\ (K_{11}, 10)]^\omega$	12.75
9	$K_4, K_7, \ldots, K_{14}$	$[(K_{12}, 15), (K_8, 7), (K_{12}, 28), (K_8, 10)]^\omega$	6.83
10	$K_4, K_6, \ldots, K_{14}$	$[(K_{12}, 15), (K_7, 7), (K_{14}, 8), (K_{12}, 15), (K_{14}, 5), (K_7, 10)]^\omega$	593
11	$K_4, \ldots, K_{14}$	$[(K_{12}, 15), (K_6, 7), (K_{13}, 8), (K_{12}, 15), (K_{13}, 5), (K_6, 10)]^\omega$	383
12	$K_3, \ldots, K_{14}$	$[(K_4, 15), (K_5, 7), (K_{11}, 8),\ (K_4, 15), (K_{11}, 5), (K_5, 10)]^\omega$	1.43
13	$K_2, \ldots, K_{14}$	$[(K_4, 10), (K_{12}, 5), (K_3, 7), (K_{10}, 8), (K_{12}, 10), (K_4, 5), (K_{10}, 5), (K_3, 10)]^\omega$	308
14	$K_1, \ldots, K_{14}$	$[(K_4, 10), (K_{14}, 5), (K_2, 7), (K_9, 8), (K_{14}, 10), (K_4, 5), (K_9, 5), (K_2, 10)]^\omega$	1.58

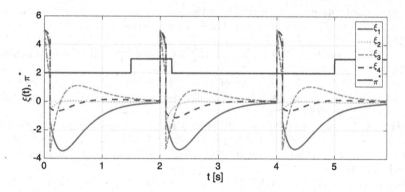

Fig. 4. Closed-loop system trajectory for Batch Reactor Process.

Figure 4 shows a simulation of the closed loop batch reactor process with $p = 3$ and step disturbances (of 0.1s width) at seconds 0, 2, and 4. It illustrates how the schedule obtained for $\underline{\sigma}_{T1}$ indeed retains the stability of the closed-loop under the considered disturbances.

References

1. Angeli, D., Sontag, E.D.: Forward completeness, unboundedness observability, and their Lyapunov characterizations. Syst. Control Lett. **38**, 209–217 (1999)
2. Anta, A., Tabuada, P.: To sample or not to sample: self-triggered control for nonlinear systems. IEEE Trans. Autom. Control **55**(9), 2030–2042 (2010)
3. Behrmann, G., Fehnker, A., Hune, T., Larsen, K.G., Pettersson, P., Romijn, J.M.T., Vaandrager, F.W.: Minimum-cost reachability for priced timed automata. In: Di Benedetto, M.D., Sangiovanni-Vincentelli, A.L. (eds.) HSCC 2001. LNCS, vol. 2034, pp. 147–161. Springer, Heidelberg (2001)
4. Branicky, M.S.: Multiple Lyapunov functions and other analysis tools for switched and hybrid systems. IEEE Trans. Autom. Control **43**(4), 475–482 (1998)

5. Cervin, A., Velasco, M., Marti, P., Camacho, A.: Optimal online sampling period assignment: theory and experiments. IEEE Trans. Control Syst. Technol. **6**(4), 902–910 (2011)
6. Chakraborty, S., Künzli, S., Thiele, L.: A general framework for analysing system properties in platform-based embedded system designs. In: DATE, vol. 3, p. 10190 (2003)
7. D'Innocenzo, A., Weiss, G., Alur, R., Isaksson, A.J., Johansson, K.H., Pappas, G.J.: Scalable scheduling algorithms for wireless networked control systems. In: IEEE International Conference on Automation Science and Engineering, CASE, pp. 409–414. IEEE (2009)
8. Goswami, D., Masrur, A., Schneider, R., Xue, C.J., Chakraborty, S.: Multirate controller design for resource-and schedule-constrained automotive ECUs. In: Proceedings of the Conference on Design, Automation and Test in Europe, pp. 1123–1126. EDA Consortium (2013)
9. Greco, L., Fontanelli, D., Bicchi, A.: Design and stability analysis for anytime control via stochastic scheduling. IEEE Trans. Autom. Control **56**(3), 571–585 (2011)
10. Green, M., Limebeer, D.J.N.: Linear Robust Control. Prentice Hall, Englewood Cliffs (1994)
11. Hespanha, J.P., et al.: Stability of switched systems with average dwell-time. In: Proceedings of the 38th IEEE Conference on Decision and Control, vol. 3, pp. 2655–2660. IEEE (1999)
12. Khalil, H.K.: Nonlinear Systems, 2nd edn. Prentice-Hall Inc., New Jersey (1996)
13. Larsen, K.G.: Priced timed automata: theory and tools. In: IARCS Annual Conference on Foundations of Software Technology and Theoretical Computer Science, FSTTCS, pp. 417–425 (2009)
14. Nešic, D., Teel, A., Carnevale, D.: Explicit computation of the sampling period in emulation of controllers for nonlinear sampled-data systems. IEEE Trans. Autom. Control **54**(3), 619–624 (2009)
15. Nešić, D., Teel, A.R., Kokotović, P.: Sufficient conditions for stabilization of sampled-data nonlinear systems via discrete-time approximations. Syst. Control Lett. **38**(4), 259–270 (1999)
16. Quagli, A., Fontanelli, D., Greco, L., Palopoli, L., Bicchi, A.: Design of embedded controllers based on anytime computing. IEEE Trans. Ind. Inf. **6**(4), 492–502 (2010)
17. Raha, R., Hazra, A., Mondal, A., Dey, S., Chakrabarti, P.P., Dasgupta, P.: Synthesis of sampling modes for adaptive control. In: IEEE International Conference on Control System, Computing and Engineering (ICCSCE), pp. 294–299. IEEE (2014)
18. Rasmussen, J.I., Larsen, K.G., Subramani, K.: Resource-optimal scheduling using priced timed automata. In: Jensen, K., Podelski, A. (eds.) TACAS 2004. LNCS, vol. 2988, pp. 220–235. Springer, Heidelberg (2004)
19. Sharifi-Kolarijani, A., Adzkiya, D., Mazo, M., Jr.: Symbolic abstractions for the scheduling of event-triggered control systems. In: Proceedings of 54st IEEE Conference on Decision and Control, Osaka, Japan, December 2015
20. Sontag, E.D.: Mathematical Control Theory, vol. 6, 2nd edn. Springer, New York (1998)
21. Sontag, E.D.: Input to state stability: basic concepts and results. In: Nistri, P., Stefani, G. (eds.) Nonlinear and Optimal Control Theory. Lecture Notes in Mathematics, vol. 1932, pp. 163–220. Springer, Berlin (2008)
22. Tabuada, P.: Event-triggered real-time scheduling of stabilizing control tasks. IEEE Trans. Autom. Control **52**(9), 1680–1685 (2007)

23. Thiele, L., Chakraborty, S., Naedele, M.: Real-time calculus for scheduling hard real-time systems. In: IEEE International Symposium on Circuits, Systems. Emerging Technologies for the 21st Century, vol. 4, pp. 101–104 (2000)
24. Weiss, G., Alur, R.: Automata based interfaces for control and scheduling. In: Bemporad, A., Bicchi, A., Buttazzo, G. (eds.) HSCC 2007. LNCS, vol. 4416, pp. 601–613. Springer, Heidelberg (2007)
25. Wiesbaden, S.A.M.: Autosar – The worldwide automotive standard for E/E systems. ATZextra worldwide 18(9), 5–12 (2013)

Real-Time Verification and Synthesis

Real-Time Synthesis is Hard!

Thomas Brihaye[1], Morgane Estiévenart[1], Gilles Geeraerts[2], Hsi-Ming Ho[1(✉)],
Benjamin Monmege[3], and Nathalie Sznajder[4]

[1] Université de Mons, Mons, Belgium
{thomas.brihaye,morgane.estievenart,hsi-ming.ho}@umons.ac.be
[2] Université libre de Bruxelles, Brussels, Belgium
gigeerae@ulb.ac.be
[3] Aix Marseille Univ, CNRS, LIF, Marseille, France
benjamin.monmege@lif.univ-mrs.fr
[4] Sorbonne Universités, UPMC, LIP6, Paris, France
nathalie.sznajder@lip6.fr

Abstract. We study the reactive synthesis problem (RS) for specifications given in Metric Interval Temporal Logic (MITL). RS is known to be undecidable in a very general setting, but on infinite words only; and only the very restrictive BResRS subcase is known to be decidable (see D'Souza *et al.* and Bouyer *et al.*). In this paper, we sharpen the decidability border of MITL synthesis. We show RS is undecidable on finite words too, and present a landscape of restrictions (both on the logic and on the possible controllers) that are still undecidable. On the positive side, we revisit BResRS and introduce an efficient on-the-fly algorithm to solve it.

1 Introduction

The design of programs that respect real-time specifications is a difficult problem with recent and promising advances. Such programs must handle thin timing behaviours, are prone to errors, and difficult to correct a posteriori. Therefore, one road to the design of correct real-time software is the use of automatic synthesis methods, that *build*, from a specification, a program which is correct by construction. To this end, *timed games* are nowadays recognised as the key foundational model for the synthesis of real-time programs. These games are played between a *controller* and an *environment*, that propose actions in the system, modelled as a *plant*. The *reactive synthesis problem* (RS) consists, given a real-time specification, in deciding whether the controller has a winning strategy ensuring that every execution of the plant consistent with this strategy (i.e., no matter the choices of the environment) satisfies the specification. As an example, consider a lift for which we want to design a software verifying certain safety conditions. In this case, the plant is a (timed) automaton, whose states record

More technical details and proofs can be found in the full version of this paper [8]. This work has been supported by The European Union Seventh Framework Programme under Grant Agreement 601148 (Cassting) and by the FRS/F.N.R.S. PDR grant SyVeRLo.

© Springer International Publishing Switzerland 2016
M. Fränzle and N. Markey (Eds.): FORMATS 2016, LNCS 9884, pp. 105–120, 2016.
DOI: 10.1007/978-3-319-44878-7_7

the current status of the lift (its floor, if it is moving, the button on which users have pushed...), as well as timing information regarding the evolution in-between the different states. On the other hand, the specification is usually given using some real-time logic: in this work, we consider mainly specifications given by a formula of MITL [2], a real-time extension of LTL. Some actions in the plant are controllable (closing the doors, moving the cart), while others belong to the environment (buttons pushed by users, exact timing of various actions inside intervals, failures...). Then, RS asks to compute a controller that performs controllable actions at the right moments, so that, for all behaviours of the environment, the lift runs correctly.

In the *untimed case*, many positive theoretical and practical results have been achieved regarding RS: for instance, when the specification is given as an LTL formula, we know that if a winning strategy exists, then there is one that can be described by a finite state machine [17]; and efficient LTL synthesis algorithms have been implemented [3,13]. Unfortunately, in the real-time setting, the picture is not so clear. Indeed, a winning strategy in a timed game might need unbounded memory to recall the full prefix of the game, which makes the real-time synthesis problem a *hard* one. This is witnessed by three papers presenting negative results: D'Souza and Madhusudan [12] and Bouyer *et al.* [4] show that RS is undecidable (on finite and infinite words) when the specification is respectively a timed automaton and an MTL formula (the two most expressive formalisms in Fig. 1). More recently, Doyen *et al.* show [11] that RS is undecidable for MITL specifications over infinite words; but leave the finite words case open.

When facing an undecidability result, one natural research direction consists in considering subcases in order to recover decidability: here, this amounts to considering fragments of the logic, or restrictions on the possible controllers. Such results can also be found in the aforementioned works. In [12], the authors consider a variant of RS, called *bounded resources reactive synthesis* (BResRS) where the number of clocks and the set of guards that the controller can use are fixed a priori, and the specification is given by means of a timed automaton. By coupling this technique with the translation of MITL into timed automata [7], one obtains a 3-EXPTIME procedure (in the finite and infinite words cases). Unfortunately, due to the high cost of translating MITL into timed automata and the need to construct its entire deterministic region automaton, this algorithm is unlikely to be amenable to implementation. Then, [4] presents an on-the-fly algorithm for BResRS with MTL specifications (MTL is a strict superset of MITL), on finite words, but their procedure runs in non-primitive recursive time.

Hence, the decidability status of the synthesis problem (with MITL requirements) still raises several questions, namely: (*i*) Can we relax the restrictions in the definition of BResRS while retaining decidability? (*ii*) Is RS decidable on finite words, as raised in [11]? (*iii*) Are there meaningful restrictions of the logic that make RS decidable? (*iv*) Can we devise an on-the-fly, efficient, algorithm that solves BResRS in 3-EXPTIME as in [12]? In the present paper, we provide answers to those questions. First, we consider the additional IRS, BPrecRS and BClockRS problems, that introduce different levels of restrictions. IRS requests the controller to be a timed automaton. BPrecRS and BClockRS are further restrictions of IRS where respectively the set of guards and the set of clocks of the controller are fixed a priori. Thus, we consider the following hierarchy of problems: RS $\supseteq$ IRS $\supseteq$ $\genfrac{}{}{0pt}{}{\mathsf{BPrecRS}}{\mathsf{BClockRS}}$ $\supseteq$ BResRS. Unfortunately, while IRS, BPrecRS and BClockRS seem to make sense in practice, they turn out to be undecidable both on finite and infinite words—an answer to points (i) and (ii). Our proofs are based on a *novel* encoding of halting problem for deterministic channel machines. By contrast, the undecidability results of [4] (for MTL) are reductions from the same problem, but their encoding relies heavily on the ability of MTL to express *punctual constraints* like 'every a event is followed by a b event *exactly* one time unit later', which is not allowed by MITL. To the best of our knowledge, our proofs are the first to perform such a reduction in a formalism that disallows punctual requirements—a somewhat unexpected result. Then, we answer point (iii) by considering a hierarchy of syntactic subsets of MITL (see Fig. 1) and showing that, for all these subsets, BPrecRS and BClockRS (hence also IRS and RS) remain undecidable, on finite and infinite words. Note that the undecidability proof of [12] cannot easily be adapted to cope with these cases, because it needs a mix of open and closed constraints; while we prove undecidable very weak fragments of MITL where only closed or only open constraints are allowed. All these negative results shape a precise picture of the decidability border for real-time synthesis (in particular, they answer open questions from [4,9,11]). On the positive side, we answer point (iv) by devising an on-the-fly algorithm to solve BResRS (in the finite words case) that runs in 3-EXPTIME. It relies on one-clock alternating timed automata (as in [4], but unlike [12] that use timed automata), and on the recently introduced *interval semantics* [7].

2   Reactive Synthesis of Timed Properties

Let Σ be a finite alphabet. A (finite) timed word[1] over Σ is a finite word $\sigma = (\sigma_1, \tau_1) \cdots (\sigma_n, \tau_n)$ over $\Sigma \times \mathbb{R}^+$ with $(\tau_i)_{1 \leqslant i \leqslant n}$ a non-decreasing sequence of non-negative real numbers. We denote by $T\Sigma^\star$ the set of finite timed words over Σ. A *timed language* is a subset L of $T\Sigma^\star$.

Timed Logics. We consider the reactive synthesis problem against various real-time logics, all of them being restrictions of Metric Temporal Logic (MTL) [14]. The logic MTL is a timed extension of LTL, where the temporal modalities are labelled with a timed interval. The formal syntax of MTL is given as follows:

$$\varphi := \top \mid a \mid \varphi \wedge \varphi \mid \neg\varphi \mid \varphi\mathsf{U}_I\varphi$$

where $a \in \Sigma$ and I is an interval over $\mathbb{R}^+$ with endpoints in $\mathbb{N} \cup \{+\infty\}$.

We consider the *pointwise semantics* and interpret MTL formulas over timed words. The semantics of a formula φ in MTL is defined inductively in the usual

---

[1] In order to keep the discussion focused and concise, we give the formal definitions for finite words only. It is straightforward to adapt them to the infinite words case.

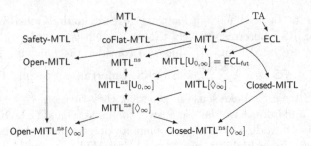

Fig. 1. All the fragments of MITL for which BPrecRS and BClockRS are undecidable (hence also RS and IRS). $A \to B$ means that A strictly contains B.

way. We recall only the semantics of U: given $\sigma = (\sigma_1, \tau_1) \cdots (\sigma_n, \tau_n) \in T\Sigma^\star$, and a position $1 \leqslant i \leqslant n$, we let $(\sigma, i) \models \varphi_1 \mathsf{U}_I \varphi_2$ if there exists $j > i$ such that $(\sigma, j) \models \varphi_2$, $\tau_j - \tau_i \in I$, and $(\sigma, k) \models \varphi_1$, for all $i < k < j$.

With $\bot := \neg\top$, we can recover the 'next' operator $\bigcirc_I \varphi := \bot\mathsf{U}_I\varphi$, and we rely on the usual shortcuts for the 'finally', 'globally' and 'dual-until' operators: $\Diamond_I \varphi := \top\mathsf{U}_I\varphi$, $\Box_I\varphi := \neg\Diamond_I\neg\varphi$ and $\varphi_1\widetilde{\mathsf{U}}_I\varphi_2 := \neg((\neg\varphi_1)\mathsf{U}_I(\neg\varphi_2))$. We also use the non-strict version of the 'until' operator $\varphi_1\overline{\mathsf{U}}_I\varphi_2$, defined as $\varphi_2 \vee (\varphi_1 \wedge \varphi_1\mathsf{U}_I\varphi_2)$ (if $0 \in I$) or $\varphi_1 \wedge \varphi_1\mathsf{U}_I\varphi_2$ (if $0 \notin I$). This notation yields the corresponding non-strict operators $\overline{\Diamond}\varphi$ and $\overline{\Box}\varphi$ in the natural way. When the interval I is the entire set of the non-negative real numbers, the subscript is often omitted. We say that σ satisfies the formula φ, written $\sigma \models \varphi$ if $(\sigma, 1) \models \varphi$, and we denote by $\mathcal{L}(\varphi)$ the set of all timed words σ such that $\sigma \models \varphi$.

We consider mainly a restriction of MTL called MITL (for Metric Interval Temporal Logic), in which the intervals are restricted to non-singular ones. We denote by Open-MITL the open fragment of MITL: in negation normal form, each subformula $\varphi_1\mathsf{U}_I\varphi_2$ has either I open or $\inf(I) = 0$ and I right-open, and each subformula $\varphi_1\widetilde{\mathsf{U}}_I\varphi_2$ has I closed. Then, a formula is in Closed-MITL if it is the negation of an Open-MITL formula. By [7], Open-MITL formulas (respectively, Closed-MITL formulas) translate to open (closed) timed automata [15], i.e., all clock constraints are strict (non-strict). Two other important fragments of MTL considered in the literature consist of Safety-MTL [16], where each subformula $\varphi_1\mathsf{U}_I\varphi_2$ has I bounded in negation normal form, and coFlat-MTL [5], where the formula satisfies the following in negation normal form: (i) in each subformula $\varphi_1\mathsf{U}_I\varphi_2$, if I is unbounded then $\varphi_2 \in$ LTL; and (ii) in each subformula $\varphi_1\widetilde{\mathsf{U}}_I\varphi_2$, if I is unbounded then $\varphi_1 \in$ LTL.

For all of these logics L, we can consider several restrictions. The restriction in which only the non-strict variants of the operators ($\overline{\Diamond}$, $\overline{\Box}$, $etc.$) are allowed is denoted by L^{ns}. The fragment in which all the intervals used in the formula are either unbounded, or have a left endpoint equal to 0 is denoted by $\mathsf{L}[\mathsf{U}_{0,\infty}]$. In this case, the interval I can be replaced by an expression of the form $\sim c$, with $c \in \mathbb{N}$, and $\sim \in \{<, >, \leqslant, \geqslant\}$. It is known that $\mathsf{MITL}[\mathsf{U}_{0,\infty}]$ is expressively equivalent to $\mathsf{ECL}_{\mathsf{fut}}$ [18], which is itself a syntactic fragment of Event-Clock Logic

(ECL). Finally, $\mathsf{L}[\Diamond_\infty]$ stands for the logic where 'until' operators only appear in the form of $\Diamond_I$ or $\Box_I$ with intervals I of the shape $[a,\infty)$ or (a,∞).

Symbolic Transition Systems. Let X be a finite set of variables, called clocks. The set $\mathcal{G}(X)$ of *clock constraints* g over X is defined by: $g := \top \mid g \wedge g \mid x \bowtie c$, where $\bowtie \in \{<, \leqslant, =, \geqslant, >\}$, $x \in X$ and $c \in \mathbb{Q}^+$. A *valuation* over X is a mapping $\nu: X \to \mathbb{R}^+$. The satisfaction of a constraint g by a valuation ν is defined in the usual way and noted $\nu \models g$, and $[\![g]\!]$ is the set of valuations ν satisfying g. For $t \in \mathbb{R}^+$, we let $\nu + t$ be the valuation defined by $(\nu + t)(x) = \nu(x) + t$ for all $x \in X$. For $R \subseteq X$, we let $\nu[R \leftarrow 0]$ be the valuation defined by $(\nu[R \leftarrow 0])(x) = 0$ if $x \in R$, and $(\nu[R \leftarrow 0])(x) = \nu(x)$ otherwise.

Following the terminology of [4,12], a *granularity* is a triple $\mu = (X, m, K)$ where X is a finite set of clocks, $m \in \mathbb{N} \setminus \{0\}$, and $K \in \mathbb{N}$. A constraint g is μ-granular if $g \in \mathcal{G}(X)$ and each constant in g is of the form $\frac{\alpha}{m}$ with an integer $\alpha \leqslant K$. A *symbolic alphabet* Γ based on (Σ, X) is a finite subset of $\Sigma \times \mathcal{G}^{\mathrm{atom}}_{m,K}(X) \times 2^X$, where $\mathcal{G}^{\mathrm{atom}}_{m,K}(X)$ denotes all atomic (X, m, K)-granular clock constraints (i.e., clock constraints g such that $[\![g]\!] = [\![g']\!]$ or $[\![g]\!] \cap [\![g']\!] = \emptyset$, for every (X, m, K)-granular clock constraint g'). Such a symbolic alphabet Γ is said μ-granular. A *symbolic word* $\gamma = (\sigma_1, g_1, R_1) \cdots (\sigma_n, g_n, R_n)$ over Γ generates a set of timed words over Σ, denoted by $tw(\gamma)$ such that $\sigma \in tw(\gamma)$ if $\sigma = (\sigma_1, \tau_1) \cdots (\sigma_n, \tau_n)$, and there is a sequence $(\nu_i)_{0 \leqslant i \leqslant n}$ of valuations with ν_0 the zero valuation, and for all $1 \leqslant i \leqslant n$, $\nu_{i-1} + \tau_i - \tau_{i-1} \models g_i$ and $\nu_i = (\nu_{i-1} + \tau_i - \tau_{i-1})[R_i \leftarrow 0]$ (assuming $\tau_0 = 0$). Intuitively, each (σ_i, g_i, R_i) means that action σ_i is performed, with guard g_i satisfied and clocks in R_i reset.

A *symbolic transition system* (STS) over a symbolic alphabet Γ based on (Σ, X) is a tuple $\mathcal{T} = (S, s_0, \Delta, S_f)$ where S is a possibly infinite set of locations, $s_0 \in S$ is the initial location, $\Delta \subseteq S \times \Gamma \times S$ is the transition relation, and $S_f \subseteq S$ is a set of accepting locations (omitted if all locations are accepting). An STS with finitely many locations is a *timed automaton* (TA) [1]. For a finite path $\pi = s_1 \xrightarrow{b_1} s_2 \xrightarrow{b_2} \cdots \xrightarrow{b_n} s_{n+1}$ of $\mathcal{T}$ (i.e., such that $(s_i, b_i, s_{i+1}) \in \Delta$ for all $1 \leqslant i \leqslant n$), the *trace* of π is the word $b_1 b_2 \cdots b_n$, and π is *accepting* if $s_{n+1} \in S_f$. We denote by $\mathcal{L}(\mathcal{T})$ the language of $\mathcal{T}$, defined as the timed words associated to symbolic words that are traces of finite accepting paths starting in s_0. We say that a timed action $(t, \sigma) \in \mathbb{R}^+ \times \Sigma$ is *enabled* in $\mathcal{T}$ at a pair (s, ν), denoted by $(t, \sigma) \in \mathsf{En}_{\mathcal{T}}(s, \nu)$, if there exists a transition $(s, (\sigma, g, R), s') \in \delta$ such that $\nu + t \models g$. The STS $\mathcal{T}$ is *time-deterministic* if there are no distinct transitions $(s, (\sigma, g_1, R_1), s_1)$ and $(s, (\sigma, g_2, R_2), s_2)$ in Δ and no valuation ν such that $\nu \models g_1$ and $\nu \models g_2$. In a time-deterministic STS $\mathcal{T} = (S, s_0, \delta, S_f)$, for all timed words σ, there is at most one path π whose trace γ verifies $\sigma \in tw(\gamma)$. In that case, we denote by $\delta(s_0, \sigma)$ the unique (if it exists) pair (s, ν) (where $s \in S$ and ν is a valuation) reached after reading $\sigma \in tw(\gamma)$.

Example 1. A time-deterministic TA $\mathcal{P}$ with a single clock x is depicted in Fig. 2. Intuitively, it accepts all timed words σ of the form $w_1 w_2 \cdots w_n$ where each w_i is a timed word such that (i) either $w_i = (b, \tau)$; (ii) or w_i is a sequence of a's

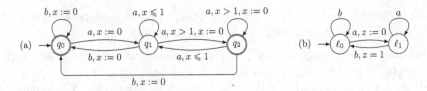

Fig. 2. (a) A time-deterministic STS $\mathcal{P}$ with $X = \{x\}$. Instead of depicting a transition per letter (a, g, R) (with g atomic), we merge several transitions; e.g., we skip the guard, when all the possible guards are admitted. $x := 0$ denotes the reset of x. (b) A time-deterministic STS $\mathcal{T}$. It is a controller to realise $\varphi = \Box(a \Rightarrow \Diamond_{\leqslant 1} b)$ with plant $\mathcal{P}$.

(starting at time stamp τ) of duration at most 1; and w_{i+1} is either of the form (b, τ'), or of the form (a, τ') with $\tau' - \tau > 1$.

Reactive Synthesis with Plant. To define our reactive synthesis problems, we partition the alphabet Σ into controllable and environment actions Σ_C and Σ_E. Following [4,12], the system is modelled by a time-deterministic TA $\mathcal{P} = (Q, q_0, \delta_{\mathcal{P}}, Q_f)$, called the *plant*[2]. Observe that the plant has accepting locations: only those runs ending in a final location of the plant will be checked against the specification. We start by recalling the definition of the general *reactive synthesis* family of problems (RS) [10,11]. It consists in a game played by the controller and the environment, that interact to create a timed word as follows. We start with the empty timed word, and then, at each round, the controller and the environment propose timed actions to be performed by the system— therefore, they must be firable in the plant $\mathcal{P}$—respectively (t, a) and (t', b), with $t, t' \in \mathbb{R}^+$, $a \in \Sigma_C$ and $b \in \Sigma_E$. The timed action with the shortest[3] delay (or the environment action if the controller decides not to propose any action) is performed, and added to the current play for the next round. If both players propose the same delay, we resolve the time non-deterministically.

On those games, we consider a parameterised family of reactive synthesis problems denoted $\mathsf{RS}_s^b(\mathcal{F})$, where $s \in \{u, d\}$; $b \in \{\star, \omega\}$; and $\mathcal{F}$ is one of the formalisms in Fig. 1. An instance of $\mathsf{RS}_s^b(\mathcal{F})$ is given by a specification $S \in \mathcal{F}$ and a plant $\mathcal{P}$, which are interpreted over finite words when $b = \star$ and infinite words when $b = \omega$. The timed language $\mathcal{L}(S)$ is a specification of desired behaviours when $s = d$ and undesired behaviours when $s = u$. Then, $\mathsf{RS}_s^b(\mathcal{F})$ asks whether there exists a strategy for the controller such that all the words in the outcome of this strategy are in $\mathcal{L}(S)$ (or outside $\mathcal{L}(S)$) when we consider desired (or undesired) behaviours (when $s = \omega$, the definition of $\mathcal{L}(S)$ must be the infinite words one). If this is the case, we say that S is *(finite-word) realisable* for the problem under study. For example, $\mathsf{RS}_u^\omega(\mathsf{MITL})$ is the reactive synthesis problem

---

[2] We assume that for every location q and every valuation ν, there exists a timed action $(t, \sigma) \in \mathbb{R}^+ \times \Sigma$ and a transition $(q, (\sigma, g, R), q') \in \delta_{\mathcal{P}}$ such that $\nu + t \models g$.

[3] Observe that this is different from [4,12], where the environment can always prevent the controller from playing, even by proposing a longer delay. We claim our definition is more reasonable in practice but all proofs can be adapted to both definitions.

where the inputs are a formula of MITL and a plant, which are interpreted over the infinite words semantics, and where the MITL formula specifies the behaviours that the controller should avoid. Unfortunately, the variants RS are too general, and a winning strategy might require unbounded memory:

Example 2. Consider the alphabet $\Sigma = \Sigma_C \uplus \Sigma_E$ with $\Sigma_C = \{b\}$ and $\Sigma_E = \{a\}$, a plant $\mathcal{P}$ accepting $T\Sigma^*$, and the specification defined by the MTL formula $\varphi = \Box((a \wedge \Diamond_{\geqslant 1} a) \Rightarrow \Diamond_{=1} b)$. Clearly, a winning strategy for the controller is to remember the time stamps $\tau_1, \tau_2, \ldots$ of all a's, and always propose to play action b one time unit later (note that if the environment blocks the time to prevent the controller from playing its b, the controller wins). However this requires to memorise an unbounded number of time stamps with a great precision.

Restrictions on RS. In practice, it makes more sense to restrict the winning strategy of the controller to be implementable by an STS, which has finitely many clocks (and if possible finitely many locations). Let us define formally what it means for an STS $\mathcal{T} = (S, s_0, \delta)$ to control a plant $\mathcal{P}$. We let $T\Sigma^*_{\mathcal{T},\mathcal{P}}$ be the *set of timed words consistent with $\mathcal{T}$ and $\mathcal{P}$*, defined as the smallest set containing the empty timed word, and closed by the following operations. Let σ be a word in $T\Sigma^*_{\mathcal{T},\mathcal{P}}$, with $(q, \nu_\mathcal{P}) = \delta_\mathcal{P}(q_0, \sigma)$, $T = 0$ if $\sigma = \varepsilon$, and $(c, T) \in \Sigma \times \mathbb{R}^+$ be the last letter of σ otherwise. Then, we extend σ as follows:

- either the controller proposes to play a controllable action (t, b), because it corresponds to a transition that is firable both in the controller and the plant. This action can be played (σ is extended by $(b, T+t)$), as well as any environment action (t', a) with $t' \leqslant t$ (the environment can overtake the controller). Formally, if $\delta(s_0, \sigma) = (s, \nu)$ is defined and $\mathsf{En}_\mathcal{T}(s, \nu) \cap \mathsf{En}_\mathcal{P}(q, \nu_\mathcal{P}) \cap (\mathbb{R}^+ \times \Sigma_C) \neq \emptyset$: for all $(t, b) \in \mathsf{En}_\mathcal{T}(s, \nu) \cap \mathsf{En}_\mathcal{P}(q, \nu_\mathcal{P}) \cap (\mathbb{R}^+ \times \Sigma_C)$, we let $\sigma \cdot (b, T+t) \in T\Sigma^*_{\mathcal{T},\mathcal{P}}$ and $\sigma \cdot (a, T + t') \in T\Sigma^*_{\mathcal{T},\mathcal{P}}$ for all $t' \leqslant t$ and $a \in \Sigma_E$ such that $(t', a) \in \mathsf{En}_\mathcal{P}(q, \nu_\mathcal{P})$.
- Or the controller proposes nothing, then the environment can play all its enabled actions. Formally, if $\delta(s_0, \sigma) = (s, \nu)$ is defined and $\mathsf{En}_\mathcal{T}(s, \nu) \cap \mathsf{En}_\mathcal{P}(q, \nu_\mathcal{P}) \cap (\mathbb{R}^+ \times \Sigma_C) = \emptyset$ and $\mathsf{En}_\mathcal{P}(q, \nu_\mathcal{P}) \cap (\mathbb{R}^+ \times \Sigma_E) \neq \emptyset$, we let $\sigma \cdot (a, T + t') \in T\Sigma^*_{\mathcal{T},\mathcal{P}}$ for all $(t', a) \in \mathsf{En}_\mathcal{P}(q, \nu_\mathcal{P}) \cap (\mathbb{R}^+ \times \Sigma_E)$.
- Otherwise, we declare that every possible future allowed by the plant is valid, i.e., we let $\sigma \cdot \sigma' \in T\Sigma^*_{\mathcal{T},\mathcal{P}}$ for all $\sigma \cdot \sigma' \in \mathcal{L}(\mathcal{P})$. This happens when the controller proposes only actions that are not permitted by the plant while the environment has no enabled actions; or when the controller lost track of a move of the environment during the past.

Then, the MTL *implementable reactive synthesis* problem $\mathsf{IRS}^*_d(\mathsf{MTL})$ (on finite words and with desired behaviours) is to decide, given a plant $\mathcal{P}$ and a specification given as an MTL formula φ, whether there exists a set of clocks X, a symbolic alphabet Γ based on (Σ, X), and a time-deterministic STS $\mathcal{T}$ over Γ such that $T\Sigma^*_{\mathcal{T},\mathcal{P}} \cap \mathcal{L}(\mathcal{P}) \subseteq \mathcal{L}(\varphi) \cup \{\varepsilon\}$.[4]

---

[4] Empty word ε is added for convenience, in case it is not already in $\mathcal{L}(\varphi)$.

While the definition of $\mathsf{IRS}_d^\star(\mathsf{MTL})$ is more practical than that of $\mathsf{RS}_d^\star(\mathsf{MTL})$, it might still be too general because the clocks and symbolic alphabet the controller can use are not fixed *a priori*. In the spirit of [4,12], we define three variants of IRS. First, the MTL *bounded-resources synthesis problem* $\mathsf{BResRS}_d^\star(\mathsf{MTL})$ is a restriction of $\mathsf{IRS}_d^\star(\mathsf{MTL})$ where the granularity of the controller is fixed: given an MTL formula φ, and a granularity $\mu = (X, m, K)$, it asks whether there exists a μ-granular symbolic alphabet Γ based on (Σ, X), and a time-deterministic STS $\mathcal{T}$ over Γ such that $T\Sigma_{\mathcal{T},\mathcal{P}}^\star \cap \mathcal{L}(\mathcal{P}) \subseteq \mathcal{L}(\varphi) \cup \{\varepsilon\}$. Second, the less restrictive MTL *bounded-precision synthesis problem* $\mathsf{BPrecRS}_d^\star(\mathsf{MTL})$ and MTL *bounded-clocks synthesis problem* $\mathsf{BClockRS}_d^\star(\mathsf{MTL})$ are the variants of IRS where *only* the precision and *only* the number of clocks are fixed, respectively. Formally, $\mathsf{BPrecRS}_d^\star(\mathsf{MTL})$ asks, given an MTL formula φ, $m \in \mathbb{N}$, and $K \in \mathbb{N}\setminus\{0\}$, whether there are a finite set X of clocks, an (X, m, K)-granular symbolic alphabet Γ based on (Σ, X), and a time-deterministic STS $\mathcal{T}$ over Γ such that $T\Sigma_{\mathcal{T},\mathcal{P}}^\star \cap \mathcal{L}(\mathcal{P}) \subseteq \mathcal{L}(\varphi) \cup \{\varepsilon\}$. $\mathsf{BClockRS}_d^\star(\mathsf{MTL})$ is defined similarly with an MTL formula φ, and a finite set of clocks X (instead of m, K) as input.

While we have defined IRS, BPrecRS, BClockRS and BResRS for MTL requirements, and in the finite words, desired behaviours case only, these definitions extend to all the other cases we have considered for RS: infinite words, undesired behaviours, and all fragments of MTL. We rely on the same notations as for RS, writing for instance $\mathsf{BPrecRS}_u^\omega(\mathsf{MITL})$ or $\mathsf{BClockRS}_d^\omega(\mathsf{coFlat\text{-}MTL})$, etc.

Example 3. Consider the instance of $\mathsf{IRS}_d^\star(\mathsf{MITL})$ where the plant accepts $T\Sigma^\star$ and the specification is $\varphi = \Box(a \Rightarrow \Diamond_{\leqslant 1} b)$. This instance is negative (φ is not realisable), since, for every time-deterministic STS $\mathcal{T}$, $(a, 0) \in T\Sigma_{\mathcal{T},\mathcal{P}}^\star$ but is not in $\mathcal{L}(\varphi)$. However, if we consider now the plant $\mathcal{P}$ in Fig. 2(a), we claim that the STS $\mathcal{T}$ with one clock z depicted in Fig. 2(b) realises φ. Indeed, this controller resets its clock z each time it sees the first a in a sequence of a's, and proposes to play a b when z has value 1, which ensures that all a's read so far are followed by a b within 1 time unit. The restrictions enforced by the plant (which can be regarded as a sort of fairness condition) ensure that this is sufficient to realise φ for $\mathsf{IRS}_d^\star(\mathsf{MITL})$. This also means that φ is realisable for $\mathsf{BPrecRS}_d^\star(\mathsf{MITL})$ with precision $m = 1$ and $K = 1$; for $\mathsf{BClockRS}_d^\star(\mathsf{MITL})$ with set of clocks $X = \{z\}$; and for $\mathsf{BResRS}_d^\star(\mathsf{MITL})$ with granularity $\mu = (\{z\}, 1, 1)$.

3   BPrecRS and BClockRS are Undecidable

Let us show that all the variants of BPrecRS and BClockRS are undecidable, whatever formalism from Fig. 1 we consider for the specification. This entails that all variants of RS and IRS are undecidable too (in particular $\mathsf{RS}_d^\star(\mathsf{ECL})$ which settles an open question of [11] negatively). To this aim, we show undecidability on the weakest formalisms in Fig. 1, namely: coFlat-MTL, Safety-MTL, Open-MITL$^{\mathrm{ns}}[\Diamond_\infty]$ and Closed-MITL$^{\mathrm{ns}}[\Diamond_\infty]$. Similar results have been shown for MTL (and for Safety-MTL as desired specifications) in [4] via a reduction from the halting problem for deterministic channel machines, but their proof depends crucially on *punctual* formulas of the form $\Box(a \Rightarrow \Diamond_{=1}b)$ which are not expressible in MITL. Our original contribution here is to adapt these ideas to a formalism without punctual constraints, which is non-trivial.

Deterministic Channel Machines. A *deterministic channel machine* (DCM) $\mathcal{S} = \langle S, s_0, s_{halt}, M, \Delta \rangle$ can be seen as a finite automaton equipped with an unbounded fifo channel, where S is a finite set of states, s_0 is the initial state, s_{halt} is the halting state, M is a finite set of messages and $\Delta \subseteq S \times \{m!, m? \mid m \in M\} \times S$ is the transition relation satisfying the following *determinism* hypothesis: (i) $(s, a, s') \in \Delta$ and $(s, a, s'') \in \Delta$ implies $s' = s''$; (ii) if $(s, m!, s') \in \Delta$ then it is the only outgoing transition from s.

The semantics is described by a graph $G(\mathcal{S})$ with nodes labelled by (s, x) where $s \in S$ and $x \in M^*$ is the channel content. The edges in $G(\mathcal{S})$ are defined as follows: (i) $(s, x) \xrightarrow{m!} (s', xm)$ if $(s, m!, s') \in \Delta$; and (ii) $(s, mx) \xrightarrow{m?} (s', x)$ if $(s, m?, s') \in \Delta$. Intuitively, these correspond to messages being *written to* or *read from* the channel. A *computation* of $\mathcal{S}$ is then a path in $G(\mathcal{S})$. The *halting problem* for DCMs asks, given a DCM $\mathcal{S}$, whether there is a computation from (s_0, ε) to (s_{halt}, x) in $G(\mathcal{S})$ for some $x \in M^*$.

Proposition 1 ([6]). *The halting problem for DCMs is undecidable.*

It should be clear that $\mathcal{S}$ has a unique computation. Without loss of generality, we assume that s_{halt} is the only state in S with no outgoing transition. It follows that exactly one of the following must be true: (i) $\mathcal{S}$ has a halting computation; (ii) $\mathcal{S}$ has an infinite computation not reaching s_{halt}; (iii) $\mathcal{S}$ is blocking at some point, i.e., $\mathcal{S}$ is unable to proceed at some state $s \neq s_{halt}$ (with only *read* outgoing transitions) either because the channel is empty or the message at the head of the channel does not match any of the outgoing transitions from s.

Finite-Word Reactive Synthesis for MITL. We now give a reduction from the halting problem for DCMs to $RS_d^*(MITL)$. The idea is to devise a suitable MITL formula such that in the corresponding timed game, the environment and the controller are forced to propose actions in turn, according to the semantics of the DCM. Each prefix of the (unique) computation of the DCM is thus encoded as a play, i.e., a finite timed word. More specifically, given a DCM $\mathcal{S}$, we require each play to satisfy the following conditions:

C1 The action sequence of the play (i.e., omitting all timestamps) is of the form $Nil_C^* s_0 a_0 s_1 a_1 \cdots$ where Nil_C is a special action of the controller and $(s_i, a_i, s_{i+1}) \in \Delta$ for each $i \geqslant 0$.

C2 Each s_i comes with no delay and no two *write* or *read* actions occur at the same time, i.e., if $(a_i, \tau)(s_{i+1}, \tau')(a_{i+1}; \tau'')$ is a substring of the play then $\tau = \tau'$ and $\tau < \tau''$.

C3 Each $m?$ is preceded exactly 1 time unit (t.u.) earlier by a corresponding $m!$

C4 Each $m!$ is followed exactly 1 t.u. later by a corresponding $m?$ if there are actions that occur at least 1 t.u. after the $m!$ in question.

To this end, we construct a formula of the form $\Phi \Rightarrow \Psi$ where Φ and Ψ are conjunctions of the conditions that the environment and the controller must adhere to, respectively. In particular, the environment must propose s_i's according to the transition relation (C1 and C2) whereas the controller is responsible for proposing $\{m!, m? \mid m \in M\}$ properly so that a correct encoding of the writing and reading of messages is maintained (C2, C3, and C4). When both players obey these conditions, the play faithfully encodes a prefix of the computation of $\mathcal{S}$, and the controller wins the play. If the environment attempts to ruin the encoding, the formula will be satisfied, i.e., the play will be winning for the controller. Conversely, if the controller attempts to cheat by, say, reading a message that is not at the head of the channel, the environment can pinpoint this error (by proposing a special action $Check^{\leftarrow}$) and falsify the formula, i.e., the play will be losing for the controller. In what follows, let $\Sigma_E = S \cup \{Check^{\leftarrow}, Check^{\rightarrow}, Lose, Nil_E\}$, $\Sigma_C = \{m!, m? \mid m \in M\} \cup \{Win, Nil_C\}$, $\varphi_E = \bigvee_{e \in \Sigma_E} e$, $\varphi_C = \bigvee_{c \in \Sigma_C} c$, $\varphi_S = \bigvee_{s \in S} s$, $\varphi_W = \bigvee_{m \in M} m!$, $\varphi_R = \bigvee_{m \in M} m?$ and $\varphi_{WR} = \varphi_W \vee \varphi_R$. Let us now present the formulas $\varphi_1, \varphi_2, \ldots$ and $\psi_1, \psi_2, \ldots$ needed to define Φ and Ψ.

We start by formulas enforcing condition C1. The play should start from s_0, alternate between E-actions and C-actions, and the controller can win the play if the environment does not proceed promptly, and vice versa for the environment:

$$\varphi_1 = \neg\big(Nil_C \overline{\mathsf{U}}(\varphi_E \wedge \neg s_0)\big) \qquad \psi_1 = \neg\big(Nil_C \overline{\mathsf{U}}(\varphi_C \wedge \neg Nil_C)\big)$$
$$\varphi_2 = \neg\overline{\Diamond}(\varphi_E \wedge \bigcirc_{\leqslant 1}\varphi_E) \qquad \psi_2 = \neg\overline{\Diamond}(\varphi_C \wedge \bigcirc_{\leqslant 1}\varphi_C)$$
$$\varphi_3 = \neg\overline{\Diamond}(\varphi_{WR} \wedge \bigcirc Win) \qquad \psi_3 = \neg\overline{\Diamond}(\varphi_S \wedge \neg s_{halt} \wedge \bigcirc Lose).$$

Both players must also comply to the semantics of $\mathcal{S}$:

$$\varphi_4 = \bigwedge_{\substack{(s,a,s') \in \Delta \\ b \notin \{s', Check^{\leftarrow}, Check^{\rightarrow}\}}} \neg\overline{\Diamond}(s \wedge \bigcirc a \wedge \bigcirc \bigcirc b) \qquad \psi_4 = \bigwedge_{\substack{s \neq s_{halt} \\ \forall s' \, (s,a,s') \notin \Delta}} \neg\overline{\Diamond}(s \wedge \bigcirc a).$$

Once the encoding has ended, both players can only propose Nil actions:

$$\varphi_5 = \neg\overline{\Diamond}\big((s_{halt} \vee Check^{\leftarrow} \vee Check^{\rightarrow} \vee Lose \vee Win) \wedge \Diamond(\varphi_E \wedge \neg Nil_E)\big)$$
$$\psi_5 = \neg\overline{\Diamond}\big((s_{halt} \vee Check^{\leftarrow} \vee Check^{\rightarrow} \vee Lose \vee Win) \wedge \Diamond(\varphi_C \wedge \neg Nil_C)\big).$$

For condition C2, we simply state that the environment can only propose delay 0 whereas the controller always proposes a positive delay:

$$\varphi_6 = \neg\overline{\Diamond}(\varphi_{WR} \wedge \bigcirc_{>0}\varphi_E) \qquad \psi_6 = \overline{\square}(\varphi_S \wedge \neg s_{halt} \wedge \bigcirc \varphi_{WR} \implies \bigcirc_{>0}\varphi_{WR}).$$

Let us finally introduce formulae to enforce conditions C3 and C4. Note that a requirement like 'every write is matched by a read *exactly* one time unit later' is easy to express in MTL, but not so in MITL. Nevertheless, we manage to translate C3 and C4 in MITL by exploiting the game interaction between the players. Intuitively, we allow the cheating player to be punished by the other. Formally, to ensure C3, we allow the environment to play a $Check^{\leftarrow}$ action after any $m?$ to check that this read has indeed occurred 1 t.u. after the corresponding $m!$. Assuming such a $Check^{\leftarrow}$ has occurred, the controller must enforce:

$$\psi^{\leftarrow} = \bigvee_{m \in M} \overline{\Diamond}(m! \wedge \overline{\Diamond}_{\leqslant 1}(m? \wedge \bigcirc Check^{\leftarrow}) \wedge \overline{\Diamond}_{\geqslant 1}(m? \wedge \bigcirc Check^{\leftarrow})).$$

Now, to ensure C4, the environment may play a $Check^{\rightarrow}$ action at least 1 t.u. after a write on the channel. If this $Check^{\rightarrow}$ is the first action that occurs more than 1 t.u. after the writing (expressed by the formula $\psi^{\rightarrow}_{fst}$), we must check that the writing has been correctly addressed, i.e., there has been an action exactly 1 t.u. after, *and* this action was the corresponding reading:

$$\psi^{\rightarrow}_{fst} = \overline{\Diamond}(\varphi_W \wedge \overline{\Diamond}_{<1}\theta^{\rightarrow}_1 \wedge \overline{\Diamond}_{\geqslant 1}\theta^{\rightarrow}_0)$$
$$\psi^{\rightarrow} = \neg\overline{\Diamond}(\varphi_W \wedge \overline{\Diamond}_{<1}\theta^{\rightarrow}_1 \wedge \overline{\Diamond}_{>1}\theta^{\rightarrow}_0) \wedge \psi^{\leftarrow}[Check^{\rightarrow}/Check^{\leftarrow}]$$

where $\psi^{\leftarrow}[Check^{\rightarrow}/Check^{\leftarrow}]$ is the formula obtained by replacing all $Check^{\leftarrow}$ with $Check^{\rightarrow}$ in $\psi^{\leftarrow}$, $\theta^{\rightarrow}_0 = \varphi_{WR} \wedge \bigcirc Check^{\rightarrow}$ and $\theta^{\rightarrow}_1 = \varphi_{WR} \wedge \bigcirc \varphi_S \wedge \bigcirc\bigcirc \theta^{\rightarrow}_0$. In the overall, we consider:

$$\varphi_7 = \bigwedge_{m \in M} \neg\overline{\Diamond}(m! \wedge \bigcirc Check^{\leftarrow})$$
$$\psi_7 = (\overline{\Diamond} Check^{\leftarrow} \Rightarrow \psi^{\leftarrow}) \wedge ((\overline{\Diamond} Check^{\rightarrow} \wedge \psi^{\rightarrow}_{fst}) \Rightarrow \psi^{\rightarrow}).$$

Now let $\Phi = \bigwedge_{1 \leqslant i \leqslant 7} \varphi_i$, $\Psi = \bigwedge_{1 \leqslant i \leqslant 7} \psi_i$ and $\Omega = \Phi \Rightarrow \Psi$.

Proposition 2. *Ω is finite-word realisable if and only if either (i) S has a halting computation, or (ii) S has an infinite computation not reaching s_{halt}.*[5]

Proof (Sketch). If (i) or (ii) is true, Ω can be realised by the controller faithfully encoding a computation of S. If E proposes $Check^{\leftarrow}$ or $Check^{\rightarrow}$, the play will satisfy ψ_7. Otherwise, if S has an infinite computation not reaching s_{halt}, the play can grow unboundedly and will satisfy all ψ's, hence Ω.

Conversely, if S is blocking, then Ω is not realisable. Indeed, either the controller encodes S correctly, but then at some point it will not be able to propose any action, and will be subsumed by the environment that will play $Lose$. Or the controller will try to cheat, by (1) inserting an action $m?$ not matched by a corresponding $m!$ 1 t.u. earlier, or (2) writing a message $m!$ that will not be read 1 t.u. later. For the first case, the environment can then play $Check^{\leftarrow}$ right after the incorrect $m?$, and the play will violate $\psi^{\leftarrow}$, hence ψ_7 and Ω. For the second case, the environment will play $Check^{\rightarrow}$ after the first action occurring 1 t.u. after the unfaithful $m!$ and the play will violate $\psi^{\rightarrow}$. □

Now let $\Omega' = \Phi \Rightarrow \Psi \wedge \Box(\neg s_{halt})$, i.e., we further require the computation not to reach s_{halt}. The following proposition can be proved almost identically.

---

[5] Observe that the proof does not require any plant (or uses the trivial plant accepting $T\Sigma^{\star}$). This entails undecidability of the 'realisability problem', which is more restrictive than $\mathsf{RS}^{\star}_d$ and another difference with respect to the proof in [4].

Proposition 3. Ω' is finite-word realisable if and only if S has an infinite computation not reaching s_{halt}.

Corollary 1. S has a halting computation if and only if Ω is finite-word realisable but Ω' is not finite-word realisable.

It follows that if $RS_d^\star(MITL)$ is decidable, we can decide whether S has a halting computation. But the latter is known to be undecidable. Hence:

Theorem 1. $RS_d^\star(MITL)$ is undecidable.

Theorem 1 and its proof are the core results from which we will derive all other undecidability results announced at the beginning of the section.

Remark 1. One may show that RS_d^ω is undecidable for formulas of the form $\Phi \Rightarrow \Psi$ where Φ and Ψ are conjunctions of Safety-MTL$[U_{0,\infty}]$ formulas by rewriting φ_i's and ψ_i's. This answers an open question of [9].

BPrecRSand BClockRSfor Safety-MTL, coFlat-MTL, and MITL. In the proof of Proposition 2, if S actually halts, the number of messages present in the channel during the (unique) computation is bounded by a number N. It follows that the strategy of C can be implemented as a bounded-precision controller (with precision $(m, K) = (1, 1)$ and N clocks) or a bounded-clocks controller (with precision $(m, K) = (\frac{1}{N}, 1)$ and a single clock). Corollary 1 therefore holds also for the bounded-precision and bounded-clocks cases, and $BPrecRS_d^\star(MITL)$ and $BClockRS_d^\star(MITL)$ are undecidable. By further modifying the formulas used in the proof of Proposition 2, we show that the undecidability indeed holds even when we allow only unary non-strict modalities with lower-bound constraints and require the constraints to be exclusively strict or non-strict, hence $BPrecRS_d^\star$ and $BClockRS_d^\star$ are undecidable too on Open-MITL$^{ns}[\lozenge_\infty]$ and Closed-MITL$^{ns}[\lozenge_\infty]$. This entails undecidability in the *undesired specifications* case because the negation of an Open-MITL$^{ns}[\lozenge_\infty]$ is a Closed-MITL$^{ns}[\lozenge_\infty]$ formula and vice-versa. Finally, we can extend our proofs to the infinite words case, hence:

Theorem 2. $RS_s^b(L)$, $IRS_s^b(L)$, $BPrecRS_s^b(L)$ and $BClockRS_s^b(L)$ are undecidable for $L \in \{Open\text{-}MITL^{ns}[\lozenge_\infty], Closed-MITL^{ns}[\lozenge_\infty]\}$, $s \in \{u, d\}$ and $b \in \{\star, \omega\}$.

This result extends the previous undecidability proofs of [11] ($RS_d^\omega(ECL)$ is undecidable), and of [12] ($IRS_d^\star(TA)$ and $IRS_u^\star(TA)$ are undecidable). In light of these previous works, our result is somewhat surprising as the undecidability proof in [12] is via a reduction from the universality problem for timed automata, yet this universality problem becomes decidable when all constraints are strict [15].

Finally, it remains to handle the cases of Safety-MTL and coFlat-MTL. Contrary to the case of MTL, the infinite-word satisfiability problem is decidable for Safety-MTL [16] and the infinite-word model-checking problem is decidable for both Safety-MTL [16] and coFlat-MTL [5]. Nevertheless, our synthesis problems remain undecidable for these fragments. In particular, the result on Safety-MTL answers an open question of [4] negatively:

Theorem 3. $RS_s^b(L)$, $IRS_s^b(L)$, $BPrecRS_s^b(L)$ and $BClockRS_s^b(L)$ are undecidable for $L \in \{Safety\text{-}MTL, coFlat\text{-}MTL\}$, $s \in \{u, d\}$ and $b \in \{\star, \omega\}$.

4   Bounded-Resources Synthesis for **MITL** Properties

We have now characterised rather precisely the decidability border for MITL synthesis problems. In light of these results, we focus now on $\mathsf{BResRS}^\star_d(\mathsf{MITL})$ (since MITL is closed under complement, one can derive an algorithm for $\mathsf{BResRS}^\star_u(\mathsf{MITL})$ from our solution). Recall that the algorithm of D'Souza and Madhusudan [12], associated with the translation of MITL into TA [2] yields a 3EXPTIME procedure for these two problems. Unfortunately this procedure is unlikely to be amenable to efficient implementation. This is due to the translation from MITL to TA and the need to determinise a region automaton, which is known to be hard in practice. On the other hand, Bouyer *et al.* [4] present a procedure for $\mathsf{BResRS}^\star_d(\mathsf{MTL})$ (which can thus be applied to MITL requirements). This algorithm is on-the-fly, in the sense that it avoids, if possible to build a full automaton for the requirement; and thus more likely to perform well in practice. Unfortunately, being designed for MTL, its running time can only be bounded above by a non-primitive recursive function. We present now an algorithm for $\mathsf{BResRS}^\star_d(\mathsf{MITL})$ that combines the advantages of these two previous solutions: it is *on-the-fly* and runs in 3EXPTIME. To obtain an on-the-fly algorithm, Bouyer *et al.* use *one-clock alternating automata* (OCATA) instead of TA to represent the MITL requirement. We follow the same path, but rely on the newly introduced *interval-based semantics* [7] for these automata, in order to mitigate the complexity. Let us now briefly recall these two basic ingredients.

OCATA and Interval Semantics. Alternating timed automata [16] extend (non-deterministic) timed automata by adding *conjunctive transitions*. Intuitively, conjunctive transitions spawn several copies of the automaton that run in parallel from the target states of the transition. A word is accepted iff *all* copies accept it. An example is shown in Fig. 3, where the conjunctive transition is the hyperedge starting from ℓ_0. In the classical semantics, an execution of an OCATA is a sequence of set of states, named *configurations*, describing the current location and clock valuation of all active copies. For example, a prefix of execution of the automaton in Fig. 3 would start in $\{(\ell_0, 0)\}$ (initially, there is only one copy in ℓ_0 with the clock equal to 0); then $\{(\ell_0, 0.42)\}$ (after letting 0.42 time units elapse); then $\{(\ell_0, 0.42), (\ell_1, 0)\}$ (after firing the conjunctive transition from ℓ_0), etc. It is well-known that all formulas φ of MTL (hence, also MITL) can be translated into an OCATA A_φ that accepts the same language [16] (with the classical semantics); and with a number of locations linear in the number of subformulas of φ. This translation is thus straightforward. This is the key advantage of OCATA over TA: the complexity of the MITL formula is shifted from the syntax to the semantics—what we need for an on-the-fly algorithm.

Then, in the *interval semantics* [7], valuations of the clocks are not *points* anymore but *intervals*. Intuitively, intervals are meant to approximate sets of (punctual) valuations: $(\ell, [a, b])$ means that there *are* clock copies with valuations a and b in ℓ, and that there *could be* more copies in ℓ with valuations in $[a, b]$. In this semantics, we can also *merge* two copies $(\ell, [a_1, b_1])$ and $(\ell, [a_2, b_2])$ into a single copy $(\ell, [a_1, b_2])$ (assuming $a_1 \leqslant b_2$), in order to keep the number of

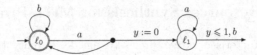

Fig. 3. An OCATA (with single clock y) accepting the language of $\Box(a \Rightarrow \Diamond_{\leqslant 1} b)$.

clock copies below a fixed threshold K. It has been shown [7] that, when the OCATA has been built from an MITL formula, the interval semantics is sufficient to retain the language of the formula, with a number of copies which is at most doubly exponential in the size of the formula.

Sketch of the Algorithm. Equipped with these elements, we can now sketch our algorithm for BResRS$_d^*$(MITL). Starting from an MITL formula φ, a plant $\mathcal{P}$ and a granularity $\mu = (X, m, K)$, we first build, in polynomial time, an OCATA $A_{\neg\varphi}$ accepting $\mathcal{L}(\neg\varphi)$. Then, we essentially adapt the technique of Bouyer *et al.* [4], relying on the interval semantics of OCATA instead of the classical one. This boils down to building a tree that unfolds the parallel execution of $A_{\neg\varphi}$ (in the interval semantics), $\mathcal{P}$ and all possible actions of a μ-granular controller (hence the *on-the-fly* algorithm). Since the granularity is fixed, there are only finitely many possible actions (i.e., guards and resets on the controller clocks) for the controller at each step. We rely on the region construction to group the infinitely many possible valuations of the clocks into finitely many equivalence classes that are represented using 'region words' [16]. The result is a finitely branching tree that might still have infinite branches. We stop developing a branch once a global configuration (of $A_{\neg\varphi}$, $\mathcal{P}$, and the controller) repeats on the branch. By the region construction *and* the interval semantics, this will happen on all branches, and we obtain a *finite tree* of size at most triply exponential. This tree can be analysed (using backward induction) as a game with a safety objective for the controller: to avoid the nodes where $\mathcal{P}$ and $A_{\neg\varphi}$ accept at the same time. The winning strategy yields, if it exists, a correct controller.

Experimental Results. We have implemented our procedure in Java, and tested it over a benchmark related to a scheduling problem, inspired by an example of [9]. This problem considers n machines, and a list of jobs that must

Table 1. Experimental results on the scheduling problem: realisable instances on the left, non-realisable on the right.

T	n	# clocks	exec. time (sec) / #nodes
1	1	0	46 / 52
1	1	1	199 / 147
1	1	2	4,599 / 1,343
2	2	1	2,632 / 645
2	2	2	18,453 / 2,358
3	3	1	182,524 / 2,297
3	3	2	>5min
4	4	0	54,893 / 667
4	4	1	>5min

T	n	# clocks	exec. time (sec) / #nodes
2	1	0	77 / 84
2	1	1	824 / 311
2	1	2	3,079 / 1,116
3	2	1	17,134 / 1698
3	2	2	>5min
4	3	0	10,621 / 540
4	3	1	>5min

be assigned to the machines. A job takes T time units to finish. The plant ensures that at least one time unit elapses between two job arrivals (which are uncontrollable actions). The specification asks that the assignment be performed in 1 time unit, and that each job has T time units of computation time. We tested this example with $T = n$, in which case the specification is realisable (no matter the number of clocks, which we make vary for testing the prototype efficiency), and with $T = n + 1$, in which case it is not. Table 1 summarises some of our results.

These results show that our prototypes can handle small but non-trivial examples. Unfortunately—as expected by the high complexities of the algorithm—they do not scale well. As future works, we will rely on the well-quasi orderings defined in [4] to introduce heuristics in the spirit of the antichain techniques [13]. Second, we will investigate zone-based versions of this algorithm to avoid the state explosion which is inherent to region based techniques.

References

1. Alur, R., Dill, D.L.: A theory of timed automata. T.C.S. **126**(2), 183–235 (1994)
2. Alur, R., Feder, T., Henzinger, T.A.: The benefits of relaxing punctuality. J. ACM **43**(1), 116–146 (1996)
3. Bohy, A., Bruyère, V., Filiot, E., Jin, N., Raskin, J.-F.: Acacia+, a tool for LTL synthesis. In: Madhusudan, P., Seshia, S.A. (eds.) CAV 2012. LNCS, vol. 7358, pp. 652–657. Springer, Heidelberg (2012)
4. Bouyer, P., Bozzelli, L., Chevalier, F.: Controller synthesis for MTL specifications. In: Baier, C., Hermanns, H. (eds.) CONCUR 2006. LNCS, vol. 4137, pp. 450–464. Springer, Heidelberg (2006)
5. Bouyer, P., Markey, N., Ouaknine, J., Worrell, J.: The cost of punctuality. In: LICS 2007, pp. 109–120. IEEE (2007)
6. Brand, D., Zafiropulo, P.: On communicating finite state machines. J. ACM **30**, 323–342 (1983)
7. Brihaye, T., Estiévenart, M., Geeraerts, G.: On MITL and alternating timed automata. In: Braberman, V., Fribourg, L. (eds.) FORMATS 2013. LNCS, vol. 8053, pp. 47–61. Springer, Heidelberg (2013)
8. Brihaye, T., Estiévenart, M., Geeraerts, G., Ho, H.-M., Monmege, B., Sznajder, N.: Real-time synthesis is hard! (full version) (2016). arXiv:1606.07124
9. Bulychev, P.E., David, A., Larsen, K.G., Li, G.: Efficient controller synthesis for a fragment of $MTL_{0,\infty}$. Acta Informatica **51**(3–4), 165–192 (2014)
10. de Alfaro, L., Faella, M., Henzinger, T.A., Majumdar, R., Stoelinga, M.: The element of surprise in timed games. In: Amadio, R.M., Lugiez, D. (eds.) CONCUR 2003. LNCS, vol. 2761, pp. 144–158. Springer, Heidelberg (2003)
11. Doyen, L., Geeraerts, G., Raskin, J.-F., Reichert, J.: Realizability of real-time logics. In: Ouaknine, J., Vaandrager, F.W. (eds.) FORMATS 2009. LNCS, vol. 5813, pp. 133–148. Springer, Heidelberg (2009)
12. D'Souza, D., Madhusudan, P.: Timed control synthesis for external specifications. In: Alt, H., Ferreira, A. (eds.) STACS 2002. LNCS, vol. 2285, pp. 571–582. Springer, Heidelberg (2002)
13. Filiot, E., Jin, N., Raskin, J.-F.: An antichain algorithm for LTL realizability. In: Bouajjani, A., Maler, O. (eds.) CAV 2009. LNCS, vol. 5643, pp. 263–277. Springer, Heidelberg (2009)

14. Koymans, R.: Specifying real-time properties with metric temporal logic. Real-Time Syst. **2**(4), 255–299 (1990)
15. Ouaknine, J., Worrell, J.B.: Universality and language inclusion for open and closed timed automata. In: Maler, O., Pnueli, A. (eds.) HSCC 2003. LNCS, vol. 2623, pp. 375–388. Springer, Heidelberg (2003)
16. Ouaknine, J., Worrell, J.: On the decidability and complexity of metric temporal logic over finite words. LMCS **3**(1), 1–27 (2007)
17. Pnueli, A., Rosner, R.: On the synthesis of an asynchronous reactive module. In: Ausiello, G., Dezani-Ciancaglini, M., Ronchi Della Rocca, S. (eds.) ICALP 1989. LNCS, vol. 372, pp. 652–671. Springer, Heidelberg (1989)
18. Raskin, J.-F.: Logics, automata and classical theories for deciding real time. Ph.D. thesis, FUNDP (Belgium) (1999)

A Boyer-Moore Type Algorithm for Timed Pattern Matching

Masaki Waga[1(✉)], Takumi Akazaki[1,2], and Ichiro Hasuo[1]

[1] University of Tokyo, Tokyo, Japan
{mwaga,ultraredrays,ichiro}@is.s.u-tokyo.ac.jp
[2] JSPS Research Fellow, Tokyo, Japan

Abstract. The *timed pattern matching* problem is formulated by Ulus et al. and has been actively studied since, with its evident application in monitoring real-time systems. The problem takes as input a *timed word/signal* and a *timed pattern* (specified either by a *timed regular expression* or by a *timed automaton*); and it returns the set of those intervals for which the given timed word, when restricted to the interval, matches the given pattern. We contribute a *Boyer-Moore* type optimization in timed pattern matching, relying on the classic Boyer-Moore string matching algorithm and its extension to (untimed) pattern matching by Watson and Watson. We assess its effect through experiments; for some problem instances our Boyer-Moore type optimization achieves speedup by two times, indicating its potential in real-world monitoring tasks where data sets tend to be massive.

1 Introduction

Importance of systems' *real-time* properties is ever growing, with rapidly diversifying applications of computer systems—cyber-physical systems, health-care systems, automated trading, etc.—being increasingly pervasive in every human activity. For real-time properties, besides classic problems in theoretical computer science such as *verification* and *synthesis*, the problem of *monitoring* already turns out to be challenging. Monitoring asks, given an execution log and a specification, whether the log satisfies the specification; sometimes we are furthermore interested in *which segment* of the log satisfies/violates the specification. In practical deployment scenarios where we would deal with a number of very long logs, finding matching segments in a computationally tractable manner is therefore a pressing yet challenging matter.

In this context, inspired by the problems of *string* and *pattern matching* of long research histories, Ulus et al. recently formulated the problem of *timed pattern matching* [20]. In their formalization, the problem takes as input a *timed signal* w (values that change over the continuous notion of time) and a *timed regular expression (TRE)* $\mathcal{R}$ (a real-time extension of regular expressions); and it returns the *match set* $\mathcal{M}(w, \mathcal{R}) = \{(t, t') \mid t < t', w|_{(t,t')} \in L(\mathcal{R})\}$, where $w|_{(t,t')}$ is the restriction of w to the time interval (t, t') and $L(\mathcal{R})$ is the set of signals that match $\mathcal{R}$.

M. Fränzle and N. Markey (Eds.): FORMATS 2016, LNCS 9884, pp. 121–139, 2016.
DOI: 10.1007/978-3-319-44878-7_8

Since its formulation timed pattern matching has been actively studied. The first offline algorithm is introduced in [20]; its application in conditional performance evaluation is pursued in [10]; and in [21] an online algorithm is introduced based on *Brzozowski derivatives*. Underlying these developments is the fundamental observation [20] that the match set $\mathcal{M}(w, \mathcal{R})$—an uncountable subset of $\mathbb{R}^2_{\geq 0}$—allows a finitary symbolic representation by inequalities.

Contributions. In this paper we are concerned with *efficiency* in timed pattern matching, motivated by our collaboration with the automotive industry on various light-weight verification techniques. Towards that goal we introduce optimization that extends the classic *Boyer-Moore* algorithm for string matching (finding a pattern string *pat* in a given word w). Specifically we rely on the extension of the latter to *pattern matching* (finding subwords of w that is accepted by an NFA $\mathcal{A}$) by Watson & Watson [24], and introduce its *timed* extension.

We evaluate its efficiency through a series of experiments; in some cases (including an automotive example) our Boyer-Moore type algorithm outperforms a naive algorithm (without the optimization) by twice. This constant speed-up may be uninteresting from the complexity theory point of view. However, given that in real-world monitoring scenarios the input set of words w can be literally *big data,*[1] halving the processing time is a substantial benefit, we believe.

Our technical contributions are concretely as follows: (1) a (naive) algorithm for timed pattern matching (Sect. 4); (2) its online variant (Sect. 4); (3) a proof that the match set allows a finitary presentation (Theorem 4.3), much like in [20]; and (4) an algorithm with Boyer-Moore type optimization (Sect. 5). Throughout the paper we let (timed) patterns expressed as *timed automata (TA)*, unlike timed regular expressions (TRE) in [10,20,21]. Besides TA is known to be strictly more expressive than TRE (see [12] and also Case 2 of Sect. 6), our principal reason for choosing TA is so that the Boyer-Moore type pattern matching algorithm in [24] smoothly extends.

Related and Future Work. The context of the current work is *run-time verification* and *monitoring* of cyber-physical systems, a field of growing research activities (see e.g. recent [11,14]). One promising application is in *conditional quantitative analysis* [10], e.g. of fuel consumption of a car during acceleration, from a large data set of driving record. Here our results can be used to efficiently isolate the acceleration phases.

Aside from timed automata and TREs, *metric* and *signal temporal logics (MTL/STL)* are commonly used for specifying continuous-time signals. Monitoring against these formalisms has been actively studied, too [7–9,13]. It is known that an MTL formula can be translated to a timed alternating automaton [18]. MTL/STL tend to be used against "smooth" signals whose changes are continuous, however, and it is not clear how our current results (on timed-stamped finite words) would apply to such a situation. One possible practical approach would be to quantize continuous-time signals.

---

[1] For example, in [6], a payment transaction record of 300 K users over almost a year is monitored—against various properties, some of them timed and others not—and they report the task took hundreds of hours.

Being *online*—to process a long timed word w one can already start with its prefix—is obviously a big advantage in monitoring algorithms. In [21] an online timed pattern matching algorithm (where a specification is a TRE) is given, relying on the timed extension of *Brzozowski derivative*. We shall aim at an online version of our Boyer-Moore type algorithm (our online algorithm in Sect. 4 is without the Boyer-Moore type optimization), although it seems hard already for the prototype problem of string matching.

It was suggested by multiple reviewers that use of *zone automata* can further enhance our Boyer-Moore type algorithm for timed pattern matching. See Remark 5.6.

Organization of the Paper. We introduce necessary backgrounds in Sect. 2, on: the basic theory of timed automata, and the previous Boyer-Moore algorithms (for string matching, and the one in [24] for (untimed) pattern matching). The latter will pave the way to our main contribution of the timed Boyer-Moore algorithm. We formulate the timed pattern matching problem in Sect. 3; and a (naive) algorithm is presented in Sect. 4 together with its online variant. In Sect. 5 a Boyer-Moore algorithm for timed pattern matching is described, drawing intuitions from the untimed one and emphasizing where are the differences. In Sect. 6 we present the experiment results; they indicate the potential of the proposed algorithm in real-world monitoring applications.

Most proofs are deferred to the appendix in [23] due to lack of space.

2 Preliminaries

2.1 Timed Automata

Here we follow [1,3], possibly with a fix to accept finite words instead of infinite. For a sequence $\overline{s} = s_1 s_2 \ldots s_n$ we write $|\overline{s}| = n$; and for i, j such that $1 \leq i \leq j \leq |s|$, $\overline{s}(i)$ denotes the element s_i and $\overline{s}(i, j)$ denotes the subsequence $s_i s_{i+1} \ldots s_j$.

Definition 2.1 (timed word). A *timed word* over an alphabet Σ is an element of $(\Sigma \times \mathbb{R}_{>0})^*$—which is denoted by $(\overline{a}, \overline{\tau})$ using $\overline{a} \in \Sigma^*$, $\overline{\tau} \in (\mathbb{R}_{>0})^*$ via the embedding $(\Sigma \times \mathbb{R}_{>0})^* \hookrightarrow \Sigma^* \times (\mathbb{R}_{>0})^*$—such that for any $i \in [1, |\overline{\tau}| - 1]$ we have $0 < \tau_i < \tau_{i+1}$. Let $(\overline{a}, \overline{\tau})$ be a timed word and $t \in \mathbb{R}$ be such that $-\tau_1 < t$. The *t-shift* $(\overline{a}, \overline{\tau}) + t$ of $(\overline{a}, \overline{\tau})$ is the timed word $(\overline{a}, \overline{\tau} + t)$, where $\overline{\tau} + t$ is the sequence $\tau_1 + t, \tau_2 + t, \ldots, \tau_{|\overline{\tau}|} + t$. Let $(\overline{a}, \overline{\tau})$ and $(\overline{a'}, \overline{\tau'})$ be timed words over Σ such that $\tau_{|\tau|} < \tau'_1$. Their *absorbing concatenation* $(\overline{a}, \overline{\tau}) \circ (\overline{a'}, \overline{\tau'})$ is defined by $(\overline{a}, \overline{\tau}) \circ (\overline{a'}, \overline{\tau'}) = (\overline{a} \circ \overline{a'}, \overline{\tau} \circ \overline{\tau'})$, where $\overline{a} \circ \overline{a'}$ and $\overline{\tau} \circ \overline{\tau'}$ denote (usual) concatenation of sequences over Σ and $\mathbb{R}_{>0}$, respectively. Now let $(\overline{a}, \overline{\tau})$ and $(\overline{a''}, \overline{\tau''})$ be arbitrary timed words over Σ. Their *non-absorbing concatenation* $(\overline{a}, \overline{\tau}) \cdot (\overline{a''}, \overline{\tau''})$ is defined by $(\overline{a}, \overline{\tau}) \cdot (\overline{a''}, \overline{\tau''}) = (\overline{a}, \overline{\tau}) \circ ((\overline{a''}, \overline{\tau''}) + \tau_{|\overline{\tau}|})$. A *timed language* over an alphabet Σ is a set of timed words over Σ.

Remark 2.2 (signal). *Signal* is another formalization of records with a notion of time, used e.g. in [20]; a signal over Σ is a function $\mathbb{R}_{\geq 0} \to \Sigma$. A timed word describes a time-stamped sequence of events, while a signal describes values of Σ that change over time. In this paper we shall work with timed words. This is for technical reasons and not important from the applicational point of view: when we restrict to those signals which exhibit only finitely many changes, there is a natural correspondence between such signals and timed words.

Let C be a (fixed) finite set of *clock variables*. The set $\Phi(C)$ of *clock constraints* is defined by the following BNF notation.

$$\Phi(C) \ni \delta = x < c \mid x > c \mid x \leq c \mid x \geq c \mid \textbf{true} \mid \delta \wedge \delta \quad \text{where } x \in C \text{ and } c \in \mathbb{Z}_{\geq 0}.$$

Absence of $\vee$ or $\neg$ does not harm expressivity: $\vee$ can be emulated with nondeterminism (see Definition 2.3); and $\neg$ can be propagated down to atomic formulas by the de Morgan laws. Restriction to **true** and $\wedge$ is technically useful, too, when we deal with intervals and zones (Definition 4.1).

A *clock interpretation* ν over the set C of clock variables is a function $\nu : C \to \mathbb{R}_{\geq 0}$. Given a clock interpretation ν and $t \in \mathbb{R}_{\geq 0}$, $\nu + t$ denotes the clock interpretation that maps a clock variable $x \in C$ to $\nu(x) + t$.

Definition 2.3 (timed automaton). A *timed automaton (TA)* $\mathcal{A}$ is a tuple $(\Sigma, S, S_0, C, E, F)$ where: Σ is a finite alphabet; S is a finite set of states; $S_0 \subseteq S$ is the set of initial states; C is the set of clock variables; $E \subseteq S \times S \times \Sigma \times \mathcal{P}(C) \times \Phi(C)$ is the set of transitions; and $F \subseteq S$ is the set of accepting states.

The intuition for $(s, s', a, \lambda, \delta) \in E$ is: from s, also assuming that the clock constraint δ is satisfied, we can move to the state s' conducting the action a and resetting the value of each clock variable $x \in \lambda$ to 0. Examples of TAs are in (7) and Figs. 7, 8, 9, 10 and 11 later.

The above notations (as well as the ones below) follow those in [1]. In the following definition (1) of run, for example, the first transition occurs at (absolute) time τ_1 and the second occurs at time τ_2; it is implicit that we stay at the state s_1 for time $\tau_2 - \tau_1$.

Definition 2.4 (run). A *run* of a timed automaton $\mathcal{A} = (\Sigma, S, S_0, C, E, F)$ over a timed word $(\overline{a}, \overline{\tau}) \in (\Sigma \times \mathbb{R}_{>0})^*$ is a pair $(\overline{s}, \overline{\nu}) \in S^* \times ((\mathbb{R}_{\geq 0})^C)^*$ of a sequence $\overline{s}$ of states and a sequence $\overline{\nu}$ of clock interpretations, subject to the following conditions: (1) $|\overline{s}| = |\overline{\nu}| = |\overline{a}| + 1$; (2) $s_0 \in S_0$, and for any $x \in C$, $\nu_0(x) = 0$; and (3) for any $i \in [0, |\overline{a}| - 1]$ there exists a transition $(s_i, s_{i+1}, a_{i+1}, \lambda, \delta) \in E$ such that the clock constraint δ holds under the clock interpretation $\nu_i + (\tau_{i+1} - \tau_i)$ (here τ_0 is defined to be 0), and the clock interpretation ν_{i+1} has it that $\nu_{i+1}(x) = \nu_i(x) + \tau_{i+1} - \tau_i$ (if $x \notin \lambda$) and $\nu_{i+1}(x) = 0$ (if $x \in \lambda$). This run is depicted as follows.

$$(s_0, \nu_0) \xrightarrow{(a_1, \tau_1)} (s_1, \nu_1) \xrightarrow{(a_2, \tau_2)} \cdots \longrightarrow (s_{|\overline{a}|-1}, \nu_{|\overline{\tau}|-1}) \xrightarrow{(a_{|\overline{a}|}, \tau_{|\overline{\tau}|})} (s_{|\overline{a}|}, \nu_{|\overline{\tau}|}) \quad (1)$$

Such a run $(\overline{s}, \overline{\nu})$ of $\mathcal{A}$ is *accepting* if $s_{|\overline{s}|-1} \in F$. The *language* $L(\mathcal{A})$ of $\mathcal{A}$ is defined by $L(\mathcal{A}) = \{w \mid \text{there is an accepting run of } \mathcal{A} \text{ over } w\}$.

There is another specification formalism for timed languages called *timed regular expressions (TREs)* [2,3]. Unlike in the classic Kleene theorem, in the timed case timed automata are strictly more expressive than TREs. See [12, Proposition 2].

Region automaton is an important theoretical gadget in the theory of timed automaton: it reduces the domain $S \times (\mathbb{R}_{\geq 0})^C$ of pairs (s, ν) in (1)—that is an *infinite* set—to its *finite* abstraction, the latter being amenable to algorithmic treatments. Specifically it relies on an equivalence relation $\sim$ over clock interpretations. Given a timed automaton $\mathcal{A} = (\Sigma, S, S_0, C, E, F)$—where, without loss of generality, we assume that each clock variable $x \in C$ appears in at least one clock constraint in E—let c_x denote the greatest number that is compared with x in the clock constraints in E. (Precisely: $c_x = \max\{c \in \mathbb{Z}_{\geq 0} \mid x \bowtie c$ occurs in E, where $\bowtie \in \{<, >, \leq, \geq\}\}$.) Writing $\mathrm{int}(\tau)$ and $\mathrm{frac}(\tau)$ for the integer and fractional parts of $\tau \in \mathbb{R}_{\geq 0}$, an equivalence relation $\sim$ over clock interpretations ν, ν' is defined as follows. We have $\nu \sim \nu'$ if:

- for each $x \in C$ we have $\mathrm{int}(\nu(x)) = \mathrm{int}(\nu'(x))$ or $(\nu(x) > c_x$ and $\nu'(x) > c_x)$;
- for any $x, y \in C$ such that $\nu(x) \leq c_x$ and $\nu(y) \leq c_y$, $\mathrm{frac}(\nu(x)) < \mathrm{frac}(\nu(y))$ if and only if $\mathrm{frac}(\nu'(x)) < \mathrm{frac}(\nu'(y))$; and
- for any $x \in C$ such that $\nu(x) \leq c_x$, $\mathrm{frac}(\nu(x)) = 0$ if and only if $\mathrm{frac}(\nu'(x)) = 0$.

A *clock region* is an equivalence class of clock interpretations modulo $\sim$; as usual the equivalence class of ν is denoted by $[\nu]$. Let α, α' be clock regions. We say α' is a *time-successor* of α if for any $\nu \in \alpha$, there exists $t \in \mathbb{R}_{>0}$ such that $\nu + t \in \alpha'$.

Definition 2.5 (region automaton). For a timed automaton $\mathcal{A} = (\Sigma, S, S_0, C, E, F)$, the *region automaton* $R(\mathcal{A})$ is the NFA $(\Sigma, S', S_0', E', F')$ defined as follows: $S' = S \times ((\mathbb{R}_{\geq 0})^C / \sim)$; on initial states $S_0' = \{(s, [\nu]) \mid s \in S_0, \nu(x) = 0$ for each $x \in C\}$; on accepting states $F' = \{(s, \alpha) \in S' \mid s \in F\}$. The transition relation $E' \subseteq S' \times S' \times \Sigma$ is defined as follows: $((s, \alpha), (s', \alpha'), a) \in E'$ if there exist a clock region α'' and $(s, s', a, \lambda, \delta) \in E$ such that

- α'' is a time-successor of α, and
- for each $\nu \in \alpha''$, (1) ν satisfies δ, and (2) there exists $\nu' \in \alpha'$ such that $\nu(x) = \nu'(x)$ (if $x \notin \lambda$) and $\nu'(x) = 0$ (if $x \in \lambda$).

It is known [1] that the region automaton $R(\mathcal{A})$ indeed has finitely many states. The following notation for NFAs will be used later.

Definition 2.6 ($Runs_{\mathcal{A}}(s, s')$). Let $\mathcal{A}$ be an NFA over Σ, and s and s' be its states. We let $Runs_{\mathcal{A}}(s, s')$ denote the set of runs from s to s', that is, $Runs_{\mathcal{A}}(s, s') = \{s_0 s_1 \ldots s_n \mid n \in \mathbb{Z}_{\geq 0}, s_0 = s, s_n = s', \forall i. \exists a_{i+1}. s_i \xrightarrow{a_{i+1}} s_{i+1}$ in $\mathcal{A}\}$.

2.2 String Matching and the Boyer-Moore Algorithm

In Sects. 2.2 and 2.3 we shall revisit the Boyer-Moore algorithm and its adaptation for pattern matching [24]. We do so in considerable details, so as to provide both technical and intuitional bases for our timed adaptation.

String matching is a fundamental operation on strings: given an input string *str* and a pattern string *pat*, it asks for the *match set*

$$\begin{array}{c}
\text{1 2 3 4 5 6 7 8 9 10 11 12 13 14 15 16 17 18 19 20 21 22 23 24} \\
str = \text{H E R E I S A S I M P L E E X A M P L E} \\
pat = \text{E X A M P L E} \\
\text{1 2 3 4 5 6 7}
\end{array}$$

Fig. 1. The string matching problem

$\{(i,j) \mid str(i,j) = pat\}$. An example (from [17]) is in Fig. 1, where the answer is $\{(18, 24)\}$.

A brute-force algorithm has the complexity $O(|str||pat|)$; known optimizations include ones by Knuth, Morris, and Pratt [15] and by Boyer and Moore [5]. The former performs better in the worst case, but for practical instances the latter is commonly used. Let us now demonstrate how the Boyer-Moore algorithm for string matching works, using the example in Fig. 1. Its main idea is to skip unnecessary matching of characters, using two *skip value functions* Δ_1 and Δ_2 (that we define later).

The bottom line in the Boyer-Moore algorithm is that the pattern string *pat* moves *from left to right*, and matching between the input string *str* and *pat* is conducted *from right to left*. In (2) is the initial configuration, and we set out with comparing the characters $str(7)$ and $pat(7)$. They turn out to be different.

A naive algorithm would then move the pattern to the right by one position. We can do better, however, realizing that the character $str(7) = $ S (that we already read for comparison) never occurs in the pattern

$$\begin{array}{l}
\text{1 2 3 4 5 6 7 8 9 10 11 12 13 14 15 16 17 18 19 20 21 22 23 24} \\
\text{H E R E I S A S I M P L E E X A M P L E} \\
\text{E X A M P L E} \\
\text{1 2 3 4 5 6 7}
\end{array} \quad (2)$$

$$\begin{array}{l}
\text{1 2 3 4 5 6 7 8 9 10 11 12 13 14 15 16 17 18 19 20 21 22 23 24} \\
\text{H E R E I S A S I M P L E E X A M P L E} \\
\text{E X A M P L E} \\
\text{1 2 3 4 5 6 7}
\end{array} \quad (3)$$

$$\begin{array}{l}
\text{1 2 3 4 5 6 7 8 9 10 11 12 13 14 15 16 17 18 19 20 21 22 23 24} \\
\text{H E R E I S A S I M P L E E X A M P L E} \\
\text{E X A M P L E} \\
\text{1 2 3 4 5 6 7}
\end{array} \quad (4)$$

pat. This means the position 7 cannot belong to any matching interval (i, j), and we thus jump to the configuration (3). Formally this argument is expressed by the value $\Delta_1(\text{S}, 7) = 7$ of the first skip value function Δ_1, as we will see later.

Here again we compare characters from right to left, in (3), realizing immediately that $str(14) \neq pat(7)$. It is time to shift the pattern; given that $str(14) = $ P occurs as $pat(5)$, we shift the pattern by $\Delta_1(\text{P}, 7) = 7 - 5 = 2$.

We are now in the configuration (4), and some initial matching succeeds ($str(16) = pat(7)$, $str(15) = pat(6)$, and so on). The matching fails for $str(12) \neq pat(3)$. Following the same reasoning as above—the character $str(12) = $ I does not occur in $pat(3)$, $pat(2)$ or $pat(1)$—we would then shift the pattern by $\Delta_1(\text{I}, 3) = 3$.

However we can do even better. Consider the table on the right, where we forget about the input *str* and shift the pattern *pat* one by one, trying to match it with *pat* itself. We are specifically interested in the segment MPLE from $pat(4)$ to $pat(7)$ (underlined in the first row)— because it is the partial match we have discovered in the configuration (4). The table shows

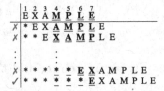

Fig. 2. Table for computing Δ_2

that we need to shift at least by 6 to get a potential match (the last row); hence from the configuration (4) we can shift the pattern *pat* by 6, which is more than the skip value in the above ($\Delta_1(I, 3) = 3$). This argument—different from the one for Δ_1—is formalized as the second skip value function $\Delta_2(3) = 6$ (Fig. 2).

We are led to the config-
uration on the right, only to
find that the first matching trial
fails ($str(22) \neq pat(7)$). Since

$$
\begin{array}{l}
\text{\scriptsize 1 2 \ 3 \ 4 \ 5 6 7 8 \ 9 \ \ 10 11 \ 12 \ 13 \ 14 \ 15 \ 16 \ 17 \ 18 \ 19 \ 20 \ 21 \ 22 23 24} \\
\text{H E R E \ I S \ A \ \ S I M P L E \ \ E X A M P L E} \\
\hspace{5.8cm}\text{E X A M P L E} \hspace{1.5cm}(5) \\
\hspace{6.1cm}\text{\scriptsize 1 \ 2 \ 3 \ 4 \ 5 \ 6 \ 7}
\end{array}
$$

$str(22) = $ P occurs in *pat* as $pat(5)$, we shift *pat* by $\Delta_1(P, 7) = 2$. This finally brings us to the configuration in Fig. 1 and the match set $\{(18, 24)\}$.

Summarizing, the key in the Boyer-Moore algorithm is to use two skip value functions Δ_1, Δ_2 to shift the pattern faster than one-by-one. The precise definition of Δ_1, Δ_2 is in Appendix A in [23], for reference.

2.3   Pattern Matching and a Boyer-Moore Type Algorithm

Pattern matching is another fundamental operation that generalizes string matching: given an input string *str* and a regular language L as a *pattern*, it asks for the *match set* $\{(i,j) \mid str(i,j) \in L\}$. For example, for *str* in Fig. 1 and the pattern $[A - Z]^*MPLE$, the match set is $\{(11, 16), (18, 24)\}$. In [24] an algorithm for pattern matching is introduced that employs "Boyer-Moore type" optimization, much like the use of Δ_2 in Sect. 2.2.

Let $str = $ cbadcdc be an input string and $dc^*\{ba \mid dc\}$ be a pattern L, for example. We can solve pattern matching by the following brute-force algorithm.

- We express the pattern as an NFA $\mathcal{A} = (\Sigma, S, S_0, E, F)$ in Fig. 3. We reverse words—$w \in L$ if and only if $w^{Rev} \in L(\mathcal{A})$—following the Boyer-Moore algorithm (Sect. 2.2) that matches a segment of input and a pattern *from right to left*.
- Also following Sect. 2.2 we "shift the pattern from left to right." This technically means: we conduct the following for $j = 1$ first, then $j = 2$, and so on. For fixed j we search for $i \in [1, j]$ such that $str(i, j) \in L$. This is done by computing the set $S_{(i,j)}$ of reachable states of $\mathcal{A}$ when it is fed with $str(i, j)^{Rev}$.

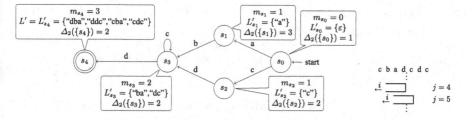

Fig. 3. The automaton $\mathcal{A}$ and skip values   **Fig. 4.** A brute-force algorithm

The computation is done step-by-step, decrementing i from j to 1:

$$S_{(j,j)} = \{s \mid \exists s' \in S_0 .\, s' \overset{str(j)}{\to} s\} \ , \text{ and } S_{(i,j)} = \{s \mid \exists s' \in S_{(i+1,j)} .\, s' \overset{str(i)}{\to} s\} \ .$$

Then (i,j) is a matching interval if and only if $S_{(i,j)} \cap F \neq \emptyset$. See Fig. 4.

The Boyer-Moore type optimization in [24] tries to hasten the shift of j. A key observation is as follows. Assume $j = 4$; then the above procedure would feed $str(1,4)^{Rev} = $ dabc to the automaton $\mathcal{A}$ (Fig. 3). We instantly see that this would not yield any matching interval—for a word to be accepted by $\mathcal{A}$ it must start with abd, cdd, abc or cdc.

Precisely the algorithm in [24] works as follows. We first observe that the shortest word accepted by $\mathcal{A}$ is 3; therefore we can start right away with $j = 3$, skipping $j = 1, 2$ in the above brute-force algorithm. Unfortunately $str(1,3) = $ cba does not match L, with $str(1,3)^{Rev} = $ abc only leading to $\{s_3\}$ in $\mathcal{A}$.

We now shift j by 2, from 3 to 5, following Fig. 5. Here

$$L' = \{\, (w(1,3))^{Rev} \mid w \in L(\mathcal{A}) \,\} = \{\text{dba}, \text{ddc}, \text{cba}, \text{cdc}\}; \quad (6)$$

that is, for $str(i,j)$ to match the pattern L its last three characters must match L'. Our previous "key observation" now translates to the fact that $str(2,4) = $ bad does not belong to L'; in the actual algorithm in [24], however, we do not use the string $str(2,4)$ itself. Instead we *overapproximate* it with the information that feeding $\mathcal{A}$ with $str(1,3)^{Rev} = $ abc led to $\{s_3\}$. Similarly to the case with L', this implies that the last two characters of $str(1,3)$ must have been in $L'_{s_3} = \{\text{ba}, \text{dc}\}$. The table shows that none in L'_{s_3} matches any of L' when j is shifted by 1; when j is shifted by 2, we have matches (underlined). Therefore we jump from $j = 3$ to $j = 5$.

L'_{s_3}	2	3	4	5
			b	a
		d	c	

L'		d	b	a
shifted		d	d	c
by 1		c	b	a
(✗)		c	d	c
L'	*	d	b	a
shifted	*	d	d	c
by 2	*	c	b	a
(✓)	*	c	d	c

Fig. 5. Table for $\Delta_2(s_3)$

This is how the algorithm in [24] works: it accelerates the brute-force algorithm in Fig. 4, skipping some j's, with the help of a skip value function Δ_2. The overapproximation in the last paragraph allows Δ_2 to rely only on a pattern L (but not on an input string str); this means that pre-processing is done once we fix the pattern L, and it is reused for various input strings str. This is an advantage in monitoring applications where one would deal with a number of input strings str, some of which are yet to come. See Appendix B in [23] for the precise definition of the skip value function Δ_2.

In Fig. 3 we annotate each state s with the values m_s and L'_s that is used in computing $\Delta_2(\{s\})$. Here m_s is the length of a shortest word that leads to s; $m = \min_{s \in F} m_s$ (that is 3 in the above example); and $L'_s = \{w(1, \min\{m_s, m\})^{Rev} \mid w \in L(\mathcal{A}_s)\}$.

It is not hard to generalize the other skip value function Δ_1 in Sect. 2.2 for pattern matching, too: instead of *pat* we use the set L' in the above (6). See Appendix B in [23].

3   The Timed Pattern Matching Problem

Here we formulate our problem, following the notations in Sect. 2.1.

Given a timed word w, the timed word segment $w|_{(t,t')}$ is the result of clipping the parts outside the open interval (t, t'). For example, for $w = \big((a, b, c), (0.7, 1.2, 1.5)\big)$, we have $w|_{(1.0, 1.7)} = \big((b, c, \$), (0.2, 0.5, 0.7)\big)$, $w|_{(1.0, 1.5)} = \big((b, \$), (0.2, 0.5)\big)$ and $w|_{(1.2, 1.5)} = \big((\$), (0.3)\big)$. Here the (fresh) *terminal character* $\$$ designates the end of a segment. Since we use open intervals (t, t'), for example, the word $w|_{(1.2, 1.5)}$ does not contain the character c at time 0.3. The formal definition is as follows.

Definition 3.1 (timed word segment). Let $w = (\overline{a}, \overline{\tau})$ be a timed word over Σ, t and t' be reals such that $0 \le t < t'$, and i and j be indices such that $\tau_{i-1} \le t < \tau_i$ and $\tau_j < t' \le \tau_{j+1}$ (we let $\tau_0 = 0$ and $\tau_{|\overline{\tau}|+1} = \infty$). The *timed word segment* $w|_{(t,t')}$ of w on the interval (t, t') is the timed word $(\overline{a'}, \overline{\tau'})$, over the extended alphabet $\Sigma \amalg \{\$\}$, defined as follows: (1) $|w|_{(t,t')}| = j - i + 2$; (2) we have $a'_k = a_{i+k-1}$ and $\tau'_k = \tau_{i+k-1} - t$ for $k \in [1, j-i+1]$; and (3) $a'_{j-i+2} = \$$ and $\tau'_{j-i+2} = t' - t$.

Definition 3.2 (timed pattern matching). The *timed pattern matching* problem (over an alphabet Σ) takes (as input) a timed word w over Σ and a timed automaton $\mathcal{A}$ over $\Sigma \amalg \{\$\}$; and it requires (as output) the *match set* $\mathcal{M}(w, \mathcal{A}) = \big\{(t, t') \in (\mathbb{R}_{\ge 0})^2 \mid t < t', w|_{(t,t')} \in L(\mathcal{A})\big\}$.

Our formulation in Definition 3.2 slightly differs from that in [20] in that: (1) we use timed words in place of signals (Remark 2.2); (2) for specification we use timed automata rather than timed

$$(7)$$

cation we use timed automata rather than timed regular expressions; and (3) we use an explicit terminal character $\$$. While none of these differences is major, introduction of $\$$ enhances expressivity, e.g. in specifying "an event a occurs, and after that, no other event occurs within 2s." (see (7)). It is also easy to ignore $\$$—when one is not interested in it—by having the clock constraint **true** on the $\$$-labeled transitions leading to the accepting states.

Assumption 3.3. In what follows we assume the following. Each timed automaton $\mathcal{A}$ over the alphabet $\Sigma \amalg \{\$\}$ is such that: every $\$$-labeled transition is into an accepting state; and no other transition is $\$$-labeled. And there exists no transition from any accepting states.

4   A Naive Algorithm and Its Online Variant

Here we present a naive algorithm for timed pattern matching (without a Boyer-Moore type optimization), also indicating how to make it into an online one. Let us fix a timed word w over Σ and a timed automaton $\mathcal{A} = (\Sigma \amalg \{\$\}, S, S_0, C, E, F)$ as the input.

First of all, a match set (Definition 3.2) is in general an infinite set, and we need its finitary representation for an algorithmic treatment. We follow [20] and use (2-dimensional) zones for that purpose.

Definition 4.1 (zone). Consider the 2-dimensional plane $\mathbb{R}^2$ whose axes are denoted by t and t'. A *zone* is a convex polyhedron specified by constraints of the form $t \bowtie c$, $t' \bowtie c$ and $t' - t \bowtie c$, where $\bowtie \in \{<, >, \le, \ge\}$ and $c \in \mathbb{Z}_{\ge 0}$.

It is not hard to see that each zone is specified by three intervals (that may or may not include their endpoints): T_0 for t, T_f for t' and T_Δ for $t' - t$. We let a triple (T_0, T_f, T_Δ) represent a zone, and write $(t, t') \in (T_0, T_f, T_\Delta)$ if $t \in T_0$, $t' \in T_f$ and $t' - t \in T_\Delta$.

In our algorithms we shall use the following constructs.

Definition 4.2 (reset, eval, solConstr, $\rho_\emptyset$, *Conf*). Let $\rho \colon C \rightharpoonup \mathbb{R}_{>0}$ be a partial function that carries a clock variable $x \in C$ to a positive real; the intention is that x was reset at time $\rho(x)$ (in the absolute clock). Let $x \in C$ and $t_r \in \mathbb{R}_{>0}$; then the partial function reset$(\rho, x, t_r) \colon C \rightharpoonup \mathbb{R}_{>0}$ is defined by: reset$(\rho, x, t_r)(x) = t_r$ and reset$(\rho, x, t_r)(y) = \rho(y)$ for each $y \in C$ such that $y \ne x$. (The last is Kleene's equality between partial functions, to be precise.)

Now let ρ be as above, and $t, t_0 \in \mathbb{R}_{\ge 0}$, with the intention that t is the current (absolute) time and t_0 is the epoch (absolute) time for a timed word segment $w|_{(t_0, t')}$. We further assume $t_0 \le t$ and $t_0 \le \rho(x) \le t$ for each $x \in C$ for which $\rho(x)$ is defined. The clock interpretation eval$(\rho, t, t_0) \colon C \rightarrow \mathbb{R}_{\ge 0}$ is defined by: eval$(\rho, t, t_0)(x) = t - \rho(x)$ (if $\rho(x)$ is defined); and eval$(\rho, t, t_0)(x) = t - t_0$ (if $\rho(x)$ is undefined).

For intervals $T, T' \subseteq \mathbb{R}_{\ge 0}$, a partial function $\rho \colon C \rightharpoonup \mathbb{R}_{>0}$ and a clock constraint δ (Sect. 2.1), we define solConstr$(T, T', \rho, \delta) = \{(t, t') \mid t \in T, t' \in T', \text{eval}(\rho, t', t) \models \delta\}$.

We let $\rho_\emptyset \colon C \rightharpoonup \mathbb{R}_{>0}$ denote the partial function that is nowhere defined.

For a timed word w, a timed automaton $\mathcal{A}$ and each $i, j \in [1, |w|]$, we define the set of "configurations": $Conf(i, j) = \{(s, \rho, T) \mid \forall t_0 \in T. \exists (\bar{s}, \bar{\nu}). (\bar{s}, \bar{\nu})$ is a run over $w(i, j) - t_0, s_{|\bar{s}|-1} = s,$ and $\nu_{|\bar{\nu}|-1} = \text{eval}(\rho, \tau_j, t_0)\}$. Further details are in Appendix C in [23].

Our first (naive) algorithm for timed pattern matching is in Algorithm 1. We conduct a brute-force breadth-first search, computing $\{(t, t') \in \mathcal{M}(w, \mathcal{A}) \mid \tau_{i-1} \le t < \tau_i, \tau_j < t' \le \tau_{j+1}\}$ for each i, j, with the aid of $Conf(i, j)$ in Definition 4.2. (The singular case of $\forall i. \tau_i \notin (t, t')$ is separately taken care of by *Immd*.) We do so in the order illustrated in Fig. 6: we decrement i, and for each i we increment j. This order—that flips the one in Fig. 4—is for the purpose of the Boyer-Moore type optimization later in Sect. 5. In Appendix C in [23] we provide further details.

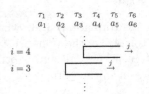

Fig. 6. i, j in our algorithms for timed pattern matching

Theorem 4.3 (termination and correctness of Algorithm 1)

1. Algorithm 1 terminates and its answer Z is a finite union of zones.

2. *For any $t, t' \in \mathbb{R}_{>0}$ such that $t < t'$, the following are equivalent: (1) there is a zone $(T_0, T_f, T_\Delta) \in Z$ such that $(t, t') \in (T_0, T_f, T_\Delta)$; and (2) there is an accepting run $(\bar{s}, \bar{\nu})$ over $w|_{(t, t')}$ of $\mathcal{A}$.*

□

As an immediate corollary, we conclude that a match set $\mathcal{M}(w, \mathcal{A})$ always allows representation by finitely many zones.

Changing the order of examination of i, j (Fig. 6) gives us an *online* variant of Algorithm 1. It is presented in Appendix D in [23]; nevertheless our Boyer-Moore type algorithm is based on the original Algorithm 1.

Algorithm 1. Our naive algorithm for timed pattern matching. See Def. 4.2 and Appendix C in [23] for details.

Require: A timed word $w = (\bar{a}, \bar{\tau})$, and a timed automaton $\mathcal{A} = (\Sigma, S, S_0, C, E, F)$.
Ensure: $\bigcup Z$ is the match set $\mathcal{M}(w, \mathcal{A})$ in Def. 3.2.
1: $i \leftarrow |w|$; $CurrConf \leftarrow \emptyset$; $Immd \leftarrow \emptyset$; $Z \leftarrow \emptyset$ ▷ *Immd and Z are finite sets of zones.*
2: **for** $s \in S_0$ **do**   ▷ *Lines 2–5 compute Immd.*
3:    **for** $s_f \in F$ **do**
4:      **for** $(s, s_f, \$, \lambda, \delta) \in E$ **do**
5:        $Immd \leftarrow Immd \cup \text{solConstr}([0, \infty), (0, \infty), \rho_\emptyset, \delta)$
6: $Z \leftarrow Z \cup \{ (T_0 \cap [\tau_{|w|}, \infty), T_f \cap (\tau_{|w|}, \infty), T_\Delta) \mid (T_0, T_f, T_\Delta) \in Immd \}$
7:        ▷ *We have added $\{ (t, t') \in \mathcal{M}(w, \mathcal{A}) \mid t, t' \in [\tau_{|w|}, \infty) \}$ to Z.*
8: **while** $i > 0$ **do**
9:    $Z \leftarrow Z \cup \{ (T_0 \cap [\tau_{i-1}, \tau_i), T_f \cap (\tau_{i-1}, \tau_i], T_\Delta) \mid (T_0, T_f, T_\Delta) \in Immd \}$
10:       ▷ *We have added $\{ (t, t') \in \mathcal{M}(w, \mathcal{A}) \mid t, t' \in [\tau_{i-1}, \tau_i] \}$ to Z.*
11:     ▷ *Now, for each j, we shall add $\{ (t, t') \in \mathcal{M}(w, \mathcal{A}) \mid t \in [\tau_{i-1}, \tau_i), t' \in (\tau_j, \tau_{j+1}] \}$.*
12:    $j \leftarrow i$
13:    $CurrConf \leftarrow \{ (s, \rho_\emptyset, [\tau_{i-1}, \tau_i)) \mid s \in S_0 \}$
14:    **while** $CurrConf \neq \emptyset$ & $j \leq |w|$ **do**
15:      $(PrevConf, CurrConf) \leftarrow (CurrConf, \emptyset)$ ▷ *Here $PrevConf = Conf(i, j-1)$.*
16:      **for** $(s, \rho, T) \in PrevConf$ **do**
17:        **for** $(s, s', a_j, \lambda, \delta) \in E$ **do**   ▷ *Read (a_j, τ_j).*
18:          $T' \leftarrow \{ t_0 \in T \mid \text{eval}(\rho, \tau_j, t_0) \models \delta \}$
19:          ▷ *Narrow the interval T to satisfy the clock constraint δ.*
20:          **if** $T' \neq \emptyset$ **then**
21:            $\rho' \leftarrow \rho$
22:            **for** $x \in \lambda$ **do**
23:              $\rho' \leftarrow \text{reset}(\rho', x, \tau_j)$ ▷ *Reset the clock variables in λ.*
24:            $CurrConf \leftarrow CurrConf \cup (s', \rho', T')$
25:            **for** $s_f \in F$ **do**   ▷ *Lines 25–31 try to insert \$ in $(\tau_j, \tau_{j+1}]$.*
26:              **for** $(s', s_f, \$, \lambda', \delta') \in E$ **do**
27:                **if** $j = |w|$ **then**
28:                  $T'' \leftarrow (\tau_j, \infty)$
29:                **else**
30:                  $T'' \leftarrow (\tau_j, \tau_{j+1}]$
31:                  $Z \leftarrow Z \cup \text{solConstr}(T', T'', \rho', \delta')$
32:      $j \leftarrow j + 1$
33:    $i \leftarrow i - 1$

---

5   A Timed Boyer-Moore Type Algorithm

Here we describe our main contribution, namely a Boyer-Moore type algorithm for timed pattern matching. Much like the algorithm in [24] skips some j's in Fig. 4 (Sect. 2.3), we wish to skip some i's in Fig. 6. Let us henceforth fix a timed word $w = (\overline{a}, \overline{\tau})$ and a timed automaton $\mathcal{A} = (\Sigma \amalg \{\$\}, S, S_0, C, E, F)$ as the input of the problem.

Let us define the *optimal* skip value function by $Opt(i) = \min\{n \in \mathbb{R}_{>0} \mid \exists t \in [\tau_{i-n-1}, \tau_{i-n}). \exists t' \in (t, \infty). (t, t') \in \mathcal{M}(w, \mathcal{A})\}$; the value $Opt(i)$ designates the biggest skip value, at each i in Fig. 6, that does not change the outcome of the algorithm. Since the function Opt is not amenable to efficient computation in general, our goal is its underapproximation that is easily computed.

Towards that goal we follow the (untimed) pattern matching algorithm in [24]; see Sect. 2.3. In applying the same idea as in Fig. 5 to define a skip value, however, the first obstacle is that the language L'_{s_3}—the set of (suitable prefixes of) all words that lead to s_3—becomes an *infinite* set in the current timed setting. Our countermeasure is to use a *region automaton* $R(\mathcal{A})$ (Definition 2.5) for representing the set.

We shall first introduce some constructs used in our algorithm.

Definition 5.1 $(\mathcal{W}(r), \mathcal{W}(\overline{s}, \overline{\alpha}))$. Let r be a set of runs of the timed automaton $\mathcal{A}$. We define a timed language $\mathcal{W}(r) = \{ (\overline{a}, \overline{\tau}) \mid$ in r there is a run of $\mathcal{A}$ over $(\overline{a}, \overline{\tau}) \}$.

For the region automaton $R(\mathcal{A})$, each run $(\overline{s}, \overline{\alpha})$ of $R(\mathcal{A})$—where $s_k \in S$ and $\alpha_k \in (\mathbb{R}_{\geq 0})^C / \sim$, recalling the state space of $R(\mathcal{A})$ from Definition 2.5—is naturally identified with a set of runs of $\mathcal{A}$, namely $\{(\overline{s}, \overline{\nu}) \in (S \times (\mathbb{R}_{\geq 0})^C)^* \mid \nu_k \in \alpha_k$ for each $k\}$. Under this identification we shall sometimes write $\mathcal{W}(\overline{s}, \overline{\alpha})$ for a suitable timed language, too.

The above definitions of $\mathcal{W}(r)$ and $\mathcal{W}(\overline{s}, \overline{\alpha})$ naturally extends to a set r of *partial runs* of $\mathcal{A}$, and to a *partial run* $(\overline{s}, \overline{\alpha})$ of $R(\mathcal{A})$, respectively. Here a partial run is a run but we do not require: it start at an initial state; or its initial clock interpretation be 0.

The next optimization of $R(\mathcal{A})$ is similar to so-called *trimming*, but we leave those states that do not lead to any final state (they become necessary later).

Definition 5.2 $(R^r(\mathcal{A}))$. For a timed automaton $\mathcal{A}$, we let $R^r(\mathcal{A})$ denote its *reachable region automaton*. It is the NFA $R^r(\mathcal{A}) = (\Sigma, S^r, S_0^r, E^r, F^r)$ obtained from $R(\mathcal{A})$ (Definition 2.5) by removing all those states which are unreachable from any initial state.

We are ready to describe our Boyer-Moore type algorithm. We use a skip value function Δ_2 that is similar to the one in Sect. 2.3 (see Figs. 3 and 5), computed with the aid of m_s and L'_s defined for each state s. We define m_s and L'_s using the NFA $R^r(\mathcal{A})$. Notable differences are: (1) here L'_s and L' are sets of *runs*, not of *words*; and (2) since the orders are flipped between Figs. 4 and 6, *Rev* e.g. in (6) is gone now.

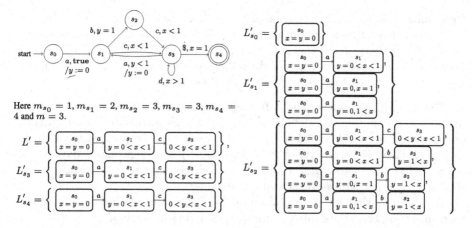

Here $m_{s_0} = 1, m_{s_1} = 2, m_{s_2} = 3, m_{s_3} = 3, m_{s_4} = 4$ and $m = 3$.

Fig. 7. An example of a timed automaton $\mathcal{A}$, and the values m_s, L'_s, L'

The precise definitions are as follows. Here $s \in S$ is a state of the (original) timed automaton $\mathcal{A}$; and we let $R^{\mathrm{r}}(s) = \{(s, \alpha) \in S^{\mathrm{r}}\}$.

$$m = \min\{|w'| \mid w' \in L(\mathcal{A})\} \quad m_s = \min\{|r| \mid \beta_0 \in S_0^{\mathrm{r}}, \beta \in R^{\mathrm{r}}(s), r \in \mathit{Runs}_{R^{\mathrm{r}}(\mathcal{A})}(\beta_0, \beta)\}$$
$$L' = \{r(0, m-1) \mid \beta_0 \in S_0^{\mathrm{r}}, \beta_f \in F^{\mathrm{r}}, r \in \mathit{Runs}_{R^{\mathrm{r}}(\mathcal{A})}(\beta_0, \beta_f)\} \tag{7}$$
$$L'_s = \{r(0, \min\{m, m_s\} - 1) \mid \beta_0 \in S_0^{\mathrm{r}}, \beta \in R^{\mathrm{r}}(s), r \in \mathit{Runs}_{R^{\mathrm{r}}(\mathcal{A})}(\beta_0, \beta)\}$$

Note again that these data are defined over $R^{\mathrm{r}}(\mathcal{A})$ (Definition 5.2); $\mathit{Runs}_{R^{\mathrm{r}}(\mathcal{A})}(\beta_0, \beta_f)$ is from Definition 2.6.

Definition 5.3 (Δ_2). Let Conf be a set of triples (s, ρ, T) of: a state $s \in S$ of $\mathcal{A}$, $\rho \colon C \rightharpoonup \mathbb{R}_{>0}$, and an interval T. (This is much like $\mathit{Conf}(i, j)$ in Definition 4.2.) We define the skip value $\Delta_2(\mathit{Conf})$ as follows.

$$d_1(r) = \min_{r' \in L'} \min\{n \in \mathbb{Z}_{>0} \mid \mathcal{W}(r) \cap (\bigcup_{r'' \in \mathrm{pref}(r'(n, |r'|))} \mathcal{W}(r'')) \neq \emptyset\}$$
$$d_2(r) = \min_{r' \in L'} \min\{n \in \mathbb{Z}_{>0} \mid (\bigcup_{r'' \in \mathrm{pref}(r)} \mathcal{W}(r'')) \cap \mathcal{W}(r'(n, |r'|)) \neq \emptyset\}$$
$$\Delta_2(\mathit{Conf}) = \max_{(s, \rho, T) \in \mathit{Conf}} \min_{r \in L'_s} \min\{d_1(r), d_2(r)\}.$$

Here $r \in \mathit{Runs}_{R^{\mathrm{r}}(\mathcal{A})}$; L' is from (7); $\mathcal{W}$ is from Definition 5.1; $r'(n, |r'|)$ is a subsequence of r' (that is a partial run); and $\mathrm{pref}(r)$ denotes the set of all prefixes of r.

Theorem 5.4 (correctness of Δ_2). *Let $i \in [1, |w|]$, and $j = \max\{j \in [i, |w|] \mid \mathit{Conf}(i, j) \neq \emptyset\}$, where $\mathit{Conf}(i, j)$ is from Definition 4.2. (In case $\mathit{Conf}(i, j)$ is everywhere empty we let $j = i$.) Then we have $\Delta_2(\mathit{Conf}(i, j)) \leq \mathit{Opt}(i)$.* $\square$

The remaining issue in Definition 5.3 is that the sets like $\mathcal{W}(r)$ and $\mathcal{W}(r'')$ can be infinite—we need to avoid their direct computation. We rely on the usual automata-theoretic trick: the intersection of languages is recognized by a product automaton.

Given two timed automata $\mathcal{B}$ and $\mathcal{C}$, we let $\mathcal{B} \times \mathcal{C}$ denote their *product* defined in the standard way (see e.g. [19]). The following is straightforward.

Proposition 5.5. *Let* $r = (\overline{s}, \overline{\alpha})$ *and* $r' = (\overline{s'}, \overline{\alpha'})$ *be partial runs of* $R(\mathcal{B})$ *and* $R(\mathcal{C})$, *respectively; they are naturally identified with sets of partial runs of* $\mathcal{B}$ *and* $\mathcal{C}$ *(Definition 5.1). Assume further that* $|r| = |r'|$. *Then we have* $\mathcal{W}(r) \cap \mathcal{W}(r') = \mathcal{W}(r, r')$, *where* (r, r') *is the following set of runs of* $\mathcal{B} \times \mathcal{C}$: $(r, r') = \left\{ \left((\overline{s}, \overline{s'}), (\overline{\nu}, \overline{\nu'}) \right) \mid (\overline{s}, \overline{\nu}) \in (\overline{s}, \overline{\alpha}) \text{ and } (\overline{s'}, \overline{\nu'}) \in (\overline{s'}, \overline{\alpha'}) \right\}$. $\qquad\square$

The proposition allows the following algorithm for the emptiness check required in computing d_1 (Definition 5.3). Firstly we distribute $\cap$ over $\bigcup$; then we need to check if $\mathcal{W}(r) \cap \mathcal{W}(r'') \neq \emptyset$ for each r''. The proposition reduces this to checking if $\mathcal{W}(r, r'') \neq \emptyset$, that is, if (r, r'') is a (legitimate) partial run of the region automaton $R(\mathcal{A} \times \mathcal{A})$. The last check is obviously decidable since $R(\mathcal{A} \times \mathcal{A})$ is finite. For d_2 the situation is similar.

We also note that the computation of Δ_2 (Definition 5.3) can be accelerated by memorizing the values $\min_{r \in L'_s} \min\{d_1(r), d_2(r)\}$ for each s.

Finally our Boyer-Moore type algorithm for timed pattern matching is Algorithm 3 in Appendix E in [23]. Its main differences from the naive one (Algorithm 1) are: (1) initially we start with $i = |w| - m + 1$ instead of $i = |w|$ (line 1 of Algorithm 1); and (2) we decrement i by the skip value computed by Δ_2, instead of by 1 (line 33 of Algorithm 1).

It is also possible to employ an analog of the skip value function Δ_1 in Sects. 2.2 and 2.3. For $c \in \Sigma$ and $p \in \mathbb{Z}_{>0}$, we define $\Delta_1(c, p) = \min_{k>0}\{k - p \mid k > m \text{ or } \exists (\overline{a}, \overline{\tau}) \in \mathcal{W}(L'). a_k = c\}$. Here m and L' are from (7). Then we can possibly skip more i's using both Δ_1 and Δ_2; see Appendix E in [23] for details. In our implementation we do not use Δ_1, though, following the (untimed) pattern matching algorithm in [24]. Investigating the effect of additionally using Δ_1 is future work.

One may think of the following alternative for pattern matching: we first forget about time stamps, time constraints, etc.; the resulting "relaxed" untimed problem can be solved by the algorithm in [24] (Sect. 2.3); and then we introduce the time constraints back and refine the interim result to the correct one. Our *timed* Boyer-Moore algorithm has greater skip values in general, however, because by using region automata $R(\mathcal{A}), R^r(\mathcal{A})$ we also take time constraints into account when computing skip values.

Remark 5.6. It was suggested by multiple reviewers that our use of region automata be replaced with that of *zone automata* (see e.g. [4]). This can result in a much smaller automaton $R(\mathcal{A})$ for calculating skip values (cf. Definition 5.3 and Case 2 of Sect. 6). More importantly, zone automata are insensitive to the time unit size—unlike region automata where the numbers c_x in Definition 2.5 govern their size—a property desired in actual deployment of timed pattern matching. This is a topic of our imminent future work.

6   Experiments

We implemented both of our naive offline algorithm and our Boyer-Moore type algorithm (without Δ_1) in C++ [22]. We ran our experiments on MacBook Air

Mid 2011 with Intel Core i7-2677M 1.80 GHz CPU with 3.7 GB RAM and Arch Linux (64-bit). Our programs were compiled with GCC 5.3.0 with optimization level O3.

An execution of our Boyer-Moore type algorithm consists of two phases: in the first *pre-processing* phase we compute the skip value function Δ_2—to be precise the value $\min_{r \in L'_s} \min\{d_1(r), d_2(r)\}$ for each s, on which Δ_2 relies—and in the latter "matching" phase we actually compute the match set.

As input we used five test cases: each case consists of a timed automaton $\mathcal{A}$ and multiple timed words w of varying length $|w|$. Cases 1 and 4 are from a previous work [20] on timed pattern matching; in Case 2 the timed automaton $\mathcal{A}$ is not expressible with a timed regular expression (TRE, see [12] and Sect. 2.1); and Cases 3 and 5 are our original. In particular Case 5 comes from an automotive example.

Our principal interest is in the relationship between execution time and the length $|w|$ (i.e. the number of events), for both of the naive and Boyer-Moore algorithms. For each test case we ran our programs 30 times; the presented execution time is the average. We measured the execution time separately for the pre-processing phase and the (main) matching phase; in the figures we present the time for the latter.

We present an overview of the results. Further details are in Appendix G in [23].

Case 1: No Clock Constraints. In Fig. 8 we present a timed automaton $\mathcal{A}$ and the execution time (excluding pre-processing) for 37 timed words w whose lengths range from 20 to 1,024,000. Each timed word w is an alternation of $a, b \in \Sigma$, and its time stamps are randomly generated according to a certain uniform distribution.

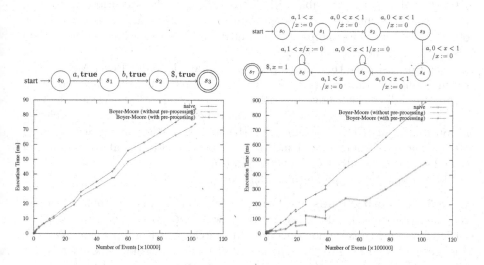

Fig. 8. Case 1: $\mathcal{A}$ and execution time   **Fig. 9.** Case 3: $\mathcal{A}$ and execution time

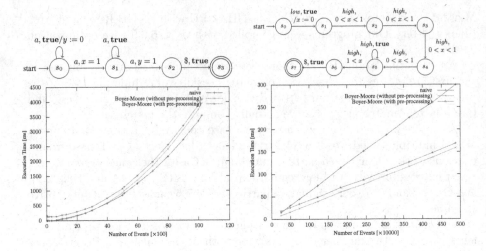

Fig. 10. Case 2: $\mathcal{A}$ and execution time   **Fig. 11.** Case 5: $\mathcal{A}$ and execution time

The automaton $\mathcal{A}$ is without any clock constraints, so in this case the problem is almost that of *untimed* pattern matching. The Boyer-Moore algorithm outperforms the naive one; but the gap is approximately 1/10 when $|w|$ is large enough, which is smaller than what one would expect from the fact that i is always decremented by 2. This is because, as some combinatorial investigation would reveal, those i's which are skipped are for which we examine fewer j's

The pre-processing phase (that relies only on $\mathcal{A}$) took $6.38 \cdot 10^{-2}$ ms. on average.

Case 2: Beyond Expressivity of TREs. In Fig. 10 are a timed automaton $\mathcal{A}$—one that is not expressible with TREs [12]—and the execution time for 20 timed words w whose lengths range from 20 to 10,240. Each w is a repetition of $a \in \Sigma$, and its time stamps are randomly generated according to the uniform distribution in the interval $(0, 0.1)$.

One can easily see that the skip value is always 1, so our Boyer-Moore algorithm is slightly slower due to the overhead of repeatedly reading the result of pre-processing. The naive algorithm (and hence the Boyer-Moore one too) exhibits non-linear increase in Fig. 10; this is because its worst-case complexity is bounded by $|w||E|^{|w|+1}$ (where $|E|$ is the number of edges in $\mathcal{A}$). See the proof of Theorem 4.3 (Appendix F.1 in [23]). The factor $|E|$ in the above complexity bound stems essentially from nondeterminism.

The pre-processing phase took $1.39 \cdot 10^2$ ms. on average.

Case 3: Accepting Runs are Long. In Fig. 9 are a timed automaton $\mathcal{A}$ and the execution time for 49 timed words w whose lengths range from 8,028 to 10,243,600. Each w is randomly generated as follows: it is a repetition of $a \in \Sigma$; a is repeated according to the exponential distribution with a parameter λ; and we do so for a fixed duration $\tau_{|\bar{\tau}|}$, generating a timed word of length $|w|$. See Table 3 in Appendix G in [23].

In the automaton $\mathcal{A}$ the length m of the shortest accepting run is large; hence so are the skip values in the Boyer-Moore optimization. (Specifically the skip value is 5 if both $\tau_i - \tau_{i-1}$ and $\tau_{i+1} - \tau_i$ are greater than 1.) Indeed, as we see from the figure, the Boyer-Moore algorithm outperforms the naive one roughly by twice.

The pre-processing phase took 7.02 ms. on average. This is in practice negligible; recall that pre-processing is done only once when $\mathcal{A}$ is given.

Case 4: Region Automata are Big. Here $\mathcal{A}$ is a translation of the TRE $\langle ((\langle p \rangle_{(0,10]} \langle \neg p \rangle_{(0,10]})^* \wedge (\langle q \rangle_{(0,10]} \langle \neg q \rangle_{(0,10]})^*) \$ \rangle_{(0,80]}$. We executed our two algorithms for 12 timed words w whose lengths range from 1,934 to 31,935. Each w is generated randomly as follows: it is the interleaving combination of an alternation of p, $\neg p$ and one of q, $\neg q$; in each alternation the time stamps are governed by the exponential distribution with a parameter λ; and its duration $\tau_{|\tau|}$ is fixed.

This $\mathcal{A}$ is bad for our Boyer-Moore type algorithm since its region automaton $R(\mathcal{A})$ is very big. Specifically: the numbers c_x in Definition 2.5 are big (10 and 80) and we have to have many states accordingly in $R(\mathcal{A})$—recall that in $\sim$ we care about the coincidence of integer part. Indeed, the construction of $R^r(\mathcal{A})$ took ca. 74s., and the construction of $R(\mathcal{A} \times \mathcal{A})$ did not complete due to RAM shortage. Therefore we couldn't complete pre-processing for Boyer-Moore. We note however that our naive algorithm worked fine. See Table 4 in Appendix G in [23].

Case 5: An Automotive Example. This final example (Fig. 11) is about anomaly detection of engines. The execution time is shown for 10 timed words w whose lengths range from 242,808 to 4,873,207. Each w is obtained as a discretized log of the simulation of the model `sldemo_enginewc.slx` in the Simulink Demo palette [16]: here the input of the model (desired rpm) is generated randomly according to the Gaussian distribution with $\mu = 2{,}000$ rpm and $\sigma^2 = 10^6$ rpm^2; we discretized the output of the model (engine torque) into two statuses, *high* and *low*, with the threshold of 40N $\cdot$ m.

This test case is meant to be a practical example in automotive applications—our original motivation for the current work. The automaton $\mathcal{A}$ expresses: the engine torque is *high* for more than 1 s (the kind of anomaly we are interested in) and the log is not too sparse (which means the log is a credible one).

Here the Boyer-Moore algorithm outperforms the naive one roughly by twice. The pre-processing phase took 9.94 ms on average.

Lacking in the current section are: detailed comparison with the existing implementations (e.g. in [20], modulo the word-signal difference in Remark 2.2); and performance analysis when the specification $\mathcal{A}$, instead of the input timed word w, grows. We intend to address these issues in the coming extended version.

Acknowledgments. Thanks are due to the anonymous referees for their careful reading and expert comments. The authors are supported by Grant-in-Aid No. 15KT0012, JSPS; T.A. is supported by Grant-in-Aid for JSPS Fellows.

References

1. Alur, R., Dill, D.L.: A theory of timed automata. Theor. Comput. Sci. **126**(2), 183–235 (1994)
2. Asarin, E., Caspi, P., Maler, O.: A Kleene theorem for timed automata. In: Proceedings of the LICS 1997, pp. 160–171. IEEE Computer Society (1997)
3. Asarin, E., Caspi, P., Maler, O.: Timed regular expressions. J. ACM **49**(2), 172–206 (2002)
4. Behrmann, G., Bouyer, P., Larsen, K.G., Pelánek, R.: Lower and upper bounds in zone-based abstractions of timed automata. STTT **8**(3), 204–215 (2006)
5. Boyer, R.S., Moore, J.S.: A fast string searching algorithm. Commun. ACM **20**(10), 762–772 (1977)
6. Colombo, C., Pace, G.J.: Fast-forward runtime monitoring — an industrial case study. In: Qadeer, S., Tasiran, S. (eds.) RV 2012. LNCS, vol. 7687, pp. 214–228. Springer, Heidelberg (2013)
7. Deshmukh, J.V., Donzé, A., Ghosh, S., Jin, X., Juniwal, G., Seshia, S.A.: Robust online monitoring of signal temporal logic. In: Bartocci, E., Majumdar, R. (eds.) RV 2015. LNCS, vol. 9333, pp. 55–70. Springer, Heidelberg (2015). doi:10.1007/978-3-319-23820-3_4
8. Dokhanchi, A., Hoxha, B., Fainekos, G.: On-line monitoring for temporal logic robustness. In: Bonakdarpour, B., Smolka, S.A. (eds.) RV 2014. LNCS, vol. 8734, pp. 231–246. Springer, Heidelberg (2014)
9. Donzé, A., Ferrère, T., Maler, O.: Efficient robust monitoring for STL. In: Sharygina, N., Veith, H. (eds.) CAV 2013. LNCS, vol. 8044, pp. 264–279. Springer, Heidelberg (2013)
10. Ferrère, T., Maler, O., Ničković, D., Ulus, D.: Measuring with timed patterns. In: Kroening, D., Păsăreanu, C.S. (eds.) CAV 2015. LNCS, vol. 9207, pp. 322–337. Springer, Heidelberg (2015)
11. Geist, J., Rozier, K.Y., Schumann, J.: Runtime observer pairs and bayesian network reasoners on-board FPGAs: flight-certifiable system health management for embedded systems. In: Bonakdarpour, B., Smolka, S.A. (eds.) RV 2014. LNCS, vol. 8734, pp. 215–230. Springer, Heidelberg (2014)
12. Herrmann, P.: Renaming is necessary in timed regular expressions. In: Pandu Rangan, C., Raman, V., Sarukkai, S. (eds.) FST TCS 1999. LNCS, vol. 1738, pp. 47–59. Springer, Heidelberg (1999)
13. Ho, H.-M., Ouaknine, J., Worrell, J.: Online monitoring of metric temporal logic. In: Bonakdarpour, B., Smolka, S.A. (eds.) RV 2014. LNCS, vol. 8734, pp. 178–192. Springer, Heidelberg (2014)
14. Kane, A., Chowdhury, O., Datta, A., Koopman, P.: A case study on runtime monitoring of an autonomous research vehicle (ARV) system. In: Bartocci, E., Majumdar, R. (eds.) RV 2015. LNCS, vol. 9333, pp. 102–117. Springer, Heidelberg (2015). doi:10.1007/978-3-319-23820-3_7
15. Knuth, D.E., Morris Jr., J.H., Pratt, V.R.: Fast pattern matching in strings. SIAM J. Comput. **6**(2), 323–350 (1977)
16. Simulink User's Guide. The MathWorks Inc., Natick (2015)
17. Boyer-Moore Fast String Searching Example. http://www.cs.utexas.edu/users/moore/best-ideas/string-searching/fstrpos-example.html
18. Ouaknine, J., Worrell, J.: On the decidability and complexity of metric temporal logic over finite words. Logical Meth. Comput. Sci. **3**(1), 1–27 (2007)

19. Pandya, P.K., Suman, P.V.: An introduction to timed automata. In: Modern Applications of Automata Theory, pp. 111–148. World Scientific (2012)
20. Ulus, D., Ferrère, T., Asarin, E., Maler, O.: Timed pattern matching. In: Legay, A., Bozga, M. (eds.) FORMATS 2014. LNCS, vol. 8711, pp. 222–236. Springer, Heidelberg (2014)
21. Ulus, D., Ferrère, T., Asarin, E., Maler, O.: Online timed pattern matching using derivatives. In: Chechik, M., Raskin, J.-F. (eds.) TACAS 2016. LNCS, vol. 9636, pp. 736–751. Springer, Heidelberg (2016). doi:10.1007/978-3-662-49674-9_47
22. Waga, M., Akazaki, T., Hasuo, I.: Code that Accompanies "A Boyer-Moore Type Algorithm for TimedPattern Matching". https://github.com/MasWag/timed-pattern-matching
23. Waga, M., Akazaki, T., Hasuo, I.: A Boyer-Moore Type Algorithm for Timed Pattern Matching (2016). CoRR, abs/1606.07207
24. Watson, B.W., Watson, R.E.: A Boyer-Moore-style algorithm for regular expression pattern matching. Sci. Comput. Program. 48(2–3), 99–117 (2003)

Abstraction Strategies for Computing Travelling or Looping Durations in Networks of Timed Automata

Raymond Devillers[1] and Hanna Klaudel[2(✉)]

[1] Département D'Informatique,
Université Libre de Bruxelles, City of Brussels, Belgium
rdevil@ulb.ac.be
[2] Laboratoire IBISC, Université D'Evry-Val D'Essonne, Evry, France
hanna.klaudel@ibisc.univ-evry.fr

Abstract. This paper shows how to abstract networks of timed automata in order to accelerate the analysis of quantitative properties such as path or cycle duration, that would otherwise suffer from the state space explosion. Two approaches are introduced, a single step strategy and an iterative one, where a part of the network of timed automata is merged and abstracted. As a consequence, the state space is reduced and model-checking is simplified. These approaches are illustrated on a case study, where the comparison is done by calculating the cycle time of one automaton in the network, both on the real network and on the two abstracted ones, showing that the method reduces significantly the runtime, or simply renders feasible the analysis of the system.

Keywords: Timed automata · State space explosion · Duration · Approximation

1 Introduction

Timed automata [1] are a powerful formalism useful to model and analyse real-time concurrent systems. They extend finite state machines by adding real-valued variables, called clocks, which evolve linearly and can be compared with integer constants in states (yielding invariants), called here locations, and along transitions (yielding guards), where some clocks may also be reset to zero; additional (Boolean or integer) variables may also be introduced, checked in guards and invariants, and updated along transitions. Networks are sets of timed automata, which may synchronise through binary communication channels, meaning that a communication involves exactly two components, one performing an emission $k!$ and the other one performing a reception $k?$ on the same channel k. Model checking may be performed on such models, in particular with tools like UPPAAL [9,12].

It is well known that the automated analysis of complex systems, with many communicating components and different orders of magnitude in the used constants, quickly faces a state explosion problem, making the analysis extremely

© Springer International Publishing Switzerland 2016
M. Fränzle and N. Markey (Eds.): FORMATS 2016, LNCS 9884, pp. 140–156, 2016.
DOI: 10.1007/978-3-319-44878-7_9

time and/or memory demanding, or even unfeasible. In such a context, this paper focuses on the computation of upper/lower bounds for the travelling time of various paths or loops in timed automata components. The objective here is to determine if the timing characteristics of the considered system are satisfactory or not, rather than to compute exact bounds (even if it may often lead to tight bounds). We use approximations, which are based on the analysis of the involved communication structure of the network and replace some parts of it by suitable abstractions. We present two approaches (a one step and an iterative one) accelerating and often simply making it possible to achieve these computations. We shall use as a running example a network of timed automata that occurred in the field of mixed reality applications [2].

Related Work. The problems arising from the fragmentation of the state space due to different orders of magnitude in the constants have already been addressed, for various variants of timed automata, and the solutions have sometimes been incorporated in tools [8,10]. The problems due to the complexity of some components have been handled in [6], for instance, where locations are merged in such a way that the added behaviours do not impact the property at hand, or in [7], where UPPAAL has been used in an industrial case study as a "structured testing" tool in order to find bounds for some activities. By contrast, the fact that the size of the state space of distributed systems increases in an exponential way with the number of components is seldom considered, except maybe in [11] where, in a very specific framework, two kinds of components may be distinguished and each kind may be analysed individually, allowing to inject the results in the analysis of the other kind, iteratively until convergence; and in [3] where the authors exploit the specificities of a 2-level real-time scheduling on a single platform. The idea we shall develop here is rather different: in order to simplify the system and make it more adequate for quantitative analyses, we shall consider subsystems and abstract the rest by simple computation nodes.

Paper's Structure: The next sections present first the necessary definitions, then introduces our running example and recalls how one may use UPPAAL to analyse a network of timed automata. Section 5 presents an abstraction strategy, available when only a few components are out of reach of a direct analysis. Section 6 shows how to proceed when no (or too few) components may be analysed. The last section concludes and discusses some possible extensions.

2   Preliminaries

Syntactically, a timed automaton is an annotated directed (and connected) graph, provided with a finite set of non-negative real variables called *clocks*; additional (Boolean or integer) variables may also be introduced. The nodes (*locations*) are annotated with *invariants*, (predicates allowing to enter or stay in a location); they may also have some qualifiers, like an *urgency* indication. The arcs are annotated with *guards* (predicates allowing to perform a move) or *communication actions*, and possibly with some clock *resets* and variable updates.

We shall not detail here the exact syntax allowed for the predicates, adopting the one used in UPPAAL. As usual, the empty predicate is interpreted as true.

In order to glue together the various components of a network of timed automata, some arcs will be classically annotated with communication actions (variable updating may also serve to materialise interactions between components, but also inside a component) which may be either of the form $k!$, meaning the emission of a signal on a channel k, or a complementary $k?$, meaning the reception of some signal on channel k, supposed to synchronise with a $k!$. A channel may also have some qualifiers, like an *urgency* indication. The absence of synchronisation action on an arc indicates an internal activity of the automaton.

Definition 1. *A timed automaton is a tuple $A = (S, s^0, X, K, V, E, I)$, where*

- *S is a set of locations and $s^0 \in S$ is the initial one,*
- *X is the set of clocks,*
- *K is the set of communication actions,*
- *V is the set of variables,*
- *$E \subseteq S \times (K \times B \times U \times 2^X) \times S$ is a set of arcs between locations, possibly annotated with a communication action in K, a guard in B, a variable update U, and a set of clock resets in 2^X,*
- *$I : S \to B$ assigns invariants to locations.*

Definition 2. *A network of timed automata is a set $\mathcal{A} = \{A_1, \ldots, A_n\}$ where each $A_i = (S_i, s_i^0, X_i, K_i, V_i, E_i, I_i)$ is an individual timed automaton, the sets S_i being disjoint.*

The semantics of a network of timed automata is that of the underlying timed automaton (synchronising together through channels and possibly also interacting through common variables and clocks) as recalled below, with the following notations. A location vector is a vector $\bar{s} = (s_1, \ldots, s_n)$; the initial location vector is $\bar{s}^0 = (s_1^0, \ldots, s_n^0)$. We denote by $s_i \xrightarrow{k,b}_{r,u} s_i'$ the arcs between locations, where k is a communication action (which may be absent), b a guard (empty guard is interpreted as true), r is a set of clocks to be reset (possibly empty), and u an update of variables (also possibly empty). The invariant predicates are composed of predicates over location vectors $I(\bar{s}) = \bigwedge_i I_i(s_i)$. We write $\bar{s}[s_i'/s_i]$ to denote the vector where the ith element s_i of $\bar{s}$ is replaced by s_i', and $\bar{s}[s_i'/s_i, s_j'/s_j]$ to denote the vector where the ith element s_i of $\bar{s}$ is replaced by s_i' while the jth element s_j of $\bar{s}$ is replaced by s_j'. A valuation is a function ν from the set of clocks to the non-negative reals, and from the set of variables to Boolean or integer values. Let $\mathbb{V}$ be the set of all clock and variable valuations, $\nu_0(y) = 0$ for each clock or integer variable y, and $\nu_0(b) = \text{false}$ for each Boolean variable b. We shall denote by $\nu \vDash F$ the fact that the valuation ν satisfies (makes true) the formula F. If r is a clock reset and u a variable update, we shall denote by $\nu[r, u]$ the valuation obtained after applying clock reset r and the variables update u to ν; and if $d \in \mathbb{R}_{>0}$ is a delay, $\nu + d$ is the valuation such that, for any clock x, $(\nu + d)(x) = \nu(x) + d$, the variables being left unchanged.

Definition 3. *The semantics of a network* $\mathcal{A} = \{A_1, \ldots A_n\}$ *is defined as a timed transition system* $(St, st_0, \rightarrow)$, *where* $St = (S_1 \times, \ldots \times S_n) \times \mathbb{V}$ *is the set of states,* $st_0 = (\bar{s}^0, \nu_0)$ *is the initial state, and* $\rightarrow \subseteq St \times St$ *is the transition relation defined by:*

- *(silent):* $(\bar{s}, \nu) \rightarrow (\bar{s}', \nu')$ *if there exists* $s_i \xrightarrow{b}_{r,u} s'_i$, *for some* i, *such that* $\bar{s}' = \bar{s}[s'_i/s_i]$, $\nu \vDash b$, $\nu' = \nu[r, u]$ *and* $\nu' \vDash I(\bar{s}')$,
- *(sync):* $(\bar{s}, \nu) \rightarrow (\bar{s}', \nu')$ *if there exist two arcs* $s_i \xrightarrow{k?,b_i}_{r_i,u_i} s'_i$ *and* $s_j \xrightarrow{k!,b_j}_{r_j,u_j} s'_j$ *with* $i \neq j$, *such that* $\nu \vDash b_i \wedge b_j$, $\bar{s}' = \bar{s}[s'_i/s_i, s'_j/s_j]$, $\nu' = \nu[r_i \cup r_j, u_i; u_j]$ *(assuming the updates* u_i *and* u_j *commute) and* $\nu' \vDash I(\bar{s}')$,
- *(timed):* $(\bar{s}, \nu) \rightarrow (\bar{s}, \nu + d)$ *if* $\forall x \in [0, 1] : \nu + x \cdot d \vDash I(\bar{s})$, *there is no urgent synchronisation possible (they have precedence on time passing), and there is no urgent location in* $\bar{s}$ *(time may not progress in an urgent location).*

3   Running Example

In order to illustrate our techniques, we shall use along the paper the running example, originated from [2] and depicted in Fig. 1 modelling an augmented reality system with a sensor I (for *inertial*), two cooperating processing units P (for *priority*) and L (for *lower*), a memory component M and two rendering loops G (for *graphical*) and H (for *haptical*).

Component I, once initialised in s_0, cyclically acquires data in s_1 and sends it on channel k_I to processing unit P. After initialisation (between s_0 and s_3), component P cyclically awaits synchronisations with components I (if available) and L (mandatory), processes data in location s_5 and sends its results to component L on channel k_P. Component L acquires data from component P, then processes them in location s_1 (which takes at least 20 and at most 60 time units), synchronises with memory M (on channel *lock*), writes data in it, which lasts between 10 and 20 time units (in location s_3), and unlocks M. Two rendering components G and H access cyclically M, read and update data in s_1 and process them in s_3.

The underlying communication/synchronisation scheme is represented in Fig. 2.

This kind of system may be handled by UPPAAL. Note that in this example all the communication channels are urgent, i.e., when one or more communications may take place, one of them must occur immediately, and we resume until no more communication is allowed (but other moves may occur before the time progresses): then the time may continue to progress. It is easy to see that no Zeno phenomenon may occur here[1]. Each component is essentially looping, possibly after an initialisation part. We shall here consider the timing characteristics of components L and G, and in particular the bounds of durations for performing their loops.

---

[1] i.e., a situation where infinitely many moves may/must occur in a finite/zero delay.

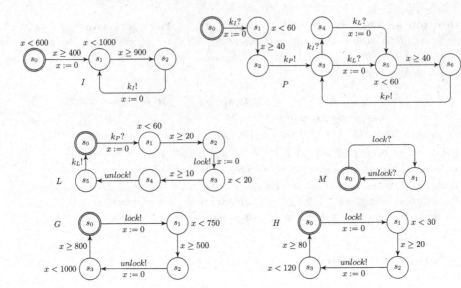

Fig. 1. Network of timed automata of Example 1 (all clocks are local and all channels are urgent).

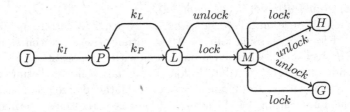

Fig. 2. Communication/synchronisation schema of the running example. The nodes represent components (individual timed automata) and the arcs the synchronisations with the direction from emitting to receiving component.

4   Timing Analysis

Before starting an estimation of the time needed to reach some location s' from location s in a component C, we may first wonder if it may not happen that one gets stuck during the travel (this phenomenon may have various causes - local or global deadlock, starvation, infinite waiting – analysed in [2,5]). This may be checked with a *leads to* property $\varphi\text{-->}\varphi'$, verifying if when φ is true it is certain that φ' will eventually become true also, for which UPPAAL has an efficient algorithm. One may thus use a query $C.s\text{-->}C.s'$ to check if it is certain to reach s' from s in C. A variant of this kind of formula is $C.s\text{-->}\neg C.s$, allowing to check that we cannot get stuck in location s. Applying this kind of formula to a loop needs however to *instrument* a bit the considered component, i.e., to add some features which do not modify the component's behaviour but allow

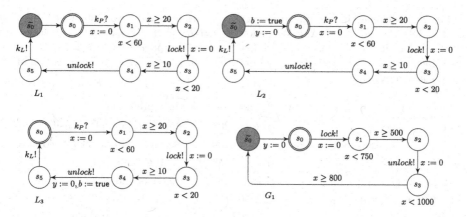

Fig. 3. Some instrumented versions of L: L_1 with added urgent location $\tilde{s}_0$, L_2 with added urgent location $\tilde{s}_0$, local clock y and Boolean variable b; L_3 with added local clock y, and Boolean variable b; and instrumented version G_1 of G with added urgent location $\tilde{s}_0$ and local clock y.

to analyse it. Indeed, the formula $C.s$ - -> $C.s$ will always return *true*, because it is satisfied by the empty path, hence does not correspond to a true looping behaviour. A general technique to solve this kind of problem is to introduce an urgent location $\tilde{s}$ (where time may not progress, represented in dark blue in the figures) before the considered location s, with all the arcs to s redirected to $\tilde{s}$. This technique is general, but even if it does not modify the original behaviour, it increases the size of the state space since it introduces a new location. However, in some circumstances, if there is a location s_1 such that it is not possible to loop without visiting it, it is enough to check the pair of formulas $C.s$ - -> $C.s_1$ and $C.s_1$ - -> $C.s$.

As an example, the instrumented version L_1 of component L is illustrated in Fig. 3, and the first three lines of Table 1 give the liveness results for L and L_1.

In order to evaluate timing characteristics, we may use UPPAAL queries of the kind $\sup\{\varphi\}$: x to compute the supremum (respectively, $\inf\{\varphi\}$: x to compute the infimum) of clock x when formula φ is true. Note that there may be an asymmetry in their usage; for instance, $\sup\{C.s\}$: $C.x$ computes the supremum of clock x when *leaving* location s in component C, while $\inf\{C.s\}$: $C.x$ computes the infimum of clock x when *entering* location s in component C.

However, to make a good use of those queries it may again be necessary to instrument a bit the considered components. First, one should add new clocks allowing to measure the interesting paths, with resets put on the arcs entering the starting point(s), unless existing clocks already do the job. Next, one may need to add urgent locations, for instance when we need to consider the maximal time to enter a location and not the time to leave it. This may also be used to differentiate the various ways to enter a location, when there are many ones. Finally, one may introduce Boolean variables (initialised to *false*) to select paths satisfying some constraints.

Table 1. Model checking results, and execution times observed for a system with Intel Core i5 1.4 GHz and 4GB RAM. We denote by ex1-L_i, for $i = 1, 2, 3$, the specification composed of all the automata of Example 1 where component L is replaced by its instrumented version L_i allowing to perform the desired request. The interpretation of ex1-G_1 is analogous.

Model	Query	Result	Time [s]	Interpretation
ex1	$L.s_0 \text{- ->} L.s_2$	true	208	first half loop of L feasible
ex1	$L.s_2 \text{- ->} L.s_0$	true	139	second half loop of L feasible
ex1-L_1	$L_1.s_0 \text{- ->} L_1.\tilde{s_0}$	true	345	loop feasible
ex1-L_2	$\inf\{L_2.\tilde{s_0}\}: L_2.y$	> 70	148	lower bound of looping time
ex1-L_2	$\sup\{L_2.\tilde{s_0}\}: L_2.y$	< 2550	150	upper bound of looping time
ex1-L_2	$\inf\{L_2.\tilde{s_0} \wedge \neg L_2.b\}: L_2.y$	≥ 1330	148	lower bound of the first loop
ex1-L_2	$\sup\{L_2.\tilde{s_0} \wedge \neg L_2.b\}: L_2.y$	< 2550	157	upper bound of the first loop
ex1-L_2	$\inf\{L_2.\tilde{s_0} \wedge L_2.b\}: L_2.y$	> 70	158	lower bound of the next loops
ex1-L_2	$\sup\{L_2.\tilde{s_0} \wedge L_2.b\}: L_2.y$	< 950	159	upper bound of the next loops
ex1-L_3	$\inf\{L_3.s_2 \wedge \neg L_3.b\}: L_3.y$	> 1320	110	lower bound of $s_0 \rightarrow s_2$ in the first loop
ex1-L_3	$\sup\{L_3.s_1 \wedge \neg L_3.b\}: L_3.y$	< 1720	111	upper bound of $s_0 \rightarrow s_2$ in the first loop
ex1-L_3	$\inf\{L_3.s_2 \wedge L_3.b\}: L_3.y$	> 60	112	lower bound of $s_5 \rightarrow s_2$ in the next loops
ex1-L_3	$\sup\{L_3.s_1 \wedge L_3.b\}: L_3.y$	< 120	113	upper bound of $s_5 \rightarrow s_2$ in the next loops
ex1-G_1	$\inf\{G_1.\tilde{s_0}\}: G_1.y$	–	int. 1h	lower bound of looping in G_1
ex1-G_1	$\sup\{G_1.\tilde{s_0}\}: G_1.y$	–	int. 1h	upper bound of looping in G_1
ex1-G_1	$G_1.s0 \text{- ->} G_1.\tilde{s_0}$	–	int. 1h	loop feasible?

For instance, for the timing analysis of component L of Example 1, one may consider its instrumented version L_2, as shown in Fig. 3, and use the pair of queries $\inf\{L_2.\tilde{s_0}\}: L_2.y$ and $\sup\{L_2.\tilde{s_0}\}: L_2.y$ to get the lower and upper bounds (respectively) of the looping time: this is also illustrated in Table 1. However, since component P has an initialisation phase before entering its true looping part, one may suspect that the first loop of L and the next ones behave differently: this is confirmed by the next four queries in the table, where the Boolean variable b in L_2 allows to distinguish the first loop from the next ones (it is also possible to unroll explicitly the first iteration(s) of the loop in order to analyse them successively; this amounts for instance to replace a looping structure α^* by a structure $\alpha(\alpha^*)$ if we want to isolate the first iteration from the next ones; we shall not do it here, but a partial unrolling will be used in the next two sections, for other reasons). For further use, we are also interested in the time to go from s_5 to s_2, and in the time to first enter s_2 (from the initial state); this may be analysed with the instrumented version L_3 of L, also shown on Fig. 3 and illustrated in Table 1: the Boolean variable b is used to distinguish the first time one enters s_2 (from s_0) from the next ones (from s_5).

Similarly, the bounds of the looping times of components G may be obtained from the instrumented version G_1, also shown on Fig. 3, and the results are detailed at the end of Table 1.

All the computations succeeded, except for the looping times of G, for which the executions were stopped after 1 hour, and the accelerations by over/under-approximations offered by UPPAAL do not help. It could happen that the bounds for the looping time of G may be obtained by allowing more execution time (and/or a much more powerful computer), but in any case this would likely be considered unsatisfactory by the end user, who probably would like to analyse many variants of the model.

Note that, to get bounds for the time needed to follow some path, one may also add the bounds for sub-paths, but the result is generally less accurate than the global estimation; this is due to the well known property that the $\inf(f_1 + f_2) \geq \inf(f_1) + \inf(f_2)$ and $\sup(f_1 + f_2) \leq \sup(f_1) + \sup(f_2)$ for any two functions f_1 and f_2, the equality being only obtained if the two functions are independent, or by mere chance, because the extrema are reached at the same points.

5   Direct Abstraction Strategy

We have seen in the previous section that the computation of timing characteristics may blow up. This is usually due to a combination of a complex system, in particular a highly distributed one, and ill balanced constants in the invariants and guards. We shall now consider strategies allowing to get around this unfortunate phenomenon in some circumstances, at least partly.

First, it may be observed that it is usually not necessary to know the exact infima and suprema, but only to be able to assert that some traveling time is not higher than some value, and possibly also not lower than some other value. Hence it is sufficient to determine an (approximate) interval $[min, max]$ encompassing the traveling time under consideration, i.e., to get an over-approximation of the true bounds. We here considered a closed interval, but sometimes we shall use open or semi-closed ones, when it is known that some extremum may not be reached.

Since one of the main sources of computation failure is the size of the system, we shall delineate a subsystem including the component we want to analyse and abstract away the interactions of this subsystem with the rest of the system, in order to isolate the subsystem and make its analysis feasible. This subsystem should be chosen with care: it should be small enough to allow the computations, but not too small to avoid uselessly large approximations (knowing that the travel time is in interval $[0, \infty]$ is not very useful). This may also be used to only keep in the subsystem components with similar constants. Also, we shall assume that the only interactions of the subsystem with the exterior is through rendez-vous on channels (no shared clock or variable), and that we are able to analyse the times taken by these communications.

In such a subsystem, we may distinguish internal components, which do not communicate with the exterior, and border components, which communicate both with the subsystem and with the exterior. The intuitive idea behind the method is then to replace those communications in the border components by one or more computation arcs, of the kind illustrated in Fig. 5, over-approximating the true time needed by those communications: guard $x \geq min$ and invariant $x \leq max$ ensure a delay in the interval $[min, max]$. Strict inequalities are also possible, for example guard $x > min$ and invariant $x < max$ ensure a delay in the interval (min, max), and analogously for other combinations. The values min and max, as well as the choice between strict or weak inequalities, should be provided by the analysis of the abstracted communication in the border component behaving in the full system.

In our example, since we want to analyse component G, we shall consider the subsystem $ss1$ (with the interior composed of M, H and G, and border component L), illustrated on top of Fig. 4. Note that the choice of the actual boundary of $ss1$ is quite arbitrary provided that it contains G, does not communicate with the rest of the system through clocks or variables, (which is the case here since all the clocks and variables are local) and the border may be analysed in the full system (which is the case in our example, as detailed in Table 1).

In general, if all the bordering components may be analysed in the full system, in order to abstract away the interactions with the exterior of the subsystem, the

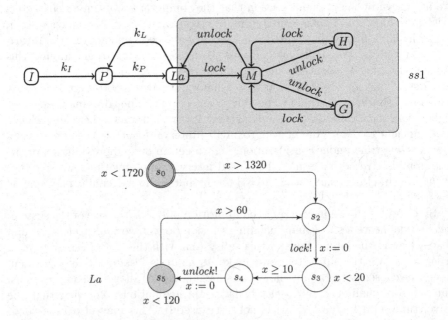

Fig. 4. Subsystem $ss1$ of Example 1, depicted within the communication scheme, and the border component La (obtained from L by abstracting the exterior of $ss1$, i.e., components I and P).

$$c := 0 \quad \xrightarrow{\hspace{3cm}} \quad s \quad \xrightarrow{\quad (c \geq min) \wedge (c \leq max) \wedge b \quad}_{r,\,u} \quad s'$$
$$(c \leq max) \vee I$$

Fig. 5. A computation arc over-approximating (by an interval $[min, max]$ on some 'computation' clock c, with the guard b, the final clock resets r and the global variable updates u) the traveling through a communication arc or phase. Clock c is reset on all the incoming arcs to s and should not be reset by other components; it is in principle a new clock introduced for the abstraction, but it may also be an existing one that is available at that point. I materialises the invariants driving the other ways to leave s, usually in the form of a disjunction of inequalities of the kind $c \leq max'$ or $c < max'$.

most direct technique is simply to replace each communication arc ($k!$ or $k?$) with the exterior by an adequate computation arc, i.e., with an interval $[min, max]$ if we know from the analysis of the component that the communication takes between min and max time units. (see Fig. 5; note that constraints of the kind $0 \leq c$ and $c \leq \infty$ may be simply dropped, and that we assumed here to have inclusive extrema, while they may be exclusive.) Also, as already noticed, in order to avoid too large approximations due to an initialisation phenomenon, it may be useful to unroll the first loop execution(s).

It may happen that a same communication arc allows to interact both with the interior and the exterior of the subsystem (in our example, if the left border of $ss1$ was shifted right so that the border becomes component M and component L is now in the exterior, channels *lock* and *unlock* connect M both to the exterior L and to the interior G and H). In this case, we should duplicate those arcs in order to separate the communications (in our modified example, this would mean replace the *lock* in M by a choice between *lock*1 and *lock*2, *lock*1 being used in L and *lock*2 in G and H, and similarly for *unlock*).

The technique we just sketched is general but it uses the least possible granularity for the abstraction of the communications with the exterior of the subsystem, which unfortunately multiplies the intermediate computations (to evaluate the min/max values) and accumulates the propagations of approximations (due to the fact already mentioned that the sum of two mins/maxs may be lower/higher than the min/max of the sum). Hence, instead of abstracting away the outside communication arcs individually, we may search the coarsest possible abstraction. This amounts to search for the largest possible *phases* of communications with the exterior (see Definition 4) and to abstract each phase by a computation arc of the kind described in Fig. 5 for the individual abstractions.

Definition 4. *A communication phase is a part of a component with a first location s and a last one s' (possibly the same) together with intermediate locations and arcs: the arcs are either computation ones or communications with the exterior of the considered subsystem; they link locations of the phase, and all arcs to/from the intermediate locations belong to the phase; moreover, all the interactions with the exterior of the phase (through clock resets, variable updates and guards) should be equivalent to what happens with a single arc, so that traveling* *through the phase may be over-approximated by a single computation arc of the form described in Fig. 5.*

For instance, for each clock reset during the phase, if its value is used outside the phase (before a further reset), one must have a reset on each arc to s' inside the phase (hence terminating the phase): all those resets yield the reset r. For each variable modified in the phase whose value is used outside the phase but in the same component (before a further modification), the final modification must be the same whatever the path from s to s'; if the value of the variable is used in another component of the subsystem, the (same) modification should only occur on all the arcs to s' inside the phase: those final modifications yield the updates u. Finally, the guard b used to summarise the guards inside the phase, should be implied by all the guards on the arcs from s inside the phase, and its value should not change during the rest of the phase. Note that we may have various phases between the same end locations s and s', and that a single communication arc always constitutes a phase by itself, but not often a maximal one.

For our example, in the (unique) border component L of subsystem $ss1$, the outside channels are k_L and k_P, and we may abstract the phase constituted by the whole path from s_5 to s_2, by a single computation arc. However, since the initial state is inside the abstracted path, we must also abstract the first time the path from s_0 to s_2 is ran; by the way, this also constitutes a partial unrolling of the first loop. We thus get the abstracted component La illustrated on the bottom of Fig. 4: the timing constraints for the computation arcs originating at locations s_0 and s_5 (depicted in blue) are those obtained by the analysis of L_3 in Table 1. The bounds for the looping time of G are then computed in the system $ss1$-La (i.e., $ss1$ with border component La). The results for the corresponding queries are presented in Table 2.

Table 2. Model checking results of G with the direct abstraction method. Notations for models are as in Table 1.

Model	Query	Result	Time [s]	Interpretation
ss1-La	$G_1.s_0 - \text{-}> G_1.\tilde{s}_0$	true	284	loop feasible
ss1-La	$\inf\{G_1.\tilde{s}_0\}: G_1.y$	≥ 8100	16	lower bound of looping in G_1
ss1-La	$\sup\{G_1.\tilde{s}_0\}: G_1.y$	< 11750	16	upper bound of looping in G_1

It may be observed that, while the computation of the looping time of component G exploded for the full system, it becomes quite immediate in the simplified and abstracted subsystem $ss1$. Of course, it is not sure that the bounds we obtained are very tight with respect to the true infimum/supremum, but they may be satisfactory with respect to the question the practitioner will ask about the behaviour of G. In particular that means that there is no deadlock or starvation phenomena.

Proposition 1. SOUNDNESS OF THE DIRECT STRATEGY

The direct strategy, consisting in replacing each arc or phase of the subsystem communicating with the exterior of the considered subsystem by a computation arc with an interval encompassing the actual delay needed to cross it in the full system, provides a correct over-approximation of the subsystem.

Proof. Obvious since the true evolutions of the components in the subsystem (in the full system) are compatible with the ones in the isolated subsystem. As a consequence, if a traveling time in a component is larger than some constant and/or smaller than another one in the isolated subsystem, this is also true in the full system; in other words, the intervals obtained for the isolated subsystem are over-approximations of the true ones, in the full system. Similarly, if it is sure from some location to reach another one in the isolated subsystem, this is also true in the full system, since this means it is not possible to escape visiting the second location.   □ 1

6 Iterated Abstraction Strategy

When one or more boundary components are too complex to be directly analysed, the technique developed in the previous section may be inefficient, because the only bounds we may use for them is $[0, \infty]$. However, we may circumvent the problem by analysing their abstractions as viewed both from the interior and the exterior of the considered subsystem.

Let us thus assume that, in a complex system to be model-checked, we consider a subsystem $ss1$ such that the direct analysis of some of its bordering components fails. Besides subsystem $ss1$, we shall also consider the subsystem $ss2$ composed of the components exterior to $ss1$ and the bordering one(s), as illustrated in the upper part of Fig. 6. If $ss2$ is still too complex, we may cut it in the same way, and at the end we shall get a family of small subsystems covering the whole system, with interior components, and with border ones communicating with at least two subsystems.

For each subsystem and each of its border components, we may then build the abstracted version of the latter, as viewed from this subsystem, in a way similar to what we have explained in the previous section.

The general idea of the iterated abstraction strategy is then to proceed in a succession of rounds. In each round, we consider successively each subsystem in some order, with each of its border components abstracting the exterior of the considered subsystem, replacing the communications with each exterior subsystem (arc or phase) by computational arcs, possibly after duplicating channels and unrolling the main loop. If the border component is analysable, the bounds and invariants will be derived as in the previous section; otherwise, they will be parameterised, and those parameters will be initialised in such a way that we are sure the induced behaviour encompasses the actual one (for instance we may use the interval $[0, \infty]$). When analysing this simplified component in its isolated subsystem, we may then estimate bounds for the communications between the

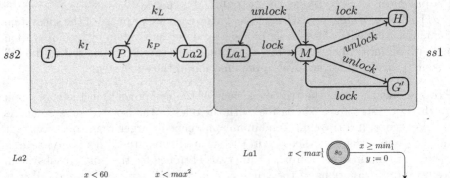

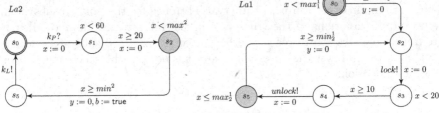

Fig. 6. Two subsystems $ss1$ and $ss2$ of Example 1' used for the iterated abstraction strategies, and the two versions of component L, abstracted as viewed from $ss2$ ($La2$) and from $ss1$ ($La1$). The superscripts for parameters min^i and max^i refer to subsystems, while subscripts identify different mins and maxs if necessary.

border component and this subsystem: this will be used to get better bounds for the abstractions of the same component when viewed from the subsystems to be considered next.

We proceed that way until no improvement is obtained when going from one round to the next one, i.e., when no bound is improved when analysing the various borders of the various subsystems, or when the practitioner considers the approximation obtained up to now is satisfactory with respect to his needs (in general, this means all the upper bounds are considered low enough), or desperate (in general because one of the lower bounds is too high, so that the situation will never be satisfactory, and it will be necessary to adapt the structure of the system).

One then may estimate bounds for the looping times (or traveling times) one is interested in. Note that, again, there is no guarantee that the obtained bounds will be very tight: all we know is that the true interval will be inside the result.

This is summarised in Algorithm 1.

Proposition 2. SOUNDNESS OF THE ITERATED STRATEGY

Starting with $[0, \infty]$ intervals, Algorithm 1 terminates, and the successive stages of the successive rounds produce correct over-approximations of the original system.

Proof. Let us assume that, at the end of the first round, the obtained intervals are smaller or equal to the initial ones (this will in particular be the case if we start with $[0, \infty]$ intervals). Then, since the intervals at the beginning of the second round are the same than at the end of the first round, during the second round the possible evolutions are compatible with the specifications of the first round, so that at the end of the second round, the obtained intervals are smaller or equal to the ones obtained at the end of the first round. Iterating the reasoning we get that the successive rounds will yield a series of nested intervals.

If, moreover, the initial intervals encompass the ones in the original system (again, this will in particular be the case if we start with $[0, \infty]$ intervals), the same kind of argument as the one used in the proof of Proposition 1 shows that, at each stage, the evolutions of the original system are compatible with the approximate components (be it internal to a subsystem or a bordering one), so that the bounds obtained for the latter are correct.

If the bounds stabilise, the algorithm terminates (possibly before, if a satisfactory situation is reached). Since the bounds of each abstracted interval at each stage are natural numbers (or ∞ for the upper bound), the only way we shall have non-stabilisation is when the successive values of an interval are of the form $[k_i, \infty]$ with increasing but unbounded k_i's (this corresponds to a very particular case where it is impossible to reach the end of an abstracted part). But then the algorithm will terminate because the situation will be considered as desperate by the end user at some point. (Note that in our experiences, we always got stabilisation, and quite fast.)   □ 2

In order to illustrate this technique, let us replace in our running example the component G by a slower one; we shall thus consider a system Example 1', which is as Example 1 except for G which has been replaced by G', in which the

---

Algorithm 1. Iterated abstraction method

Data: network of timed automata N, a property ϕ to be analysed in a
      subsystem S of N
Result: analysis of ϕ in an approximated subsystem S
Construct a family of subsystems including S, covering N;
foreach subsystem **do**
  | Determine the bordering components of it and construct its abstracted
  | version ;
end
Choose the initial values of the min/max parameters;
Choose an ordering of the subsystems;
repeat
  | Analyse the subsystems cyclically, following the chosen ordering, and
  | determine new approximate values for the min/max parameters;
until *no progress is made, or the situation is judged satisfactory or desperate by*
the end user;
Analyse ϕ in the abstracted version of S, approximated with the final parameter
values;

---

computation interval for s_1 has been changed to $[3100, 4200)$, and that of s_3 to $[5000, 7500)$. We also consider the instrumented version G'_1, defined in the same way as G_1.

Since automatic analyses are usually made complicated, even unfeasible, when there are different orders of magnitudes in the constants of a system, we may expect new difficulties with respect to the case of Example 1: indeed, all the queries of Table 1 now blow up.

We shall use the decomposition in subsystems illustrated on top of Fig. 6. There is thus still a unique border, L, and its (parameterised) abstracted variants as viewed by subsystems $ss1$ and $ss2$ are shown on the bottom of this figure.

The iteration then takes the form of rounds, which stabilise very fast:

Round 1:

Step 1: Since the problem arises from G', we shall first consider subsystem $ss2$, with L replaced by $La2$ (see Fig. 6), with the initial parameters $min^2 = 0$ and $max^2 = \infty$ (which amounts to drop the constraints on min^2, max^2). (Note that we could have used $min^2 = 10$, since a closer look at L shows that at least 10 time units are spent between $lock!$ and $unlock!$, but this will not be necessary). We may then use the queries shown on top of Table 3 to obtain a first estimation of min^1_1, max^1_1, min^1_2 and max^1_2.

Step 2: With the bounds obtained in the previous step, analyse component $La1$ in $ss1$, and search for the bounds min^2 and max^2 with the next two queries in Table 3.

Round 2:

Step 1: With the bounds obtained in step 2 of round 1, analyse component $La2$ in $ss2$, and search for the next estimation of the bounds min^1_1, max^1_1, min^1_2 and max^1_2 with the next four queries in Table 3. Since no improvement is obtained with respect to the results of round 1, we may stop the iterations, and estimate the bounds for the looping time of G' and $La1$ in $ss1$, as shown by the last queries in Table 3 (for L, we do not need true computations: the approximate bounds for the loop, after some initialisation, is given by the sums of the bounds of the two half-loops, from s_2 to s_5 and from s_5 to s_2).

We may observe that, while none of the components L and G were analysable in the original system of Example 1', with our iterated abstraction strategy no computation took more than a few seconds (but the loop feasibility which takes a few minutes), leading to bounds that satisfied the practitioners at the origin of this kind of system.

Table 3. Results and execution times of the iterative abstraction process for Example 1'. Notations for models as in Table 1.

Round 1	Step1			
model	query	result	time [s]	interpretation
$ss2$-$La2$	$\inf\{La2.s_2 \wedge \neg La2.b\}: La2.y$	≥ 1320	< 1	min_1^1
$ss2$-$La2$	$\sup\{La2.s_1 \wedge \neg La2.b\}: La2.y$	< 1720	< 1	max_1^1
$ss2$-$La2$	$\inf\{La2.s_2 \wedge La2.b\}: La2.y$	≥ 60	< 1	min_2^1
$ss2$-$La2$	$\sup\{La2.s_1 \wedge La2.b\}: La2.y$	< 120	< 1	max_2^1
Round 1	**Step2**			
model	query	result	time [s]	interpretation
$ss1$-$La1$	$\inf\{La1.s_5\}: La1.y$	> 10	2	min^2
$ss1$-$La1$	$\sup\{La1.s_4\}: La1.y$	< 4280	2	max^2
Round 2	**Step1**			
model	query	result	time [s]	interpretation
$ss2$-$La2$	$\inf\{La2.s_2 \wedge \neg La2.b\}: La2.y$	≥ 1320	< 1	min_1^1
$ss2$-$La2$	$\sup\{La2.s_1 \wedge \neg La2.b\}: La2.y$	< 1720	< 1	max_1^1
$ss2$-$La2$	$\inf\{La2.s_2 \wedge La2.b\}: La2.y$	≥ 60	< 1	min_2^1
$ss2$-$La2$	$\sup\{La2.s_1 \wedge La2.b\}: La2.y$	< 120	< 1	max_2^1
	Final analysis			
model	query	result	time [s]	interpretation
$ss1$-$La1$	$G_1'.s_0 - -> G_1'.\tilde{s}_0$	true	2125	loop of G' feasible
$ss1$-$La1$	$\inf\{G_1'.\tilde{s}_0\}: G_1'.y$	≥ 8100	18	lower bound of looping in G'
$ss1$-$La1$	$\sup\{G_1'.\tilde{s}_0\}: G_1'.y$	< 11750	18	upper bound of looping in G'
$ss1$-$La1$	$min_2^1 + min^2$	> 70	0	lower bound of looping in $La1$
$ss1$-$La1$	$max_2^1 + max^2$	< 4400	0	upper bound of looping in $La1$

7 Conclusion and Future Work

We proposed and showed the soundness of two abstraction methods allowing to accelerate (or make possible) the model-checking analysis of timed properties of components of networks of timed automata. We illustrated on a typical example how the abstraction strategy may help in analysing the timing properties of a network of timed automata when a state space explosion occurs. We also applied our iterative strategy on the behaviour of component L in our first example, with the same decomposition since the system has the same structure, and we observed that only a fraction of second is necessary to analyse each of the three steps, compared to a few minutes in the direct analysis summarised in Table 1 (and in this case the obtained bounds are exactly the same).

Example 1 has not been chosen on purpose: it arose in one of our previous works, as a solution to deadlock problems occurring in a small but realistic model of augmented reality application, but we should of course examine how our techniques apply to larger realistic systems. We should also derive good ways to decompose a large system into subsystems of adequate size and characteristics. Finally, in addition to local analyses like the loop or travelling time bounds, we could be interested in the time needed to transfer an information from a source component to a consumer one, like in our example from a sensor to a rendering loop.

Acknowledgements. We are grateful to Jean-Yves Didier, Mathieu Moine and Johan Arcile for their ideas in the early stage of this work. We would like also to thank the anonymous referees for their careful reading and inspiring suggestions.

References

1. Alur, R., Dill, D.L.: A theory of timed automata. Theoret. Comput. Sci. **126**(2), 183–235 (1994)
2. Arcile, J., Didier, J., Klaudel, H., Devillers, R., Rataj, A.: Indefinite waitings in MIRELA systems. ESSS 2015, pp. 5–18 (2015). http://dx.doi.org/10.4204/EPTCS.184.1
3. Carnevali, L., Pinzuti, A., Vicario, E.: Compositional verification for hierarchical scheduling of real-time systems. IEEE Trans. Softw. Eng. **39**(5), 638–657 (2013)
4. Devillers, R., Didier, J.-Y., Klaudel, H.: Specifications, Implementing Timed Automata: The "Sandwich" Approach. ACSD 2013, pp. 226–235. IEEE (2013)
5. Devillers, R., Didier, J.-Y., Klaudel, H., Arcile, J.: Deadlock and temporal properties analysis in mixed reality applications. ISSRE 2014. IEEE, pp. 55–65 (2014)
6. Finkbeiner, B., Peter, H.-J., Schewe, S.: Synthesising certificates in networks of timed automata. IET Softw. **4**(3), 222–235 (2010)
7. Hendriks, M., Verhoef, M.: Timed automata based analysis of embedded system architectures. In: Workshop on Parallel and Distributed Real-Time Systems (2006)
8. Hendriks, M., Larsen, K.: Exact acceleration of real-time model checking. Electr. Notes Theor. Comput. Sci. **65**(6), 120–139 (2002)
9. Larsen, K.G., Pettersson, P., Yi, W.: UPPAAL in a nutshell. Int. J. Softw. Tools Technol. Transf. **1**(1–2), 134–152 (1997)
10. Möller, M.O.: Parking can get you there faster- model augmentation to speed up real-time model-checking. Electr. Notes Theor. Comput. Sci. **65**(6), 202–217 (2002)
11. Perathoner, S., et al.: Influence of different abstractions on the performance analysis of distributed hard real-time systems. Design Autom. Emb. Sys. **13**(1–2), 27–49 (2009)
12. UPPAAL. http://www.uppaal.org/

Distributed Algorithms for Time Optimal Reachability Analysis

Zhengkui Zhang$^{(\boxtimes)}$, Brian Nielsen, and Kim G. Larsen

Department of Computer Science, Aalborg University, Aalborg, Denmark
{zhzhang,bnielsen,kgl}@cs.aau.dk

Abstract. Time optimal reachability analysis is a novel model based technique for solving scheduling and planning problems. After modeling them as reachability problems using timed automata, a real-time model checker can compute the fastest trace to the goal states which constitutes a time optimal schedule. We propose distributed computing to accelerate time optimal reachability analysis. We develop five distributed state exploration algorithms, implement them in UPPAAL enabling it to exploit the compute resources of a dedicated model-checking cluster. We experimentally evaluate the implemented algorithms with four models in terms of their ability to compute near- or proven-optimal solutions, their scalability, time and memory consumption and communication overhead. Our results show that distributed algorithms work much faster than sequential algorithms and have good speedup in general.

1 Introduction

Time optimal reachability (TOR) analysis is a novel model based technique for solving scheduling and planning problems [1,16]. After modeling these problems using timed automata, a real-time model checker such as UPPAAL [6] and KRO-NOS [12] can compute the fastest trace to the goal states which constitutes a time optimal schedule, because the trace carries actions of the model and timing information of these actions to the goal states. TOR allows natural modeling of real-time behavior, constrains and interactions of components, as well as flexible choices of efficiently implemented search algorithms inside model checkers.

However the well-known state-space explosion problem may arise when the number of components in the model is large. In [20] we developed swarm algorithms to mitigate this problem and accelerate TOR. The core idea is employing a large number of parallel UPPAAL instances or agents with randomized search strategies to search the state spaces independently, thus finding different traces to the goal state in parallel and avoiding local optimality. The advantages of this approach are: (1) easy to implement; (2) find optimal (or near optimal) results fast without exploring the full state-space. A weak point however is the lack of data parallelism nor sharing of the explored state-space, thus the execution time is hardly reduced and memory is limited to that of a single instance.

This work has been supported by Danish National Research Foundation – Center for Foundations of Cyber-Physical Systems, a Sino-Danish research center.

M. Fränzle and N. Markey (Eds.): FORMATS 2016, LNCS 9884, pp. 157–173, 2016.
DOI: 10.1007/978-3-319-44878-7_10

In this paper, we extend our previous work in [20] by developing distributed algorithms that may accelerate TOR in three ways. First, the state-space is now partitioned and distributed among distributed CPU and memory resources so that multiple worker processes now share the state-space exploration workload, thus the execution time may potentially be shortened greatly. Second, more traces/state-space will be explored in parallel, thus the fastest trace will be potentially found even faster than the swarm algorithms. Third, the disjoint parts of state-space are stored in the distributed memory, allowing fully use the memory of a cluster and handle even larger models than swarm algorithms.

Related Work. Because time optimal reachability involves the notion of cost and optimality, *branch and bound* (B&B) is used for efficient state-space exploration. By a bounding function and the current best solution to the goal states, B&B can effectively prune parts of the state-space that guarantee not to lead to an optimal solution [13] thus avoiding enumerating the entire state-space. Behrmann *et al.* presented a branch-and-bound minimal-cost reachability algorithm on the priced timed automata (PTA) in [7,8].

The earliest and monumental distributed model checker is the parallel Murφ verifier proposed in 1997 [17]. Its design delineated the cornerstone upon which other distributed model checkers were built thereafter such as distributed UPPAAL [5,9], DIVINE [3], LTSMIN [11], etc. Meanwhile, enormous research efforts have been made to improve the state-space generation algorithm, the partition algorithm, the state storage data structure, the communication and control mechanism, as well as many other technical issues. Since 2006 multi-core CPUs became pervasive inside PC, HPC and embedded markets, DIVINE, LTSMIN and FDR3 [14] exploit multi-core shared memory technique to achieve even better performance on the modern hardware architecture. DIVINE also made fruitful attempts to accelerate model checking using GPUs from 2009 [4].

Contribution. We developed five distributed TOR algorithms and implemented them in the UPPAAL model checker to accelerate TOR analysis. In addition to sharing explored states, worker processes exchange computed better costs to the goal states. This enables each worker to prune its local state-space efficiently by B&B, hence need less execution time and memory consumption.

D-BFS: distributed breath-first search. Each worker runs local BFS while exchanging states with other workers.

D-BFS^S: distributed strict order BFS (also named *level synchronized* BFS). A synchronization protocol will ensure all workers completely explore states on the same current BFS level before moving on to the next level.

D-DFS: distributed depth-first search. Same principle as D-BFS except traversing depth-first.

D-DFS^G: distributed greedy DFS. In addition to D-DFS, each worker always picks the successor state of the lowest cost in each iteration.

D-RDFS: distributed random depth-first search. Same principle as D-DFS with a randomly picked successor state.

It is worth noting that in distributed BFS/DFS/DFS^G/RDFS, their global search orders only approximate BFS/DFS/DFS^G/RDFS. Due to the varying communication delay or workload on computing nodes, states are received in nondeterministic order from run to run. This influences the successor states generation locally and changes the number of states explored [9]. Another important observation is that in UPPAAL BFS often completes explorations much faster than DFS/RDFS because DFS/RDFS can cause higher degree of *fragmentation* of the underlying symbolic state-space requiring many more symbolic states. The motivation of D-BFS^S is to keep this strong point of BFS. However BFS has an inherent drawback that it typically only reports results late when it has searched nearly all states, making it infeasible for very large state-spaces.

We employ the following metrics to compare the algorithms:

Metric 1: time to find the optimal result (t_{opt}). The minimum runtime to find the fastest trace (or schedule) to the goal states. Users wish to get the optimal result fast even before an algorithm terminates.

Metric 2: time to completely explore the state-space and terminate thus proving the optimal result (t_{prov}). Users prefer an algorithm to terminate fast.

Metric 3: time to progressively improved solutions (a.k.a. *near optimal* solutions). It shows how fast the results converge to the optimal as a function of running time. In scheduling problems, the absolute optimal solution is not always required, but a sufficiently good one may suffice. Particularly when algorithms cannot terminate due to time or memory constrains, faster converge speed produces better near optimal results that are closer to the optimality.

Metric 4: memory consumption and communication overhead of algorithms. Smaller memory consumption improves scalability by allowing bigger state-space. Smaller communication overhead improves computing speed.

Outline. The rest of the paper is organized as follows. Section 2 recalls the definitions of timed automata and sequential TOR algorithm. Section 3 explains the distributed TOR algorithms. Section 4 shows benchmark experiment results of the sequential and distributed TOR algorithms. Section 5 concludes.

2 Sequential Time Optimal Reachability

This section recalls timed automaton and the sequential time-optimal reachability algorithm. For brevity parallel composition of timed automata is omitted.

2.1 Timed Automata

Let $X = \{x, y, ...\}$ be a finite set of clocks. We define $\mathcal{B}(X)$ as the set of clock constraints over X generated by grammar: $g, g_1, g_2 ::= x \bowtie n \mid x - y \bowtie n \mid g_1 \wedge g_2$, where $x, y \in X$ are clocks, $n \in \mathbb{N}$ and $\bowtie \in \{\leq, <, =, >, \geq\}$.

Definition 1. A Timed Automaton (TA) [2] is a 6-tuple $\mathcal{A} = (L, \ell_0, X, \Sigma,$ $E, Inv)$ where: L is a finite set of locations; $\ell_0 \in L$ is the initial location; X is a finite set of non-negative real-valued clocks; Σ is a finite set of actions; $E \subseteq L \times \mathcal{B}(X) \times \Sigma \times 2^X \times L$ is a finite set of edges, each of which contains a source location, a guard, an action, a set of clocks to be reset and a target location; $Inv : L \to \mathcal{B}(X)$ sets an invariant for each location. For simplicity an edge $(\ell, g, a, r, \ell') \in E$ is written as $\ell \xrightarrow{g,a,r} \ell'$.

Definition 2. The semantics of a timed automaton $\mathcal{A}$ is a Timed Transition System (TTS) $S_{\mathcal{A}} = (Q, Q_0, \Sigma, \to)$ where: $Q = \{(\ell, v) \mid (\ell, v) \in L \times \mathbb{R}^X_{\geq 0}$ and $v \models Inv(\ell)\}$ are states, $Q_0 = (\ell_0, 0)$ is the initial state, Σ is the finite set of actions, $\to \subseteq Q \times (\Sigma \cup \mathbb{R}_{\geq 0}) \times Q$ is the transition relation defined separately for action $a \in \Sigma$ and delay $d \in \mathbb{R}_{\geq 0}$ as:

(1) $(\ell, v) \xrightarrow{a} (\ell', v')$ if there is an edge $(\ell \xrightarrow{g,a,r} \ell') \in E$ such that $v \models g$, $v' = v[r \mapsto 0]$ and $v' \models Inv(\ell')$;

(2) $(\ell, v) \xrightarrow{d} (\ell, v + d)$ such that $v \models Inv(\ell)$ and $v + d \models Inv(\ell)$.

Definition 3. A trace ρ of $\mathcal{A}$ can be expressed in $S_{\mathcal{A}}$ as a sequence of alternative delay and action transitions starting from the initial state: $\rho = q_0 \xrightarrow{d_1} q_0' \xrightarrow{a_1}$ $q_1 \xrightarrow{d_2} q_1' \xrightarrow{a_2} \cdots \xrightarrow{d_n} q_{n-1}' \xrightarrow{a_n} q_n \cdots$, where $a_i \in \Sigma$, $d_i \in \mathbb{R}_{\geq 0}$, q_i is state (ℓ_i, v_i), and q_i' is reached from q_i after delay d_{i+1}. State q (or q') is reachable if there exists a finite trace with the final state of q (or q'). Let $Exec_{\mathcal{A}}$ denotes the set of traces of $\mathcal{A}$ and $Exec_{\mathcal{A}}^f$ denotes the set of finite traces.

Definition 4. The span of a finite trace $\rho \in Exec_{\mathcal{A}}^f$ is defined as the finite sum $\Sigma_{i=1}^n d_i$. For a given state (ℓ, v), the minimum span of reaching the state $\texttt{MinSpan}(\ell, v)$ is the infimum of the spans of finite traces ending in (ℓ, v). For a given location ℓ, the minimum span of reaching the location $\texttt{MinSpan}(\ell)$ is the infimum of spans of finite traces ending in (ℓ, v) for all possible v.

2.2 Sequential Time Optimal Reachability Algorithm

The real-time model checker UPPAAL works by exploring a finite *symbolic reachability graph*, where the nodes are *symbolic states*. A symbolic state is a pair (ℓ, Z), where $\ell \in L$ is a location, and $Z = \{v \mid v \models g_z, g_z \in \mathcal{B}(X)\}$ is a convex set of clock valuations called *zone* [15], which is normally efficiently represented and stored in memory as *difference bound matrices* (DBM) [10]. Besides, we denote the action and delay transitions between symbolic states uniformly as $\rightsquigarrow$.

Definition 5. The cost function on a symbolic state (ℓ, Z) is defined as $\texttt{MinCost}(\ell, Z) = \inf\{\texttt{MinSpan}(\ell, v) \mid v \in Z\}$. It is the span of a finite symbolic trace ending in (ℓ, Z).

Algorithm 1. Sequential Time Optimal Reachability

WAITING $\longleftarrow \{(\ell_0, Z_0)\}$, PASSED $\longleftarrow \emptyset$, COST $\longleftarrow \infty$

Procedure Main()

1   **while** WAITING $\neq \emptyset$ **do**
2   select (ℓ, Z) from WAITING
3   **if** $(\ell, Z) \models$ Goal **then**
4   **if** MinCost$(\ell, Z) <$ COST **then**
5   COST $\longleftarrow$ MinCost(ℓ, Z)
6   **else if** $(\ell, Z) \not\subseteq$ PASSED **and** MinCost$(\ell, Z) <$ COST **then**
7   add (ℓ, Z) to PASSED
8   **forall the** (m, D) *such that* $(\ell, Z) \rightsquigarrow (m, D)$ **do**
9   add (m, D) to WAITING

10   **return** COST

UPPAAL keeps track of the trace span by including an implicit clock ψ in addition to the original set of clocks X of the model. Clock ψ drifts as the global elapsing time and remains unaffected from resets or guards or invariants in the model. Thus the zone Z is now over $X \cup \{\psi\}$; and MinCost(ℓ, Z) is calculated on-the-fly by evaluating the lower bound of ψ in Z.

Algorithm 1 shows the sequential TOR algorithm that computes the minimum span to reach the goal states satisfying the proposition Goal. WAITING and PASSED keep unexplored and explored symbolic states respectively; and WAITING has the initial state. COST maintains the current best result that is infinity initially. Inside procedure Main, whenever WAITING is not empty, an unexplored state is popped from WAITING in a loop. If the state is a goal state, COST is updated. This implies a near optimal schedule to the goal is found. If the state is not goal state, it is subject to symbolic state inclusion checking and B&B elimination rule at line 6. A symbolic state (ℓ, Z) is included in PASSED and discarded if $\exists (\ell, H) \in$ PASSED s.t. $Z \subseteq H$ [10,15]. That is, a previously explored state with the same location has an equal or larger zone than the current state. The same state is pruned if its cost function is no less than the current COST. If the state gets through the two tests on line 6, it is added to PASSED as already explored, and then its successor states are generated and added to WAITING.

3 Distributed Time Optimal Reachability

This section describes the distributed time optimal reachability algorithms that extends the sequential version with state-space partitioning and message passing. Each algorithm is uniform and executed by all worker processes in a cluster.

3.1 Distributed Algorithm

Algorithm 2 shows the distributed algorithms: D-BFS, D-DFS, D-DFS^G and D-RDFS. A key activity of this algorithm is partitioning and distributing the state-space. A partition function uniquely computes the ID of a process that a symbolic state belongs to, hence divides the entire state-space into disjoint subsets on all processes. We use a hash function to partition; and the hash value is only calculated on the location ℓ^1. The reason is that the inclusion checking of a symbolic state requires looking up all states with the same location in PASSED. Therefore, in distributed settings all states of the same location will destine to the same process for deterministic and easy inclusion checking. The other key work of this algorithm is message passing and handling. We define two messages: (1) UPDATE carries better costs; (2) STATE carries symbolic states.

Definition 6. *Let N be the set of worker processes and p denote the local process ID. The partition function is a total mapping:* Hash $: L \rightarrow N$ *from the set of locations to the set of processes. Process p is the* owner *of a symbolic state (ℓ, Z) if* Hash$(\ell) = p$. *A symbolic state is a* local *state if it is generated on its owner process, otherwise it is an* emigrant *state.*

Definition 7. *A process is* active *when doing local search or receiving messages. Initially all processes are active. A process is* idle *when its waiting list is empty and receiving no messages. Computation can* terminate *if all processes are idle and the network has no message in transit.*

Three new variables are used: ECOST maintains external better cost received from the network, ACTIVE specifies process status (active or idle), and TERMINATE controls the Main loop. At the beginning of each iteration, Ecost compares with Cost. If Ecost is smaller, a better cost has been found by another process, and Cost is updated. If Cost is smaller, the current process finds a better cost, which is assigned to Ecost and then broadcasted. Line 5 marks process to idle according to Definition 7. The remaining lines inside Main resembles the local search in the sequential algorithm, except at line 14 a successor state is hashed to compute its owner process ID and sent out if it does not belong to the current process p. When the root process becomes idle, it invokes the termination detection procedure CheckTerm based on the well-known token-based Safra protocol [18]. Line 20 updates Ecost on reception of a cost message. Line 21 adds a received emigrant state into WAITING.

The computation starts at the process p that owns the initial state $s_0 = (\ell_0, Z_0)$ determined by Hash. Successor states s'_i are generated by local search on s_0, meanwhile Hash computes the owner process ID of s'_i. If s'_i belongs to a different process r than p, it is sent to process r. Otherwise it is stored locally for future exploration. Once process r receives a state, it stores it in its WAITING and eventually starts to generate successors from it; and the partition function works in a similar fashion. Gradually all processes start to work. Finally the entire state-space is generated, and no unexplored successor states could be found. When all processes become idle and no message is in transit, the computation can stop.

---

[1] For real UPPAAL models, the location is a vector of locations from each parallelly composed timed automata and the values of all discrete variables in the model.

Algorithm 2. Distributed Time Optimal Reachability for
D-BFS/D-DFS/D-DFS^G/D-RDFS

(Local Variables)

WAITING $\longleftarrow$ $\begin{cases} \{(\ell_0, Z_0)\} & \text{if } p = \text{Hash}(\ell_0), \\ \emptyset & \text{otherwise.} \end{cases}$ PASSED $\longleftarrow$ $\emptyset$, COST $\longleftarrow$ ∞

TERMINATE $\longleftarrow$ FALSE, ACTIVE $\longleftarrow$ TRUE, ECOST $\longleftarrow$ ∞

(Message Types)
UPDATE, STATE

Procedure Main()

```
1   while ¬TERMINATE do
2       if ECOST < COST then  COST ←— ECOST
3       if COST < ECOST then  UpdateE(COST), Broadcast(UPDATE, COST)
4       if WAITING = ∅ then
5           if receive no message then  ACTIVE ←— FALSE, CheckTerm()
6           continue
7       select (ℓ, Z) from WAITING, ACTIVE ←— TRUE
8       if (ℓ, Z) ⊨ Goal then
9           if MinCost(ℓ, Z) < COST then
10              COST ←— MinCost(ℓ, Z)
11      else if (ℓ, Z) ∉ PASSED and MinCost(ℓ, Z) < COST then
12          add (ℓ, Z) to PASSED
13          forall the (m, D) such that (ℓ, Z) ↝ (m, D) do
14              if (r ←— Hash(m)) ≠ p then  Send(STATE, (m, D), r)
15              else add (m, D) to WAITING
16   return COST
```

Procedure UpdateE(NEWCOST)

```
17   if NEWCOST < ECOST then  ECOST ←— NEWCOST
```

Procedure CheckTerm() // Safra protocol [18]

```
18   if p = root and all processes are idle and no message in transit then
19       TERMINATE ←— TRUE on all processes
```

(Message Processing Rules)

```
20   When receive UPDATE⟨NCOST⟩: UpdateE(NCOST), ACTIVE ←— TRUE.
21   When receive STATE⟨(n, F)⟩: add (n, F) to WAITING, ACTIVE ←— TRUE.
```

3.2 Distributed Algorithm for Strict BFS

Algorithm 3 highlights the changes on Algorithm 2 to make a distributed strict BFS. NLQ stands for the next level queue that collects the states on the next BFS level. WAITING keeps states on the current BFS level. Lines 2 to 5 explore states on one level and generate successor states for the next level, which are either sent out or stored in NLQ. The emigrant states received from the network are also stored in NLQ at line 13. After exhausting the states on the current level in WAITING, all processes synchronize on the condition that each process

---

Algorithm 3. Distributed Time Optimal Reachability for D-BFS^S

NLQ ⟵ ∅

Procedure Main()

```
1    while ¬TERMINATE do
2        while WAITING ≠ ∅ do
             same code as lines 2 to 3 and 7 to 12 in Algorithm 2
3            forall the (m, D) such that (ℓ, Z) ⤳ (m, D) do
4                if (r ⟵ Hash(m)) ≠ p then  Send(STATE, (m, D), r)
5                else  add (m, D) to NLQ

6        Await(Synchronize(receive all STATE messages) or TERMINATE)
7        if TERMINATE then  break
8        Swap(WAITING, NLQ)
9        if WAITING = ∅  and  receive no message then
10           ACTIVE ⟵ FALSE, CheckTerm()

11       if ECOST < COST then  COST ⟵ ECOST
12       return COST
```

13 When receive STATE⟨(n, F)⟩: add (n, F) to NLQ, ACTIVE ⟵ TRUE.

has completely harvested all STATE messages from the network into NLQ. After line 8 WAITING contains the states for the next BFS level and NLQ is empty.

4   Experiments

We developed a new version of UPPAAL implementing the distributed algorithms. The implementation involves three key tasks: (1) build a communication module by the MPI library; (2) interact with UPPAAL's internal memory management to fetch send-out states or insert received states; (3) implement the distributed search orders with the support from (1) and (2). We applied several optimization techniques [19] to improve communication such as: asynchronous communication, buffering states and sending them in packets, and packet compression.

We ran benchmark experiments in a cluster with 9 computing nodes. Each node has 1 Tb memory (NUMA architecture) and 64 cores at the frequency of 2.3 GHz (4 AMD Opteron 6376 Processors each with 16 cores), a 1 TB SATA disk and the Infiniband interconnection. All five distributed algorithms were executed 10 runs for every core setting: 1, 2, 4, 8, 16, 32, 64, 128, 256, 512. These core settings follow an even mapping topology as the (nodes, cores-per-node) pairs: $1 \rightarrow (1,1), 2 \rightarrow (2,1), 4 \rightarrow (4,1), 8 \rightarrow (4,2), 16 \rightarrow (4,4), 32 \rightarrow (4,8), 64 \rightarrow (4,16), 128 \rightarrow (4,32), 256 \rightarrow (4,64), 512 \rightarrow (8,64)$. For instance, 2 cores are mapped to 2 nodes with 1 core on each node; 32 cores are mapped to 4 nodes with 8 cores on each node.

4.1   Models

We use the same models as in [20]. The first three models are up-scaled versions of those in normal UPPAAL distribution by adding more parallel components. The last model is transformed from an industrial task graph benchmark[2].

Job-Shop-6 (jb-6). Six people want to read a single piece of four-section newspaper. Each person has his own preferred reading sequence, and can spend different time on each section. When one person is reading a section, others who are also interested in it must wait. The objective is to find the time optimal schedule for all six people to finish reading.

Aircraft-Landing-15 (alp-15). 15 aircrafts need to land on two runways. Each aircraft has a preferred target landing time. It can also speed up and land earlier or stay longer in the air and land later if necessary. Furthermore, aircrafts cannot land back to back on the same runway due to wake turbulence by the previous aircraft. Thus there are certain minimum constraints on the separation delay between aircrafts of different sizes. The objective is to find the time optimal schedule for all aircrafts to land safely.

Viking-Bridge-15 (vik-15). 15 vikings want to cross a bridge in the darkness. The bridge is damaged and can only carry two people at the same time. To find the way over the bridge the vikings need to bring a torch, but the group has only one torch to share. The 15 members of the group need different time to cross the bridge (one-way), which for simplicity is classified into four levels: 5, 10, 20 and 25 time units. The objective is to find the time optimal schedule for those 15 vikings to cross the bridge safely.

Task-Graph-88 (task-88). A robot control program has 88 computational tasks each of which has precedence constraints (predecessor tasks) among [0,3] and processing time among [1,111]. A task can start only if all its predecessor tasks complete. Now the control program is going to be assigned to four heterogeneous processors at the speeds of [1,1,2,4]. The objective is to compute a non-preemptive schedule that minimizes the time for all tasks to terminate.

4.2   Time to Find or Prove Optimal Result (Metric 1 & 2)

Tables 1, 2, 3 and 4 show for models Job-Shop-6, Job-Shop-8 and Viking-Bridge-15 the median runtime to reach optimal cost (t_{opt} corresponding to metric 1), and the median runtime to prove optimal cost (t_{prov} corresponding to metric 2). We want to know how the distributed algorithms scale with an increasing number of cores denoted by #C (#C=1 for sequential algorithms). We set the 4-h time bound for the experiments; and "-" indicates timeout.

Job-Shop-6. For the sequential algorithms, DFS[G] has the best t_{opt} and BFS has the best t_{prov}. DFS is the slowest for both t_{opt} and t_{prov}.

---

[2] http://www.kasahara.elec.waseda.ac.jp/schedule/stgarc_e.html.

Table 1. Runtime (sec) of Job-Shop-6

#C	BFS				DFS		DFS^G		RDFS	
	t_{opt}	t_{prov}			t_{opt}	t_{prov}	t_{opt}	t_{prov}	t_{opt}	t_{prov}
1	100	100			7411	9309	6	175	616	2125

#C	D-BFS		D-BFS^S		D-DFS		D-DFS^G		D-RDFS	
	t_{opt}	t_{prov}	t_{opt}	t_{prov}	t_{opt}	t_{prov}	t_{opt}	t_{prov}	t_{opt}	t_{prov}
2	246	246	153	153	467	1398	301	842	532	1505
4	346	390	88	88	53	419	15	311	23	401
8	98	129	33	33	1	199	1	158	2	187
16	58	73	23	23	1	116	1	88	1	112
32	28	38	16	16	1	62	1	63	1	60
64	18	31	14	14	1	34	1	32	1	34
128	12	15	16	16	1	17	1	21	1	17
256	8	11	38	39	2	11	1	9	2	11
512	6	10	70	72	2	17	1	10	2	19

For the distributed algorithms, D-BFS runs slower than BFS at lower core settings (2 to 8), and a speed-up requires more cores. D-BFS^S is much more competitive. We note that UPPAAL is highly optimized for single core execution, and therefore requires several cores to offset initialization and message passing overhead. Further, the *core mapping topology* leads to high communication latency especially at 2 and 4 cores where each core is mapped to one computing node using an (infiniband) network that is relatively slower than the internal bus within a node. The intensive state exchange on the single channel between 2 cores will also incur a *communication channel congestion*. The congestion fades when using more cores. If we map 2 and 4 cores on the same computing node as shown in Table 2, t_{prov} is improved by 40 % for D-BFS^S, and 15 % for D-BFS.

Table 2. Runtime (sec) for cores on same node

#C	D-BFS		D-BFS^S	
	t_{opt}	t_{prov}	t_{opt}	t_{prov}
2	195	195	95	95
4	340	352	53	53
8	107	118	29	29

The difference between BFS (D-BFS) and D-BFS^S is caused by the symbolic states. BFS is good at building larger zones (see Sect. 1). But since D-BFS only approximates BFS, it causes more *fragmentation* at 2 and 4 cores where workers consequently generate and communicate more symbolic states. Using more cores from 16 to 512 cores, D-BFS steadily reduces execution time for t_{opt} and t_{prov}. D-BFS^S runs faster than D-BFS at core settings (2 to 64). Above 128 cores t_{opt} and t_{prov} slow down indicating higher level synchronization overhead.

Comparing the three remaining depth-first based distributed algorithms, they all have a noticeable t_{opt} of merely 1 or 2 s above 8 cores. D-DFS^G seems overall to be a good choice, despite sligtly less speedup.

Job-Shop-8. This is an enlarged version of Job-Shop-6. This experiment shows that when all sequential algorithms confront timeout, the distributed algorithms can terminate normally and prove the optimal result. D-BFS^S can already terminates at 4 cores while other algorithms need more than 16 cores. It also has the best t_{prov}; and shows a linear speedup from 4 to 128 cores. D-DFS^G has extremely good t_{opt}.

Aircraft-Landing-15. All distributed algorithms show similar pattern as Job-Shop-6. A

Table 3. Runtime (sec) of Job-Shop-8

#C	BFS			DFS^G	
	t_{opt}	t_{prov}		t_{opt}	t_{prov}
1	-	-		849	-

#C	D-BFS		D-BFS^S		D-DFS^G	
	t_{opt}	t_{prov}	t_{opt}	t_{prov}	t_{opt}	t_{prov}
2	-	-	-	-	6249	-
4	-	-	9295	9295	366	-
8	-	-	4900	4900	1	-
16	8881	13050	2568	2568	1	-
32	5390	7276	1315	1315	1	13293
64	3157	4623	693	663	2	7956
128	2052	2470	450	450	2	4406
256	1335	1495	260	260	4	2547
512	1012	1231	365	365	11	1773

"-": denotes 4-h timeout.

difference is that D-BFS has much faster t_{opt} above 8 cores and somewhat faster t_{prov} than D-BFS^S at higher core settings (in Appendix A).

Viking-Bridge-15. This model is good for BFS, but extremely bad for DFS/RDFS that suffer timeout. We observed from the log files that this model produces solutions with a wide cost spectrum from 638195 to 220 and decrement step of just one. This explains why DFS^G is also 30 times slower than BFS because it gets trapped by the fine grained local optimal (as depicted in Fig. 2).

No distributed algorithms could beat BFS without using enough many cores. D-BFS and D-BFS^S show pool speedup. The good news is that D-DFS and D-RDFS can complete in half an hour above 4 cores and present linear speedup in t_{opt} and t_{prove} until 128 cores. D-DFS^G confronts heavy fragmentation and timeout at 2 and 4 cores. But using enough many workers avoids local optimal, and D-DFS^G gains the best t_{opt} and t_{prov} among all algorithms.

Task-Graph-88. The table for this model is absent because the model is too large for all algorithms to complete within the 4-h time bound. But we show how the near optimal results converge according to runtime in Sect. 4.3.

Conclusions. (1) D-DFS^G can find the optimal result very fast in general followed by D-DFS/D-RDFS. (2) D-DFS/D-RDFS have good speedup on the time to prove. (3) For larger models, distributed algorithms provide results while the sequential algorithms cannot, with D-BFS^S in many cases being the fastest to terminate. (4) D-BFS/D-DFS^G may be slower than the optimized sequential BFS/DFS^G at low core settings due to fragmentation. (5) The exact performance may depend on the characteristics of the model.

Table 4. Runtime (sec) of Viking-Bridge-15

#C	BFS				DFS		DFS^G		RDFS	
	t_{opt}	t_{prov}			t_{opt}	t_{prov}	t_{opt}	t_{prov}	t_{opt}	t_{prov}
1	66	66			-	-	2016	2146	-	-
#C	D-BFS		D-BFS^S		D-DFS		D-DFS^G		D-RDFS	
	t_{opt}	t_{prov}	t_{opt}	t_{prov}	t_{opt}	t_{prov}	t_{opt}	t_{prov}	t_{opt}	t_{prov}
2	533	559	125	125	-	-	-	-	-	-
4	308	314	106	106	956	1058	-	-	868	980
8	400	430	70	70	439	515	181	267	458	520
16	165	196	41	41	216	280	71	115	173	246
32	115	120	31	31	116	183	28	69	82	132
64	64	69	23	23	40	63	14	32	41	69
128	32	36	61	61	20	49	8	24	17	34
256	50	55	113	114	15	24	6	11	14	23
512	21	25	165	168	16	34	13	18	17	36

"-": denotes 4-h timeout.

4.3   Results Versus Time (Metric 3)

Figures 1, 2 and 3 show how near optimal results improve with running time for Job-Shop-6, Viking-Bridge-15 and Task-Graph-88. The sample window is 2 min. For the distributed algorithms, we look at the intermediate core setting of 32.

Job-Shop-6. For the sequential algorithms, DFS^G is the fastest in finding the optimal result of 62 at 6 s. BFS reports 62 at 100 s. DFS reports no results within the sample window. RDFS only reports near optimal results from 72 to 68. For the distributed algorithms, D-DFS/D-DFS^G/D-RDFS reach the optimal result immediately at 1 s. D-BFS/D-BFS^S reach the optimal result at 28 s and 16 s respectively. Compared with the best of our swarm algorithms (S-Agent) presented in [20], finding the optimal took 13 s.

Aircraft-Landing-15. It shows the similar pattern as Job-Shop-6.

Viking-Bridge-15. For the sequential algorithms, BFS finds the optimal result of 220 at 66 s. DFS/RDFS are omitted because they only report results far exceeding 220. DFS^G gets trapped by the local optimal within the cost range from 285 to 265. For the distributed algorithms, D-DFS^G reports the best quality near optimal results and reaches the optimal at 28 s. D-BFS^S finds the optimal result at 31 s. Both are faster than sequential BFS. D-RDFS/D-DFS/D-BFS report near optimal results from high to low quality.

Task-Graph-88. BFS based algorithms BFS/D-BFS/D-BFS^S are omitted because they report no result even in 4 h. Only DFS based algorithms can report near optimal results. For the sequential algorithms, DFS^G/RDFS/DFS find results from high to low quality. For the distributed algorithms, D-DFS is

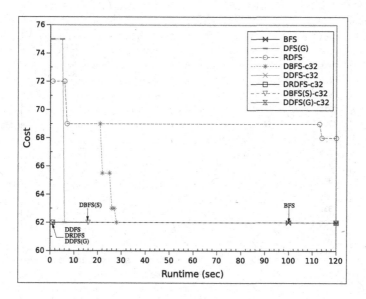

Fig. 1. Cost vs. Runtime for Job-Shop-6

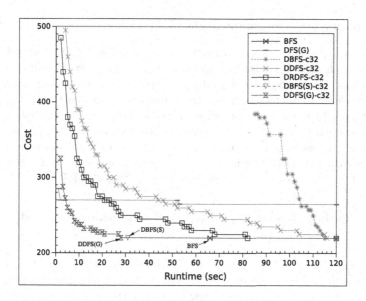

Fig. 2. Cost vs. Runtime for Viking-Bridge-15

superior among all algorithms. Compared with the best of our swarm algorithms (S-Agent, included in the plot) presented in [20], D-DFS finds better solutions faster and reaches the highest quality result of 328 as early as 46 s.

Conclusions. D-DFS/D-DFS^G/D-RDFS are generally very fast at finding near optimal results.

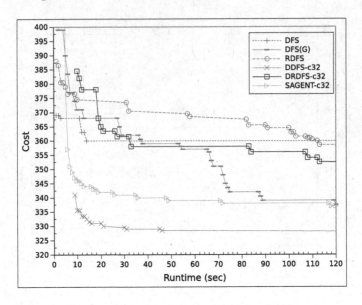

Fig. 3. Cost vs. Runtime for Task-Graph-88

4.4   Memory and Communication (Metric 4)

Table 5 shows statistics about memory consumption and communication overhead. For each model, column M shows the total memory (in GB) consumed by all UPPAAL processes. Distributed algorithms will generate more states than sequential algorithms, because emigrant states are generated by multiple workers and then sent to the owner process. These emigrant states contribute to the computation and communication overhead. Column R compares the amount of emigrant states generated and transmitted against the state-space size. Taking jb-6 as an example, D-BFS generates a large amount of emigrant states that is 14.7 times the state-space, but the factor is only 3.9 for D-BFS^S.

Table 5. Resident memory (GB) and communication overhead

Models	jb-6	alp-15	vik-15	Models	jb-6			alp-15			vik-15		
	M	M	M		M	R	C%	M	R	C%	M	R	C%
BFS	0.19	0.15	0.48	D-BFS	1.71	14.7	26.3	1.17	14.7	23.5	3.25	15.4	63.3
				D-BFS^S	0.67	3.9	62.5	0.67	4.0	56.3	1.31	2.8	77.4
DFS	2.54	0.16	*19.51*	D-DFS	1.77	14.9	45.2	1.14	22.0	45.8	6.22	20.9	64.5
DFS^G	0.22	0.12	2.57	D-DFS^G	1.82	14.6	27.6	1.33	23.1	44.7	3.93	10.8	58.0
RDFS	0.85	0.25	*19.47*	D-RDFS	1.82	14.5	36.7	1.18	21.3	47.6	5.15	16.1	59.8

Distributed algorithms are at 32 cores. *Italic* font denotes 4-h timeout.

Column C shows the portion of the communication time out of the total execution time in percentage. Because a lot of emigrant states are transmitted, the communication overhead of distributed algorithms is also high (up about 47 % of the total execution time). For D-BFS^S, this may be even higher due to the level synchronization overhead.

Distributed algorithms normally consume more memory than their sequential counterparts. The average scale ratio is 5 times for the three models. There are three reasons. First, when a UPPAAL process initiates prior to local search, it consumes about 13 MB memory for core data structures and libraries. Then 32 UPPAAL processes will consume 416 MB that already double the size of some sequential algorithms' peak memory usage. Second, MPI allocates system buffers for message passing. Third, UPPAAL's internal memory management only marks obsolete memory slots for re-use to store newly explored states rather than returning them to the operation system (quite sensibly expecting to save time for repeated page (re-)allocation). When a distributed algorithm is running however, more memory is used mainly because it receives and stores a large number of emigrant states from the network as indicated by the R columns which approximate 14 times the size of the state-space for most distributed algorithms.

Conclusions. The distributed algorithms have memory, computation and communication overhead. There may be several ways to optimize memory management and communication (e.g. caching more emigrant states locally). However, we have currently decided against implementing these, in part because the performance is quite reasonable, and in part because we envision that the most effective approach will be to incorporate multi-core shared memory techniques that provides more fine-grained parallelism, better locality and lower communication and synchronization overhead. However, implementing an efficient (lockless or lock-free) multi-core and thread-safe version of the internal exploration and optimized memory layout in UPPAAL requires great care.

5   Conclusions

We developed five distributed algorithms to accelerate timed optimal reachability analysis. We performed four benchmark experiments in terms of ability to compute near- or proven-optimal solutions, scalability, time and memory consumption and communication overhead. The experiment results are very promising. Based on the evaluation we conclude: (1) D-BFS^S can terminate fast thus prove the optimal result for large models; (2) D-DFS/D-DFS^G/D-RDFS are good at finding (near-) optimal results. For the future work, we will develop parallel and distributed algorithms applying multi-core shared memory as the significant optimization. We will develop hybrid algorithms that combine the benefits as well as the state-of-the-art advances from distributed and swarm verification [20].

A   Results for Runtime

Table 6. Runtime (sec) of Aircraft-Landing-15

#C	BFS				DFS		DFS^G		RDFS	
	t_{opt}	t_{prov}			t_{opt}	t_{prov}	t_{opt}	t_{prov}	t_{opt}	t_{prov}
1	155	155			71	419	5	135	184	935

#C	D-BFS		D-BFS^S		D-DFS		D-DFS^G		D-RDFS	
	t_{opt}	t_{prov}	t_{opt}	t_{prov}	t_{opt}	t_{prov}	t_{opt}	t_{prov}	t_{opt}	t_{prov}
2	422	454	134	135	77	408	13	351	193	628
4	71	243	69	69	1	345	< 1	207	2	326
8	4	86	42	42	< 1	139	< 1	123	< 1	140
16	7	39	26	26	< 1	80	< 1	66	< 1	82
32	11	34	16	16	< 1	48	< 1	47	< 1	42
64	5	14	11	11	1	22	< 1	21	1	23
128	2	10	15	16	1	12	< 1	14	1	14
256	1	8	28	29	< 1	9	< 1	7	< 1	9
512	1	8	49	51	< 1	17	< 1	10	< 1	15

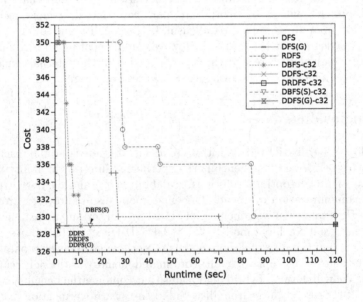

Fig. 4. Cost vs. Runtime for Aircraft-Landing-15

References

1. Abdeddaim, Y., Asarin, E., Maler, O.: Scheduling with timed automata. Theor. Comput. Sci. **354**(2), 272–300 (2006)
2. Alur, R., Dill, D.L.: A theory of timed automata. Theor. Comput. Sci. **126**(2), 183–235 (1994)
3. Barnat, J., Brim, L., Češka, M., Ročkai, P.: DiVinE: parallel distributed model checker (tool paper). In: HiBi/PDMC, pp. 4–7. IEEE (2010)
4. Barnat, J., Bauch, P., Brim, L., Ceska, M.: Designing fast LTL model checking algorithms for many-core gpus. J. Parallel Distrib. Comput. **72**(9), 1083–1097 (2012)
5. Behrmann, G.: Distributed reachability analysis in timed automata. STTT **7**(1), 19–30 (2005)
6. Behrmann, G., David, A., Larsen, K.G.: A tutorial on UPPAAL. In: Bernardo, M., Corradini, F. (eds.) SFM-RT 2004. LNCS, vol. 3185, pp. 200–236. Springer, Heidelberg (2004)
7. Behrmann, G., Fehnker, A., Hune, T., Larsen, K.G., Pettersson, P., Romijn, J.M.T.: Efficient guiding towards cost-optimality in UPPAAL. In: Margaria, T., Yi, W. (eds.) TACAS 2001. LNCS, vol. 2031, pp. 174–188. Springer, Heidelberg (2001)
8. Behrmann, G., Fehnker, A., Hune, T., Larsen, K.G., Pettersson, P., Romijn, J.M.T., Vaandrager, F.W.: Minimum-cost reachability for priced timed automata. In: Di Benedetto, M.D., Sangiovanni-Vincentelli, A.L. (eds.) HSCC 2001. LNCS, vol. 2034, pp. 147–161. Springer, Heidelberg (2001)
9. Behrmann, G., Hune, T., Vaandrager, F.W.: Distributing timed model checking - how the search order matters. In: Emerson, E.A., Sistla, A.P. (eds.) CAV 2000. LNCS, vol. 1855, pp. 216–231. Springer, Heidelberg (2000)
10. Bengtsson, J.E., Yi, W.: Timed automata: semantics, algorithms and tools. In: Desel, J., Reisig, W., Rozenberg, G. (eds.) Lectures on Concurrency and Petri Nets. LNCS, vol. 3098, pp. 87–124. Springer, Heidelberg (2004)
11. Blom, S., van de Pol, J., Weber, M.: LTSMIN: distributed and symbolic reachability. In: Touili, T., Cook, B., Jackson, P. (eds.) CAV 2010. LNCS, vol. 6174, pp. 354–359. Springer, Heidelberg (2010)
12. Bozga, M., Daws, C., Maler, O., Olivero, A., Tripakis, S., Yovine, S.: Kronos: a model-checking tool for real-time systems. In: Vardi, M.Y. (ed.) CAV 1998. LNCS, vol. 1427. Springer, Heidelberg (1998)
13. Fehnker, A.: Bounding and Heuristics in Forward Reachability Algorithms. UB Nijmegen [Host] (2000)
14. Gibson-Robinson, T., Armstrong, P., Boulgakov, A., Roscoe, A.W.: FDR3 — a modern refinement checker for CSP. In: Ábrahám, E., Havelund, K. (eds.) TACAS 2014 (ETAPS). LNCS, vol. 8413, pp. 187–201. Springer, Heidelberg (2014)
15. Larsen, K.G., Pettersson, P., Yi, W.: Model-checking for real-time systems. In: FCT, pp. 62–88 (1995)
16. Niebert, P., Tripakis, S., Yovine, S.: Minimum-time reachability for timed automata. In: IEEE Mediteranean Control Conference (2000)
17. Stern, U., Dill, D.L.: Parallelizing the Murφ verifier. In: Grumberg, O. (ed.) CAV 1997. LNCS, vol. 1254, pp. 256–267. Springer, Heidelberg (1997)
18. Tel, G.: Introduction to Distributed Algorithms, 2nd edn. Cambridge University Press, New York (2001)
19. Verstoep, K., Bal, H.E., Barnat, J., Brim, L.: Efficient large-scale model checking. In: IPDPS, pp. 1–12 (2009)
20. Zhang, Z., Nielsen, B., Larsen, K.G.: Time optimal reachability analysis using swarm verification. In: SAC SVT, pp. 1634–1640 (2016)

Workload Analysis

Scenario-Aware Workload Characterization Based on a Max-Plus Linear Representation

Gustavo Patino Alvarez[1(✉)] and Wang Jiang Chau[2]

[1] SISTEMIC Group, University of Antioquia, Medellin, Colombia
adolfo.patino@udea.edu.co
[2] Laboratory of Microelectronics (LME), University of São Paulo,
São Paulo, Brazil
jcwang@lme.usp.br

Abstract. This paper describes an event analytical model for the workload characterization of multimedia applications with several scenarios of operation. This model describes the application tasks as timed actors of a Scenario-Aware Dataflow Graph (SADF), so that the multiple application scenarios are defined in terms of the variable execution times previously identified in the timing characterization of every application task. A Max-Plus linear representation between the input and output event sequences of the SADF Graph states the basis of a model of scenario-based workload curves and a model of scenario-based service curves that allow to characterize the behavioral dynamism of the application in its design phase. By a detailed study, we show the applicability of our model for the performance evaluation of a multimedia application, whose tasks are implemented in general purpose processors.

Keywords: Application scenarios · Max-plus algebra · Linear time-varying system · Multimedia application · Network calculus · Service curves · Variable execution time · Workload curves

1 Introduction

Nowadays, the performance evaluation in the design of complex embedded real-time systems is assessed through extensive system-level simulations, regardless of how many, and which, workload scenarios are simulated. Such simulations can never achieve, in a reasonable time, the total coverage required for complete performance verification. To verify that an embedded system meets the time constraints imposed on all possible workload scenarios, such workload can be characterized by formal analytical approaches which usually return performance limits of worst-case.

Many multimedia and stream processing applications are implemented as a main loop that read, process and write individual event streams. An event can be a bit (belonging to a bitstream), a JPEG marker, a macroblock, a video frame, an audio sample or a network packet. The data-flow model of computation called Synchronous Dataflow (SDF) has traditionally been used in the modeling of digital signal processing applications (DSP) [1]. Due to the similar structure between DSP applications and multimedia applications, the SDF graphs also provide a good degree of expressiveness

© Springer International Publishing Switzerland 2016
M. Fränzle and N. Markey (Eds.): FORMATS 2016, LNCS 9884, pp. 177–194, 2016.
DOI: 10.1007/978-3-319-44878-7_11

for modeling multimedia applications [2]. The SDF model has great potential analysis to measure accurate performance metrics, which are very important in the worst-case performance evaluation of such systems. However, the limitation of this model is its inability to represent variable execution times in the set of actors corresponding to the application tasks; from this fact, the universe of the executions of such application is represented by a single scenario of execution, usually referred to as one of the worst case. As result, any measure of performance, or workload characterization, is often distant from what the application will actually exposes, when implemented in a hardware platform.

In multimedia applications, a scenario is defined as the behavior of a task for a specific type of input event/data, such that the set of scenarios should cover all possible input events. The concept of scenarios has been used for long time in different design approaches, including hardware and software design for embedded systems [3]. In this paper, we concentrate on so-called application scenarios [4], so that a characterization algorithm of application tasks identifies the different application scenarios according to the amount of execution time estimated for the several operation flows in the source code that implements each application task.

The techniques introduced in [5–7] and also in this paper, allow these scenarios to be treated individually within an analytical characterization. The Scenario-Aware Dataflow (SADF) model [6] characterizes each scenario, or operation mode, individually by a specific Synchronous Dataflow (SDF) graph, so that each SDF graph models the tasks with constants rates associated with their worst-case execution times (WCET) [8]. A SADF model is also characterized by an explicit specification of the possible order in which certain scenarios are executed in the application. Thus, the SADF model can specify a sequence of scenarios by means of a Finite State Machine [7], or stochastically by means of a Markov chain [6]. In both cases, each state is marked with a scenario; and different states can be marked with the same scenario.

The fundamental characteristics of the workload to be captured in a workload model of these multimedia applications are the ones that affect the timing properties of resources and request flows, as well as their respective interactions. One must take into account the dynamic behavior, viewed upon as a collection of the different tasks behaviors [8]. The authors of [10] have proposed a dynamic solution of the SDF graph viewed as a linear model in Max-Plus Algebra [9], which has features of a linear discrete time-varying system in order to make explicit the dynamic behavior of certain application.

In this paper we extend the previous solution to the SADF graph; from a mathematical point of view, it is described a way to derive formal analytical expressions based on a linear model in Max-Plus Algebra in order to depicts the generation of event sequences, according to the iterations of a SADF graph and considering the collection of the different application scenarios and the variable execution demand found in the characterization of each application task. Thus, with such linear model it is possible to characterize all scenario sequences using the concepts of scenario-based workload curves and scenario-based service curves.

The remaining of this paper is organized as follows: Sect. 2 explains some preliminary concepts about timing characterization using Variability Characterization Curves. Also in Sect. 2 some important definitions related to Synchronous Dataflow

Graph are briefly described. Section 3 presents the SADF graph as a Linear Max-Plus Model, and the dynamical representation of this graph by a state space model, whose solution states the basis for the scenario-based workload curves and scenario-based service curves explained in Sect. 4. Section 5 summarizes the timing characterization proposed in this paper, describing a workload characterization analysis flow considering the mathematical concepts shown in the previous sections. Section 6 exposes the analysis of a JPEG decoder used as a use case in our experiments. Finally, Sect. 7 concludes our paper.

2 Preliminaries

In this Section we will discuss some specification formalisms and their relationships.

2.1 Variability Characterization Curves

The Variability Characterization Curves (VCCs) can be used to quantify the characteristics of the best-case and worst-case in some kind of sequences [11]. These sequences may be consecutive stream objects belonging to a streaming, or sequences of consecutive time intervals of a specific length. A VCC $\mathcal{V}$ is defined as a pair $(\mathcal{V}^l(k), \mathcal{V}^u(k))$, where k represents the length of the sequence. Let the function P be the measure of some property within a sequence, such that $P(n)$ denotes the increasing measure of this property for the first n elements of the sequence [11].

Definition - Upper VCC: An upper VCC for the set of increasing functions P is an increasing function $\mathcal{V}^u(k)$ which satisfies the condition:

$$\mathcal{V}^u(k) = \sup_{i \geq 0}\{P(i+k)-P(i)\} \tag{2.1a}$$

Definition – Lower VCC: A lower VCC for the set of increasing functions P is an increasing function $\mathcal{V}^u(k)$ which satisfies the condition:

$$\mathcal{V}^l(k) = \inf_{i \geq 0}\{P(i+k)-P(i)\} \tag{2.1b}$$

Therefore, $\mathcal{V}^l(k)$ and $\mathcal{V}^u(k)$ provide an upper and lower limit of the measure P for all its subsequences of length k within a larger sequence [11].

A single VCC can serve as a compact abstraction of a whole class of sequences, or functions, with a similar variability of worse-case or better-case. Thus, the VCCs represent an attractive way to capture various aspects of the behavior of a system in the context of heterogeneous embedded systems-design [12].

2.2 SDF Model

In the dynamic execution of SDF graphs, two essential operations characterize their timed behavior: *Synchronization* and *Delay*. *Synchronization* is observed each time a specific actor needs to wait for sufficient input tokens to be able to fire; while the *Delay* is observed each time an actor begins a firing and takes a fixed amount of time before completing and producing the respective output tokens. This fixed amount of time is defined as the actor execution time. These two features correspond to the Maximum and Addition operations of the Max-Plus Algebra [9]. If T is the number of tokens required for an actor to start a firing, and for each $\tau \in T$, t_τ is the time when the token becomes available, then the start time of the actor firing is given by:

$$\max_{\tau \in T} t_\tau \tag{2.2a}$$

Let e be the execution time of this actor, then the output tokens produced by the actor become available for consumption by other actors at:

$$\max_{\tau \in T} t_\tau + e \tag{2.2b}$$

which is a Max-Plus expression [13].

As an illustration of the behavior of a SDF graph, Fig. 1 depicts a graph which shows an iteration composed by four fires, one from each actor in the graph.

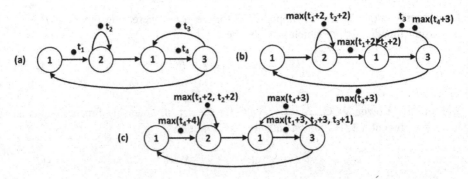

Fig. 1. Example of a self-timed execution of a SDF graph.

In the initial state (a), the second actor from the left consumes the tokens marked with t_1 and t_2. Consequently, the fire occurs at a time $max(t_1, t_2)$ and ends at a time $max(t_1 + 2, t_2 + 2)$ creating two new tokens with such timestamp. At the same state, the fourth actor consumes the token marked with t_4 and a fire occurs at a time $max(t_4)$ and ends at a time $max(t_4 + 3)$ creating two new tokens with this timestamp in state (b). Once in state (b), the first actor fires consuming the token marked with $max(t_4 + 3)$, so that the firing ends at $max(t_4 + 4)$ creating a new token in state (c). Since in state (b) the third actor also has tokens on its inputs, it can fire consuming the tokens marked with $max(t_1 + 2, t_2 + 2)$ and t_3. This fire occurs at a time $max(t_1 + 2, t_2 + 2, t_3)$ and ends at a time $max(t_1 + 3, t_2 + 3, t_3 + 1)$, thus creating a new token with this timestamp in state (c). Due to these fires, the graph takes back to the original state, but with the symbolic tokens representing the temporal impact of a single iteration. This graph dynamics is called a self-timed execution of an SDF graph [14].

The dynamics of this SDF graph, considering the production times of each token in a single iteration, can be described by the next Max-Plus representation:

$$t(k+1) = \begin{bmatrix} max(t_1 - \infty, t_2 - \infty, t_3 - \infty, t_4 + 4) \\ max(t_1 + 2, t_2 + 2, t_3 - \infty, t_4 - \infty) \\ max(t_1 - \infty, t_2 - \infty, t_3 - \infty, t_4 + 3) \\ max(t_1 + 3, t_2 + 3, t_3 + 1, t_4 - \infty) \end{bmatrix}$$

$$= \begin{bmatrix} -\infty & -\infty & -\infty & 4 \\ 2 & 2 & -\infty & -\infty \\ -\infty & -\infty & -\infty & 3 \\ 3 & 3 & 1 & -\infty \end{bmatrix} \begin{bmatrix} t_1(k) \\ t_2(k) \\ t_3(k) \\ t_4(k) \end{bmatrix}$$

Thus, $t(k+1) = \mathbf{M}t(k)$, where $\mathbf{M}$ is the Max-Plus matrix of the SDF graph. According to execution of the SDF graph, a $e_{m,n}$ value in the column m and row n of the matrix $\mathbf{M}$ specifies that there is a minimum distance $e_{m,n}$ between the timestamps of the token m, in the previous iteration k, to the token n, in the new iteration $k+1$, considering the dependencies in the graph. An entry $-\infty$ means that there is no any dependency between such tokens. Thereby, in our example, $e_{1,4}$ means that between the timestamps of tokens $t_1(k+1)$ and $t_4(k)$ there is a distance of 4 clock cycles.

2.3   SADF Model

The Fig. 2a describes a FSM-based Scenario-Aware Dataflow (FSM-SADF) model [7], which consists of a directed graph representing the connection between tasks A, B, C and D of the application, and the execution times for each task with respect to the two possible scenarios a and b, such that task B has an execution time of 2 clock cycles when performed in the scenario a, and an execution time of 3 clock cycles when performed in the scenario b. The Finite State Machine (FSM) shown in Fig. 2b is the possible execution sequence of the scenarios a and b within the overall implementation of the application.

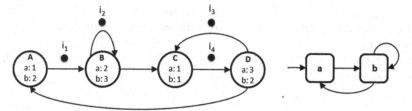

a. Example of a SADF Graph with four tokens and two possible scenarios {a,b}.

b. FSM used to define the possible execution order of scenarios {a,b} in the SADF Graph.

Fig. 2. Example of a SADF graph.

Initially, the SADF graph has a specific distribution of its initial tokens along the graph. This distribution remains unchanged with the individual iterations performed by the graph, regardless of the scenario that is being executed. At the end of an iteration, the production times of this collection of initial tokens capture the starting point for the next iteration, whenever the application is running in the same or in another scenario.

As it was shown in Sect. 2.2, a SDF graph without explicit input and output actors is simply characterized by its matrix $\mathbf{M}$, so that the timed behavior is governed by the following equation $i(k+1) = \mathbf{M}i(k)$, where $i(k)$ is the vector of production times of tokens in the graph [5]. In a SADF graph, each individual scenario is modeled by a SDF graph, such that a matrix $\mathbf{M}(\sigma)$ characterizes every scenario $\sigma \in \Sigma$, where σ is the set of all possible scenarios in the SADF. Thus, if the iteration k is performed in the scenario σ, then,

$$i(k+1) = \mathbf{M}(\sigma)i(k) \tag{2.3}$$

which is a Max-Plus expression for the vector of production times of tokens, $i(k+1)$. For instance, related to Fig. 2, the matrices associated with each scenario are as follows:

$$\mathbf{M}(a) = \begin{bmatrix} -\infty & -\infty & -\infty & 4 \\ 2 & 2 & -\infty & -\infty \\ -\infty & -\infty & -\infty & 3 \\ 3 & 3 & 1 & -\infty \end{bmatrix} \quad \mathbf{M}(b) = \begin{bmatrix} -\infty & -\infty & -\infty & 4 \\ 3 & 3 & -\infty & -\infty \\ -\infty & -\infty & -\infty & 2 \\ 4 & 4 & 1 & -\infty \end{bmatrix}$$

Formally, a SADF graph is modeled as a set of all scenarios and their corresponding SDF graphs modeled by matrices $\mathbf{M}(\sigma)$. The combination of the state machine, and the multiplication of Max-Plus matrices, is called Max-Plus Automata [9], which represents a system with linear dynamic variation with time, according to the different scenarios of operation related to the automata states.

A Max-Plus automata is a tuple $\mathcal{A} = (\Sigma, \mathbf{M}, \mathcal{M})$ consisting of a finite set Σ of scenarios, a mapping $\mathbf{M}$, which assigns to each scenario $\sigma \in \Sigma$ a Max-Plus matrix $\mathbf{M}(\sigma)$, and a morphism $\mathcal{M}$ on finite sequences of scenarios, which maps such sequences to a Max-Plus matrix, such that:

$$\mathcal{M}(\sigma_1, \cdots \sigma_k) = \mathbf{M}(\sigma_k) \cdots \mathbf{M}(\sigma_1) \tag{2.4}$$

The Eq. (2.4) is the matrix product in the Max-Plus notation, between the various matrices associated with each scenario within the sequence $\bar{\sigma} = \sigma_1, \cdots \sigma_k$, a product defined from the matrix related to the last scenario σ_k, until the matrix related to the first scenario σ_1.

Thus, $\mathcal{M}(\bar{\sigma})i(0)$ captures the production times of tokens in the SADF after the scenario sequence $\bar{\sigma}$, where $i(0)$ is the initial condition of production times of tokens.

3 Max-Plus Linear Representation of a SADF Graph

In the case of the SADF graphs, the linear Max-Plus model is represented in Fig. 3, where the system matrix varies according to the scenario sequence executed in the application up to the iteration k. In view of this Max-Plus linear representation proposed for the SADF graph, where the graph matrix varies with each iteration according to the matrix product defined by the morphism $\mathcal{M}$, the linear model in Max-Plus has features of a time-varying system [10], but in our case the new set of state equations is defined as:

$$
\begin{aligned}
i(k+1) &= \mathbf{M}(\sigma_{k+1})i(k) \oplus B(\sigma_{k+1})x(k) \\
y(k) &= Ci(k) \oplus Dx(k)
\end{aligned}
\tag{3.1}
$$

where the matrices $\mathbf{M}$, B, C and D represent the mutual dependencies between inputs, outputs and internal state of the graph, such that, in each iteration of an execution of the SADF graph, the matrix $\mathbf{M}$ defined must be the one related to the scenario performed in that moment by the graph, the same denoted in Eq. (2.3) and considering that the initial condition for each new scenario corresponds to the state vector of the last execution in the previous scenario.

Due to this mathematical description for the state space of the SADF graph, which corresponds to a discrete time-varying linear model in Max-Plus, the analytical treatment that can be given is similar to that found in classical linear discrete time-varying systems [10].

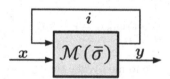

Fig. 3. Max-Plus linear representation of a SADF graph.

3.1 Solution to the State-Space Equations in SADF

The solution for the state vector in Eq. (3.1) can be described by a Max-Plus finite product, where for an iteration k of the SADF graph, the state vector is defined by

$$
i(k) = \bigotimes_{s=1}^{k} \mathbf{M}(\sigma_s)i(0) \oplus \bigoplus_{n=0}^{k-1}\left[\bigotimes_{s=n+2}^{k}\mathbf{M}(\sigma_s)\right]B(\sigma_{n+1})x(n)
\tag{3.2a}
$$

Or also:

$$
i(k) = \bigotimes_{s=1}^{k}\mathbf{M}(\sigma_s)i(0) \oplus \bigoplus_{n=1}^{k}\left[\bigotimes_{s=k}^{k-n+2}\mathbf{M}(\sigma_s)\right]B(\sigma_{k-n+1})x(k-n)
\tag{3.2b}
$$

By using Eq. (3.2b) in the output variable of the SADF graph in Eq. (3.1), the resulting expression for the output set is

$$y(k) = C \bigotimes_{s=1}^{k} \mathbf{M}(\sigma_s)i(0) \oplus Dx(k)$$

$$\oplus C \bigoplus_{n=1}^{k} [\bigotimes_{s=k}^{k-n+2} \mathbf{M}(\sigma_s)]B(\sigma_{k-n+1})x(k-n) \tag{3.3}$$

As with the classic linear time-varying systems, it is possible to define a state transition matrix $\mathbf{\Phi}(k,p)$ described by:

$$\mathbf{\Phi}(k,p) = \begin{cases} M(\sigma_k)M(\sigma_{k-1})\cdots M(\sigma_p), & k \geq p \geq 0 \\ E, & p > k \end{cases} \tag{3.4}$$

Or also:

$$\mathbf{\Phi}(k,p) = \begin{cases} \bigotimes_{s=p}^{k} \mathbf{M}(\sigma_s), & k \geq p \geq 0 \\ E, & p > k \end{cases} \tag{3.5}$$

where E is the identity matrix in Max-Plus Algebra [9]. In this way, substituting Eq. (3.5) in Eq. (3.3), the new expression to describe the graph output becomes:

$$y(k) = C\mathbf{\Phi}(k,1)i(0) \oplus Dx(k)$$

$$\bigoplus_{n=1}^{k} \mathbf{\Phi}(k,k-n+2)B(\sigma_{k-n+1})x(k-n) \tag{3.6}$$

From Eq. (3.6), it is possible to modify the summation index to include within the series the response component associated with matrix D. Thus, we define the function $\mathbf{h}(k,n)$ as:

$$\mathbf{h}(k,n) = \begin{cases} D & n = 0 \\ C\mathbf{\Phi}(k,k-n+2)B(\sigma_{k-n+1}) & n > 0 \end{cases} \tag{3.7}$$

And the output of the SADF graph can be rewritten as:

$$y(k) = C\mathbf{\Phi}(k,1)i(0) \oplus \bigoplus_{n=0}^{k} \mathbf{h}(k,n)x(k-n) \tag{3.8}$$

This equation represents the Max-Plus vector of the output traces of a SADF graph for each iteration k, given a specific sequence of scenarios $\bar{\sigma} = \sigma_1, \cdots \sigma_k$, defined possibly by a finite state machine.

4   Variability Characterization Curves for SADF Graphs

In this Section, the concept of Variability Characterization Curves (VCCs) described in Sect. 2.1 will be used to present the workload curves and service curves based on scenarios, whose definitions are contribution of this paper.

4.1   Scenario-Based Workload Curve

Given a multimedia application represented by a SADF graph, characterized by a set of possible scenarios Σ, and where each execution of the application corresponds to the execution of a sequence of scenarios $\bar{\sigma} = \sigma_1, \cdots \sigma_k$ related to the execution of k iterations within the graph, every scenario in this sequence has associated one Max-Plus matrix specified in terms of the execution times of the multiple application tasks. These execution times are assumed as variables according to each executed scenario [5, 8].

Let $m_{i,j}$ be the task execution time related to node i, j of the SADF graph, when it is referred to the scenario σ_s. Thus, given any subsequence of α scenarios covered in descending order from each scenario σ_β performed as the last one in the sequence, the following expression defines the component i, j of the matrix that results of the matrix product associated to this subsequence of α scenarios within the SADF graph:

$$\psi_{i,j}(\alpha, \beta) = \bigotimes_{s=\beta}^{\beta-\alpha+1} m_{i,j}(\sigma_s) \qquad 0 \le i, j \le n; n, \alpha, \beta \in Z_{>0} \qquad (4.1)$$

In this way, a matrix of $n \times n$, denoted by $\Psi(\alpha, \beta)$, covers these real components. In Max-Plus notation, the matrix $\Psi(\alpha, \beta)$ is defined as:

$$\Psi(\alpha, \beta) = \bigotimes_{s=\beta}^{\beta-\alpha+1} M(\sigma_s) \qquad \alpha, \beta \in Z_{>0} \qquad (4.2)$$

Given a sequence of scenarios $\bar{\sigma} = \sigma_a, \cdots \sigma_k$, the matrix $\Psi(\alpha, \beta)$ is a product with decreasing sub-index related to the given sequence, containing an α number of matrices. Thus, σ_β is the scenario associated with the first matrix evaluated within each subsequence of scenarios. As an example, consider the sequence of scenarios $\bar{\sigma} = \sigma_2, \cdots \sigma_5$, such that the matrix $\Psi(\alpha, \beta)$ is the product of Max-Plus matrices, $M(\sigma_s)$. In this case, the number of matrices in the sequence is $\alpha = 4$, and the last scenario in the sequence is $\sigma_\beta = \sigma_5$, so that the matrix $\Psi(\alpha, \beta)$ is evaluated as:

$$\Psi(4, 5) = M(\sigma_5)M(\sigma_4)M(\sigma_3)M(\sigma_2)$$

In order to find the maximum and the minimum for the Max-Plus product of execution times between all the possible sequences of scenarios, it is defined the workload curves based on scenarios, which consider the maximum and minimum of each component $\psi_{i,j}(\alpha, \beta)$ for all possible scenarios where σ_β corresponds to the last scenario in every possible subsequence.

$$\psi_{i,j}^u(\alpha) = \max_{\forall \beta} \big(\psi_{i,j}(\alpha, \beta)\big) \qquad 0 \le i,j \le n; n, \alpha, \beta \in Z_{>0} \qquad (4.3)$$

In this expression, $\psi_{i,j}^u(\alpha)$ is defined as the upper workload curve based on application scenarios for the task i,j, given a sequence of scenarios of length α. This set (i,j) of upper workload curves based on scenarios refers to the matrix $\mathbf{\Psi}^u(\alpha)$ described by Eq. (4.4):

$$\mathbf{\Psi}^u(\alpha) = \max_{\forall \beta}(\mathbf{\Psi}(\alpha, \beta)) \qquad \alpha, \beta \in Z_{>0} \qquad (4.4)$$

In a simpler way, the matrix $\mathbf{\Psi}^u(\alpha)$ is the one containing the larger elements resulting from the Max-Plus product of execution times for every application task, given each subsequence of size α, finished in the scenario σ_β. With this consideration, the matrix $\mathbf{\Psi}^u(\alpha)$ can be defined as an upper matrix curve of scenarios.

In the same way, it is possible to define the set of lower curves based on application scenarios for the task i,j:

$$\psi_{i,j}^l(\alpha) = \min_{\forall \beta} \big(\psi_{i,j}(\alpha, \beta)\big) \qquad 0 \le i,j \le n; n, \alpha, \beta \in Z_{>0} \qquad (4.5)$$

such that it also defines a lower matrix curve of scenarios $\mathbf{\Psi}^l(\alpha)$, composed by the several lower curves $\psi_{i,j}^l(\alpha)$.

$$\mathbf{\Psi}^l(\alpha) = \min_{\forall \beta}(\mathbf{\Psi}(\alpha, \beta)) \qquad \alpha, \beta \in Z_{>0} \qquad (4.6)$$

These concepts described here about workload curves based on application scenarios and matrix curves of scenarios, are closely related to the concept of workload curve defined in [8], so that the mathematical expressions of Eq. (4.1) to Eq. (4.6) are an extension of the mathematical specification used to define the workload curves in [8].

4.2   Scenario-Based Service Curve

Such as in classical linear systems, in the Max-Plus linear model the impulse response also allows a fully characterization of an application or system modeled by the graph SDF [5], such that various features and performance measures can be assessed by knowing the explicit representation of the impulse response. One of these features is the service that is provided by the system modeled as a dataflow graph. In [15] the service curve model defined within the theoretical framework of Network Calculus was described in a way that a system is said to offer a service curve $S(t)$ if, for all $t \ge 0$, it satisfies:

$$D(t) \ge \min_{\tau \in [0,t]} \{A(\tau) + S(t - \tau)\} = A \otimes S(t) \qquad (4.7)$$

where $A(t)$ is the cumulative function of packet arrival at a network, $D(t)$ is the cumulative function of packet departure in the network, and the operator $\otimes$ is referred in this case as the Min-Plus convolution [15].

The service curves can be regarded as the impulse response of a linear system, such that in case of the Network Calculus model the description of services curves is based on the Min-Plus Algebra. If a system implements $S(t)$ both as the lower and the upper service curve, the Eq. (4.7) only describes the equality, and $S(t)$ is referred as an exact service curve [15].

Nevertheless, one of the main characteristics of the classical linear time-varying systems is that they do not have an impulse response in the usual sense of its definition [10]. Thus, in the case of SADF graph it is necessary to define an approximation of the function $\mathbf{h}(k,n)$ in Eq (3.7), so that it may be likely to know an approach to a possible impulse response, which may lead to the definition of limits of the service provided by the application or system modeled by a SADF graph.

Considering the expression that describes the function $\mathbf{h}(k,n)$, the following expression is an expansion of Eq. (3.7):

$$\mathbf{h}(k,n) = \begin{cases} D & n = 0 \\ CB(\sigma_{k-n+1}) & n = 1 \\ C\Psi(n-1,k)B(\sigma_{k-n+1}) & n > 1 \end{cases} \tag{4.8}$$

In order to find the maximum and minimum limits of $\mathbf{h}(k,n)$ for all possible options of the initial scenario σ_k, it is necessary to define two functions $\mathbf{h}^u(n)$ and $\mathbf{h}^l(n)$ to represent, respectively, the maximum and minimum limit of function $\mathbf{h}(k,n)$, for all k. This is,

$$\mathbf{h}^l(n) \leq \mathbf{h}(k,n) \leq \mathbf{h}^u(n) \tag{4.9}$$

Thus $\mathbf{h}^u(n)$ is defined as:

$$\mathbf{h}^u(n) = \max_{\forall k} \begin{cases} D & n = 0 \\ CB(\sigma_{k-n+1}) & n = 1 \\ C\Psi(n-1,k)B(\sigma_{k-n+1}) & n > 1 \end{cases} \tag{4.10}$$

and $\mathbf{h}^l(n)$ is defined as:

$$\mathbf{h}^u(n) = \min_{\forall k} \begin{cases} D & n = 0 \\ CB(\sigma_{k-n+1}) & n = 1 \\ C\Psi(n-1,k)B(\sigma_{k-n+1}) & n > 1 \end{cases} \tag{4.11}$$

Grouping these analyzes and approximations, the upper limit of $\mathbf{h}(k,n)$ is described by:

$$\mathbf{h}^u(n) = \begin{cases} D & n = 0 \\ CB_{max} & n = 1 \\ C\Psi^u(n-1)B_{max} & n > 1 \end{cases} \tag{4.12}$$

This expression summarizes all possible sequences of length $n-1$, so that the elements of the matrix $\Psi^u(n-1)$ correspond to the greatest multiplications of execution times of every task, given each scenario sequence of length $n - 1$ assessed. In the same way, it is possible to obtain the lower limit of $\mathbf{h}(k, n)$ defined as:

$$\mathbf{h}^l(n) = \begin{cases} D & n = 0 \\ CB_{min} & n = 1 \\ C\Psi^l(n-1)B_{min} & n > 1 \end{cases} \qquad (4.13)$$

Thus, for an application represented by a SADF graph, the service $S(k)$ has the following limits:

$$S^l(k) \leq S(k) \leq S^u(k) \qquad (4.14)$$

where, according to Eqs. (4.12) and (4.13),

$$\begin{aligned} S^l(k) &= \mathbf{h}^l(n) \quad \text{and,} \\ S^u(k) &= \mathbf{h}^u(n) \end{aligned} \qquad (4.15)$$

5 Workload Characterization Analysis Flow Based on Application Scenarios

Step A: This step corresponds to the Characterization Analysis Flow of the variable execution times of each application software task under analysis [16] (Fig. 4).

Step B: In this step, the specification of the application by a KPN model, or by a generic Application Tasks Graph (APTG), communicated via FIFO channels, is used to model the application as a SADF graph.

Step C: This step is basically to build the several matrices associated to each application scenario.

Step D: Given the SADF graph and the set of matrices associated to the scenarios, the step D computes the workload matrix curves defined by Eq (4.4) and (4.6).

Step E: Using the workload matrix curves computed in step D, step E determines the scenarios-based service curves, defined in Eqs. (4.15), (4.12) and (4.13), which give an upper and lower limit of the time the application may take to process k consecutive events (Sect. 4.2).

Step F: Finally, in step F, the service curve model and an arrival events function are used to estimate the limits on the output events generated from the application, and the limits of performances measures like throughput. Finally, the result of this analysis flow is a numerical estimation of these limits.

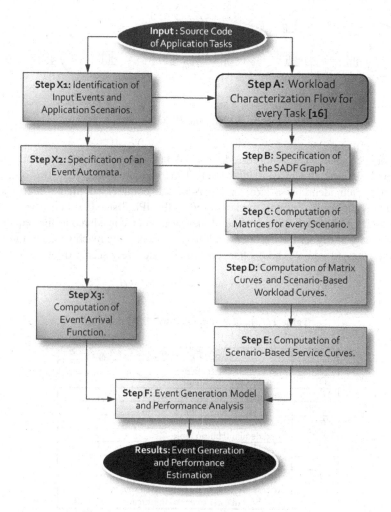

Fig. 4. Analysis flow developed for this paper.

6 Use Case

6.1 The JPEG Decoder

The JPEG decoder is a process capable of reconstructing image data from a stream of compressed image data, encoded under the JPEG standard [17].

The decoder takes the compressed image data as its input and subsequently applies a variable length decoding (VLD), zigzag scan and inverse quantization (IQZZ), inverse discrete cosine transform (IDCT), a color conversion (CC) and a last process (Raster) for putting the pixel values for the minimal coded unit (MCU) in place in the image, writing the image to disk when the conversion is complete. Figure 5 shows the JPEG decoder depicted as a Kahn Process Network (KPN) [18], annotated with buffer

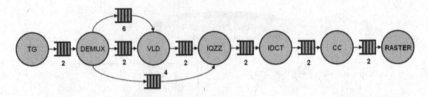

Fig. 5. KPN of the JPEG decoder

sizes between tasks. The compressed image data forms a byte stream input for the decoder. This byte stream contains so-called markers. A marker is a two-byte combination, which identifies a structural part of the compressed image data. Table 1 summarizes the most common markers used in the JPEG standard [17].

In the JPEG decoder, the sequence of markers can be considered as the sequence of input events that trigger the decoder, such that the finite state machine shown in Fig. 6 represents the order how markers happen and activate every scenario inside of Demux task.

Table 1. Markers supported by JPEG decoder

Marker	Action
SOI	Allow decoding of image.
EOI	Stop decoding of image.
APP	Read segment from input stream.
COM	Read segment from input stream.
DRI	Set restart interval.
DQT	Load dequantization table.
DHT	Load Huffman table.
SOF	Process frame header.
SOS	Process start of scan header; Process all MCUs in compressed image data; Send EOI marker over communications channel.

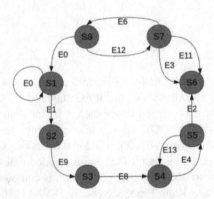

Fig. 6. Event automata for the input event sequence of the JPEG decoder

Table 2. Extreme execution times of every task according to the multiple JPEG application scenarios.

Worst-case Execution Time for every task on each scenario					
Scenario	vld	iqzz	idct	cc	Raster
1	166	365	1108	498	708
2	259	365	1108	1665	1346
3	332	365	1108	498	1965
4	397	365	1108	1665	708
5	431	365	1108	498	1346
6	467	365	1108	1665	1965
7	563	365	1108	498	708
8	628	365	1108	1665	1346
9	667	365	1108	498	1965
10	734	365	1108	1665	708
11	797	365	1108	498	1346
12	860	365	1108	1665	1965

Considering the values of these execution times for each task, as given in Table 2, twelve different matrices associated with each scenario are set for the JPEG encoder. Every execution time has been defined in clock cycles considering a Simplescalar processor running at 100 MHz [16].

6.2 Scenario-Based Services Curves

From the matrices of the several scenarios, and considering a certain input event sequence, the expressions Eqs. (4.3) and (4.5) were implemented in ScicosLab [19] to obtain the scenario matrix curves. With these curves, it is possible to calculate the sequences of service curves (lower and upper) for the JPEG decoder shown in the graph of Fig. 6.

The calculation was made in Scicoslab implementing the proposed expressions for each curve $S^l(k)$ and $S^u(k)$, explained in Sect. 4.2 by Eqs. (4.15), (4.12) and (4.13). Figs. 7 and 8 depict the curves calculated considering a maximum of iterations of $k = 10$ and $k = 50$, respectively. They describe the service provided by the application, such that this service is defined as the execution time the application needs to process a sequence of events related to a sequence of scenarios executed in the application up to the iteration k. Consequently, Figs. 7 and 8 show the upper and lower limit of the time the application may take to process k consecutive events associated to k consecutive scenarios executed in the application.

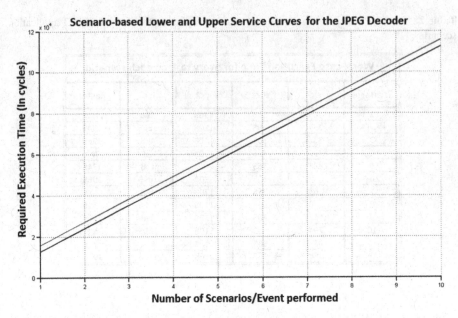

Fig. 7. Scenario-based service curves for JPEG decoder ($k = 1..10$).

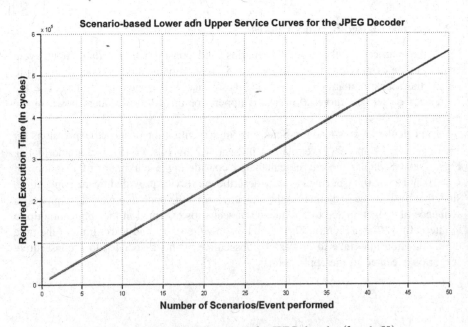

Fig. 8. Scenario-based service curves for JPEG decoder ($k = 1..50$).

7   Conclusions

In consideration of the different operation scenarios that make explicit the dynamic behavior of certain application, the modeling based on a SADF model of computation shows a timing behavior that has been analyzed as a linear model in a state space based on Max-Plus Algebra, so that the presence of several scenario sequences over time adds a timing variation to the linear model. From a mathematical point of view, it is possible to derive formal analytical expressions that describe the generation of event sequences by according to the iterations of a SADF graph. Also considering the full range of possible application scenarios and the variable execution demand that is found in the characterization of each application task, it is possible to characterize the set of all scenario sequences using the concepts of scenario-based workload curves and scenario-based service curves described in this paper, which allow to characterize the behavioral dynamism of an application in its design phase by describing the service (or execution time) that the application requires to process a sequence of events associated to a sequence of scenarios executed in the application. A JPEG decoder was used to test our methodology.

Acknowledgement. The given work was supported by CAPES (in Brazil), University of São Paulo (USP), and by CODI at the University of Antioquia (UdeA).

References

1. Schaumont, P.: A Practical Introduction to Hardware/Software Codesign -, 2nd edn. Springer, Heidelberg (2013). ISBN 978-1-4614-3736-9
2. Stuijk, S., Basten, T., Mesman, B., Geilen, M.: Predictable embedding of large data structures in multiprocessor networks-on-chip. In: Proceedings of the Conference on Design, Automation and Test in Europe, DATE 2005, vol. 1, pp. 254–255. IEEE Computer Society, Washington (2005). doi:http://dx.doi.org/10.1109/DATE.2005.244
3. Rosson, M.B., Carroll, J.M.: Scenario-based design. In: Jacko, J.A., Sears, A. (eds.) The human-computer interaction handbook, pp. 1032–1050. L. Erlbaum Associates Inc., Hillsdale (2002)
4. Gheorghita, S.V., Basten, T., Corporaal, H.: Application scenarios in streaming-oriented embedded-system design. IEEE Des. Test **25**(6), 581–589 (2008). doi:10.1109/MDT.2008. 158
5. Geilen, M., Stuijk, S.: Worst-case performance analysis of synchronous dataflow scenarios. In: Proceedings of the Eighth IEEE/ACM/IFIP International Conference on Hardware/Software Codesign and System Synthesis (CODES/ISSS 2010), pp. 125–134. ACM, New York (2010). doi:http://dx.doi.org/10.1145/1878961.1878985
6. Theelen, B.D., Geilen, M.C.W., Basten, T., Voeten, J.P.M., Gheorghita, S.V., Stuijk, S.: A scenario-aware data flow model for combined long-run average and worst-case performance analysis. In: Proceedings of the 4th ACM-IEEE International Conference on Formal Methods and Models for Codesign (MEMOCODE), pp. 185–194. IEEE Computer Society Press (2006)

7. Skelin, M., Wognsen, E.R., Olesen, M.C., Hansen, R.R., Larsen, K.G.: Model checking of finite-state machine-based scenario-aware dataflow using timed automata. In: 10th IEEE International Symposium on Industrial Embedded Systems (SIES), Siegen (2015). doi:10.1109/SIES.2015.7185065

8. Maxiaguine, A., Künzli, S., Thiele, L.: Workload characterization model for tasks with variable execution demand. In: Proceedings of the Conference on Design, Automation and Test in Europe, DATE 2004, vol. 2. IEEE Computer Society, Washington (2004)

9. Baccelli, F.L., Cohen, G., Olsder, G.J., Quadrat, J.-P.: Synchronization and Linearity: An Algebra for Discrete Event Systems. Wiley, Hoboken (2001). http://www.rocq.inria.fr/metalau/cohen/SED/book-online.html

10. Addad, B., Amari, S., Lesage, J.-J.: Linear time-varying (Max, +) representation of conflicting timed event graphs. In: 10th International Workshop on Discrete Event Systems, August 2010, pp. 310–315, Berlin, Germany (2010)

11. Maxiaguine, A., Zhu, Y., Chakraborty, S., Wong, W.-F.: Tuning SoC platforms for multimedia processing: identifying limits and tradeoffs. In: Proceedings of the 2nd IEEE/ACM/IFIP International Conference on Hardware/Software Codesign and System Synthesis, 08–10 September 2004, Stockholm, Sweden (2004)

12. Liu, Y., Chakraborty, S., Ooi, W.T.: Approximate VCCs: a new characterization of multimedia workloads for system-level MpSoC design. In: Proceedings. 42nd Design Automation Conference, 2005, pp. 248–253 (2005) doi:10.1109/DAC.2005.193810

13. Geilen, M.: Synchronous dataflow scenarios. ACM Trans. Embed. Comput. Syst. 10(2), Article 16, 31 pp. (2011). doi:http://dx.doi.org/10.1145/1880050.1880052

14. Geilen, M.: Reduction techniques for synchronous dataflow graphs. In: Proceedings of the 46th Annual Design Automation Conference (DAC 2009), pp. 911–916. ACM, New York (2009). doi:http://dx.doi.org/10.1145/1629911.1630146

15. Fidler, M.: Survey of deterministic and stochastic service curve models in the network calculus. IEEE Commun. Surv. Tutorials 12(1), 59–86 (2010)

16. Gustavo, A.P.A., Gonzalez, J., Chau, W.J., Strum, M.: Workload and task characterization based on operation modes timing analysis. In: 2012 IEEE International SOC Conference (SOCC), pp. 248–253, 12-14 September 2012

17. Meijer, S., Kienhuis, B., Turjan, A., de Kock, E.: A process splitting transformation for kahn process networks. In: 2007 Design, Automation & Test in Europe Conference & Exhibition, Nice, pp. 1–6 (2007)

18. Kahn, G.: The semantics of a simple language for parallel programming. Inf. Process. 74, 471–475 (1974). North-Holland

19. SCICOSLAB. http://www.scicoslab.org

A Novel WCET Semantics
of Synchronous Programs

Michael Mendler[1], Partha S. Roop[2,4](✉), and Bruno Bodin[3]

[1] Bamberg University, Bamberg, Germany
[2] University of Auckland, Auckland, New Zealand
p.roop@auckland.ac.nz
[3] University of Edinburgh, Edinburgh, UK
[4] Mercator Fellow, Bamberg University, Bamberg, Germany

Abstract. Semantics for synchronous programming languages are well known. They capture the execution behaviour of reactive systems using precise formal operational or denotational models for verification and unambiguous semantics-preserving compilation. As synchronous programs are highly time critical, there is an imminent need for the development of an execution time aware semantics that can be used as the formal basis of WCET tools. To this end we propose such a compositional semantics for synchronous programs. Our approach, which is algebraic and based on formal power series in min-max-plus algebra, combines in one setting both the linear system theory for timing and constructive Gödel-Dummet logic for functional specification of synchronisation behaviour. The developed semantics is illustrated using a running example in the SCCharts language.

1 Introduction

The synchronous paradigm [4] is ideal for designing safety critical, real-time systems in aviation, automotive and industrial automation. The issue of timing correctness is at the heart of such systems and is the topic of our interest. In this paper, we concentrate on Esterel [5] style imperative synchronous languages (ISP) and their graphical counter parts such as Argos [17], SyncCharts [2], and SCCharts [23]. Semantics of such languages are well known [5,17,23]. These semantics primarily express execution behaviour using unambiguous mathematical notation. However, these semantics are time-abstract and unsuitable from the point of view of worst case execution time (WCET) analysis.

Existing WCET techniques for ISP [20,21,24] have been largely guided by heuristics using general-purpose analysis tools such as ILP, model-checking, SAT-solving, and micro-architectural modelling. The evaluations of the methods are based on empirical benchmarking. Systematic studies of semantic soundness and computational complexity of WCET heuristics are rare. To master the complexity of the WCET problem for ISP, so we believe, it will be necessary to balance the trade-off between efficiency and precision in a semantic model that permits the tight coupling of function and timing and is applicable at all levels of

© Springer International Publishing Switzerland 2016
M. Fränzle and N. Markey (Eds.): FORMATS 2016, LNCS 9884, pp. 195–210, 2016.
DOI: 10.1007/978-3-319-44878-7_12

abstraction, from high-level ISP programs down to low-level assembly or hardware, while also being abstract and language-independent. This paper proposes such a WCET semantics of synchronous languages based on logic and algebra. The application of this semantics outlined here is based on some, arguably strong, assumptions. First, we consider that programs are executed on precision timed architectures [10]. These simplify static timing analysis without sacrificing throughput by using thread-interleaved pipelines without pipeline speculation. They also use scratchpad memories instead of caches and are devoid of timing anomalies. This assumption may be relaxed to some extent by compositional use of techniques for architecture modelling [7]. Second, we assume that for each synchronous thread there is sufficient computation between two state boundaries. This assumption is essential for the annotation of timing cost with every transition of a synchronous thread. Third, we assume that concurrency is modelled by thread interleaving rather than multi-processing. Note, however, that this work is mainly theoretical. Our motivating running example does not necessarily demonstrate the most general use of the proposed algebraic semantics.

An overview of the paper is as follows. We introduce a running example with hierarchy, concurrency, and reactivity using an SCChart [23], which is presented in Sect. 2. We propose input-output Boolean tick cost automata (IO-BTCA) as an intermediate representation of synchronous threads. This is presented in Sect. 3. As our main contribution we develop an expressive constructive logic of formal power series extending Gödel-Dummett's intuitionistic logic as an algebraic semantics for IO-BTCA and their compositions. The theory is expounded in Sect. 4 and its application is illustrated Sect. 5 using the running example. Conclusions relative to related work is presented in Sect. 7.

2   Illustrative SCCharts Example

We use the SCCharts language to model the running example as shown in Fig. 1a. The figure is annotated with the key features of the language used in this example. This language is a synchronous Statecharts [14] and the reader is referred to [23] for a detailed discussion on the language. The *sequencer* needs a start input signal to make progress from its initial state Disabled to the state Enabled. The state Enabled implements the actual specification of reaction: *after two ticks receiving the input* a, *the output* done *is emitted*. The sequencer uses local signals b, c and d to synchronize three concurrent threads cC, cA and cB (also called *regions*). Each thread is specified using a finite state machine with a unique start state e.g. $A0$, $B0$ and $C0$, indicated using bold circumferences. Each transition is labelled as i/o, where i is the guard that must be true for the transition to trigger, and o is the output part that is emitted when the transition is taken. Transitions are *non-immediate* and cannot be taken in the same tick when their source state is entered, except when they are marked as *immediate* using a dotted arrow as seen in Fig. 1b. Concurrent regions are nested within a higher-level region. The first thread cA synchronizes with the second thread cB and the third thread cC using the local signals b, c, d. The three concurrent

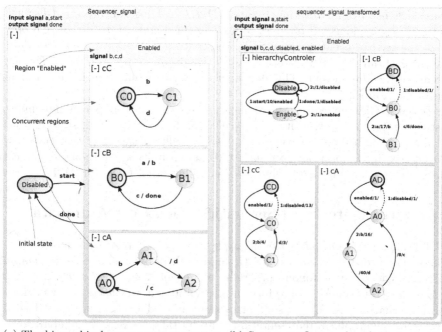

(a) The hierarchical, concurrent sequencer as it is seen in a SCChart visualizer.

(b) Sequencer flattened with timing back-annotations.

Fig. 1. Running sequencer example.

threads have 36 possible configurations. Due to synchronous execution, however, only the three combinations $A0/B0/C0$, $A1/B1/C1$ and $A2/B1/C0$ are feasible. WCET analysis techniques for synchronous programs must detect such infeasibility to ensure tightness.

Intermediate representation without preemption. The hierarchical transition in Fig. 1a is a weak preemption transition enabled by done. When this happens, all three threads are preempted and the behaviour moves to the initial state Disabled. Weak preemptions indicate causality i.e. the body terminates by generating an event that leads to the preemption transition being taken. Preemptions are handled in conventional semantics by introducing a separate hierarchical concurrency operator [17]. However, in the compilation chain towards executable sequential code, structural translation rules typically "compile away" the hierarchical transitions, which simplify WCET analysis.

Figure 1b shows the model generated after this structural translation. Each hierarchical region may be restructured by introducing one concurrent region per level of hierarchy. The concurrent region acts as a **controller** to activate and deactivate the appropriate sub-region (in the original specification). For example, we have introduced the region hC (hierarchyController) that waits until the start event to send an enable command to the other three concurrent regions.

These regions have an additional state $AD/BD/CD$ to indicate their disabled status. These regions can progress to their enabled state state $A0/B0/C0$ only when the **enable** event is provided by the controller. We have used *immediate* transitions from $A0/B0/C0$ to their respective disable state $AD/BD/CD$ upon receipt of the *done* event. This emulates the weak preemption in the original specification in Fig. 1a.

To aid WCET analysis, transitions are annotated with upper bound timing cost. For instance the transition t_{C1C0} leading from state $C1$ to state $C0$ has an upper bound timing cost of $\mathsf{wcet}(t_{C1C0}) = 3$ while t_{B0B1} has $\mathsf{wcet}(t_{B0B1}) = 17$. The timing annotations seen in Fig. 1b are entirely fictive though technical feasibility of obtaining these values has been illustrated earlier in [11, 16].

3 Intermediate Level Semantics: Tick Cost Automata

WCET analysis is formulated over graph representations of conventional programs. We propose to model the timing-enriched behaviour of a sequential (single-threaded) synchronous program as an *input-output Boolean tick cost automaton* (IO-BTCA). Following the convention in SCCharts, we will draw non-immediate transitions as solid arrows and immediate transitions as dashed arrows, in the graphical representation of an IO-BTCA. Also, we label a transition t with the triple $grd(t)/del(t)/act(t)$. A state which has at least one non-immediate transition exiting from it is called a *pause* state. All other states are *transient* states. We say an automaton *pauses* if control reaches a pause state and the guards of all immediate transitions leaving the state, if any, are false. An immediate transition whose guard is true must be taken in the same tick in which the state is entered. The activation of a non-immediate transition is checked only in the next tick.

Definition 1. *An* input-output Boolean tick cost automaton *(IO-BTCA) is* $M = \langle Q, e, I, O, \to, e \rangle$, *where* $Q = states(M)$ *is a finite set of* states *with a distinguished* entry *state* $e = entry(M) \in Q$. $I = In(M)$ *and* $O = Out(M)$ *denote the set of* input *and* output *signals, respectively. The transition relation* $\to$ *is partitioned into the set of* immediate transitions $\to_i$ *and* non-immediate *transitions* $\to_n$, *i.e.*, $\to = \to_i \uplus \to_n$. *Each type of transitions is a relation* $\to \subseteq Q \times \mathcal{B}(I) \times \mathbb{N} \times 2^O \times Q$, *where* $\mathcal{B}(I)$ *denotes the set of Booleans over* I. *A transition* $t = (q_1, b, d, o, q_2) \in \to$ *connects a source state* q_1 *with a target state* q_2. *It is labelled by a Boolean guard* $b = grd(t)$ *over* I *specifying the condition under which the transition triggers, a delay* $d = del(t)$ *describing its worst case timing cost and a set of emitted signals* $o = act(t)$.

WCET of an IO-BTCA. An example of an IO-BTCA is shown in Fig. 2. This automaton A has transient states $A0$, $A5$ and $A6$ drawn as solid circles, and pause states $A1$, $A2$, $A3$ and $A4$ drawn as two half-circles. The transient entry node $A6$ is indicated by a transition arrow without source state. Each pause state is split into two parts. The upper half of each pause state represents the *surface* of the state. When the surface is reached, it can be left immediately in

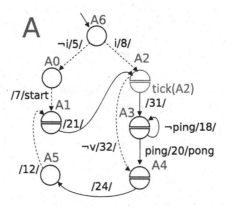

Fig. 2. A IO-BTCA A to illustrate the different features of the model. Immediate transitions are dashed arrows and non-immediate transition are plain arrows.

the same tick. As an example, on the state $A2$, if the condition $\neg v$ is true, it goes directly to $A4$. If there is no activated transition out of the surface, the control flow pauses there to wait for the clock tick. The occurrence of the clock tick switches activation to the lower half of the state, called the *depth*, from where the successive tick then is started. To express the synchronising behaviour of the clock tick we always use q for the surface and $tick(q)$ for the depth of a pause state in an IO-BTCA. This is indicated only for state $A2$ in Fig. 2 but applies to all other pause states, too.

Following the terminology of [19] we distinguish two types of execution paths in an IO-BTCA. A *sink path* starts in $entry(A)$, passes through immediate transitions ends in a pause state. An *internal path* starts the automaton in some pause state $tick(Ai)$ (the depth part) at the beginning of the tick, then activates a sequence of transitions and finally pauses in the surface of another pause state Aj.

Parallel composition of IO-BTCAs. Consider the synchronous multi-threaded composition cA‖cB‖cC shown in Fig. 3. The IO-BTCAs run concurrently and signals emitted by one machine are broadcast to the others. This may trigger a chain reaction of transition executions which are all executed in the same tick. The ticks are synchronised so that when one component pauses it stops and waits for the others to complete any sequence of enabled immediate transitions they may have. The composition cA‖cB‖cC pauses when *each* of cA, cB and cC pauses. For simplicity we look at the subsystem cA‖cB only. Note that from the 12 possible joint configurations of cA‖cB only 5 are actually reachable, while 7 state pairs do not align. The states which do align are indicated in Fig. 3 by the horizontal lines connecting the three automata. Without consideration of this alignment the possible maximum WCET for this example would be over-approximated $40 + 17 + 13 = 70$, induced by the transitions $A1 \rightarrow A2$, $B0 \rightarrow B1$ and $C0 \rightarrow CD$. But this is infeasible. As the tick lines show no two of

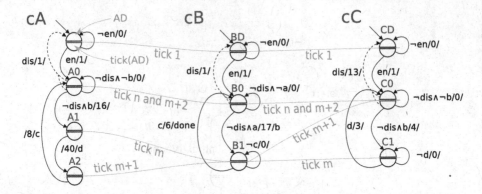

Fig. 3. Three IO-BTCAs representing the threads cA, cB and cC in our running example of Fig. 1b.

them can occur in the same tick. The actual WCET of cA‖cB‖cC in arbitrary environments is 43.

4   Min-Max-Plus Semantics of IO-BTCA

Here we present the semantics of IO-BTCA in terms of denotational fixed point equations. We show that the synchronous reaction behaviour and tick cost of every IO-BTCA can be described as a recursive equation system in the algebra of max-plus formal power series [3]. More details on these semantics can be found in an additional report [18].

4.1   Min-Max-Plus Algebra

Semi-ring structure. Our timing analysis will be expressed in the discrete max-plus structure over natural numbers $(\mathbb{N}_\infty, \oplus, \odot, 0, 1)$ where $\mathbb{N}_\infty =_{df} \mathbb{N} \cup \{-\infty, +\infty\}$ and $\oplus$ stands for the maximum and $\odot$ for addition on $\mathbb{N}_\infty$. Both binary operators are commutative, associative and have the neutral elements $0 =_{df} -\infty$ and $1 =_{df} 0$, respectively, i.e., $x \oplus 0 = x$ and $x \odot 1 = x$. The constant 0 is absorbing for $\odot$, i.e., $x \odot 0 = 0 \odot x = 0$. In particular, $-\infty \odot +\infty = -\infty$. Addition $\odot$ distributes over max $\oplus$, i.e., $x \odot (y \oplus z) = x + max(y, z) = max(x + y, x + z) = (x \odot y) \oplus (x \odot z)$. However, $\oplus$ does not distribute over $\odot$, for instance, $4 \oplus (5 \odot 2) = max(4, 5 + 2) = 7$ while $(4 \oplus 5) \odot (4 \oplus 2) = max(4, 5) + max(4, 2) = 9$. This induces on $\mathbb{N}_\infty$ a (commutative, idempotent) semi-ring. The choice of notation[1] $\odot$ and $\oplus$ highlights the multiplicative and additive nature, respectively, of the operators. Following convention, multiplicative expressions $x \odot y$ are written also without $\odot$ simply as $x\,y$ and $\odot$ is assumed to bind more strongly than $\oplus$.

---

[1] In [3] the constants $-\infty$ and 0 are symbolised as ϵ and e, respectively. Alain Girault suggested to us the notation 0 and 1 which we find more suggestive.

Logical interpretation. $\mathbb{N}_\infty$ is not only a semi-ring but also a lattice structure with the natural ordering $\leq$. Meet and join, respectively, are $x \wedge y = min(x, y)$ and $x \vee y = max(x, y) = x \oplus y$. With its two infinities $-\infty$ and $+\infty$ the order structure $(\mathbb{N}_\infty, \leq, -\infty, +\infty)$ is a complete lattice. This means we can construct least and greatest solutions of fixed-point equations by taking infinite join $\bigvee$ and meet $\bigwedge$, respectively.

Max-plus algebra (over integers and real numbers) is well-known and widely exploited for discrete event system analysis (see, e.g., [3,12]). What is rarely exploited, however, is the fact that the lattice structure of this algebra also supports logical reasoning, built around the *min* operation. The logical view is natural for our application where the values in $\mathbb{N}_\infty$ represent stabilisation times and measure the presence or absence of a signal during a tick. The bottom element $0 = -\infty$ indicates that a signal is *absent*, i.e., is never going to become active. Logically, this corresponds to falsity, usually written $\bot$. A signal with an upper bound stabilisation time of $+\infty$ on the other hand is known to become *present eventually*, though we cannot give an upper bound. This is simple logical truth, normally written $\top$. All other stabilisation values $d \in \mathbb{N}$ codify *bounded presence* which are forms of truth stronger than $\top$. On these multi-valued forms of truth (aka "presence") the minimum operation $\wedge$ acts like logical conjunction while the maximum $\oplus$ is logical disjunction $\vee$. The behaviour of $\top = +\infty$ and $\bot = -\infty = 0$ with respect to $\wedge$ and $\vee$ follows the classical Boolean truth tables. However, a logic is not a logic without negation. The natural *implication* operation $\supset$ is given such that $x \supset y = y$ if $y < x$, $+\infty$ otherwise. This defines the residual with respect to minimum $\wedge$, i.e., $x \supset y$ is the largest element z such that $x \wedge z \leq y$. Implication internalises the ordering relation in the sense that $x \supset y = \top$ iff $x \leq y$. It generates a *negation operation* in the usual way as $\neg x =_{df} x \supset \bot$ with the property that $\neg x = \top$ if $x = \bot$ and $\neg x = \bot$ if $x \geq 0$. This turns the lattice $\mathbb{N}_\infty$ into an *intuitionistic logic* or a (complete) Heyting algebra [22]. In fact, the specific Heyting algebra $(\mathbb{N}_\infty, \wedge, \vee, \supset, \bot, \top)$ is Gödel-Dummet logic, called **LC**, which is decidable and completely axiomatised by the laws of intuitionistic logic plus the linearity axiom $(x \supset y) \vee (y \supset x)$, see [9].

Intuitionistic logic. For us both the semiring structure $(\mathbb{N}_\infty, \oplus, \odot, 0, 1)$ and the logical interpretation $(\mathbb{N}_\infty, \wedge, \vee, \supset, \bot, \top)$ are equally important. The former to calculate WCET timing and the latter to express signals and reaction behaviour. Both are overlapping with the identities $\oplus = \vee$ and $0 = \bot$. Every element in $\mathbb{N}_\infty$ is at the same time a delay value and a constructive truth value. Every algebraic expression is at the same time the computation of a WCET and a logical activation condition. This makes min-max-plus algebra an ideal candidate to specify the constructive semantics of synchronous programming, at the exception that negation does not behave like in classical logic. Specifically, the law of the excluded middle $x \vee \neg x = \top$ fails to hold. For instance, if an Esterel program has a feedback cycle in which it emits a signal a if a is absent, this would be specified by $\neg a \supset a$. In classical logic we could prove (by case analysis) that necessarily $a = \top$, i.e., a is present (eventually). This is inconsistent with the constructive semantics of Esterel in which the program would be rejected as non-causal. Intuitionistic Gödel-Dummet logic is causality-sensitive: $\neg a \supset a$ has an infinite number of solutions, viz. all $a \geq 0$. So, the program has no unique (bounded) response on signal a, thus explaining why it must be rejected. In this paper we do not expand on constructiveness analysis and so do not exploit the intuitionistic nature of the logic.

4.2   Formal Max-Plus Power Series

The structure $\mathbb{N}_\infty$ plays the role of scalars in the algebra of IO-BTCAs where automata are specified with formal power series over $\mathbb{N}_\infty$. These are obtained by freely adjoining to $\mathbb{N}_\infty$ a formal variable X to represent the synchronous tick that separates one instant from the next. More specifically, a *(max-plus) formal power series*, *fps* for short, is a (finite or ω-infinite) sequence

$$A = \bigoplus_{i \geq 0} a_i X^i \; = \; a_0 \oplus a_1 X \oplus a_2 X^2 \oplus a_3 X^3 \cdots \tag{1}$$

with $a_i \in \mathbb{N}_\infty$ and where exponentiation is repeated multiplication, i.e., $X^0 = \mathbb{1}$ and $X^{k+1} = X X^k = X \odot X^k$. A formal power series stores an infinite sequence of numbers $a_0, a_1, a_2, a_3, \ldots$ as the scalar coefficients of the base polynomials X^i.

Such a power series may model an automaton's timing behaviour measuring the time cost to complete each tick or to reach a given state in given tick. If $a_i = \mathbb{0}$ then this means that A is not executed during the tick i and thus not contributing to the tick cost, or that a given state A is not reachable during this tick. This contrasts with $a_i = \mathbb{1}$ which means A is executed during tick i but with zero cost, or that the state A is active at the beginning of the tick. If $a_i > \mathbb{0}$ then automaton A is executed taking at most a_i time to finish tick i, or state A is reached within a_i-time during the selected tick. We can evaluate A with $X = \mathbb{1}$, written $A[\mathbb{1}]$, and obtain the worst-case reaction time across all ticks.

However, A could also be used to model a signal. In this context, $a_i = \mathbb{0}$ is equivalent to the signal being absent in tick i, $a_i = \mathbb{1}$ implies that s is present from the beginning of the tick, and $a_i > \mathbb{0}$ would mean that A becomes present during tick i with a maximal delay of a_i.

The tick sequences we will generate from finite state IO-BTCA are *rational*, i.e., ultimately periodic. These have the form $A = A_\tau \oplus X^k A_\phi$ where the first part $A_\tau = t_0 \oplus t_1 X \oplus \cdots \oplus t_k X^k$ is a finite initial *transient* sequence and the second part $A_\phi = r_0 X \oplus \cdots \oplus r_{n-1} X^n \oplus X^n A_\phi$ a finite *recurrent* loop. For notational convenience we will write such a rational series A in short form as $A = t_0{:}t_1{:}\cdots{:}t_k{:}(r_0\, r_1 \cdots r_{n-1})^\omega$. When $n = 1$ we call A an *ultimately constant* fps.

5   Modelling Signal-Dependent WCET

We will now show how our min-max-plus algebra can fully express the synchronous semantics of a IO-BTCA, in particular how it captures signal dependency and tick alignment of the timing, at different levels of precision. Rather than presenting a general semantic translation we illustrate the procedure using the example in Fig. 1b. We will derive for each automaton M a fps wcet(M) for the sequence of tick costs generated by M when started in its initial state. Moreover, we will derive for each state $S \in states(M)$ its worst case *activation* behaviour. This is a fps wcet(S) that gives for each tick the maximum waiting time for S to become active. If S is reachable in tick n then wcet(S)(n) $\geq \mathbb{1}$, otherwise wcet(S)(n) $= \mathbb{0}$. The value wcet(S)(i) $= \top$ would indicate unbounded reachability but without a specified upper bound. These fps are defined purely algebraically by recursive equation systems following the automaton's structure. The reason why wcet(M) and wcet(S) exist as unique least fixed point solutions is that $(\mathbb{N}_\infty[X], \leq, \mathbb{0})$ is a complete partial ordering and the operations appearing in the recursion are continuous.

5.1   The WCET of IO-BTCAs

Let us now consider the IO-BTCA cC, seen in Fig. 3. Since no state in cC is visited more than once during any tick, the cost wcet(cC)(i) of tick i is the worst case delay wcet(S)(i) of reaching any state $S \in \{CD, C0, C1\}$ in cC during tick i. Once we have wcet(S) $= \bigoplus_i$ wcet(S)(i) for each state $S \in \{CD, C0, C1\}$ we obtain the total tick cost as the sum (tick-wise maximum)

$$\text{wcet}(\mathsf{cC}) = \text{wcet}(CD) \oplus \text{wcet}(C0) \oplus \text{wcet}(C1). \tag{2}$$

Observe how the Eq. (2) later repeated in the Eq. (11) can constitute a max-plus definition of the WCET timing of our parallel system Enabled. Crucially for precision, however, this is the max-plus on formal time series and also these time series are parametric in signals.

We specify the timings wcet(S) of the states S inside cC in reaction to the input signals in terms of a mutually recursive system of min-max-plus recurrence equations. Here is state CD:

$$\text{wcet}(CD)(0) = \mathbb{1} \tag{3}$$

$$\begin{aligned}
\text{wcet}(CD)(n+1) = {} & (\neg en(n+1) \wedge (0 \odot (\mathbb{1} \wedge \text{wcet}(CD)(n)))) \\
& \oplus (dis(n+1) \wedge (13 \odot \text{wcet}(C0)(n+1))) \\
& \oplus (dis(n+1) \wedge (13 \odot (\mathbb{1} \wedge \neg dis(n) \wedge \text{wcet}(C0)(n)))). \tag{4}
\end{aligned}$$

These equations are directly extracted from the structure of cC. The first Eq. (3) says that state CD can be reached before the first tick with max cost $\mathbb{1} = 0$. This is correct since CD is the initial state of cC and we assume that the start up is delay-free. The second Eq. (4) looks at the cost of activating CD in some later tick $n + 1$. If CD is reachable at all in tick $n + 1$, then there are only two possibilities for where the control flow can arrive from:

(i) Control has already paused in state CD in the previous tick n and signal en is absent now in tick $n+1$. This activates the delay-free self-loop on CD.

(ii) Control has reached $C0$ in the same tick $n+1$ and immediately continues along immediate $C0 \to CD$ with *additional* cost 13.

(iii) Control has paused in $C0$ in tick n with *dis* being absent, while now in tick $n+1$ signal *dis* is present.

The recurrences (3)–(4) can be lifted to fps, thus eliminating tick count n:

$$\mathsf{wcet}(CD) = \mathbb{1} \oplus (\neg en \wedge (0 \odot tick(\mathsf{wcet}(CD)))) \oplus (dis \wedge (13 \odot \mathsf{wcet}(C0)))$$
$$\oplus (dis \wedge (13 \odot tick(\neg dis \wedge \mathsf{wcet}(C0)))) \tag{5}$$

where $tick(A) =_{df} X \odot (\mathbb{1}^{\omega} \wedge A)$ computes a "start time" for state A in each tick: We have $tick(A)(n+1) = \mathbb{1}$ if $A(n) \geq \mathbb{1}$ and $tick(A)(n+1) = 0$ if $A(n) = 0$.

The equations for cost series $\mathsf{wcet}(C0)$ and $\mathsf{wcet}(C1)$ are obtained similarly:

$$\mathsf{wcet}(C0) = (\neg b \wedge \neg dis \wedge (0 \odot tick(\neg dis \wedge \mathsf{wcet}(C0))))$$
$$\oplus (d \wedge (3 \odot tick(\mathsf{wcet}(C1)))) \oplus (en \wedge (1 \odot tick(\mathsf{wcet}(CD)))) \tag{6}$$
$$\mathsf{wcet}(C1) = (\neg dis \wedge b \wedge (4 \odot tick(\neg dis \wedge \mathsf{wcet}(C0))))$$
$$\oplus(\neg d \wedge (0 \odot tick(\mathsf{wcet}(C1)))). \tag{7}$$

The simultaneously recursive Eqs. (5)–(7) can be vectorised

$$(\mathsf{wcet}(CD), \mathsf{wcet}(C0), \mathsf{wcet}(C1)) = [\![\mathsf{cC}]\!](\mathsf{wcet}(CD), \mathsf{wcet}(C0), \mathsf{wcet}(C1)),$$

in which $[\![\mathsf{cC}]\!]$, for any fixed signals en, dis, b, d is a continuous function in the complete semi-lattice $(\mathbb{N}_{\infty}[X]^3, \leq, \oplus, (0, 0, 0))$. Its least solution is obtained by fixed point iteration $\bigoplus_{n \geq 0} [\![\mathsf{cC}]\!]^n$ where $[\![\mathsf{cC}]\!]^0 = (0, 0, 0)$ and $[\![\mathsf{cC}]\!]^{n+1} = [\![\mathsf{cC}]\!]([\![\mathsf{cC}]\!]^n)$.

Approximative WCET. With (5)–(7) at hand the cost series (2) is completely specified in reaction to the signals in the environment in which cC is running. Using the Eqs. (5)–(7) directly is possible via the equational laws of min-max-plus algebra over $\mathbb{N}_{\infty}[X]$ but computationally costly. Therefore we are now going to discuss two natural abstractions that introduce over-approximation on the tick costs for the benefit of computational efficiency. The first and most drastic abstraction ignores signals dependency altogether giving tick costs $\mathsf{wcet}_{abs}(M) \geq \mathsf{wcet}(M)$ and $\mathsf{wcet}_{abs}(S) \geq \mathsf{wcet}(S)$. This will give polynomial complexity. The second abstraction keeps signal dependencies for local analysis but ignores the environment. This gives local costs $\mathsf{wcet}_{loc}(M)$ and $\mathsf{wcet}_{loc}(S)$ which are worst-case over all environments. This yields more precise results, $\mathsf{wcet}_{abs}(M) \geq \mathsf{wcet}_{loc}(M) \geq \mathsf{wcet}(M)$ and $\mathsf{wcet}_{abs}(S) \geq \mathsf{wcet}_{loc}(S) \geq \mathsf{wcet}(S)$ but has NPTIME complexity.

Signal abstraction. We start with full signal abstraction where we do not bother to make any assumption on signals. Branching on signals is modelled by full non-determinism. We exploit monotonicity of $[\![cC]\!]$ and abstract from the signals using the upper approximations $s \leq \mathsf{T}^\omega$ and $\neg s \leq \mathsf{T}^\omega$ for every signal $s \in In(\mathsf{cC})$. This simplifies the Eqs. (5)–(7) for $\mathrm{wcet}(s)$ into equations for approximations $\mathrm{wcet}_{abs}(s) \geq \mathrm{wcet}(s)$:

$$\mathrm{wcet}_{abs}(CD) = \mathbb{1} \oplus tick(\mathrm{wcet}_{abs}(CD)) \oplus 13 \odot \mathrm{wcet}_{abs}(C0)$$
$$\oplus\, 13 \odot tick(\mathrm{wcet}_{abs}(C0)) \tag{8}$$

$$\mathrm{wcet}_{abs}(C0) = tick(\mathrm{wcet}_{abs}(C0)) \oplus (3 \odot tick(\mathrm{wcet}_{abs}(C1)))$$
$$\oplus(1 \odot tick(\mathrm{wcet}_{abs}(CD))) \tag{9}$$
$$\mathrm{wcet}_{abs}(C1) = (4 \odot tick(\mathrm{wcet}_{abs}(C0))) \oplus tick(\mathrm{wcet}_{abs}(C1)), \tag{10}$$

considering that $\mathsf{T} \wedge x = x$, $\mathbb{0} \oplus x = x$ and $0 \odot x = x$. This abstracted system $[\![cC]\!]_{abs}$ corresponds to the automaton cC from Fig. 3 stripped of all IO signals. By direct calculations unfolding (8)–(10) we find that the sequence $[\![cC]\!]^1_{abs}, [\![cC]\!]^2_{abs}, [\![cC]\!]^3_{abs}, \ldots$ has the limit solution

$$\mathrm{wcet}_{abs}(CD) = 0{:}14{:}14{:}16^\omega \quad \mathrm{wcet}_{abs}(C0) = 0{:}1{:}1{:}3^\omega \quad \mathrm{wcet}_{abs}(C1) = 0{:}0{:}4^\omega.$$

From this we get the approximation $\mathrm{wcet}(\mathsf{cC}) \leq \mathrm{wcet}_{abs}(\mathsf{cC})$ where $\mathrm{wcet}_{abs}(\mathsf{cC}) = \mathrm{wcet}_{abs}(CD) \oplus \mathrm{wcet}_{abs}(C0) \oplus \mathrm{wcet}_{abs}(C1) = 0{:}14{:}14{:}16^\omega$. Solving the equation system for $\mathrm{wcet}_{abs}(S)$ amounts to computing the longest path, between all reachable states for a given tick. Let $reachable(M, n) =_{df} \{S \in states(M) \mid \mathrm{wcet}_{abs}(S)(n) \geq \mathbb{1}\}$ be all of M's reachable states in tick n. One can show that $\mathrm{wcet}_{abs}(S)(n{+}1)$ is the maximal length of any internal path of M starting in any state in $R_n = reachable(M, n)$ and ending in S. This is computable in polynomial time. However, determining the sequence of subsets $R_0, R_1, R_2, \ldots$ reachable in each tick incurs a potential combinatorial explosion. In principle, every subset of states can occur as the set R_n. As we increase the tick count, exponentially many such state combinations may appear. Hence, it is not clear if the initial transient part of a cost series $\mathrm{wcet}_{abs}(s)$ is polynomially bounded for general IO-BTCA. However, we can show it is in PTIME for the special automata generated from SCCharts such as Enabled. The special feature is that the initial states CD, BD, AD (in fact all states) have self loops in which the environment can idle the automaton for as many ticks as it wants. As a consequence, the reachability of a state is monotonic. We call these *patient* IO-BTCA.

Tick alignment abstraction. For *general* IO-BTCAs a polynomially solvable WCET problem is obtained if we not only abstract from signals but also from the tick alignment of costs. This is a single worst case value $\mathrm{wcet}_{abs}(S)[\mathbb{1}] \in \mathbb{N}_\infty$ over all ticks. First consider that $tick(\mathrm{wcet}_{abs}(S))[\mathbb{1}] = \mathbb{1}$ iff S is reachable from the initial state by any path and $tick(\mathrm{wcet}_{abs}(S))[\mathbb{1}] = \mathbb{0}$ otherwise. Thus, $tick(\mathrm{wcet}_{abs}(S))[\mathbb{1}]$ is computable in polynomial time. The laws $(A \oplus B)[\mathbb{1}] = A[\mathbb{1}] \oplus B[\mathbb{1}]$ and $(d \odot A)[\mathbb{1}] = d \odot A[\mathbb{1}]$ permit us to replace all references to $tick(\mathrm{wcet}_{abs}(S))[\mathbb{1}]$ by $\mathbb{0}$ or $\mathbb{1}$ in equation system for $[\![M]\!]_{abs}$. The result is merely a max-plus equation system in variables $\mathrm{wcet}_{abs}(S)[\mathbb{1}] \in \mathbb{N}_\infty$ which can be solved by max path algorithms in polynomial time. This is the same as finding the max cost internal path from the set of reachable states. From the Eqs. (8)–(10) we obtain $\mathsf{wcet}_{abs}(CD)[1] = 16$, $\mathsf{wcet}_{abs}(C0)[1] = 3$ and $\mathsf{wcet}_{abs}(C1)[1] = 4$. The polynomial efficiency is achieved by solving the abstracted equation system in $\mathbb{N}_\infty$ rather then solving the original system over $\mathbb{N}_\infty[X]$ and then abstracting the result. On the other hand, of course, the tick aligned solutions $\mathsf{wcet}_{abs}(CD) = 0{:}14{:}14{:}16^\omega$, $\mathsf{wcet}_{abs}(C0) = 0{:}1{:}1{:}3^\omega$ and $\mathsf{wcet}_{abs}(C1) = 0{:}0{:}4^\omega$ are more informative and more precise in compositional WCET analysis.

Environment abstraction. This leads us to our second level of abstraction: Let $\mathsf{wcet}_{loc}(S)$ be the worst case under arbitrary environment signals. In general, $\mathsf{wcet}(S) \leq \mathsf{wcet}_{loc}(S) \leq \mathsf{wcet}_{abs}(S)$. Computing $\mathsf{wcet}_{loc}(S)$ is the same as solving a max cost executable path problem for each of the sets $reachable(M, n)$ of reachable state combinations, where we check sensitisation conditions arising from the transition guards. In a worst-case environment there is no coupling between ticks and so this satisfiability problem can be solved independently at every tick. In summary, for each tick n the feasibility of a state S being a possible starting state $S \in reachable(M, n)$ can be expressed by a logical expression in a polynomial number of Boolean signal statuses. The key observation again is that for patient IO-BTCA, even under signal control, the reachable set is monotonically increasing $reachable(M, n) \subseteq reachable(M, n + 1)$. More concretely, by induction, if we know the set $reachable(M, n)$ of states reachable in tick n, then these are the feasible start states of tick $n + 1$. We replace each occurrence of $\mathsf{wcet}(S)(n + 1)$ in the system equations of M by 1 if $S \in reachable(M, n)$ and by 0 otherwise. We then search for the maximal cost feasible path beginning in any state from $reachable(M, n)$, taking into account the signals conditions and the signals emitted by M in this tick. Solving the Boolean satisfiability conditions can be done in NPTIME. In the other direction, it is easy to show that the computation of $\mathsf{wcet}(S)$ is NP-hard. Any SAT can be coded into a patient IO-BTCA using only immediate transition so that $\mathsf{wcet}(S) = 1$ if the SAT is satisfiable and $\mathsf{wcet}(S) = 0$, otherwise.

Contextual dependency. The sequence $\mathsf{wcet}_{loc}(cC)$ is obtained by local analysis and it describes the worst-case under all possible environments. For specific environments the cost may be smaller. For instance, if en and dis are both constant true, expressed by the condition $en \wedge dis = \top^\omega$, then cC cycles along transitions between CD and $C0$ in each tick. This yields the cost series $\mathsf{wcet}_{cond}(CD) = 0{:}14^\omega \leq \mathsf{wcet}_{loc}(CD) = 0{:}14{:}14{:}16^\omega$.

5.2   The WCET of a Composition of IO-BTCAs

The cost series $\mathsf{wcet}(\mathsf{Enabled}) = \bigoplus_{i \geq 0} \mathsf{wcet}(\mathsf{Enabled})(i)\, X^i$ of the node $\mathsf{Enabled}$ in Fig. 1b is the parallel composition (tick-wise addition) of the constituent automata's tick cost series,

$$\mathsf{wcet}(\mathsf{Enabled}) = \mathsf{wcet}(hC) \parallel \mathsf{wcet}(cA) \parallel \mathsf{wcet}(cB) \parallel \mathsf{wcet}(cC). \qquad (11)$$

Following the previously defined worst case in an arbitrary environment wcet_{loc}, we calculate those abstracted series $\mathsf{wcet}_{loc}(\mathsf{hC}) = 0{:}10^{\omega}$, $\mathsf{wcet}_{loc}(\mathsf{cA}) = 0{:}2{:}16{:}40^{\omega}$, $\mathsf{wcet}_{loc}(\mathsf{cB}) = 0{:}2{:}17^{\omega}$ and $\mathsf{wcet}_{loc}(\mathsf{cC}) = 0{:}14{:}14{:}16^{\omega}$. For patient IO-BTCA the length of these sequences is polynomial.

Modelling a max-plus approach. At the top-level we are not actually interested in the cost series but merely its worst-case $\mathsf{wcet}(\mathsf{Enabled}) = \mathsf{wcet}(\mathsf{Enabled})[1]$ over all ticks. Instead of computing the parallel composition of the time sequences in $\mathbb{N}_{\infty}[X]$ we may compose their worst-case values in $\mathbb{N}_{\infty}$. Specifically,

$$\mathsf{wcet}_{loc}(\mathsf{Enabled})[1]$$
$$= (\mathsf{wcet}_{loc}(\mathsf{hC}) \parallel \mathsf{wcet}_{loc}(\mathsf{cA}) \parallel \mathsf{wcet}_{loc}(\mathsf{cB}) \parallel \mathsf{wcet}_{loc}(\mathsf{cC}))[1]$$
$$\leq \mathsf{wcet}_{loc}(\mathsf{hC})[1] \odot \mathsf{wcet}_{loc}(\mathsf{cA})[1] \odot \mathsf{wcet}_{loc}(\mathsf{cB})[1] \odot \mathsf{wcet}_{loc}(\mathsf{cC})[1]$$
$$= 10 + 40 + 17 + 16 = 83.$$

This is the so-called *max-plus* approach [19], which takes sum of the maximal tick cost from each parallel component. This calculation can be done in linear time but incurs a loss of precision in general.

Modelling a tick alignment sensitive approach. Both the locally abstracted series $\mathsf{wcet}_{loc}(M)$ and their collapsed worst case $\mathsf{wcet}_{loc}(M)[1]$ suffer from one major deficiency compared to the exact specification $\mathsf{wcet}(M)$: The local view does not account for *tick alignment*. The worst case depends on the environment sensitising in one and the same tick all the transitions whose cost adds up to the value $\mathsf{wcet}_{loc}(M)[1]$. But in a parallel system the environment of M is constrained and may not be able to exercise the sequence of sensitisations to reach the worst case configuration. In order to get tighter WCET results practical approaches have used full state space exploration [1], *context-sensitive* WCET analysis [15] or iterative narrowing using flow facts generated by model checking [20], or *tick expressions* [24]. All these approaches depend on preserving some or all of the sequencing information of the IO-BTCAs and their synchronisation via signals to detect incompatibility of local states or transitions.

Indeed, for $\mathsf{Enabled}$ in Fig. 1b to exhibit the worst case $\mathsf{wcet}_{loc}(\mathsf{Enabled})[1] = 83$ we must activate in the same tick the transitions $Disable \rightarrow Enable$ from hC, $C1 \rightarrow C0 \rightarrow CD$ from cC, $B0 \rightarrow B1$ in cB and $A1 \rightarrow A2$ in cA. However, these transitions do not align. As indicated by the horizontal tick lines in Fig. 3, it is not possible for the environment of $Enabled$ to drive the automata so the states $DisableC$, $A1$, $B0$ and $C0$ become simultaneously active in the same tick.

Practically, let us define $\mathsf{clk}(S) = \mathsf{T}^{\omega} \odot \mathsf{wcet}(S)$ as the *clock* of S giving full reachability information for a state S across all ticks and depending on all signals. If $\mathsf{clk}(S)(n) = \perp = -\infty$ then S is not reachable in tick n, while if $\mathsf{clk}(S)(n) = \mathsf{T} = +\infty$ then S is reachable. We intersect the two clocks $\mathsf{clk}(DisableC) \wedge \mathsf{clk}(A1)$ and use the recursive definitions from the specification of hC and cA to find that $\mathsf{clk}(DisableC) \wedge \mathsf{clk}(A1) = \perp^{\omega}$, i.e., both clock are incompatible.

We exploit this pairwise incompatibility information to run a second iteration of our local analysis, this time however, tracking the states $DisableC$ and $A1$.

We use $\text{wcet}_{A1}(S)$ which retains information on the dependency on (the clock of) state $A1$. It is more informative than $\text{wcet}_{abs}(S)$ but less informative than $\text{wcet}(S)$. Recalculating the abstraction for the full program

$$\text{wcet}(\text{Enabled}) \leq (\text{wcet}_{DisableC}(\text{hC}) \parallel \text{wcet}_{A1}(\text{cA})) \parallel \text{wcet}_{abs}(\text{cB}) \parallel \text{wcet}_{abs}(\text{cC})$$
$$= 0{:}12{:}26{:}41^\omega \parallel 0{:}2{:}17^\omega \parallel 0{:}14{:}14{:}16^\omega = 0{:}28{:}57{:}74^\omega$$

yields a tighter worst-case abstraction than the max-plus result $0{:}28{:}57{:}83^\omega$.

6 Related Work

The algebraic formulation of [19] for Esterel is closest to our approach. However, this does not consider the issue of tick alignment and signal dependencies. Logothetis et al. [16] show how to instrument the compilation process of Quartz for back-annotations of WCET timing into timed Kripke structures (TKS) modelling synchronous programs. However, timing semantics is not integrated into the algebraic semantics unlike our model.

Our work may be seen in the tradition of data-flow analyses for general imperative programs. Blieberger [6] presents WCET analysis using generating functions in plus-mult linear algebra considering loop counts. However, this semantics is not developed for signal dependencies and tick alignment, unlike the proposed approach. Max-plus algebra is also used for streaming applications to model actor firing times and execution dependencies [12]. Those techniques have been used, among other things, to solve throughput evaluation. The throughput of a streaming application is comparable to the WCET of a synchronous language. More recently, those techniques were extended using iterative narrowing [13] that, we believe, follows a similar direction as the iterative feasibility analysis we presented in Sect. 5.2.

Unlike the above references, it is essential to also consider architectural modelling for effective timing analysis. In our framework, we have assumed the precision timed architectures [10]. These architectures are non-speculative and have enabled us to focus on the nuances of synchronous programming instead of architectural modelling. However, our formulation could be extended in the future, along the lines of [7,8]. UPPAAL is used for precise micro-architectural modelling, including the modelling of architectures with timing anomalies, as illustrated in [7]. These works consider a network of timed automata for such models, unlike a network of IO-BTCAs considered in our semantics. Hence in our formulation it will be sufficient to consider model checking using bounded integers rather than real-valued clocks, as illustrated already in [21].

7 Conclusions

Design of safety-critical systems need both functional and timing correctness. Synchronous languages offer a deterministic concurrency model that is ideal for the design of such systems. To ensure timing correctness, several WCET analysis techniques have been developed. However, the study of timing correctness, from a semantic viewpoint is lacking, which could provide a sound basis for the design of WCET analysis tools. This paper, for the first time, develops a comprehensive semantics of synchronous languages using min-max-plus Gödel-Dummett algebra. The proposed semantics is compositional and may be used to describe the WCET behaviour of an individual thread (an automaton) or the composition of a set of threads. To facilitate precise analysis, the approach formalises the modelling of signals and the signal dependency between the threads. It also models, precisely, the tick-based lock-step execution of the threads, by formalising the *tick alignment problem* [21]. While the semantics enables precise approaches for analysis, it also facilitates abstractions and over-approximations. By abstracting a given feature, the designer may trade-off precision for scalability. Thus, the approach paves the way for the design of suitable analysis algorithms for WCET computation, that are founded on these sound semantics. In the near future, we will develop timing analysis tools for the SCCharts language by leveraging the developed semantics. We will also consider architectural modelling to support complex pipelines and memory architectures, unlike the PRET approach followed in this proposal. Another direction of future research would involve operational semantics of IO-BTCA structures and notions of simulation and equivalence among these structures unlike the fps-based semantics developed here.

Acknowledgment. We thank our anonymous reviewers and Insa Fuhrmann for the constructive feedback. We acknowledge the Precision-Timed Synchronous Reactive Processing (PRETSY2) project by the German Research Foundation DFG (ME 1427/6-2, HA 4407/6-2). Partha Roop acknowledges the research and study leave from Auckland University. Bruno Bodin acknowledges funding from the EPSRC grant PAMELA EP/K008730/1.

References

1. Andalam, S., Roop, P.S., Girault, A.: Pruning infeasible paths for tight wcrt analysis of synchronous programs. In: Design, Automation Test in Europe Conference (DATE), pp. 1–6, March 2011
2. André, C.: Synccharts: A visual representation of reactive behaviors. Rapport de recherche tr95-52, Université de Nice-Sophia Antipolis (1995)
3. Baccelli, F.L., Cohen, G., Olsder, G.J., Quadrat, J.-P.: Synchronisation and Linearity. Wiley, Chichester (1992)
4. Benvenist, A., Caspi, P., Edwards, S.A., Halbwachs, N., Le Guernic, P., de Simone, R.: The synchronous languages 12 years later. Proc. IEEE **91**(1), 64–83 (2003)
5. Berry, G.: The foundations of Esterel. In: Proof, Language, and Interaction, pp. 425–454 (2000)
6. Blieberger, J.: Data-flow frameworks for worst-case execution time analysis. Real-Time Syst. **22**(3), 183–227 (2002)
7. Cassez, F., Béchennec, J.-L.: Timing analysis of binary programs with UPPAAL. In: ACSD, pp. 41–50 (2013)

8. Dalsgaard, A.E., Olesen, M., Toft, M., Hansen, R.R., Larsen, K.G.: Metamoc: modular execution time analysis using model checking. In: OASIcs-OpenAccess Series in Informatics, vol. 15. Schloss Dagstuhl-Leibniz-Zentrum fuer Informatik (2010)

9. Dummett, M.: A propositional calculus with a denumerable matrix. J. Symbolic Logic **24**, 97–106 (1959)

10. Edwards, S.A., Lee, E.A.: The case for the precision timed (PRET) machine. In: Proceedings of the 44th Annual Design Automation Conference, pp. 264–265. ACM (2007)

11. Fuhrmann, I., Broman, D., Smyth, S., von Hanxleden, R.: Towards interactive timing analysis for designing reactive systems. Reconciling performace and predictability (RePP 2014) satellite event of ETAPS 2014. Technical report, Also as Technical report: EECS Department, University of California, Berkeley, UCB/EECS-2014-26 (2014)

12. Geilen, M., Stuijk, S.: Worst-case performance analysis of synchronous dataflow networks. In: CODES+ISSS 2010, Scottsdale, Arizona, USA, ACM, October 2010

13. De Groote, R., Hölzenspies, P.K.F., Kuper, J., Smit, G.J.M.: Incremental analysis of cyclo-static synchronous dataflow graphs. ACM Trans. Embed. Comput. Syst. (TECS) **14**(4), 68 (2015)

14. Harel, D.: Statecharts: a visual formalism for complex systems. Sci. Comput. Program. **8**(3), 231–274 (1987)

15. Ju, L., Huynh, B.K., Chakraborty, S., Roychoudhury, A.: Context-sensitive timing analysis of Esterel programs. In: Proceedings of the 46th Annual Design Automation Conference, DAC 2009, pp. 870–873. ACM, New York, NY, USA (2009)

16. Logothetis, G., Schneider, K., Metzler, C.: Generating formal models for real-time verification by exact low-level runtime analysis of synchronous programs. In: International Real-Time Systems Symposium (RTSS), pp. 256–264. IEEE Computer Society, Cancun, Mexico (2003)

17. Maraninchi, F., Rémond, Y.: Argos: an automaton-based synchronous language. Comput. Lang. **27**(1), 61–92 (2001)

18. Mendler, M., Roop, P.S., Bodin, B.: A novel wcert semantics of synchronous programs. Technical report, University of Bamberg, Nr. 101 (2016)

19. Mendler, M., von Hanxleden, R., Traulsen, C.: WCRT algebra and interfaces for Esterel-style synchronous processing. In: Proceedings of the Design, Automation and Test in Europe Conference (DATE 2009), Nice, France, April 2009

20. Raymond, P., Maiza, C., Parent-Vigouroux, C., Carrier, F., Asavoae, M.: Timing analysis enhancement for synchronous programs. Real-Time Syst. **51**, 192–220 (2015)

21. Roop, P.S., Andalam, S., von Hanxleden, R., Yuan, S., Traulsen, C.: Tight WCRT analysis of synchronous C programs. In: Proceedings of the 2009 International Conference on Compilers, Architecture, and Synthesis for Embedded Systems - CASES 2009, p. 205 (2009)

22. van Dalen, D.: Intuitionistic logic. In: Gabbay, D., Guenthner, F. (eds.) Handbook of Philosophical Logic, vol. III, pp. 225–339. Reidel, Dordrecht (1986). Chap. 4

23. von Hanxleden, R., Duderstadt, B., Motika, C., Smyth, S., Mendler, M., Aguado, J., Mercer, S., O'Brien, O.: SCCharts: sequentially constructive statecharts for safety-critical applications. In: Proceedings of ACM SIGPLAN Conference on Programming Language Design and Implementation (PLDI 2014). ACM, Edinburgh, UK, June 2014

24. Wang, J.J., Roop, P.S., Andalam, S.: ILPc: a novel approach for scalable timing analysis of synchronous programs. In: CASE 2013 (2013)

Worst-Case Execution Time Analysis
for Many-Core Architectures with NoC

Stefanos Skalistis[(✉)] and Alena Simalatsar

École Polytechnique Fédérale de Lausanne, Station 14, 1015 Lausanne, Switzerland
{stefanos.skalistis,alena.simalatsar}@epfl.ch

Abstract. The optimal deployment of data streaming applications onto multi-/many-core platforms providing real-time guarantees requires to solve the application *partitioning/placement, buffer allocation*, task *mapping* and *scheduling* optimisation problem using the tasks Worst-Case Execution Time (WCET). In turn, task WCET varies due to interferences that tasks experience when accessing shared resources, which vary depending on the solutions of the optimisation problem. To break this cyclic dependency we propose a detailed interference-based method that first over-approximates WCET based on the solution for application *partitioning/placement* and then tightens it by pruning out the interferences from tasks not overlapping in memory access and time. We prove that the derived bounds are safe. We have found that interferences on average amount to 10 % of WCET, and were able to improve the latency-guarantee up to 34 %.

1 Introduction

In the last several years there has been an increasing demand for novel methodologies for safe and efficient deployment of data-streaming applications into many-core architectures. *Many-core* architectures, having up to several hundreds of processing elements, are often organised as a set of clusters interconnected with a *network-on-chip* (NoC), with each cluster implementing a multi-core architecture. In *many-core* architectures, any data-exchange between two processing cores residing on the same cluster is performed through a shared memory, similarly to multi-core architectures. On the contrary, exchanging data across clusters is carried out by copying data from the source cluster shared memory to the target cluster memory, utilising the NoC.

The optimal deployment of a data streaming application, i.e. applications with data-dependent tasks which process data and exchange them via communication buffers, on a many-core architecture is a multi-criteria optimisation problem. To provide real-time guarantees on task deployment such optimisation must be based on the estimation of safe and tight bounds for the tasks' WCET. We consider that the WCET of such tasks is composed of (i) their Worst-Case Computation Time (WCCT) when executed in isolation, which includes the time to fetch/deposit data, plus (ii) the delay due to interferences from other tasks when accessing shared resources, i.e. memory banks, buses and/or the

© Springer International Publishing Switzerland 2016
M. Fränzle and N. Markey (Eds.): FORMATS 2016, LNCS 9884, pp. 211–227, 2016.
DOI: 10.1007/978-3-319-44878-7_13

NoC. However, computing the interferences requires the knowledge of (i) the task scheduling and mapping into cores, and (ii) the communication buffers mapping into memory banks. This results in a vicious cycle, with WCETs and the solutions of the optimisation problem depending on each other. To address this problem some approaches, e.g. [8], assume that two parallel tasks sharing a resource at any time of execution will definitely interfere. In [14] the WCET is acquired by static analysis tools such as aiT [1]. Approaches like [12] allocate resources such that there are no interferences at all. The first two approaches can largely overestimate the WCET, while the third one may result in undermining the overall performance.

In this paper we propose a simple and accurate interference-based WCET analysis of tasks for a data steaming application deployed on a many-core architecture. Considering that breaking the vicious cycle is not the main focus of this paper, we only briefly present an approach to solve the multi-criteria optimisation problem so as to outline our interference-based WCET analysis. The multi-criteria optimisation problem is decomposed into two stages *partitioning/placement* and *buffer allocation, task mapping and scheduling* the solutions of which we acquire, using methods of [15]. There, the problem is formulated in terms of constraints and given to an SMT solver to provide solutions. Given the solution of the *partitioning/placement*, derived using the WCCT, we compute a safe over-approximation of the WCET of every task by accounting for all possible interferences. The over-approximated WCETs are then used to derive the *buffer allocation* and task *mapping* and *scheduling*. Subsequently, we use these solutions to tighten task WCET, by excluding interferences from tasks that do not overlap in space, i.e. memory and bus arbiters, and time. The *scheduling* is then updated to account for the tighter WCET, by adjusting the starting time of tasks but preserving the order of task execution. We prove that the derived WCET bound is safe. As an example of a many-core architecture in this paper we consider the architecture of Kalray MPPA-256 [10].

The main contribution of this paper is an accurate interference-based WCET analysis for many-core architectures with NoC, applied to break the vicious cycle between WCET estimation and *buffer allocation, task mapping and scheduling*.

The rest of the paper is organised as follows. Section 2 discusses the related work. Section 3 presents the models, functions and notation used throughout the paper. Section 4 presents the WCET analysis applied for the Kalray MPPA-256 architecture [10], and the iterative method to tighten the WCET bounds is presented in Sect. 4.4. The evaluation of the approach is presented in Sect. 5.

2   Related Work

The evolution from single core to multi- and many-core architectures has raised a question of optimal use of shared resources, e.g. processing cores, memories, buses and NoCs. Thus, optimal deployment of tasks with data dependencies, onto a many-core platform is regarded as a multi-criteria optimisation problem [5,9,11, 15,16]. We will focus on works that, similarly to ours, consider that the WCET of a task is composed of (i) their WCCT plus (ii) the delay due to interferences.

In [13] the authors propose an ILP formulation of the task scheduling and mapping problem for multi-core architectures with caches. They consider different communication times for data exchange between the tasks mapped to the same core (e.g. when communication happens through caches) and two different cores (e.g. with the access to shared memory). In [3] the authors are presenting an upper bound estimation of the WCET for a memory-centric architecture by proposing a memory-aware execution to compute the delays due to memory contention. They consider a hierarchical memory organisation with one shared memory block and dedicated caches for each processing element (PE), where groups of PEs are organised in a small number of clusters. The access to the shared memory is realised through Data Memory Access (DMA) units, while the access delays are derived experimentally for different sizes of memory blocks. The approaches of [3,13] are suitable for architectures with a small number of clusters having simple inter-cluster communication, e.g. TI Keystone II^{TM} [17]. There have been works dedicated to WCET analysis for the tasks with data dependencies deployed onto a many-core architecture. In [7] authors present the approach to compute the WCET of tasks running on Kalray MPPA-256 platform by assuming that the maximum number of interfering tasks when accessing the shared memory within a cluster is equal to the number of cluster cores; this assumption does not hold as we have noticed in our experiments.

In [8] the authors are presenting a theory for mixed-criticality scheduling on cluster-based many-core architectures with shared resources developed within the CERTAINTY project. To derive a feasible schedule the authors are estimating the Worst-Case Response Time (WCRT) of tasks, in our paper called WCET. The tasks are scheduled with the FTTS mixed-criticality scheduling policy that repeats over a hyper-cycle divided into frames and sub-frames, the beginning of which is synchronised among each core of a cluster. Each sub-frame contains only the tasks of the same criticality level, which ensures that resource contention may happen only among the tasks with the same criticality level. The tasks' WCRT, for the same level of criticality, is composed of their worst-case execution time (i.e. WCCT in our paper), the total delay due to memory accesses with no interference from other tasks, and the worst-case delay encountered due to contention on shared resources. However, the approach to the computation of such delays depends on the application and the architecture models, the mapping of the tasks and buffers onto processing elements and memory blocks, respectively, as well as on the set of considered shared resources. In [8] the authors are considering a mixed-criticality periodic task set that resembles the Cycle-Static Dataflow (CSDF) model [2] enhanced with criticality levels. Our model considers one iteration with no criticality levels but with a detailed representation of the communication mechanism over the NoC. Also, in addition to the collisions when accessing shared memory blocks accounted in [8], we are considering the collisions happening at shared buses. Moreover, we are presenting a mechanism of tightening the upper bound of the WCET by reducing the set of potentially interfering tasks using the task scheduling, pruning out the tasks non-overlapping in time, which is considered highly complex for the models used in [8].

3   Preliminaries

In this section we present the models for the application and the many-core platform considered in our analysis with the set of functions defining application *partitioning/placement*, used to derive the unified system model, and *mapping* and *scheduling* on a platform that serves as an input to our analysis.

In the rest of the paper, for any tuple, e.g. $Y = (A, B, C)$, we will use a superscript notation to denote its respective components, e.g. A^Y, B^Y, and C^Y. We will also denote with $\mathbb{N}_0$ (resp. $\mathbb{N}_+$) the set of natural numbers that contains (resp. does not contain) zero.

3.1   The Platform Architecture Model

We define a many-core architecture as a set of *identical* multi-cores, hereafter *clusters*, interconnected via a NoC. Within a cluster, processing cores exchange data through a shared memory, hereafter *cluster memory*. The data transfer between cores located on different clusters is handled by the NoC. We will call the data exchange between processing cores on different clusters as *inter-cluster* and between cores on the same cluster as *intra-cluster* communication. Similarly to [15,16] we model the platform architecture as:

Definition 1 (Platform architecture model). *A platform architecture model is a tuple $P = (X, K, M, N)$ where:*

- *X is the set of clusters*
- *K is the set of processing cores per cluster*
- *M is the set of memory banks per cluster*
- *N is the set of NoC channels of a NoC interface.*

We assume that each cluster has one NoC interface connected, with multiple channels, to a single dedicated NoC router [4]. Notice that the set of all cores (resp. NoC channels) in the architecture is $X \times K$ (resp. $X \times N$).

Memory Access Model. The cluster memory is organised in several sets of memory banks where each set is arbitrated by a single arbiter accessible through data buses, the access to which is also arbitrated. Thus for any memory operation, we consider two arbitration points: (i) one before the data bus that connects a core to the set of memory banks and (ii) another one before a set of memory banks arbitrated by a dedicated arbiter. The data fetch and deposit from/to the memory is performed as sequence of word-by-word memory operations. A single-word memory operation is called a *request*. The memory requests delays for a task with no interference in any of the arbiters is accounted in the WCCT of the task. However, if a request interferes with other requests either in the bus or memory arbiter, extra delays will be introduced due to conflicts, which is proportional to the number of conflicting requests. Since the extra delays are caused by the interference at the arbitration points, we consider each set of memory banks coordinated by the same arbiter as a single memory bank.

Definition 2 (Arbitration constants). *The following single-conflict arbitration constants are defined in cycles:*

- $ad_{Bus} \in \mathbb{N}_+$ *is the arbitration delay for a request to access a shared bus*
- $ad_{Mem} \in \mathbb{N}_+$ *is the arbitration delay for a request to access a memory bank*

A single-conflict arbitration delay is the worst-case delay that any request may incur if it conflicts with only one other request. If $n + 1$ requests conflict at the same time, then in the worst-case any request will suffer n times the single-conflict arbitration delay.

The NoC Model. The NoC is composed of a set of routers, connected in a mesh topology. Each cluster has a dedicated *NoC interface* [4] with a dedicated router. Each NoC interface has several channels handling multiple data-flows in parallel and two dedicated elements to transmit and receive data, respectively, thus avoiding interference between these two processes.

In our model the data transfer between two clusters occurs in three stages. The first stage is *initialisation*, when the NoC interface is configured with the memory addresses from where to fetch/deposit the data and the NoC channel that should be used for the transfer. During the initialisation phase, both the core and the NoC interface are considered to be "busy" for a constant amount of time, called *initialisation delay*. The second stage is the *transfer*, during which the NoC channel fetches the data, forms the packets and forwards them to the target cluster over the NoC. The NoC interface of the target cluster receives the data and places them in the memory. The transfer time depends on the data size and distance between two clusters. The third stage is *finalisation* when the core that initialised the transfer polls the NoC interface to check if all the data have been transferred, so as to release the memory space occupied by the data. The act of polling, if it is non-blocking, keeps both processing core and the NoC interface "busy" for a constant time, called *polling delay*; otherwise, the core is blocked until all data are injected into the NoC, in addition to the polling delay.

This way, the NoC model accounts for several platform-dependent constants related to communication over the NoC, which are considered in our analysis. For two clusters $x, x' \in X$, we define the distance $\|x, x'\|$ as the minimum number of routers that a packet, sent from x to x', has to traverse.

Definition 3 (NoC constants). *For a platform architecture model P, we define the following timing constants (in cycles):*

- $id_{NoC} \in \mathbb{N}_+$ *is the initialization delay of the NoC interface*
- $dpb_{NoC}^{\|x,x'\|} \in \mathbb{N}_+$ *is the delay per byte for transferring data between two clusters with distance $\|x, x'\|$*
- $pd_{NoC} \in \mathbb{N}_+$ *is the NoC interface polling delay*

We assume, that these values are known and bounded for a platform P.

3.2 Application Model

An application composed of a set of *computation tasks* with dependencies is modelled as a task graph that is a directed acyclic graph (DAG) $G = (V, E)$, with V being a set of tasks and E a set of dependencies among these tasks. The tasks communicate through bounded FIFOs, one for each $e \in E$ of the graph.

Definition 4 (Annotated task graph). *An annotated task graph is a tuple* (V, E, d, σ) *where* (V, E) *is a task graph and:*

- $d : V \rightarrow \mathbb{N}_+$ *is the* delay function, *which represents the* execution time $d(v)$ *for a task* $v \in V$ *when executed in isolated environment with no interference.*
- $\sigma : E \rightarrow \mathbb{N}_0$ *is the* data-size function *which represents the* amount of data, *in words, sent from the source to the target task, that is for* $e = (v, v') \in E$, $\sigma(e)$ *denotes the amount of data produced by* v *and consumed by* v', *respectively.*

An *application* is an annotated task graph $A = (V_C, E_C, d_C, \sigma_C)$, containing only *computation tasks* (V_C^A) and their dependencies (E_C^A).

3.3 Application Deployment onto the Platform

The deployment of an application onto a platform is the mapping of tasks to processing cores and their dependencies to communication elements or memory blocks. For tasks placed on different clusters which communicate through FIFOs, we duplicate the FIFOs, one for each clusters, and introduce communication tasks that handle data transfer over NoC. We will call the *unified system model*, this communication-aware model which accounts for system computation and communication behaviours.

Given an application model A and a placement function p, we derive a *unified system model* (see Fig. 1).

Deriving the Unified System Model. To derive the *unified system model* the solution to the *partitioning/placement* stage is required. Given a task graph G and a platform model P we denote with $p : V \rightarrow X$, the *placement function* that assigns tasks to clusters. For an application model A, a platform model P, and a placement function p, let E_{in}^A (resp. E_{ex}^A) denote the data-exchange among tasks residing in the same cluster (resp. in different clusters):

$$E_{in}^A = \{(v, v') \in E^A \mid p(v) = p(v')\}, \quad E_{ex}^A = E \setminus E_{in}^A$$

According to our NoC model, for two tasks $(v, v') \in E_{ex}^A$, we denote with $i_{v,v'}$, $t_{v,v'}$, and $f_{v,v'}$ new *communication tasks* performing the NoC interface initialisation, the data transfer and the NoC interface polling, respectively. Let I, T and F denote their full sets, respectively. Since there exists only one NoC interface per cluster, which can execute only one initialisation communication task at a time, every per cluster projection of I, i.e. I_x as defined in Table 1, must be totally ordered.

Table 1. Projections of sets and task graph $G = (V, E)$

Per cluster x	$V_x \overset{def}{=} \{v \in V \mid p(v) = x\}$	$E_x \overset{def}{=} E \cap (V_x)^2$	$G_x \overset{def}{=} (V_x, E_x)$
Per element ϵ	$V_\epsilon \overset{def}{=} \{v \in V \mid p\mu_E(v) = \epsilon\}$	$E_\epsilon \overset{def}{=} E \cap (V_\epsilon)^2$	$G_\epsilon \overset{def}{=} (V_\epsilon, E_\epsilon)$

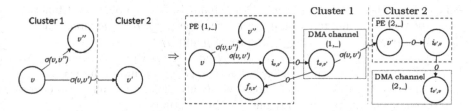

Fig. 1. Application model (left) and corresponding unified system model (right).

Definition 5 (Unified system model). *Given an application model A, a platform model P and a placement function p, the system model is an annotated task graph $S = (V, E, d, \sigma)$, such that:*

- $V = V_C^A \cup V_T$ *where V_C^A is the set of computation tasks of the application and $V_T = \{i_{v,v'}, i_{v',v}, t_{v,v'}, t_{v',v}, f_{v,v'} \mid (v, v') \in E_{ex}^A\}$ is the set of communication tasks introduced for the data-exchange among clusters;*
- $E = E_{in}^A \cup E_T^S \cup E_I^S$, *where $E_T^S = \{(v, i_{v,v'}), (i_{v,v'}, t_{v,v'}), (t_{v,v'}, v'), (v', i_{v',v}), (i_{v',v}, t_{v',v}), (t_{v,v'}, f_{v,v'}) \mid (v, v') \in E_{ex}^A\}$ is the set of dependencies introduced, among computation and communication tasks, by dependent computation tasks placed on different clusters and $E_I^S = \{(i_i, i_{i+1}) \mid i_i, i_{i+1} \in I_x, \forall i \in [1, |I_x| - 1], \forall x \in X\}$, is a totally ordered set of dependencies for NoC initialisation tasks for each cluster;*
- *The delay function $d : V \to \mathbb{N}_+$ is defined as:*

$$d(v) = \begin{cases} d^A(v) & v \in V^A, \\ id_{NoC} & v = i_{v_1, v_2}, \\ dpb_{NoC}^{\|p(v1), p(v2)\|} * \sigma^A(v_1, v_2) & v = t_{v_1, v_2}, \\ pd_{NoC} & v = f_{v_1, v_2}; \end{cases}$$

for $v_1, v_2 \in V^A$, such that $(v_1, v_2) \in E_{ex}^A$;
- *The data-size function $\sigma : E \to \mathbb{N}_+$ is defined as:*

$$\sigma(v, v') = \begin{cases} \sigma^A(v, v') & (v, v') \in E_{in}^A, \\ \sigma^A(v_1, v') & v = t_{v_1, v'} \wedge (v_1, v') \in E_{ex}^A, \\ \sigma^A(v, v_1) & v' = i_{v, v_1} \wedge (v, v_1) \in E_{ex}^A, \\ 0 & otherwise. \end{cases}$$

The *unified system model* is build based only on the solution of the application *partitioning* and *placement*, which are computed using methods of [15] based on the WCCT of tasks. This model serves as an input to the first over-approximations of the tasks' WCET. The WCET tightening requires the solutions for optimal *buffer allocation* or *memory mapping* and task *mapping* and *scheduling* functions of the corresponding optimisation problem.

Given a unified system model S and a platform model P we denote with $\mu_E : V \to (K \cup N)$ the *task mapping* function, which maps tasks to a platform element, i.e. either processing cores or NoC channels. Given a placement function p and the task mapping function μ_E, we derive the *global task mapping* function $p\mu_E : V \to X \times (K \cup N)$ as the product of p and μ_E.

With $s : V^S \to \mathbb{N}_+$ we denote the *scheduling* function which associates a start time to each task, such that for each $\epsilon \in X \times (K \cup N)$ and each $(v, v') \in E_\epsilon$, the inequality $s(v) + d(v) < s(v')$ holds, since any platform element ϵ, i.e. core or NoC channel, can execute only one task at any time.

4   Interference-Based WCET Analysis

To perform WCET analysis for a task, one needs to estimate the amount of interferences introduced by other tasks when accessing shared resources, e.g. buses, memory, NoC, etc. We distinguish two types of interference:

- **Intra-cluster:** where two tasks v, v', either computation or communication, placed to the same cluster compete for shared resources;
- **Inter-cluster:** where a computation task v and a transfer task t of different clusters are trying to access the same memory bank.

Potentially, any pair of tasks v, v' mapped on the same cluster can interfere when simultaneous accessing the same data-bus and/or the same memory bank. Therefore, the first WCET over-approximation is computed as the sum of the tasks WCCT time and the delays caused by the over-approximation of interference sets done based on the *unified system model*.

For a unified system model S and a task $v \in V^S$, both its predecessors and successors can not possibly interfere with v due to the data dependencies.

Definition 6. *Given a task graph $G = (V, E)$ and a task $v \in V$, we denote by $pred(v)$ (resp. $succ(v)$) its immediate predecessor (resp. successor) set and with $pred^*(v)$ (resp. $succ^*(v)$) its transitive closure.*

Given a unified system model S, let $\mathcal{P}_v$ denote the set of tasks possibly executed in parallel with v as:

$$\mathcal{P}_v^{over} = \left\{ v' \in V^S \setminus v \mid v' \notin pred^*(v) \cup succ^*(v) \right\}$$

and $\mathcal{P}_{v\,x}^{over} = \mathcal{P}_v^{over} \cap V_x^S$ its projection on cluster $x \in X$.

For a task $v \in V^S$ mapped onto a cluster $x \in X$, let the intra-cluster, i.e. memory and bus, and inter-cluster interference sets of tasks potentially conflicting with v on a memory bank and/or a bus $\mathcal{M}_v^{over}$, $\mathcal{B}_v^{over}$, and $\mathcal{C}_v^{over}$, respectively, be:

$$\mathcal{M}_v^{over} = \{v' \in \mathcal{P}_{v\ x}^{over}\} \qquad \mathcal{B}_v^{over} = \{v' \in \mathcal{P}_{v\ x}^{over}\}$$
$$\mathcal{C}_v^{over} = \{t_{v_1,v_2} \in \mathcal{P}_v^{over} \cap (T \setminus T_x) \mid p(v_2) = p(v)\}$$

Notice that $\mathcal{C}_v^{over}$ does not include transfer tasks placed to the same cluster as v, since the interference from them is accounted in the $\mathcal{M}_v^{over}$ and $\mathcal{B}_v^{over}$ sets.

From this point we analyse interferences for the Kalray MPPA-256 platform and its arbitration policies, but can be adapted for other architectures as well.

4.1 Kalray MPPA-256 Architecture

The architecture of Kalray MPPA-256 consists of 256 processing cores grouped in compute clusters each comprising 16 processing cores and 2MB of shared memory, which consists of 16 independent memory banks organised in two sides, *left* and *right*. The memory bank arbiter gives priority to requests received from NoC (NoC Rx), while all other requests, e.g., from processing cores and NoC transmit (NoC Tx), are arbitrated in a round robin fashion.

Processing cores are organised in pairs, each pair shares two data-buses, one for each of the memory sides. This way, when one core of a pair accesses one memory side and the other core of the same pair accesses the other memory side, there is no conflict [6]. For instance, a request from a core k to memory bank m will get an interference delay (i) due to the bus arbiter if the other core paired with k is accessing a memory bank of the same side as m, and (ii) due to the memory arbiter if any core or the NoC interface accesses memory bank m at the same time (see Fig. 2).

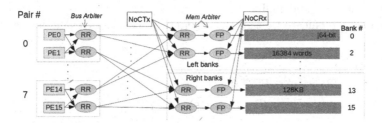

Fig. 2. Compute cluster reference architecture with arbitration points (RR stands for Round Robin and FP for Fixed Priority).

The NoC of the Kalray MPPA-256 performs the data transfers with guaranteed services by network traffic shaping that bounds the communication delay under certain threshold for the amount of communicated data [6]. We consider the packet transfer over NoC and packet handling by the NoC Rx as a unique operation performed within the *transfer tasks* t.

We model the Kalray platform as $P = (X, K, M, N)$, where $X = \{x_0, \ldots, x_{15}\}$, $K = \{pe_0, \ldots, pe_{15}\}$, $M = \{m_0, \ldots, m_{15}\}$, and $N = \{c_0, \ldots, c_7\}$. We also consider the memory sides of Kalray as separate sets $Left = \{m_{2k} | 0 \leq k \leq 7\}$ and $Right = \{m_{2k+1} | 0 \leq k \leq 7\}$).

4.2   Intra-cluster Interference

To identify the tasks interferences when accessing the same memory banks or buses, we introduce the memory mapping and shared bus functions. Recall that for a data-dependency e between two tasks, the amount of memory required for that data exchange is $\sigma(e)$. For clarity we assume that each data exchange occurs using a single memory bank.

Given a task graph $G = (V, E)$, let $E_{\sigma>0}$ be the set of non-zero data-size dependencies; we denote with $\mu_M : E_{\sigma>0} \to M$ the *memory mapping* function which associates a dependency, i.e. a buffer, to a memory bank. We extend the *memory mapping* function for tasks, i.e. $\mu_M : V \to 2^M$, such that it defines the set of memory banks that a given task accesses to fetch or deposit data:

$$\mu_M(v) = \bigcup_{e\in(\{v\}\times succ(v))\cup(pred(v)\times\{v\})} \mu_M(e)$$

We also define the *global memory mapping* function $p\mu_M : V \to 2^{X\times M}$ as the product of p and μ_M.

Given a set of processing cores K and memory banks M, we define an architecture specific *shared buses* predicate $sbus : K \times K \times M \times M \to \mathbb{B}$ as:

$$sbus(k, k', m, m') = \begin{cases} 1 & same\_pair(k, k') \wedge (m, m' \in Left \vee m, m' \in Right) \\ 0 & otherwise, \end{cases}$$

where $same\_pair(k, k')$ is true iff k, k' belong to the same processing pair, i.e. pe_0 and pe_1, pe_2 and pe_3, etc.

Given the task and buffer *mapping*, i.e. solutions for $p\mu_E$ and $p\mu_M$ function, and $sbus$ predicate we tighten the interference sets by excluding tasks not interfering in space:

$$\mathcal{P}_v = \{v' \in P_v^{over} \,|\, p\mu_E(v) \neq p\mu_E(v')\}$$
$$\mathcal{M}_v = \{v' \in \mathcal{P}_{vx} \,|\, p\mu_M(v) \cap p\mu_M(v') \neq \emptyset\}$$
$$\mathcal{B}_v = \left\{v' \in \mathcal{P}_{vx} \,\middle|\, \begin{array}{l} \forall m \in \mu_M(v), \forall m' \in \mu_M(v'), \\ sbus(\mu_E(v), \mu_E(v'), m, m') = 1 \end{array}\right\}$$

In the Kalray architecture, the memory arbiter allows to read or write only one word at a time. Therefore, we introduce a function $\tilde{\sigma}_m(v)$ that defines the number of times task $v \in V^S$ accesses memory bank m to read or write data:

$$\tilde{\sigma}_m(v) = \sum_{v'\in pred(v)\wedge p\mu_M((v',v))=m} \sigma(v', v) + \sum_{v'\in succ(v)\wedge p\mu_M((v,v'))=m} \sigma(v, v')$$

For two tasks v, v' mapped to pe_0, pe_1 belonging to the same pair using the same memory bank m the worst-case interference due to the bus (resp. memory) arbitration is the sum of all the requests to banks of the same side (resp. to the common memory bank) times the arbitration delay ad_{Bus} (resp. ad_{Mem}).

Definition 7 (Memory/Bus interference). *Given a unified system model S the memory interference function $if_{mem}(v, \mathcal{V})$ defines the interference of task $v \in V^S$ caused by taskset $\mathcal{V} \subseteq V^S \setminus v$ on memory arbiters:*

$$if_{mem}(v, \mathcal{V}) = ad_{Mem} * \sum_{v' \in \mathcal{V}} \sum_{m \in (p\mu_M(v) \cap p\mu_M(v'))} \min\left(\tilde{\sigma}_m(v), \tilde{\sigma}_m(v')\right)$$

Similarly, the bus interference function $if_{bus}(v, \mathcal{V})$ defines the interference of task v caused by taskset $\mathcal{V}$ on bus arbiters:

$$if_{bus}(v, \mathcal{V}) = ad_{Bus} * \sum_{v' \in \mathcal{V}} \sum_{m \in p\mu_M(v)} \sum_{m' \in p\mu_M(v')} \left(\begin{array}{c} sbus(p\mu_E(v), p\mu_E(v'), m, m') \\ * \min\left(\tilde{\sigma}_m(v), \tilde{\sigma}_m(v')\right) \end{array} \right)$$

For every v, the two functions are monotonically nondecreasing in $V^S \setminus v$.

Based on $\mathcal{M}_v$, $\mathcal{B}_v$ we can compute the maximum intra-cluster interference for the execution of task v as the sum of $if_{mem}(v, \mathcal{M}_v)$ and $if_{bus}(v, \mathcal{B}_v)$. Apparently this is still a safe over-approximation of the actual interference, since the execution of some tasks in the memory and bus may not overlap in time.

4.3 Inter-cluster Interference

Inter-cluster interference occurs when a communication transfer task t_{v_1,v_2} placed on cluster x' writes to the memory of cluster x thus interfering with the tasks placed on cluster x. In Kalray MPPA-256, these write requests have priority over any other request.

Similarly to Sect. 4.2, given the memory mapping function we exclude tasks that do not interfere in space:

$$\mathcal{C}_v = \{t_{v_1,v_2} \in C_v^{over} \mid p\mu_M(v) \cap p\mu_M(t_{v_1,v_2}) \neq \emptyset\}$$

Definition 8 (Communication interference delay). *Given a unified system model S the communication interference function $if_{com} : (v, \mathcal{V})$ defines the interference of task $v \in V^S$ caused by taskset $\mathcal{V} \subseteq T \setminus T_{p(v)}$ on the memory arbiter:*

$$if_{com}(v, \mathcal{V}) = ad_{Mem} * \sum_{v' \in \mathcal{V}} \sum_{m \in p\mu_M(v) \cap p\mu_M(v')} \tilde{\sigma}_m(v')$$

Using $\mathcal{C}_v$ we can compute the inter-cluster interference as $if_{com}(v, \mathcal{C}_v)$, which is an over-approximation that will be improved in Sect. 4.4

4.4 Deriving Tight WCET Estimations

For a task v we can derive its WCET, i.e. $d_{wc}(v)$, by computing the delay due to interferences with other tasks and adding them to the tasks WCCT, i.e. $d(v)$.

For a task $v \in V^S$, given the $\mathcal{M}_v$, $\mathcal{B}_v$, $\mathcal{C}_v$, the corresponding memory, bus and communication-induced memory interference sets, respectively, we compute the WCET of v, similarly to [7,8], as:

$$d_{wc}(v) \overset{def}{=} d(v) + if_{mem}(v, \mathcal{M}_v) + if_{bus}(v, \mathcal{B}_v) + if_{com}(v, \mathcal{C}_v) \qquad (1)$$

Prior to the solutions of *task mapping and scheduling*, we acquire the WCET over-approximation of task v, denoted as $d_{wc}^{over}(v)$, by applying Eq. 1 using the interference sets $\mathcal{M}_v^{over}$, $\mathcal{B}_v^{over}$ and $\mathcal{C}_v^{over}$.

To tighten this WCET estimation, given a solution of *task mapping and scheduling*, we reduce the interference sets by excluding tasks that do not overlap (i) in space, using the interference sets $\mathcal{M}_v$, $\mathcal{B}_v$ and $\mathcal{C}_v$ established in the previous sections, and (ii) in time using the scheduling function s. We consider that the execution of tasks v and v' overlaps in time if the task v' start or ends within the execution of v and vice versa, which is formalised with the following predicate:

$$in^i(v, v') = \max\left(s(v), s(v')\right) \leq \min\left(s(v) + d_{wc}^i(v), s(v') + d_{wc}^i(v')\right)$$

This way we introduce an iterative method to improve the initial interference sets. For every task $v \in V^S$, let $\mathcal{M}_v^i$, $\mathcal{B}_v^i$, $\mathcal{C}_v^i$ be the corresponding interference sets at the i-th iteration; we can calculate the worst-case delay time $d_{wc}^i(v)$ by applying Eq. 1 to those sets.

Starting from the first iteration we can compute, the updated interference sets for every task $v \in V^S$ according to the following equations:

$$\mathcal{M}_v^{i+1} = \mathcal{M}_v^i \setminus \{v' \in \mathcal{M}_v^i \mid \overline{in^i(v, v')}\} \qquad \mathcal{M}_v^0 = \mathcal{M}_v$$
$$\mathcal{B}_v^{i+1} = \mathcal{B}_v^i \setminus \{v' \in \mathcal{B}_v^i \mid \overline{in^i(v, v')}\} \quad \text{with} \quad \mathcal{B}_v^0 = \mathcal{B}_v$$
$$\mathcal{C}_v^{i+1} = \mathcal{C}_v^i \setminus \{v' \in \mathcal{C}_v^i \mid \overline{in^i(v, v')}\} \qquad \mathcal{C}_v^0 = \mathcal{C}_v$$

The method iterates until it converges, that is when none of the sets is updated, yielding the reduced interference sets $\mathcal{M}_v^{tight}$, $\mathcal{B}_v^{tight}$ and $\mathcal{C}_v^{tight}$ for any task $v \in V^S$. Applying Eq. 1 using these interference sets we acquire the tighetened WCET $d_{wc}^{tight}(v)$ for each task $v \in V^S$.

Lemma 1. *At each iteration, only non-interfering tasks are excluded and the interference sets do not increase in size.*

Proof. Two tasks v, v' can interfere iff their execution overlaps. By definition of the *in* predicate only non-overlapping, and thus non-interfering tasks, are excluded from the interference sets. Also, since the method does not update the schedule, at every iteration each set either remains the same or it is reduced. □

Theorem 1 (Convergence). *The iterative method will eventually converge.*

Proof. Since interference sets do not increase in size, the method will converge. □

Lemma 2. *For any task $v \in V^S$ at iteration i, the WCET estimation of task v $d_{wc}^i(v)$ is less than or equal the WCET $d_{wc}^{i-1}(v)$ at the previous iteration.*

Proof. Lets assume that there exists a task $v \in V^S$ such that $d_{wc}^i(v) > d_{wc}^{i-1}(v)$; then by applying Eq. 1 we deduce that at least one of the following holds:

$$if_{mem}(v, \mathcal{M}_v^i) > if_{mem}(v, \mathcal{M}_v^{i-1})$$
$$if_{bus}(v, \mathcal{B}_v^i) > if_{bus}(v, \mathcal{B}_v^{i-1})$$
$$if_{com}(v, \mathcal{C}_v^i) > if_{com}(v, \mathcal{C}_v^{i-1})$$

By monotonicity of the if_{mem}, if_{bus} and if_{com} we conclude that either $\mathcal{M}_v^i \supset \mathcal{M}_v^{i-1}$ or $\mathcal{B}_v^i \supset \mathcal{B}_v^{i-1}$ or $\mathcal{C}_v^i \supset \mathcal{C}_v^{i-1}$ holds, which contradicts with Lemma 1.   □

Theorem 2 (Safety). *The iterative method is safe, that is for every task $v \in V^S$, the actual task execution time $d_{act}(v)$ is less than or equal to $d_{wc}^{tight}(v)$ which is less than or equal to $d_{wc}^{over}(v)$.*

Proof. For any task $v \in V^S$, since $d_{wc}^{over}(v)$ is a safe over-approximation, implies that $d_{act}(v) \leq d_{wc}^{over}(v)$ holds. Due to Lemma 2 we deduce that $d_{wc}^{tight}(v) \leq d_{wc}^{over}(v)$. We also know from Lemma 1 that the tight WCET $d_{wc}^{tight}(v)$ has not excluded any interfering task v'. Therefore, $d_{act}(v) \leq d_{wc}^{tight}(v)$ which combined with the previous statements leads to $d_{act}(v) \leq d_{wc}^{tight}(v) \leq d_{wc}^{over}(v)$.   □

Corollary 1 (Latency guarantee). *Let $L = \max\limits_{v \in V^S}(s(v) + d(v))$ be the total latency; the tighetened latency L_{wc}^{tight} is greater than the actual latency L_{act} and less than the overestimated latency L_{wc}^{over}, i.e. $L_{act} \leq L_{wc}^{tight} \leq L_{wc}^{over}$.*

For each solution of the SMT solver the scheduling function is updated to account for the tight WCET, such that the tasks' starting time is updated, without introducing new interference, while preserving the order of tasks execution.

5 WCET Analysis Evaluation

To evaluate the applicability and benefits of the interference-based WCET analysis method, we conducted experiments on a subset of StreamIt [18] benchmarks and a JpegDecoder. The benchmark set used consists of 8 distinct applications, differing in the amount of computation for a single element of input, memory requirements and access patterns, etc. Specifically, the sorting algorithms (InsertionSort, MergeSort and CompCount) have complicated memory access patterns, but are not as heavy computationally, compared to Beamformer, DCT and JpegDecoder. We also modelled DCT in 10 different ways, to study the impact of different levels of model parallelism.

The WCCT of tasks was obtained by profiling them on a single core of the Kalray MPPA-256, with disabled caches and instruction prefetch buffer. We chose to profile instead of using existing tools, to avoid the over-approximation of interferences that such tools introduce. The arbitration constants used for Kalray platform are summarised in Table 2.

To acquire solutions for the *partitioning/placement* and the *mapping* and *scheduling* subproblems, we used the StreamExplorer tool [15], which provides

Table 2. Kalray MPPA-256 constants

Memory arbiter ad_{Mem}	7 cycles
Bus arbiter ad_{Bus}	4 cycles
Initialization delay id_{NoC}	1000 cycles
Polling delay pd_{NoC}	100 cycles

near-optimal solutions. Each of the solutions, varying in size from 3 up to 200 tasks, is analysed with our method acquiring an over-approximated (d_{wc}^{over}) and a tight (d_{wc}^{tight}) WCET for each task; for some solutions there was no interference at all, due to small number of tasks being deployed, or solutions with low parallelisation resulting in almost serialised schedules. Such cases are not included as they provide no significant information for our evaluation. In all figures the benchmarks are in increasing order of average number of tasks.

To outline the impact of interference, in Fig. 3, for each benchmark, we present the ratio between the delay due to interference (if^{tight}) and the average WCET (d_{wc}^{tight}) over all tasks of a particular benchmark. The average delay over all benchmarks is approximately 7 % if we exclude matrix multiplication (MatrixMult), which raises the total average delay up to 10 %. The MatrixMult benchmark is a special case, since it uses simple computational operations but requires that a significant amount of data shared among tasks. This results in having many parallel tasks accessing the same memory bank, and thus an increased number of mutual interference. Based on that, we can conclude that in several cases the interference introduced by the parallel execution of tasks can have a significant impact on the worst-case execution time of tasks, especially in highly-parallel applications where data can not be partitioned nicely.

Notice that, in Fig. 3, a set of the benchmarks (e.g. InsertionSort, Dct9, etc.) have $if^{tight}/d_{wc}^{tight}$ ratio equal to zero. This is the result of excluding sources of interference through our iterative method, the impact of which is illustrated

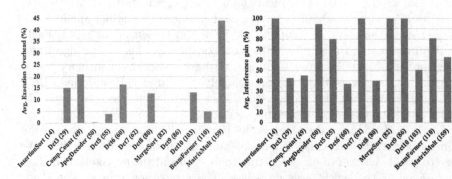

Fig. 3. Interference/execution-time ratio.

Fig. 4. Avg. % reduction of interference.

Table 3. Average worst-case (over-approximated) latency of all benchmarks (in Kcycles)

Benchmark	Lat.	Benchmark	Lat.	Benchmark	Lat.	Benchmark	Lat.
Dct1 (6)	91	Dct6 (60)	177	InsertionSort (14)	64	Fft (96)	253
Dct2 (9)	153	Dct7 (62)	174	RadixSort (31)	138	BeamFormer (110)	159
Dct3 (29)	130	Dct8 (80)	147	Comp.Count (49)	106	MatrixMult (159)	1087
Dct4 (53)	106	Dct9 (86)	125	JpegDecoder (50)	516		
Dct5 (55)	170	Dct10 (103)	190	MergeSort (82)	87		

in Fig. 4, which shows the percentage of interference excluded from the original over-approximation. In some cases, e.g. RadixSort (not included), our method did not detect any interferences due to the absence of shared resources after the application deployment onto the platform. In general, however, our approach was able to exclude on average approximately 73 % of the initially over-approximated interferences, with a peak of 100 % for all solutions of four benchmarks.

The number of sources of interference has a direct impact on the estimated value of the WCET, thus a reduction of the interference sets leads to tightening the WCET estimation. We observed on average a tightening of 5 % up to 10 % of the tasks' WCET. This is illustrated in Fig. 5, where the average WCET reduction, over all tasks of each benchmark, is presented. MatrixMult, which exhibits the highest degree of interference, experiences the most dramatic reduction. In most cases the results show that the count of interfering tasks is less than the number of cluster elements (i.e. ≤ 15), but for MatrixMult up to 22.

Recall that after the WCET tightening we recompute the scheduling function to account for WCET reduction. In Fig. 6, we compare the latency of the whole application computed with the over-approximated WCET (the values of which are in Table 3 for reference) to the latency computed with the tightened WCET. We can observe that the latency improvement varies significantly. For some cases,

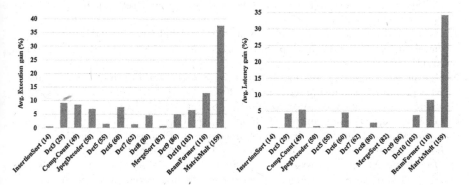

Fig. 5. Avg. % reduction of execution time.

Fig. 6. Avg. % reduction of latency.

e.g. MergeSort, even though there was noticeable reduction of tasks' WCETs, the latency improvement is still less than 1 %. Similarly, for all benchmarks, the latency improvement is slightly lower than the WCET estimiation tightening. This is expected since the WCET reduction can have at most a linear effect on overall latency if those tasks are in the schedule's critical path. This is an important finding as it proves that a significant amount of interference has no impact on the total guaranteed latency. Still, we achieve an average latency-guarantee improvement of 5 %, up to 34 %, which is significant when providing latency guarantees.

6   Conclusion

We have presented an accurate estimation of the upper bound for the WCET of tasks for an application with data dependencies deployed onto a many-core architecture. Our proposal yielded an improvement of the WCET upper bound by 5 % to 10 % compared to the over-approximation methods commonly used in literature. We can also conclude that excluding sources of interferences can have significant impact on tasks' WCET, most of which is also reflected in a corresponding improvement of overall application latency.

Acknowledgment. The research work of this paper was funded by the Swiss Confederation through the UltrasoundToGo project of the Nano-Tera.ch initiative.

References

1. aiT: the industry standard for static timing analysis. http://www.absint.com/ait/
2. Bilsen, G., Engels, M., Lauwereins, R., Peperstraete, J.: Cycle-static dataflow. IEEE Trans. Sig. Process. **44**(2), 397–408 (1996)
3. Burgio, P., Marongiu, A., Valente, P., Bertogna, M.: A memory-centric approach to enable timing-predictability within embedded many-core accelerators. In: 2015 CSI Symposium on Real-Time and Embedded Systems and Technologies (RTEST), pp. 1–8, October 2015
4. Cota, É., de Amory, A.M., Lubaszewski, M.S.: Reliability, Availability and Serviceability of Networks-on-chip. Springer Science & Business Media, New York (2011)
5. Cotton, S., Maler, O., Legriel, J., Saidi, S.: Multi-criteria optimization for mapping programs to multi-processors. In: 2011 6th IEEE International Symposium on Industrial Embedded Systems (SIES), pp. 9–17. IEEE (2011)
6. de Dinechin, B.D., van Amstel, D., Poulhiès, M., Lager, G.: Time-critical computing on a single-chip massively parallel processor. In: Proceedings of the Conference on Design, Automation & Test in Europe, DATE 2014, pp. 97:1–97:6. European Design and Automation Association, 3001 Leuven, Belgium (2014)
7. Dkhil, A., Louise, S., Rochange, C.: Worst-case communication overhead in a many-core based shared-memory model (regular paper). In: Junior Researcher Workshop on Real-Time Computing, Nice, pp. 53–56. University of Amsterdam, 16/10/2013-18/10/2013, Octobre 2013. http://www.uva.nl

8. Giannopoulou, G., Stoimenov, N., Huang, P., Thiele, L., de Dinechin, B.: Mixed-criticality scheduling on cluster-based manycores with shared communication and storage resources. Real-Time Syst. **51**, 1–51 (2015)
9. Kadayif, I., Kandemir, M., Sezer, U.: An integer linear programming based approach for parallelizing applications in on-chip multiprocessors. In: DAC 2002, pp. 703–706. ACM, New York (2002)
10. Kalray. Kalray MPPA-256 (2015)
11. Legriel, J., Le Guernic, C., Cotton, S., Maler, O.: Approximating the pareto front of multi-criteria optimization problems. In: Esparza, J., Majumdar, R. (eds.) TACAS 2010. LNCS, vol. 6015, pp. 69–83. Springer, Heidelberg (2010)
12. Nelson, A., Goossens, K., Akesson, B.: Dataflow formalisation of real-time streaming applications on a composable and predictable multi-processor soc. J. Syst. Archit. **61**(9), 435–448 (2015)
13. Nguyen, V.A., Hardy, D., Puaut, I.: Scheduling of parallel applications on many-core architectures with caches: bridging the gap between WCET analysis and schedulability analysis. In: 9th Junior Researcher Workshop on Real-Time Computing (JRWRTC 2015), Lille, France, November 2015
14. Srinivasan, A., Baruah, S.: Deadline-based scheduling of periodic task systems on multiprocessors. Inf. Process. Lett. **84**(2), 93–98 (2002)
15. Tendulkar, P., Poplavko, P., Galanommatis, I., Maler, O.: Many-core scheduling of data parallel applications using smt solvers. In: 2014 17th Euromicro Conference on Digital System Design (DSD), pp. 615–622. IEEE (2014)
16. Tendulkar, P., Poplavko, P., Maler, O.: Symmetry breaking for multi-criteria mapping and scheduling on multicores. In: Braberman, V., Fribourg, L. (eds.) FORMATS 2013. LNCS, vol. 8053, pp. 228–242. Springer, Heidelberg (2013)
17. Texas Instruments Inc. The 66AK2H12 keystone II Processor
18. Thies, W., Amarasinghe, S.: An empirical characterization of stream programs and its implications for language and compiler design. In: Proceedings of the 19th International Conference on Parallel Architectures and Compilation Techniques, PACT 2010, pp. 365–376. ACM, New York (2010)

Timed Multiset Rewriting and the Verification of Time-Sensitive Distributed Systems

Max Kanovich[1,5], Tajana Ban Kirigin[2], Vivek Nigam[3(✉)], Andre Scedrov[4,5], and Carolyn Talcott[6]

[1] University of London and University College, London, UK
mik@dcs.qmul.ac.uk
[2] University of Rijeka, Rijeka, Croatia
bank@math.uniri.hr
[3] Federal University of Paraíba, João Pessoa, Brazil
vivek@ci.ufpb.br
[4] University of Pennsylvania, Philadelphia, USA
scedrov@math.upenn.edu
[5] National Research University Higher School of Economics, Moscow, Russia
[6] SRI International, Menlo Park, USA
clt@csl.sri.com

Abstract. Time-Sensitive Distributed Systems (TSDS), such as applications using autonomous drones, achieve goals under possible environment interference (*e.g.*, winds). Moreover, goals are often specified using explicit time constraints which must be satisfied by the system *perpetually*. For example, drones carrying out the surveillance of some area must always have *recent pictures*, *i.e.*, at most M time units old, of some strategic locations. This paper proposes a Multiset Rewriting language with explicit time for specifying and analysing TSDSes. We introduce two properties, *realizability* (some trace is good) and *survivability* (where, in addition, all admissible traces are good). A good trace is an infinite trace in which goals are perpetually satisfied. We propose a class of systems called *progressive timed systems* (PTS), where intuitively only a finite number of actions can be carried out in a bounded time period. We prove that for this class of systems both the realizability and the survivability problems are PSPACE-complete. Furthermore, if we impose a bound on time (as in bounded model-checking), we show that for PTS, realizability becomes NP-complete, while survivability is in the Δ_2^p class of the polynomial hierarchy. Finally, we demonstrate that the rewriting logic system Maude can be used to automate time bounded verification of PTS.

1 Introduction

The recent years have seen an increasing number of applications where computing is carried out in all sorts of environments. For example, drones are now being used to carry out tasks such as delivering packages, monitoring plantations and railways. While these distributed systems should still satisfy well-known safety

© Springer International Publishing Switzerland 2016
M. Fränzle and N. Markey (Eds.): FORMATS 2016, LNCS 9884, pp. 228–244, 2016.
DOI: 10.1007/978-3-319-44878-7_14

(*e.g.*, drones should not run out of energy) and liveness properties (*e.g.*, freedom of livelock), they are also subject to *quantitative constraints* leading to new verification problems with explicit time constraints.

Consider, as our running example, the scenario where drones monitor some locations of interest such as infested plantation areas[1], whether rail tracks are in place[2], or locations with high risk of being trespassed. Drones should take a picture of each one of these points. Moreover, for each point, there should be *a recent picture, i.e.*, not more than M time units old for some given M. That is, the drones should collectively have a set of *recent pictures* of all sensitive locations. In order to achieve this goal, drones may need to fly consuming energy and they may need to return to the base station to recharge their batteries. The environment may interfere as there might be winds that may move the drone to some direction or other flying objects that may block a drone's progression.

When designing such as system, engineers should specify the behavior of drones, *e.g.*, where to move, when to take a picture, when to return to a base station, etc. A verification problem, called *realizability problem*, is to check, whether under the given time constraints, the specified system can achieve the assigned goal, *e.g.*, always collect a recent picture of the sensitive locations.

In many settings, the drones themselves or the environment may behave non-deterministically. For example, if a drone wants to reach a point to the northeast, it may first chose to either move north or east, both being equally likely. Similarly, there might be some wind at some location causing any drone under the wind's effect to move in the direction of the wind. A stronger property that takes into account such non-determinism is to check whether for all possible outcomes (of drone actions or environment interference), the specified system can achieve the assigned goal. We call this property *survivability*.

In our previous work [12,13,16], we proposed a timed Multiset Rewriting (MSR) framework for specifying compliance properties which are similar to *quantitative safety properties* investigating the complexity of a number of decision problems. These properties were defined over the set of *finite traces, i.e.*, the execution of a finite number of actions. Realizability and survivability, on the other hand, are similar to *quantitative liveness problems*, defined over infinite traces.

The transition to properties over infinite traces leads to many challenges as one can easily fall into undecidability fragments of verification problems. A main challenge is to identify the syntatical conditions on specifications so that the survivability and feasibility problems fall into a decidable fragment and at the same time interesting examples can be specified. Also the notion that a system satisfies a property perpetually implies that the desired property should be valid at all time instances independent of environment interference. Another issue is that systems should not be allowed to perform an unbounded number of actions in a single time instance a problem similar to the Zeno paradox.

---

[1] See (http://www.terradrone.pt/) – In Portuguese.
[2] See http://fortune.com/2015/05/29/bnsf-drone-program/.

The main contribution of this paper is threefold:

1. We propose a novel class of systems called *progressive timed systems* (PTS) (Sect. 2), specified as timed MSR theories, for which, intuitively, only a finite number of actions can be carried out in a bounded time. We demonstrate that our drone example belongs to this class (Sect. 3). We define a language for specifying realizability and survivability properties (Sect. 4) demonstrating that many interesting problems in Time-Sensitive Distributed Systems (TSDS) can be specified using our language;

2. We investigate (Sect. 5) the complexity of deciding whether a given system satisfies realizability and survivability. While these problems are undecidable in general, we show that they are PSPACE-complete for PTS. We also show that when we bound time (as in bounded-model checking) the realizability problem for PTS is NP-complete and survivability is in the Δ_2^p class of the polynomial hierarchy (P^{NP}) [22].

3. Finally (Sect. 6), we show that the rewriting logic tool Maude [6] can be used to automate the analysis of TSDS. We implemented the drone scenario described above following the work of Talcott *et al.* [25] and carried out a number of simulations with different instances of this scenario. Our simulations demonstrate that specifiers can quickly find counter-examples where their specifications do not satisfy time bounded survivability.

We conclude by discussing related and future work (Sect. 7). All missing proofs can be found in our companion technical report [15].

2   Timed Multiset Rewriting Systems

Assume a finite first-order typed alphabet, Σ, with variables, constants, function and predicate symbols. Terms and facts are constructed as usual (see [9]) by applying symbols of correct type (or sort). We assume that the alphabet contains the constant $z : Nat$ denoting zero and the function $s : Nat \to Nat$ denoting the successor function. Whenever it is clear from the context, we write n for $s^n(z)$ and $(n + m)$ for $s^n(s^m(z))$.

Timestamped facts are of the form $F@t$, where F is a fact and $t \in \mathbb{N}$ is natural number called *timestamp*. (Notice that timestamps are *not* constructed by using the successor function.) There is a special predicate symbol $Time$ with arity zero, which will be used to represent global time. A *configuration* is a multiset of ground timestamped facts, $\mathcal{S} = \{Time@t, F_1@t_1, \ldots, F_n@t_n\}$, with a single occurrence of a $Time$ fact. Configurations are to be interpreted as states of the system. Consider the following configuration where the global time is 4.

$$\mathcal{S}_1 = \big\{ Time@4, Dr(d1, 1, 2, 10)@4, Dr(d2, 5, 5, 8)@4, P(p1, 1, 1)@3, P(p2, 5, 6)@0 \big\} \quad (1)$$

Fact $Dr(dId, x, y, e)@t$ denotes that drone dId is at position (x, y) at time t with e energy units left in its battery; fact $P(pID, x, y)@t$ denotes that the point to be monitored by pId is at position (x, y) and the last picture of it was taken at time t. Thus, the above configuration denotes a scenario with two drones at positions $(1, 2)$ and $(5, 5)$ and energy left of 10 and 8, and two points to be monitored at positions $(1, 1)$ and $(5, 6)$, where the former has been taken a photo at time 3 and the latter at time 0.

Configurations are modified by multiset rewrite rules which can be interpreted as actions of the system. There is only one rule that modifies global time:

$$Time@T \longrightarrow Time@(T + 1) \tag{2}$$

where T is a time variable. Applied to a configuration, $\{Time@t, F_1@t_1, \ldots, F_n@t_n\}$, it advances global time by one, resulting in $\{Time@(t + 1), F_1@t_1, \ldots, F_n@t_n\}$.

The remaining rules are *instantaneous* as they do not modify global time, but may modify the remaining facts of configurations (those different from $Time$). Instantaneous rules have the form:

$$Time@T, W, F_1@T_1', \ldots, F_n@T_n' \mid C \longrightarrow Time@T, W, Q_1@(T + D_1), \ldots, Q_m@(T + D_m) \tag{3}$$

where $D_1, \ldots, D_m$ are natural numbers, $W = W_1@T_1, \ldots, W_n@T_n$ is a set of timestamped predicates possibly with variables, and C is the guard of the action which is a set of constraints involving the variables appearing in the rule's pre-condition, *i.e.* the variables $T, T_1, \ldots, T_p, T_1', \ldots, T_n'$. Following [8] we say that $F_1@T_1', \ldots, F_n@T_n'$ are consumed by the rule and $Q_1@(T + D_1), \ldots, Q_m@(T + D_m)$ are created by the rule. (In a rule, we color red the consumed facts and blue the created facts.)

Constraints may be of the form:

$$T > T' \pm N \quad \text{and} \quad T = T' \pm N \tag{4}$$

where T and T' are time variables, and $N \in \mathbb{N}$ is a natural number. All variables in the guard of a rule are assumed to appear in the rule's pre-condition. We use $T \geq T' \pm N$ to denote the disjunction of $T > T' \pm N$ and $T = T' \pm N$.

A rule $W \mid C \longrightarrow W'$ can be *applied on a configuration* S if there is a ground substituition σ, such that $W\sigma \subseteq S$ and $C\sigma$ is true. The resulting configuration is $(S \setminus W) \cup W'\sigma$. We write $S \longrightarrow_r S_1$ for the one-step relation where configuration S is rewritten to S_1 using an instance of rule r.

Definition 1. *A timed MSR system $\mathcal{A}$ is a set of rules containing only instantaneous rules (Eq. 3) and the tick rule (Eq. 2).*

A *trace* of a timed MSR $\mathcal{A}$ starting from an initial configuration S_0 is a sequence of configurations where for all $i \geq 0$, $S_i \longrightarrow_{r_i} S_{i+1}$ for some $r_i \in \mathcal{A}$.

$$S_0 \longrightarrow S_1 \longrightarrow S_2 \longrightarrow \cdots \longrightarrow S_n \longrightarrow \cdots$$

In the remainder of this paper, we will consider a particular class of timed MSR, called *progressive timed MSR* (PTS), which are such that only a finite number of actions can be carried out in a bounded time interval which is a natural condition for many systems. We built PTS over balanced MSR taken from our previous work [11,17]. The balanced condition is necessary for decidability of problems (such as reachability as well as the problems introduced in Sect. 4).

Definition 2. *A timed MSR $\mathcal{A}$ is* balanced *if for all instantaneous rules $r \in \mathcal{A}$, r creates the same number of facts as it consumes, that is, in Eq. (3), $n = m$.*

Proposition 1. *Let $\mathcal{A}$ be a balanced timed MSR. Let $\mathcal{S}_0$ be an initial configuration with exactly m facts. For all possibly infinite traces $\mathcal{P}$ of $\mathcal{A}$ starting with $\mathcal{S}_0$, all configurations $\mathcal{S}_i$ in $\mathcal{P}$ have exactly m facts.*

Definition 3. *A timed MSR $\mathcal{A}$ is* progressive *if $\mathcal{A}$ is balanced and for all instantaneous rules $r \in \mathcal{A}$:*

- *rule r creates at least one fact with timestamp greater than the global time, that is, in Eq. (3), at least one $D_i \geq 1$;*
- *rule r consumes only facts with timestamps in the past or at the current time, that is, in Eq. (3), the set of constraints $\mathcal{C}$ contains the set $\mathcal{C}_r = \{T \geq T_i' \mid F_i @ T_i', 1 \leq i \leq n\}$.*

The following proposition establishes a bound on the number of instances of instantaneous rules appearing between two consecutive instances of Tick rules, while the second proposition formalizes the intuition that PTS always move forward.

Proposition 2. *Let $\mathcal{A}$ be a PTS, $\mathcal{S}_0$ an initial configuration and m the number of facts in $\mathcal{S}_0$. For all traces $\mathcal{P}$ of $\mathcal{A}$ starting from $\mathcal{S}_0$, let*

$$\mathcal{S}_i \longrightarrow_{Tick} \longrightarrow \mathcal{S}_{i+1} \longrightarrow \cdots \longrightarrow \mathcal{S}_j \longrightarrow_{Tick} \longrightarrow \mathcal{S}_{j+1}$$

be any sub-sequence of $\mathcal{P}$ with exactly two instances of the Tick rule, one at the beginning and the other at the end. Then $j - i < m$.

Proposition 3. *Let $\mathcal{A}$ be a PTS. In all infinite traces of $\mathcal{A}$ the global time tends to infinity.*

For readability, we will assume from this point onwards that for all rules r, the set of its constraints implicitly contains the set $\mathcal{C}_r$ as shown in Definition 3, not writing $\mathcal{C}_r$ explicitly in our specifications.

Finally, notice that PTS has many syntactical conditions, e.g., balanced condition (Definition 2), time constraints (Eq. 4), instantaneous rules (Eq. 3). Each one of these conditions have been carefully developed as without any of them important verification problems, such as the reachability problem, becomes undecidable as we show in our previous [13]. Thus these conditions are needed also for infinite traces. The challenge here of allowing infinite traces is to make sure time advances. The definition of PTS is a simple and elegant way to enforce this. Moreover, as we show in Sect. 3, it is still possible to specify many interesting examples including our motivating example and still prove the decidability of our verification problems involving infinite traces (Sect. 5).

3   Programming Drone Behavior Using PTS

Figure 1 depicts the macro rules of our motivating scenario where drones are moving on a fixed grid of size $x_{max} \times y_{max}$, have at most e_{max} energy units and take pictures of some points of interest. We assume that there are n such points $p_1, \ldots, p_n$, where n is fixed, a base station is at position (x_b, y_b), and that the drones should take pictures so that all pictures are recent, that is, the last time a photo of it was taken should not be more than M time units before the current time of any moment.

Clearly if drones choose non-deterministically to move some direction without a particular strategy, they will fail to achieve the assigned goal. A strategy is specified by using time constraints. For this example, the strategy would depend on the difference $T - T_i$, for $1 \leq i \leq n$, specifying the time since the last picture of the point p_i that is the set of time constraints:

$$T(d_1, \ldots, d_n) = \{T - T_1 = d_1, \ldots, T - T_n = d_n\}$$

where for all $1 \leq i \leq n$ we instantiate d_i by values in $\{0, \ldots, M\}$.

$Time@T, \mathcal{P}(p_1, \ldots, p_n), Dr(Id, X, Y, E + 1)@T \mid doMove(Id, X, Y, E + 1, T, T_1, \ldots, T_n, north) \longrightarrow$
$\qquad Time@T, \mathcal{P}(p_1, \ldots, p_n), Dr(Id, X, Y + 1, E)@(T + 1)$

$Time@T, \mathcal{P}(p_1, \ldots, p_n), Dr(Id, X, Y + 1, E + 1)@T \mid doMove(Id, X, Y + 1, E + 1, T, T_1, \ldots, T_n, south) \longrightarrow$
$\qquad Time@T, \mathcal{P}(p_1, \ldots, p_n), Dr(Id, X, Y, E)@(T + 1)$

$Time@T, \mathcal{P}(p_1, \ldots, p_n), Dr(Id, X + 1, Y, E + 1)@T \mid doMove(Id, X + 1, Y, E + 1, T, T_1, \ldots, T_n, west) \longrightarrow$
$\qquad Time@T, \mathcal{P}(p_1, \ldots, p_n), Dr(Id, X, Y, E)@(T + 1)$

$Time@T, \mathcal{P}(p_1, \ldots, p_n), Dr(Id, X, Y, E + 1)@T \mid doMove(Id, X, Y, E + 1, T, T_1, \ldots, T_n, east) \longrightarrow$
$\qquad Time@T, \mathcal{P}(p_1, \ldots, p_n), Dr(Id, X, Y, E)@(T + 1)$

$Time@T, \mathcal{P}(p_1, \ldots, p_n), Dr(Id, x_b, y_b, E)@T \mid doCharge(Id, E, T, T_1, \ldots, T_n) \longrightarrow$
$\qquad Time@T, \mathcal{P}(p_1, \ldots, p_n), Dr(Id, x_b, y_b, E + 1)@(T + 1)$

$Time@T, Pt(p_1, X_1, Y_1)@T_1, \ldots, Pt(p_i, X, Y)@T_i, \ldots, Pt(p_n, X_n, Y_n)@T_n, Dr(Id, X, Y, E)@T$
$\quad \mid doClick(Id, X, Y, E, T, T_1, \ldots, T_i, \ldots, T_n) \longrightarrow$
$Time@T, Pt(p_1, X_1, Y_1)@T_1, \ldots, Pt(p_i, X, Y)@T, \ldots, Pt(p_n, X_n, Y_n)@T_n, Dr(Id, X, Y, E - 1)@(T + 1)$

$Time@T, Dr(Id, X, Y, E)@T \mid hasWind(X, Y, north) \longrightarrow Time@T, Dr(Id, X, Y + 1, E)@(T + 1)$

$Time@T, Dr(Id, X, Y + 1, E)@T \mid hasWind(X, Y, south) \longrightarrow Time@T, Dr(Id, X, Y, E)@(T + 1)$

$Time@T, Dr(Id, X + 1, Y, E)@T \mid hasWind(X, Y, west) \longrightarrow Time@T, Dr(Id, X, Y, E)@(T + 1)$

$Time@T, Dr(Id, X, Y, E)@T \mid hasWind(X, Y, east) \longrightarrow Time@T, Dr(Id, X + 1, Y, E)@(T + 1)$

Fig. 1. Macro rules specifying the scenario where drones take pictures of points of interest. Here $\mathcal{P}(p_1, \ldots, p_n)$ denotes $P(p_1, X_1, Y_1)@T_1, \ldots, P(p_n, X_n, Y_n)@T_n$. Moreover, we assume that the Drone stay in a grid of size $x_{max} \times y_{max}$ and have at most e_{max} energy units.

For example, the macro rule with $doMove(Id, X, Y, E + 1, T, T_1, \ldots, T_n, north)$ in Fig. 1 is replaced by the set of rules:

$Time@T, \mathcal{P}(p_1, \ldots, p_n), Dr(d1, 0, 0, 1)@T \mid T(0, \ldots, 0), DoMv(d1, 0, 0, 1, 0, \ldots, 0, north) \longrightarrow$
$\qquad Time@T, \mathcal{P}(p_1, \ldots, p_n), Dr(Id, 0, 1, 0)@(T + 1)$
$Time@T, \mathcal{P}(p_1, \ldots, p_n), Dr(d1, 0, 0, 1)@T \mid T(0, \ldots, 1), DoMv(d1, 0, 0, 1, 0, \ldots, 1, north) \longrightarrow$
$\qquad Time@T, \mathcal{P}(p_1, \ldots, p_n), Dr(Id, 0, 1, 0)@(T + 1)$
$\ldots$

$Time@T, \mathcal{P}(p_1, \ldots, p_n), Dr(d2, x_{max}, y_{max} - 1, e_{max})@T$
$\quad \mid T(M, \ldots, M), DoMv(d2, x_{max}, y_{max} - 1, e_{max}, M, \ldots, M, north) \longrightarrow$
$\qquad Time@T, \mathcal{P}(p_1, \ldots, p_n), Dr(Id, x_{max}, y_{max}, e_{max} - 1)@(T + 1)$

where *doMove* is function that returns a boolean value depending on the desired behavior of the drone.

Finally, there are macro rules for moving the drone, taking a picture, charging, and macro specifying winds. While most of the rules have the expected result, we explain the click and wind rules. The click rule is applicable if the drone is at the same position, (X, Y), as a point of interest p_i. If applied, the timestamp of the fact $P(p_i, X, Y)$ is updated to the current time T. The wind rule is similar to the move rules moving the drone to some direction, but does not cause the drone to consume its energy.

In our implementation, we used a more sophisticated approach described in [25] using soft-constraints to specify a drone's strategy. It can be translated as a PTS by incorporating the strategy used as described above.

Other Examples. Finally, there are a number of other examples which we have been investigating and that can are progressive. In [24], we model a simplified version of a package delivery systems inspired by Amazon's Prime Air service. In [25], we model a patrolling bot which moves from one point to another. All these examples seem to be progressive.

Other examples besides those involving drones also seem to be progressive. For example, in our previous work, we specify a monitor for clinical trials [13] using our timed MSR framework with discrete time. This specification seems to be also progressive.

4   Quantitative Temporal Properties

In order to define quantitative temporal properties, we review the notion of critical configurations and compliant traces from our previous work [16]. *Critical configuration specification* is a set of pairs $\mathcal{CS} = \{\langle \mathcal{S}_1, \mathcal{C}_1 \rangle, \ldots, \langle \mathcal{S}_n, \mathcal{C}_n \rangle\}$. Each pair $\langle \mathcal{S}_j, \mathcal{C}_j \rangle$ is of the form:

$$\langle \{F_1 @ T_1, \ldots, F_p @ T_p\}, \mathcal{C}_j \rangle$$

where $T_1, \ldots, T_p$ are time variables, $F_1, \ldots, F_p$ are facts (possibly containing variables) and $\mathcal{C}_j$ is a set of time constraints involving only the variables $T_1, \ldots, T_p$. Given a critical configuration specification, $\mathcal{CS}$, we classify a configuration $\mathcal{S}$ as *critical* if for some $1 \leq i \leq n$, there is a grounding substitution, σ, mapping time variables in $\mathcal{S}_i$ to natural numbers and non time variables to terms such that:

- $\mathcal{S}_i\sigma \subseteq \mathcal{S}$;
- all constraints in $\mathcal{C}_i\sigma$ are valid.

where substitution application $(\mathcal{S}\sigma)$ is defined as usual [9].

Example 1. We can specify usual safety conditions which do not involve time. For example, a drone should never run out of energy. This can be specified by using the following set of critical configuration specification:

$$\{\langle \{Dr(Id, X, Y, 0) @ T\}, \emptyset \rangle \mid Id \in \{d1, d2\}, X \in \{0, \ldots, x_{max}\}, Y \in \{0, \ldots, y_{max}\}\}$$

Example 2. The following critical configuration specification specifies a quantitative property involving time:

$$\{\langle\{P(p_1, x_1, y_1)@T_1, Time@T\}, T > T_1 + M\rangle, \ldots, \langle\{P(p_n, x_n, y_n)@T_n, Time@T\}, T > T_n + M\rangle\}$$

Together with the specification in Fig. 1, this critical configuration specification specifies that the last pictures of all points of interest $(p_1, \ldots, p_n$ located at $(x_1, y_1), \ldots, (x_n, y_n))$ should have timestamps no more than M time units old.

Example 3. Let the facts $St(Id)@T_1$ and $St(empty)@T_1$ denote, respectively, that at time T_1 the drone Id entered the base station to recharge and that the station is empty. Moreover, assume that only one drone may be in the station to recharge, which would be specified by adding the following rules specifying the drone landing and take off, where st is a constant symbol denoting that a drone landed on the base station:

$$Time@T, Dr(Id, x_b, y_b)@T, St(empty)@T_1 \longrightarrow Time@T, Dr(Id, st, st)@(T+1), St(Id)@T$$

$$Time@T, Dr(Id, st, st)@T, St(Id)@T_1 \longrightarrow Time@T, Dr(Id, x_b, y_b)@(T+1), St(empty)@T$$

Then, the critical configuration specification $\{\langle\{St(Id)@T_1, Time@T\}, T > T_1 + M_1\rangle \mid Id \in \{d1, d2\}\}$ specifies that one drone should not remain too long (more than M_1 time units) in a base station not allowing other drones to charge.

Definition 4. *A trace of a timed MSR is compliant for a given critical configuration specification if it does not contain any critical configuration.*

We will be interested in survivability which requires checking whether, given an initial configuration, all possible infinite traces of a system are compliant. In order to define a sensible notion of survivability, however, we need to assume some conditions on when the Tick rule is applicable. With no conditions on the application of the Tick rule many timed systems of interest, such as our main example with drones, do not satisfy survivability as the following trace containing only instances of the Tick rule could always be constructed:

$$\mathcal{S}_1 \longrightarrow_{Tick} \mathcal{S}_2 \longrightarrow_{Tick} \mathcal{S}_3 \longrightarrow_{Tick} \mathcal{S}_4 \longrightarrow_{Tick} \cdots$$

Imposing a *time sampling* is a way to avoid such traces where the time simply ticks. They are used, for example, in the semantics of verification tools such as Real-Time Maude [21]. In particular, a time sampling dictates when the Tick rule must be applied and when it cannot be applied. This treatment of time is used both for dense and discrete times in searching and model checking timed systems.

Definition 5. *A (possibly infinite) trace $\mathcal{P}$ of a timed MSR $\mathcal{A}$ uses a lazy time sampling if for any occurrence of the Tick rule $\mathcal{S}_i \longrightarrow_{Tick} \mathcal{S}_{i+1}$ in $\mathcal{P}$, no instance of any instantaneous rule in $\mathcal{A}$ can be applied to the configuration $\mathcal{S}_i$.*

In lazy time sampling instantaneous rules are given a higher priority than the Tick rule. Under this time sampling, a drone should carry out one of the rules in Fig. 1 at each time while time can only advance when all drones have carried out their actions for that moment. This does not mean, however, that the drones will satisfy their goal of always having recent pictures of the points of interest as this would depend on the behavior of the system, *i.e.*, the actions carried out by the drones. Intuitively, the lazy time sampling does not allow the passing of time if there are scheduled drone actions at the current time. Its semantics reflects that all undertaken actions do happen.

In the remainder of this paper, we fix the time sampling to lazy time sampling.

We leave for future work investigating whether our complexity results hold for other time samplings.

4.1   Verification Problems

The first property we introduce is realizability. Realizability is useful for increasing one's confidence in a specified system, as clearly a system that is not realizable can not accomplish the given tasks (specified by a critical specification) and therefore, the designer would need to reformulate it. However, if a system is shown realizable, the trace, $\mathcal{P}$, used to prove it could also provide insights on the sequence of actions that lead to accomplishing the specified tasks. This may be used to refine the specification reducing possible non-determinism.

Definition 6. *A timed MSR $\mathcal{A}$ is realizable (resp., n-time-bounded realizable) with respect to the lazy time sampling, a critical configuration specification $\mathcal{CS}$ and an initial configuration S_0 if there exists a trace, $\mathcal{P}$, that starts with S_0 and uses the lazy time sampling such that:*

1. *$\mathcal{P}$ is compliant with respect to $\mathcal{CS}$;*
2. *Global time tends to infinity (resp., global time advances by exactly n time units) in $\mathcal{P}$.*

The second condition that global time tends to infinity, which implies that only a finite number of actions are performed in a given time. Another way of interpreting this condition following [1] is of a liveness condition, that is, the system should not get stuck. The first condition, on the other hand, is a safety condition as it states that no bad state should be reached. Thus the feasibility problem (and also the survivability problem introduced next) is a combination of a liveness and safety conditions. Moreover, since $\mathcal{CS}$ involve time constraints, it is a quantitative liveness and safety property.

The n-time-bounded realizability problem is motivated by bounded model checking. We look for a finite compliant trace that spreads over a n units of time, where n is fixed.

As already noted, realizability could be useful in reducing non-determinism in the specification. In many cases, however, it is not desirable and even not possible to eliminate the non-determinism of the system. For example, in open distributed systems, the environment can play an important role. Winds, for example, may affect drones' performances such as the speed and energy required to move from one point to another. We would like to know whether for all possible decisions taken by agents and under the interference of the environment, the given timed MSR accomplishes the specified tasks. *If so, we say that a system satisfies survivability.*

Definition 7. *A timed MSR $\mathcal{A}$ satisfies* survivability *(resp., n-time-bounded* survivability*) with respect to the lazy time sampling, a critical configuration specification $\mathcal{CS}$ and an initial configuration $\mathcal{S}_0$ if it is realizable (resp., n-time-bounded realizable) and if all infinite traces (resp. all traces with exactly n instances of the Tick rule), $\mathcal{P}$, that start with $\mathcal{S}_0$ and use the lazy time sampling are such that:*

1. $\mathcal{P}$ *is compliant with respect to $\mathcal{CS}$;*
2. *The global time tends to infinity (resp., no condition).*

5   Complexity Results

Our complexity results, for a given PTS $\mathcal{A}$, an initial configuration $\mathcal{S}_0$ and a critical configuration specification $\mathcal{CS}$, will mention the value D_{max} which is an upper-bound on the natural numbers appearing in $\mathcal{S}_0$, $\mathcal{A}$ and $\mathcal{CS}$. D_{max} can be inferred syntactically by simply inspecting the timestamps of $\mathcal{S}_0$, the D values in timestamps of rules (which are of the form $T + D$) and constraints in $\mathcal{A}$ and $\mathcal{CS}$ (which are of the form $T_1 > T_2 + D$ and $T_1 = T_2 + D$). For example, the $D_{max} = 1$ for the specification in Fig. 1.

The size of a timestamped fact $F@T$, written $|F@T|$ is the total number of alphabet symbols appearing in F. For instance, $|P(s(z), f(a, X), a)@12| = 7$. For our complexity results, we assume a bound, k, on the size of facts. For example, in our specification in Fig. 1, we can take the bound $k = |x_{max}| + |y_{max}| + |e_{max}| + 5$. Without this bound (or other restrictions), any interesting decision problem is undecidable by encoding the Post correspondence problem [8].

Notice that we do not always impose an upper bound on the values of timestamps.

Assume throughout this section the following: (1) Σ – A finite alphabet with J predicate symbols and E constant and function symbols; $\mathcal{A}$ – A PTS constructed over Σ; m – The number of facts in the initial configuration $\mathcal{S}_0$; $\mathcal{CS}$ – A critical configuration specification constructed over Σ; k – An upper-bound on the size of facts; D_{max} – An upper-bound on the numeric values of $\mathcal{S}_0, \mathcal{A}$ and $\mathcal{CS}$.

5.1   PSPACE-Completeness

In order to prove the PSPACE-completeness of realizability and survivability problems, we review the machinery introduced in our previous work [13] called δ-configuration.

For a given D_{max} the *truncated time difference* of two timed facts $P@t_1$ and $Q@t_2$ with $t_1 \leq t_2$, denoted by $\delta_{P,Q}$, is defined as follows:

$$\delta_{P,Q} = \begin{cases} t_2 - t_1, \text{ provided } t_2 - t_1 \leq D_{max} \\ \infty, \text{ otherwise} \end{cases}$$

Let $\mathcal{S} = Q_1@t_1, Q_2@t_2, \ldots, Q_n@t_n$, be a configuration of a timed MSR $\mathcal{A}$ written in canonical way where the sequence of timestamps $t_1, \ldots, t_n$ is non-decreasing. The δ-configuration of $\mathcal{S}$ for a given D_{max} is
$$\delta_{\mathcal{S}, D_{max}} = [Q_1, \delta_{Q_1, Q_2}, Q_2, \ldots, Q_{n-1}, \delta_{Q_{n-1}, Q_n}, Q_n] \ .$$
In our previous work [13,16], we showed that a δ-configuration is an equivalence class on configurations. Namely, for a given D_{max}, we declare $\mathcal{S}_1$ and $\mathcal{S}_2$ equivalent, written $\mathcal{S}_1 \equiv_{D_{max}} \mathcal{S}_2$, if and only if their δ-configurations are exactly the same. Moreover, we showed that there is a bisimulation between (compliant) traces over configurations and (compliant) traces over their δ-configurations in the following sense: if $\mathcal{S}_1 \longrightarrow \mathcal{S}_2$ and $\mathcal{S}_1 \equiv_{D_{max}} \mathcal{S}_1'$, then there is a trace $\mathcal{S}_1' \longrightarrow \mathcal{S}_2'$ such that $\mathcal{S}_2 \equiv_{D_{max}} \mathcal{S}_2'$. This result appears in [16, Corollary 7].

Therefore, in the case of balanced timed MSRs, we can work on traces constructed using δ-configurations. Moreover, the following lemma establishes a bound on the number of different δ-configurations.

Lemma 1. *Assume* $\Sigma, \mathcal{A}, \mathcal{S}_0, m, \mathcal{CS}, k, D_{max}$ *as described above. The number of different δ-configurations, denoted by* $L_\Sigma(m, k, D_{max})$ *is such that*
$$L_\Sigma(m, k, D_{max}) \le (D_{max} + 2)^{(m-1)} J^m (E + 2mk)^{mk}.$$

Infinite Traces. Our previous work only dealt with *finite traces*. The challenge here is to deal with infinite traces and in particular the feasibility and survivability problems. These problems are new and as far as we know have not been investigated in the literature (see Sect. 7 for more details).

PSPACE-hardness of both the realizability and survivability can be shown by adequately adapting our previous work [17]. We therefore show PSPACE-membership of these problems.

Recall that a system is realizable if there is a compliant infinite trace $\mathcal{P}$ in which the global time tends to infinity. Since $\mathcal{A}$ is progressive, we get the condition on time from Proposition 3. We, therefore, need to construct a compliant infinite trace. The following lemma estrablishes a criteria:

Lemma 2. *Assume* $\Sigma, \mathcal{A}, \mathcal{S}_0, m, \mathcal{CS}, k, D_{max}$ *as described above. If there is a compliant trace (constructed using δ-configurations) starting with (the δ-representation of) $\mathcal{S}_0$ with length $L_\Sigma(m, k, D_{max})$, then there is an infinite compliant trace starting with (the δ-representation of) $\mathcal{S}_0$.*

Assume that for any given timed MSR $\mathcal{A}$, an initial configuration $\mathcal{S}_0$ and a critical configuration specification $\mathcal{CS}$ we have two functions $\mathcal{N}$ and $\mathcal{X}$ which check, respectively, whether a rule in $\mathcal{A}$ is applicable to a given δ-configuration and whether a δ-configuration is critical with respect to $\mathcal{CS}$. Moreover, let $\mathcal{T}$ be a function implementing the lazy time sampling. It takes a timed MSR and a δ-configuration of that system, and returns 1 when the tick must be applied and 0 when it must not be applied. We assume that $\mathcal{N}$, $\mathcal{X}$ and $\mathcal{T}$ run in Turing time bounded by a polynomial in $m, k, \log_2(D_{max})$. Notice that for our examples this is the case. Because of Lemma 2, we can show that the realizability problem is in PSPACE by searching for compliant traces of length $L_\Sigma(m, k, D_{max})$

(stored in binary). To do so, we rely on the fact that PSPACE and NPSPACE are the same complexity class [23].

Theorem 1. *Assume Σ a finite alphabet, $\mathcal{A}$ a PTS, an initial configuration $\mathcal{S}_0$, m the number of facts in $\mathcal{S}_0$, $\mathcal{CS}$ a critical configuration specification, k an upper-bound on the size of facts, D_{max} an upper-bound on the numeric values in $\mathcal{S}_0, \mathcal{A}$ and $\mathcal{CS}$, and the functions $\mathcal{N}, \mathcal{X}$ and $\mathcal{T}$ as described above. There is an algorithm that, given an initial configuration $\mathcal{S}_0$, decides whether $\mathcal{A}$ is realizable with respect to the lazy time sampling, $\mathcal{CS}$ and $\mathcal{S}_0$ and the algorithm runs in space bounded by a polynomial in m, k and $log_2(D_{max})$.*

The polynomial is in fact $log_2(L_\Sigma(m, k, D_{max}))$.

We now consider the survivability problem. Recall that in order to prove that $\mathcal{A}$ satisfies survivability with respect to the lazy time sampling, $\mathcal{CS}$ and $\mathcal{S}_0$, we must show that $\mathcal{A}$ is realizable and that for all infinite traces $\mathcal{P}$ starting with $\mathcal{S}_0$ (Definition 7):

1. $\mathcal{P}$ is compliant with respect to $\mathcal{CS}$;
2. The global time in $\mathcal{P}$ tends to infinity.

Checking that a system is realizable is PSPACE-complete as we have just shown. Moreover, the second property (time tends to infinity) follows from Proposition 3 for progressive timed MSR. It remains to show that all infinite traces using the lazy time sampling are compliant, which reduces to checking that *no critical configuration is reachable* from the initial configuration $\mathcal{S}_0$ by a trace using the lazy time sampling. This property can be decided in PSPACE by relying on the fact that PSPACE, NPSPACE and co-PSPACE are all the same complexity class [23]. Therefore, survivability is also in PSPACE as states the following theorem.

Theorem 2. *Assume $\Sigma, \mathcal{A}, \mathcal{S}_0, m, \mathcal{CS}, k, D_{max}$ and the functions $\mathcal{N}, \mathcal{X}$ and $\mathcal{T}$ as described in Theorem 1. There is an algorithm that decides whether $\mathcal{A}$ satisfies the survivability problem with respect to the lazy time sampling, $\mathcal{CS}$ and $\mathcal{S}_0$ which runs in space bounded by a polynomial in m, k and $log_2(D_{max})$.*

Corollary 1. *Both the realizability and the survivability problem for PTS are PSPACE-complete when assuming a bound on the size of facts.*

5.2   Complexity Results for n-Time-Bounded Systems

We now consider the n-time-bounded versions of the Realizability and Survivability problems (Definitions 6 and 7).

The following lemma establishes an upper-bound on the length of traces with exactly n instances of tick rules for PTS. It follows immediately from Proposition 2.

Lemma 3. *Let n be fixed and assume $\Sigma, \mathcal{A}, \mathcal{S}_0, m, \mathcal{CS}, k, D_{max}$ as described in Theorem 1. For all traces $\mathcal{P}$ of $\mathcal{A}$ with exactly n instances of the Tick rule, the length of $\mathcal{P}$ is bounded by $(n + 2) * m + n$.*

We can check in polynomial time whether a trace is compliant and has exactly n Ticks. Therefore, the n-time-bounded realizability problem is in NP as stated by the following theorem.

Theorem 3. *Let n be fixed and assume $\Sigma, \mathcal{A}, \mathcal{S}_0, m, \mathcal{CS}, k, D_{max}$ and the functions $\mathcal{N}, \mathcal{X}, \mathcal{T}$ as described in Theorem 1. The problem of determining whether $\mathcal{A}$ is n-time-bounded realizable with respect to the lazy time sampling, $\mathcal{CS}$ and $\mathcal{S}_0$ is in NP with $\mathcal{S}_0$ as the input.*

For NP-hardness, we encode the NP-hard problem 3-SAT as an n-time-bounded realizability problem as done in our previous work [14].

Recall that for n-time-bounded survivability property, we need to show that:

1. $\mathcal{A}$ is n-time-bounded realizable with respect to $\mathcal{CS}$;
2. All traces using the lazy time sampling with exactly n ticks are compliant with respect to $\mathcal{CS}$.

As we have shown, the first sub-problem is NP-complete. The second sub-problem is reduced to checking that no critical configuration is reachable from $\mathcal{S}_0$ by a trace using the lazy time sampling with less or equal to n ticks. We do so by checking whether a critical configuration is reachable. This is similar to realizability which we proved to be in NP. If a critical configuration is reachable then $\mathcal{A}$ does not satisfy the second sub-problem, otherwise it does satisfy. Therefore, deciding the second sub-problem is in co-NP. Thus the n-timed survivability problem is in a class containing both NP and co-NP, *e.g.*, Δ_2^p of the polynomial hierarchy (P^{NP}) [22].

Theorem 4. *Let n be fixed and assume $\Sigma, \mathcal{A}, \mathcal{S}_0, m, \mathcal{CS}, k, D_{max}$ and the functions $\mathcal{N}, \mathcal{X}, \mathcal{T}$ as described in Theorem 1. The problem of determining whether $\mathcal{A}$ satisfies n-time-bounded survivability with respect to the lazy time sampling, $\mathcal{CS}$ and $\mathcal{S}_0$ is in the class Δ_2^p of the polynomial hierarchy (P^{NP}) with input $\mathcal{S}_0$.*

6 Bounded Simulations

For our bounded simulations, we implemented a more elaborated version of our running scenario in Maude using the machinery described in [25]. Our preliminary results are very promising. We are able to model-check fairly large systems for the bounded survivability.

We consider N drones which should have recent pictures, *i.e.*, at most M time units old, of P points distributed in a grid $x_{max} \times y_{max}$, where the base station is at position $(\lceil x_{max}/2 \rceil, \lceil y_{max}/2 \rceil)$, and drones have maximum energy of e_{max}. Drones use soft-constraints, which take into account the drone's position, energy, and pictures, to rank their actions and they perform any one the best ranked actions. Drones are also able to share information with the base station.

Our simulation results are depicted in Table 1. We model-checked the n-timed survivability of the system where $n = 4 \times M$. We varied M and the maximum

Table 1. N is the number of drones, P the number of points of interest, $x_{max} \times y_{max}$ the size of the grid, M the time limit for photos, and e_{max} the maximum energy capacity of each drone. We measured st and t, which are, respectively, the number of states and time in seconds until finding a counter example if F (fail), and until searching all traces with exactly $4 \times M$ ticks if S (success).

Exp 1: ($N = 1, P = 4, x_{max} = y_{max} = 10$)		Exp 3: ($N = 2, P = 9, x_{max} = y_{max} = 20$)	
$M = 50, e_{max} = 40$	F, $st = 139, t = 0.3$	$M = 100, e_{max} = 500$	F, $st = 501, t = 6.2$
$M = 70, e_{max} = 40$	F, $st = 203, t = 0.4$	$M = 150, e_{max} = 500$	F, $st = 1785, t = 29.9$
$M = 90, e_{max} = 40$	S, $st = 955, t = 2.3$	$M = 180, e_{max} = 500$	S, $st = 2901, t = 49.9$
		$M = 180, e_{max} = 150$	F, $st = 1633, t = 25.6$

Exp 2: ($N = 2, P = 4, x_{max} = y_{max} = 10$)		Exp 4: ($N = 3, P = 9, x_{max} = y_{max} = 20$)	
$M = 30, e_{max} = 40$	F, $st = 757, t = 3.2$	$M = 100, e_{max} = 150$	F, $st = 3217, t = 71.3$
$M = 40, e_{max} = 40$	F, $st = 389, t = 1.4$	$M = 120, e_{max} = 150$	F, $st = 2193, t = 52.9$
$M = 50, e_{max} = 40$	S, $st = 821, t = 3.2$	$M = 180, e_{max} = 150$	S, $st = 2193, t = 53.0$
		$M = 180, e_{max} = 100$	F, $st = 2181, t = 50.4$

energy capacity of drones e_{max}. Our implementation [25] finds counter examples quickly (less than a minute) even when considering a larger grid (20×20) and three drones.[3]

We can observe that our implementations can help specifiers to decide how many drones to use and with which energy capacities. For example, in Exp 3, drones required a great deal of energy, namely 500 energy units. Adding an additional drone, Exp 4, reduced the energy needed to 150 energy units. Finally, the number of states may increase when decreasing M because with lower values of M, drones may need to come back more often to the base station causing them to share information and increasing the number of states.

7   Related and Future Work

This paper introduced a novel sub-class of timed MSR systems called progressive which is defined by imposing syntactic restrictions on MSR rules. We illustrated with examples of Time Sensitive Distributed Systems that this is a relevant class of systems. We also introduced two verification problems which may depend on explicit time constraints, namely realizability and survivability, defined over infinite traces. We showed that both problems are PSPACE-complete for progressive timed systems, and when we additionally impose a bound on time, realizability becomes NP-complete and survivability is in Δ_2^p of the polynomial hierarchy. Finally, we demonstrated by experiments that it is feasible to analyse fairly large progressive systems using the rewriting logic tool Maude.

---

[3] Although these scenarios seem small, the state space grow very fast: the state space of our largest scenario has an upper bound of $(400 \times 399 \times 398) \times (150 \times 150 \times 150) \times (180 \times 4) \times (180)^9 \geq 3.06 \times 10^{37}$ states.

Others have proposed languages for specifying properties which allow explicit time constraint. We review some of the timed automata, temporal logic and rewriting literature.

Our progressive condition is related to the *finite-variability assumption* used in the temporal logic and timed automata literature [2,3,10,18,19]: in any bounded interval of time, there can be only finitely many observable events or state changes. Similarly, progressive systems have the property that only a finite number of instantaneous rules can be applied in any bounded interval of time (Proposition 2). Such a property seems necessary for the decidability of many temporal verification problems.

As we discussed in much more detail in the Related Work section of our previous work [13], there are some important differences between our timed MSR and timed automata [2,3] on both the expressive power and decidability proofs. For example, a description of a timed MSR system uses first order formulas with variables, whereas timed automata are able to refer only to transition on ground states. That is, timed MSR is essentially a first-order language, while timed automata are propositional. If we replace a first order description of timed MSR by all its instantiations, that would lead to an exponential explosion. Furthermore, in contrast with the timed automata paradigm, in timed MSR we can manipulate in a natural way the facts both in the past, in the future, and in the present. Finally, our model uses discrete times, while timed automata uses dense times. It seems, however, possible to extend our results to dense times given our previous work [12]. We leave this investigation to future work.

The temporal logic literature has proposed many languages for the specification and verification of timed systems. While many temporal logics include quantitative temporal operators, *e.g.* [18,19], this literature does not discuss notions similar to realizability and survivability notions introduced here. In addition to that, our specifications are executable. Indeed, as we have done here, our specifications can be executed in Maude.

The work [1,5] classifies traces and sets of traces as safety, liveness or properties that can be reduced to subproblems of safety and liveness. Following this terminology, properties relating to both of our problems of realizability and survivability (that involve infinite traces) contain elements of safety as well as elements of liveness. Properties relating to the n-time-bounded versions of realizability and survivabilty could be classified as safety properties. We do not see how to express this in the terms of [1,5]. We intend to revisit this in future work.

Real-Time Maude is a tool for simulating and analyzing real-time systems. Rewrite rules are partitioned into instantaneous rules and rules that advance time, where instantaneous rules are given priority. Time advance rules may place a bound on the amount of time to advance, but do not determine a specific amount, thus allowing continual observation of the system. Time sampling strategies are used to implement search and model-checking analyses. Ölveczky and Messeguer [20] investigate conditions under which the maximal time sampling strategy used in Real-Time Maude is complete. One of the conditions required is tick-stabilizing which is similar to progressive and the finite variability assumption in that one assumes a bound on the number of actions applicable in a finite time.

Cardenas *et al.* [4] discuss possible verification problems of cyber-physical systems in the presence of malicious intruders. They discuss surviving attacks, such as denial of service attacks on the control mechanisms of devices. We believe that our progressive timed systems can be used to define sensible intruder models and formalize the corresponding survivability notions. This may lead to the automated analysis of such systems similar to the successful use of the Dolev-Yao intruder model [7] for protocol security verification. Given the results of this paper, for the decidability of any security problem would very likely involve a progressive timed intruder model.

Finally, we believe it is possible to extend this work to dense times given our previous work [12]. There we assume a Tick rule of the form $Time@T \longrightarrow Time@(T+\epsilon)$. However, we do not consider critical configuration specifications. We are currently investigating how to incorporate the results in this paper with the results of [12].

Acknowledgments. Kanovich's research was partially supported by EPSRC. Scedrov's research was partially supported by ONR and by AFOSR MURI. Kanovich's and Scedrov's work on this paper was partially carried out within the framework of the Basic Research Program at the National Research University Higher School of Economics (HSE) and partially supported within the framework of a subsidy by the Russian Academic Excellence Project '5–100'. Talcott was partially supported by NSF grant CNS-1318848 and ONR grant N00014-15-1-2202. Nigam and Talcott were partially supported by Capes Science without Borders grant 88881.030357/2013-01. Nigam was partially supported by Capes and CNPq.

References

1. Alpern, B., Schneider, F.B.: Recognizing safety and liveness. Distrib. Comput. **2**(3), 117–126 (1987)
2. Alur, R., Henzinger, T.A.: Logics and models of real time: a survey. In: de Bakker, J.W., Huizing, C., de Roever, W.P., Rozenberg, G. (eds.) REX Workshop. LNCS, vol. 600, pp. 74–106. Springer, Heidelberg (1991)
3. Alur, R., Madhusudan, P.: Decision problems for timed automata: a survey. In: Bernardo, M., Corradini, F. (eds.) SFM-RT 2004. LNCS, vol. 3185, pp. 1–24. Springer, Heidelberg (2004)
4. Cárdenas, A.A., Amin, S., Sastry, S.: Secure control: towards survivable cyber-physical systems. In: ICDCS, pp. 495–500 (2008)
5. Clarkson, M.R., Schneider, F.B.: Hyperproperties. J. Comput. Secur. **18**(6), 1157–1210 (2010)
6. Clavel, M., Durán, F., Eker, S., Lincoln, P., Martí-Oliet, N., Meseguer, J., Talcott, C.: All About Maude: A High-Performance Logical Framework. LNCS. Springer, Heidelberg (2007)
7. Dolev, D., Yao, A.: On the security of public key protocols. IEEE Trans. Inf. Theory **29**(2), 198–208 (1983)
8. Durgin, N.A., Lincoln, P., Mitchell, J.C., Scedrov, A.: Multiset rewriting and the complexity of bounded security protocols. J. Comput. Secur. **12**(2), 247–311 (2004)
9. Herbert, B., Enderton, H.B.: A Mathematical Introduction to Logic. Academic Press, Salt lake city (1972)

10. Faella, M., Legay, A., Stoelinga, M.: Model checking quantitative linear time logic. Electron. Notes Theoret. Comput. Sci. **220**(3), 61–77 (2008)
11. Kanovich, M., Kirigin, T.B., Nigam, V., Scedrov, A.: Bounded memory Dolev-Yao adversaries in collaborative systems. Inf. Comput. **238**, 233–261 (2014)
12. Kanovich, M., Kirigin, T.B., Nigam, V., Scedrov, A., Talcott, C.: Discrete vs. dense times in the analysis of cyber-physical security protocols. In: Focardi, R., Myers, A. (eds.) POST 2015. LNCS, vol. 9036, pp. 259–279. Springer, Heidelberg (2015)
13. Kanovich, M., Kirigin, T.B., Nigam, V., Scedrov, A., Talcott, C.: A rewriting framework and logic for activities subject to regulations. Math. Struct. Comput. Sci. (2015). (online) doi:10.1017/S096012951500016X
14. Kanovich, M., Ban Kirigin, T., Nigam, V., Scedrov, A.: Bounded memory protocols and progressing collaborative systems. In:.Crampton, J., Jajodia, S., Mayes, K. (eds.) ESORICS 2013. LNCS, vol. 8134, pp. 309–326. Springer, Heidelberg (2013)
15. Kanovich, M., Kirigin, T.B., Nigam, V., Scedrov, A., Talcott, C.: Timed multiset rewriting and the verification of time-sensitive distributed systems. CoRR, abs/1606.07886 (2016)
16. Kanovich, M.I., Kirigin, T.B., Nigam, V., Scedrov, A., Talcott, C.L., Perovic, R.: A rewriting framework for activities subject to regulations. In: RTA, pp. 305–322 (2012)
17. Kanovich, M.I., Rowe, P., Scedrov, A.: Collaborative planning with confidentiality. J. Autom. Reason. **46**(3–4), 389–421 (2011)
18. Laroussinie, F., Schnoebelen, P., Turuani, M.: On the expressivity and complexity of quantitative branching-time temporal logics. Theoret. Comput. Sci. **297**(1), 297–315 (2003)
19. Lutz, C., Walther, D., Wolter, F.: Quantitative temporal logics: PSPACE and below. In: TIME, pp. 138–146 (2005)
20. Ölveczky, P.C., Meseguer, J.: Abstraction and completeness for real-time maude. Electron. Notes Theoret. Comput. Sci. **176**(4), 5–27 (2007)
21. Ölveczky, P.C., Meseguer, J.: The real-time maude tool. In: Ramakrishnan, C.R., Rehof, J. (eds.) TACAS 2008. LNCS, vol. 4963, pp. 332–336. Springer, Heidelberg (2008)
22. Papadimitriou, C.H.: Computational Complexity. Academic Internet Publ, Ventura (2007)
23. Savitch, W.J.: Relationship between nondeterministic and deterministic tape classes. J. Comput. Syst. Sci. **4**, 177–192 (1970)
24. Talcott, C., Arbab, F., Yadav, M.: Soft agents: exploring soft constraints to model robust adaptive distributed cyber-physical agent systems. In: De Nicola, R., Hennicker, R. (eds.) Wirsing Festschrift. LNCS, vol. 8950, pp. 273–290. Springer, Heidelberg (2015)
25. Talcott, C., Nigam, V., Arbab, F., Kappé, T.: Formal specification and analysis of robust adaptive distributed cyber-physical systems. In: Formal Methods for the Quantitative Evaluation of Collective AdaptiveSystems (2016)

Author Index

Printed in the United States
By Bookmasters